# Sovereign Equality and Moral Disagreement

## PREMISES OF A PLURALIST INTERNATIONAL LEGAL ORDER

BRAD R. ROTH

OXFORD
UNIVERSITY PRESS

OXFORD
UNIVERSITY PRESS

*Oxford University Press, Inc., publishes works that further Oxford University's objective of excellence in research, scholarship, and education.*

Oxford New York
Auckland Cape Town Dar es Salaam Hong Kong Karachi Kuala Lumpur Madrid Melbourne
Mexico City Nairobi New Delhi Shanghai Taipei Toronto

With offices in
Argentina Austria Brazil Chile Czech Republic France Greece Guatemala Hungary Italy
Japan Poland Portugal Singapore South Korea Switzerland Thailand Turkey Ukraine Vietnam



Published by Oxford University Press, Inc.
198 Madison Avenue, New York, New York 10016



---

Library of Congress Cataloging-in-Publication Data

Roth, Brad R.
Sovereign equality and moral disagreement: premises of a pluralist international legal order / Brad R. Roth.
p. cm.
Includes bibliographical references and index.
ISBN 978-0-19-534266-6 (hardback: alk. paper)
1. Sovereignty. I. Title.
KZ4041.R383 2011
341.26–dc22

2011010843

---

1 2 3 4 5 6 7 8 9

Printed in the United States of America on acid-free paper

# Contents

# Acknowledgments

It is impossible to thank all of the interlocutors whose insights have had an influence on the development of this work over time. By acknowledging some of them, I do not mean to implicate them; many of those to whom I owe the most appreciation are those who have consistently expressed their disagreement with various aspects of my argument.

I will start with two of my most important teachers: the late Oscar Schachter, with whom I studied while pursuing my LL.M. at Columbia Law School; and Jeremy Waldron, with whom I studied while pursuing my Ph.D. at the University of California at Berkeley. My gratitude extends to a much longer list of teachers, but I could not have written this particular book without previously having had the benefit of the tutelage of these two.

I owe special thanks to many colleagues at Wayne State in both the Department of Political Science and the Law School, but in particular to James Chalmers, Gregory H. Fox, and Kevin Deegan-Krause for supplying a constant flow of ideas, and to Anthony Dillof and Vincent Wellman for commenting on one of the chapters. Through the wonders of electronic mail, I have had the continual benefit of the virtual presence of several colleagues at some remove, including Ken Anderson; Tom Ginsburg; Mary Ellen O'Connell; Mark Osiel; Andreas Paulus; and especially, Jamie Mayerfeld. Many others have made themselves available to discuss discrete topics—far too many to name—but notably Jean d'Aspremont, David Berry, Daniel Bodansky, Christopher Borgen, Allen Buchanan, Michael Byers, Anthony Colangelo, Javier Couso, Norman Farrell, Anne Herbert, Elizabeth Kiss, Susan Marks, Madeline Morris, Georg Nolte, John Parry, Jarna Petman, Steve Ratner, Darryl Robinson, Leila Nadya Sadat, Peter Spiro, Chandra Lekha Sriram, Beth Van Schaack, and Christopher Waters. I am also grateful to the Wayne State University Department of Political Science, Law School, and Humanities Center for the support that they have provided.

This book draws together themes of work that has been published in various venues over many years. The author would like to thank the publishers of the following articles and book chapters for granting me permission to adapt significant portions of my prior work for incorporation into this book. Chapter 2 includes material from "What Ever Happened to Sovereignty? Reflections on International Law Methodology," in Charlotte Ku & Thomas G. Weiss eds., *Toward Understanding Global Governance* (Academic Council on the United Nations System, 1998), pp. 69–100. Chapters 3 and 4 are based largely on "The Enduring Significance of State Sovereignty," *Florida Law Review* 56 (2004), 1017–50; and "State Sovereignty, International Legality, and Moral Disagreement," in Tomer Broude & Yuval Shany eds., *The Shifting Allocation of Authority in International Law* (Oxford: Hart Publishing Co., 2008), pp. 123–61. Chapter 4 also integrates portions of "Anti-Sovereigntism, Liberal Messianism, and Excesses in the Drive against Impunity," *Finnish Yearbook of International Law* (a Brill publication) 12 (2001), 17–45. Chapter 5 draws heavily on "Bending the Law, Breaking It, or Developing It? The United States and the Humanitarian Use of Force in the Post-Cold War Era," in Michael Byers & Georg Nolte eds., *United States Hegemony and the Foundations of the International Law* (Cambridge University Press, 2003), pp. 232–63. Chapter 6 is an adaptation of "Secessions, Coups, and the International Rule of Law: Assessing the Decline of the Effective Control Doctrine," *Melbourne Journal of International Law* 11 (2010), 393–440. Chapter 7 is an adaptation of "Coming to Terms with Ruthlessness: Sovereign Equality, Global Pluralism, and the Limits of International Criminal Justice," *Santa Clara Journal of International Law* 8 (2010), 231–88.

Brad R. Roth
December 26, 2010

# Sovereign Equality and Moral Disagreement

# 1

# A Different Sovereignty Discourse

## *Sovereign Equality as a Response to Disagreement*

## I. Sovereignty Discourses

In the currently predominant discourse among scholars of international law and international political morality, the word "sovereignty" is laden with unfavorable connotations. Principally, it refers to an unconquered domain: a realm of lawlessness that incrementally diminishes as international legality advances, or a realm of impersonal state interests that stubbornly resists the incursions of human rights. Defenders of sovereignty most frequently are heard, not so much to challenge these oppositions, as to reaffirm them from the opposite side—most audaciously, perhaps, in a National Defense Strategy pronouncement of the George W. Bush administration that identified international legal processes as tools of America's enemies.[1] This discourse, on both sides, is one of sovereignty *versus* international law and human rights, of state-centered realism *versus* liberal internationalism.

There is a second sovereignty discourse, arising in reaction against the first, that differs nominally, but only by virtue of a redefinition of the term. In this second discourse, sovereign right is replaced by sovereign responsibility. Sovereignty is characterized here not only as a creature of international legality, but as reducible to a set of capacities that, by their very nature, can never be authentically exercised in

[1] "Our strength as a nation state will continue to be challenged by those who employ a strategy of the weak, using international fora, judicial processes, and terrorism." United States Department of Defense, *The National Defense Strategy of the United States of America* (March 2005) <http://www.defenselink.mil/news/Mar2005/d20050318nds2.pdf>, at 5; *see also* David Cole, "What Bush Wants to Hear," *N.Y. Rev. Books*, 52:18 (Nov. 17, 2005), 8, at 12. Critics of legal constraints on antiterrorism measures have coined the term "lawfare" to express this point. *See* Charles J. Dunlap, Jr., "Law and Military Interventions: Preserving Humanitarian Values in 21st Conflicts" (Harvard Kennedy School Workshop Paper, 2001), available at <http://www.hks.harvard.edu/cchrp/Web%20Working%20Papers/Use%20of%20Force/Dunlap2001.pdf>.

resistance to the implementation of international legal norms. Ironically, this discourse, albeit seemingly antithetical, equally lent itself (however much to the consternation of its originators) to invocation by Bush administration officials:

> Sovereignty entails obligations. One is not to massacre your own people. Another is not to support terrorism in any way. If a government fails to meet these obligations, then it forfeits some of the normal advantages of sovereignty, including the right to be left alone inside your own territory. Other governments, including the United States, gain the right to intervene.[2]

In this modified discourse, whereas an antiquated notion of sovereignty empowers resistance to the dictates of international law and natural justice, a supposed modern understanding concedes state authority only insofar as harmonious with a larger design. Old oppositions remain but are expressed in new terminology; "humanitarian intervention," implying a challenge to a state's sovereignty, is rebranded in terms of "responsibility to protect," implying that external forces are merely fulfilling the defaulting state's own mandate.[3]

This book suggests a discourse very different from both of those above. Unlike the first discourse above, the book will speak of sovereignty as a theme unifying a small but crucial set of existing doctrines of the present international legal order and will defend that set of doctrines as responsive to fundamental human interests. It will speak, not of sovereignty *versus* international law, but of sovereignty *within* international law. It will speak, not of sovereignty *versus* human rights, but of the two concepts playing distinct and incommensurable roles within a single legal order. But unlike the second discourse above, the book will use the concept of sovereignty not to explain away existing tensions, but instead to locate the sources of tension within the project of international legality itself. It will argue that seemingly retrograde international legal norms reflect second-order moral considerations that properly limit unilateral exertions, even where those exertions are in furtherance of just causes.[4]

[2] Richard Haass, Director of Policy Planning for the George W. Bush State Department, quoted in Nicolas Lemann, "The Next World Order," *New Yorker*, Apr. 1, 2002, available at <http://www.newyorker.com/archive/2002/04/01/020401fa_FACT1>; for commentary, *see* Jose Alvarez, "Notes from the President: The Schizophrenias of R2P," *ASIL News.* 23:3 (2007), available at <http://www.asil.org/newsletter/president/pres070927.html>.

[3] *See generally* International Commission on Intervention and State Sovereignty, *The Responsibility to Protect* (December 2001) [hereinafter ICISS Report], available at <http://www.iciss.ca/pdf/Commission-Report.pdf>.

[4] As Joseph Raz has explained, doing "what ought to be done, *all things considered*," does not necessarily equate to acting on one's own assessment of the merits of the case, because deference to authority may, under certain conditions, count as a valid "second-order" moral reason for forbearing from such action. Joseph Raz, *The Authority of Law: Essays on Law and Morality* (Oxford: Clarendon Press, 1979), at 27.

This book's central contention is that international law's highest and best uses remain those given pride of place in the United Nations Charter: the establishment of a platform for peaceful accommodation among states representing a diversity of interests and values, and the protection of weak political communities from overbearing projections of power by strong foreign states.[5] This contention is by no means a denial that the international legal order accomplishes, and properly further aspires to accomplish, far more, including the advancement of substantive justice within states. But however true it may be that, as David Mitrany famously wrote in 1943, "the problem of our time is not how to keep nations peacefully apart but how to bring them actively together,"[6] keeping nations peacefully apart is indispensable to bringing them actively together. For collectivities as for individuals, cooperation is too great of a risk without a set of secure baseline entitlements.[7] And while many actors other than states affect global affairs to an ever greater extent, states remain uniquely important, with unique capacities for both beneficence and maleficence.[8]

The claim for the normative significance of state sovereignty is partly based on an attribution to discrete political communities of an ample, though not unlimited, moral right to be wrong about justice; outsiders, even when objectively correct in condemning internal practices, have a presumptive moral obligation not to interfere coercively in collective enterprises of which they are not a part and in which they hold no direct and permanent stake. However, the boundaries of the international legal order's pluralism need to be considerably broader than any first-order moral consideration, such as self-determination, alone would dictate. The contours of a legal right to self-determination and of the associated right to non-intervention need to reflect not only a political community's moral interest in deciding its own fate (for better or worse) but also its moral interest in, and empirical concern for, protection from the risk of objectively harmful interference by self-interested, arrogant, or sophomoric intermeddlers. The international legal order must both, as a matter of policy, constrain cross-border exercises of power by presumptively

[5] The first two "Purposes" of the Organization listed in Article 1 are "To maintain international peace and security" and "To develop friendly relations among nations based on respect for the principle of equal rights and self-determination of peoples." U.N. Charter, arts. 1(1), 1(2). Consequently, "The Organization is based on the principle of the sovereign equality of all its Members," *id.*, art. 2(1), and all states are bound to "refrain in their international relations from the threat or use of force against the territorial integrity or political independence of any state," *id.*, art. 2(4).

[6] David Mitrany, *A Working Peace System* (Chicago: Quadrangle Books, 1966), 28.

[7] For a discussion of how rights establish baselines that facilitate cooperative behavior, *see* Jeremy Waldron, *Liberal Rights: Collected Papers, 1981–1991* (Cambridge Univ. Press, 1993), pp. 370–91.

[8] *See* Robert Jackson, "Sovereignty and its Presuppositions: Before 9/11 and After," 55 *Pol. Stud.* 297 (2007) (arguing that disparagement of the contemporary significance of the state is largely unwarranted).

untrustworthy actors and, as a matter of politics, maintain broad-based support in a diverse and (at least moderately) distrustful international community.

As a corrective to discourses that fail to reflect the intricate balance of considerations that the United Nations Charter-based order embodies, this book intends a radical statement, albeit in service of a set of moderate prescriptions. For this purpose, what is required is a zealous defense, not of the international legal order's furtherance of human rights, justice, and democracy, but rather of that order's continued resistance to many efforts undertaken in the name of those goals. Rather than regarding the legal impediments to those efforts as artifacts of the past, to be progressively overcome by the forces of enlightenment, or as stubborn political realities that represent the regrettable limits of righteousness in a world still dominated by self-interested power holders, this book will champion those impediments affirmatively as matters of principle, to be upheld—at least presumptively—even in the face of morally compelling causes. It will affirm the continued significance of state sovereignty, not exclusively as newly harmonized with supranational authority in the form of "sovereignty as responsibility," but also in continued tension with supranational authority in the form of a presumptive *domaine réservé*. It will argue for maintaining fidelity to sovereignty-oriented legal doctrines, even where they protect the perpetrators, rather than the victims, of human rights violations, and even where they protect authoritarian regimes at the expense of would-be democratizers. It will, in short, give an unvarnished explication and bold (though not altogether unqualified) defense of the most unpopular characteristics of existing international legal doctrines.

The purpose of this radical statement is not to insist that state-centric legal doctrines remain rigid in the face of humanitarian challenges but to restore balance to a discussion that has to come to ascribe moral rectitude only to the critics of those (highly circumscribed) sovereign prerogatives that international law continues to recognize. The book seeks, not to obscure the interests of human beings grievously harmed by the abuse of sovereign prerogative, but to illuminate the human interests that would be jeopardized were the legal prerogatives currently attaching to sovereign states to be eradicated. It will by no means lament recent human-rights-oriented developments in international law (most of which the author supports), but will caution against unwarranted extrapolations that may have the ultimate effect of spurring undue dissatisfaction with international law as it actually is. In the face of compelling causes that cry out for remedial cross-border impositions, this book stands not for the conservative proposition that "hard cases make bad law," but for the moderate proposition that "extreme cases generate bad dicta."

## II. Why Invoke the Language of Sovereignty?

As will be detailed in Chapter 3, the term sovereignty is rife with ambiguity. It was not without some justification that Louis Henkin characterized the concept as "a mistake, indeed a mistake built upon mistakes, which has barnacled an unfortunate mythology."[9] Indeed, many invocations of sovereignty amount to nostalgia for a world that never was,[10] to apologism for the unbridled pursuit of national interests, to a simple repudiation of the rule of law, or merely to empty rhetoric. It might well be suggested that this book's arguments could be made more clearly and persuasively without reference to a word that seems destined to prompt misunderstanding and, among the book's primary audience, hostility.

The instant project nonetheless insists on a rehabilitation of sovereignty as a conceptual tool. It does so because sovereignty uniquely captures phenomena that withstand both the objective and normative changes of the present era.

The objective aspect is the more straightforward one. Amid the spectacularly increased prominence of international trade and investment, interstate migration, potent non-state actors (whether for-profit, humanitarian, or terrorist), and boundary-transcending information technology, the state's importance has diminished markedly in all respects ***except*** those to which the concept of sovereignty most directly pertains. Most essentially, there remains no substitute for a presumptive monopoly of the last word on public order in any given territory. A crisis of territorial order—occasioning unmediated, and therefore often armed, social conflict—remains as consequential to human well-being in this era as in any other. One may be a citizen of the world in one's own mind, and indeed may have more subjectively meaningful connections with interlocutors halfway around the world than with one's neighbors, but hardly anyone's way of life can withstand a collapse of accord over what counts as public order in one's home territory.

Moreover, however increasingly the character of social life is affected by nongovernmental decisions, state-level acts and omissions remain foundational to life in any given society. Cutting-edge scholarship is naturally drawn to how much of social life has changed, at the expense of how much has remained the same. Political decision-making still matters, and its primary locus remains the state. By contrast to all other modes of social organization, the state maintains a unique capacity to address social problems, within and without its own borders, by coordinating the efforts of large numbers of individuals through subordination to a set of collective decisions. For "us" to address large-scale social problems, there must effectively be an "us," whose contributions can be aggregated to a critical mass, and upon whom decisions about such contributions can be made binding. It is primarily the contours of the state that demarcate this "us," and the authority ascribed to the state that renders this "us" effective. Insofar as democratic participation remains a viable aspiration, sovereignty is what there is to be democratic ***about***.

[9] Louis Henkin, "Human Rights and State 'Sovereignty,'" 25 *Ga. J. Int'l & Comp. L.* 31 (1995/96).

[10] For an account of how little genuine autonomy states have ever really enjoyed, see Stephen D. Krasner, *Sovereignty: Organized Hypocrisy* (Princeton, NJ: Princeton University Press, 1999).

In relation to normative developments, sovereignty's significance is as a necessary—and distinctively paradoxical—qualification to the expansion of international law's coverage. As Chapter 3 will discuss in detail, state sovereignty cannot be reduced to what remains after international law has spoken its piece. Even though state sovereignty is best characterized as itself a creature of international law, this characterization does not imply a sweeping subordination of state-level to global-level legal authority. Rather, the two sources of authority interact by the terms of a highly nuanced—and frequently contested—arrangement. As elaborated more fully in the following chapters, this arrangement has three distinctive themes, to the paradoxes of which only the word "sovereignty" can do justice.

First, lawmaking in the international order remains predicated on the notional "consent" of the individual states subject to it. No international legislature has authority to impose norms on a non-consenting state. To be sure, consent to international lawmaking is often imputed through ingenious methodological devices, rather than derived from an actual expression of governmental will. Nonetheless, a state's freedom of action and exclusivity of territorial control remain the default positions that a claim of international legal obligation must, by some authoritative justification, overcome.[11] Relatedly, amenability to international adjudication is subject to rigorous standards of formal consent, and domestic-court adjudication of a foreign state's breach of international obligation is largely blocked by international norms of sovereign immunity.

Second, and more remarkably, bindingness on the international plane does not, by itself, imply penetration of the domestic legal order. Acts of state that violate international norms are breaches of obligation, but they are not thereby rendered null and void internally. The internal legal force of those acts, in turn, creates legal facts that international law, by the operation of its own doctrines, must acknowledge.[12] Consequently, the binding norm coexists with, rather than extinguishes, a state's sovereign authority in regard to the very same subject matter.

This point may sound abstruse, but it is of great significance to both public officials and ordinary citizens who act in accordance with their state's internationally wrongful decisions. As a presumptive matter, international law holds them harmless

[11] Though substantially misleading even when it was first articulated, the so-called "*Lotus* Principle" remains a viable starting point for international law-finding: "Restrictions on the independence of States cannot . . . be presumed." *S.S. "Lotus" (France v. Turkey)*, 1927 P.C.I.J. (ser. A) No. 10, at 18 (Sept. 7).

[12] Such doctrines include *nullum crimen sine lege*, lawful combatancy, and "permanent sovereignty over natural resources." For example, as noted in Chapter Three, a state's unlawful expropriation of a foreign national's interest in land or other natural resources does not fail to yield internationally recognized title to the property, even while it incurs liability for a breach of legal obligation; a subsequent purchaser of that interest is not fairly understood to be "trafficking in stolen property."

for their participation in their state's breaching acts—acts for which the state, as a corporative entity, bears responsibility.[13]

The result is paradoxical. The renunciation of a practice is not, in itself, a renunciation of the capacity to authorize the practice. Where the renounced practice is authorized in breach of obligation, the same act is rendered lawful and unlawful simultaneously, on coexisting legal planes. Such a tension, though intuitive when two coequal states have valid jurisdiction over the same conduct, is counterintuitive as between international and state authority, because the authority of the encompassing unit would seem naturally to subsume that of the units encompassed, as is true within both unitary and federal models of internal order. But in the international order, the tension between encompassing and encompassed authorities has no automatic resolution, precisely because the encompassed units, even while legally bound, remain legally ***sovereign***.[14]

Third, the international system's foundational norms stress the inviolability of a state's territorial integrity and political independence, as against the threat or use of force or "extreme economic or political coercion." This inviolability is presumed to withstand even the target state's own violation of international legal norms. Whereas intuition may associate one actor's obligation to obey a norm with another actor's license to do whatever is necessary to effect compliance with the norm, the international order, while providing some scope for recourse to countermeasures, places durable limits on unilateral cross-border exercises of coercion and force. These limits potentially render the norm, in effect, obligatory but not compulsory.[15]

There is an additional and more sweeping paradox that only the word "sovereignty" can capture. Internally, the rule of law is about subjecting sovereign authority itself to law: sovereignty as "constituted" by legal norms. But the international rule of law, based on the sovereign equality of states, is an accommodation among territorial communities that bear an underlying capacity (*pouvoir constituant*) to overthrow constituted domestic authority (*pouvoir constitué*). Domestic constitutions, far from constituting the units of the international order, are made, unmade, and remade by those units. Although these events may occur in ways that violate

[13] International law thus confers a "substantive defence," available to "any de jure or de facto State agent" performing official acts, establishing that the "violation is not legally imputable to [the agent] but to his state." Antonio Cassese, *International Criminal Law* (Oxford Univ. Press, 2003) at 266.

[14] Of course, a state "may not invoke the provisions of its internal law as justification for its failure to perform" its international legal obligations. Vienna Convention on the Law of Treaties, 1155 U.N.T.S. 331 (opened for signature, 1969), art. 27. But to say that an act is in breach of international law is not, in itself, to say that the act is *ultra vires* of the capacities ascribed to the state by international law, and thereby incapable of creating internationally cognizable legal facts.

[15] For example, at least as a presumptive matter, one state may not engage in law enforcement on the territory of another sovereign state, even if the latter is harboring criminals in breach of international legal obligation.

international legal norms, such violations have not—except in extraordinary circumstances—impaired the acknowledgment of the legal facts to which the events have given rise; the legal standing of governments to assert rights, incur obligations, and confer immunities on behalf of their states has not, as a general matter, depended on those governments having been constituted in accordance with previously effective internal legal norms.[16] Thus, the rule of law is not a seamless web; international law has generally (albeit with some prominent recent exceptions) operated to protect, against coercive external interference, the successful overthrow of existing legal orders. Only the word "sovereignty" can make such a legal relationship intelligible.

Moreover, the sovereignty construct serves as a uniquely appropriate lens through which to view the international order's approach to the working out of clashing conceptions of legitimate and just internal public order. Whether or not ideological differences lead to contrasting positions on public order norms as applied in ordinary circumstances, these differences manifest themselves crucially at moments of crisis, where the issue is not the presumptive norm itself, but the existence *vel non* of overriding considerations. The concept of a juridical last word on public order in a territory is most pertinent not to the norm but to "the exception," understood in both the ordinary and the Schmittian term-of-art senses of that term. As Carl Schmitt insisted in the domestic constitutional context, sovereignty is "the authority to suspend valid law"; "sovereign is he who decides on the exception."[17] So, too, is sovereignty the power to produce a valid public act in breach of a binding international obligation.

The question of sovereignty focuses attention on the dynamic rather than the static aspects of global pluralism—on what happens, not in the ordinary course, but in the heat of political struggle, when abstract consensus gives way to a clash of underlying political moralities. That certain measures are universally reprehended, others things being equal, does not mean that these measures are universally reprehended when the moral stakes of political defeat are perceived to be unacceptably high. The events that most tend to occasion calls for extraordinary cross-border impositions—as opposed to such standard responses to human rights violations as denunciations and boycotts—involve, not measures practiced in stable times and defended on their individual merits in contradiction to generally accepted human rights standards, but crisis-prompted departures from uncontroverted norms. Respect for a state's sovereignty is a matter, not of approving the state's "exceptional"

[16] See Chapter 6. For a book-length treatment of this phenomenon, see Brad R. Roth, *Governmental Illegitimacy in International Law* (Oxford Univ. Press, 1999).

[17] Carl Schmitt, *Political Theology: Four Chapters on the Concept of Sovereignty* [1922], trans. George Schwab (Cambridge, Mass.: The MIT Press, 1985), at 5. "[T]he authority to suspend valid law—be it in general or in a specific case—is . . . the actual mark of sovereignty." *Id.* at 9.

disrespect for human rights, nor of forbearing from due sanctions against such conduct, but of holding inviolable the state's ultimate authority within its territory, notwithstanding wrongfulness in the use of that authority.

## III. Neither Moral Relativism nor Natural Justice: Sovereignty Equality as a Legal Response to Moral Disagreement

In stressing the components of international law that continue to reflect sovereignty considerations, this book advocates an approach to legal interpretation that emphasizes social sources of law at the expense of reliance on first-order moral truths. It is thus understandable that some may imagine this project to be dependent on an embrace of legal positivism, as opposed to natural law.

Yet this is not the case. To the contrary, this book seeks to implement what Ronald Dworkin calls a "moral reading" of law. According to Dworkin, "judges should decide hard cases by interpreting the political structure of their community in the following, perhaps special way: by trying to find the best justification they can find, in principles of political morality, for the structure as a whole . . . ."[18] But "the structure as a whole" in this case finds justification in the need for accommodation among bearers of conflicting interests and values. Although legal interpretation is inherently a purposive process, the purposes to be fulfilled are not the first-order moral purposes of the jurist, but the second-order moral purposes associated with upholding a morally worthwhile system of cooperation among the non-like-minded. A tendentious approach to interpretation that fails to keep faith with the explicitly and implicitly negotiated terms of accommodation vitiates the legitimacy of the legal outcome.

This book embraces the idea that "law as it is" can never be truly sealed off from "law as it ought to be." Indeed, as is acknowledged in Chapter 7, the term "law" implies an orientation toward predictability and accountability in the exercise of power, and to apply that term to edicts reflecting a systemic repudiation of those aims would tend to create a misimpression. But to associate law with some irreducible set of purposes is not to accept the proposition that "an unjust law is no law at all" (a phrase most often intended figuratively rather than literally), for law is needed precisely to bridge disagreement about the content of justice.

What this book opposes, then, is not naturalistic reasoning as such, but a particular brand of it that disregards accepted international legal processes in favor of resort to first principles. As Dworkin points out, a naturalist jurist must sometimes uphold one party's "right to a consistent application of the public order," notwithstanding

[18] Ronald A. Dworkin, "'Natural' Law Revisited," 34 *U. Fla. L. Rev.* 165, 165 (1982).

the other party's "right to a better public order."[19] As to the consistent application of the existing global public order, this book will contend that the imperatives of peace and cooperation morally justify a juridical responsibility to maintain a working accommodation among states parties that espouse conflicting visions of substantive justice. This contention, far from being based on any notion of moral relativism or skepticism, is based on a claim for the objective moral significance of the (equally objective) existence and (potentially ruinous) consequences of moral disagreement.

The proliferation of widely accepted human rights instruments, from the 1948 Universal Declaration of Human Rights onward, may seem to legitimate wide-ranging extrapolations from these documents, on the ground that such extrapolations implement a universal understanding or intuition about justice that transcends political and cultural divides. On such an account, those who transgress that understanding are not only in the wrong: they know that they are in the wrong or at least are on notice of it. Where this is so, a narrow interpretation of legal instruments might be seen as accommodating cynicism rather than moral disagreement.

As Chapter 4 will detail, there are at least two reasons to take a skeptical approach to such claims for universal public order norms. First, apparent consensus on abstractions frequently dissolves at the level of application. In the face of concrete circumstances, adherents of differing "comprehensive" moral doctrines, who endorsed the abstractions for differing reasons, will interpret the same abstract norms in conflicting ways or assign them conflicting priorities. Second, consensus as to the presumptive wrongfulness of particular conduct often gives way to discord about under which adverse conditions the presumption is overcome. Agreement as to inadmissible means typically fails to hold in the face of sufficiently grave threats to what some see as morally imperative ends.

Because the international order's mechanisms for lawmaking, adjudication, and coercive implementation rely to so great an extent on consent and consensus, the temptations to circumvent these mechanisms in the name of substantive justice are formidable. Indeed, there undoubtedly are times when the benefits of licensing the exercise of power in the name of substantive justice exceed the overall detriments, all things considered. But it needs to be remembered that the targets of such action often hold precisely this view about the moral imperativeness of their own measures. A durable framework for international interaction will necessarily require—at least in the main—forbearance from unilateralism, even in the pursuit of an objectively correct vision of justice.

If international law is valued for nothing beyond its contribution to the pursuit of a particular conception of substantive justice, then norms and doctrines that block the most direct path to that end appear as obstacles to be circumvented, not

[19] Dworkin, *supra*, at 186.

limits to be respected. The result may be to undermine the perceived legitimacy of institutional constraints on untrusted and untrustworthy powers who, through unilateral invocations of universal principles, seek license to impose justice as they see it.[20]

## IV. The Equal Sovereignty of Weak States

To speak of sovereignty within international law—or "sovereign equality"—is to speak principally of the sovereignty of weak states. Contrary to the rhetoric of anxious champions of "American exceptionalism,"[21] strong states have little need to invoke the legal prerogatives at issue, for they have the political and economic clout to protect not only their baseline entitlements, but far more. Powerful and influential states are unlikely to have norms imposed on them without their input or consent, nor are their officials likely to face serious risks of extraterritorial prosecution for their participation in acts of state, nor are they menaced by threats of economic strangulation or military intervention.

Of course, no one imagines the sovereign equality of states to be either a substantive equality or an absolute guarantee of respect for sovereignty. States are equal in respect to the rudimentary legal presumptions discussed above; in all other respects, they are radically unequal, with the weak being subject to a wide range of economic and political pressures to yield to the will of the wealthier and more powerful. Moreover, each of the presumptions discussed above can be overcome: norms can be imposed on persistently objecting states where "the international community of States as a whole" manifests an insistence to this effect[22]; norms of international penal liability can develop to authorize extraterritorial prosecution of state officials for acts committed inside national territory and within official capacity; and the Security Council, with nine affirmative votes out of fifteen and the acquiescence of

[20] A considerable amount of literature already points the way. *See, e.g.*, W. Michael Reisman, "Sovereignty and Human Rights in Contemporary International Law," 84 *Am. J. Int'l L.* 866, 875 (1990) (justifying "unilateral vindication of clear violations of rights when multilateral possibilities do not obtain" on the ground that "rights without remedies are not rights at all"); Reisman, "Unilateral Actions and the Transformations of the World Constitutive Process: The Special Problem of Humanitarian Intervention," 11 *Euro. J. Int'l L.* 3, 15 (2000) (contending that "as the norms in question—international human rights norms—derive from a broader decision process than the body assigned to enforce those norms, the broader decision process sustains the norms and seeks alternative modes of enforcement").

[21] For a critique of the hostility to international law in some conservative circles in the United States, see Peter J. Spiro, "The New Sovereigntists: American Exceptionalism and Its False Prophets," 79 *Foreign Aff.* 9 (2000).

[22] *See* Vienna Convention on the Law of Treaties, *supra*, art. 53 (defining *jus cogens*, or "peremptory" norms).

each of the five Permanent Members (P5), can require crippling economic sanctions and authorize the use of force.

Yet the presumptions remain formidable. For example, the P5 veto, seemingly an affront to the idea of equality among states, actually operates as a bulwark of sovereign equality, since it guarantees, in all but the most uncontroversial cases, a Security Council deadlock that leaves in force the default rules (including non-intervention norms).

Sovereign prerogative's continued robustness within international law, such as it is, is mainly owing, not to the dead hand of the 1648 Peace of Westphalia or even to the United Nations Charter itself, but to the struggles of Third World political movements, first against colonialism and then against the perceived threat of neocolonialist domination. From the late 1950s to the late 1980s, governments of the lesser-developed countries, speaking through such organs as the Non-Aligned Movement and the Group of 77 (G-77), successfully played off the Cold War blocs against each other so as to obtain influence over the ground rules of the international order. Though they failed in the crucial aspects of their most ambitious effort, the creation of a New International Economic Order (NIEO), they succeeded in transforming the United Nations Charter's vague principle of self-determination into a right of sovereign independence for colonial territories, and in converting Charter references to sovereign equality and non-intervention into legal strictures against the most heavy-handed cross-border exercises of power, forcible and otherwise, that strong states have historically employed to prevail upon weak states. They extracted the acquiescence of the great powers in authoritative affirmations that "Every State has an inalienable right to choose its political, economic, social and cultural systems, without interference in any form by another State," and that "No State may use or encourage the use of economic, political or any other type of measures to coerce another State in order to obtain from it the subordination of the exercise of its sovereign rights and to secure from it advantages of any kind."[23]

Emblematic of the Third World's political accomplishments in this period was the decision of the International Court of Justice in *Nicaragua v. United States*.[24] Issued in response to U.S. sponsorship of an armed insurgency fighting to overthrow the Nicaraguan government, the judgment affirmed the legal significance of General Assembly pronouncements on non-intervention and repudiated a U.S. effort to rationalize the indirect use of force by invocation of Nicaragua's own transgressions (both real and imagined).[25] The Court's firm (some would say, rigid) interpretation

[23] Declaration on Principles of International Law Concerning Friendly Relations and Co-operation Among States in Accordance with the Charter of the United Nations [hereinafter] "Friendly Relations Declaration"), G.A. Res. 2625 (1970) (adopted without a vote).

[24] Military and Paramilitary Activities (Nicaragua v. U.S.), 1986 I.C.J. 14 (June 27).

[25] See the discussion in Chapter 3.

of Charter constraints on cross-border exertions was, from the standpoint of weak states, a shining instance of a legal body "speaking truth to power." Although there was no direct way to prevail upon the United States to comply with the decision—Security Council enforcement requiring the acquiescence of each of the five veto-bearing Permanent Members—the U.S. legal defeat presented significant diplomatic obstacles to the continuation of the aggressive policy, and likely contributed (albeit rather undramatically) to the policy's curtailment.[26]

Given the sovereign equality regime's history and its distinctive worth to weak states, it is somewhat surprising to see the disparagement of sovereignty-oriented norms emanating from "progressive" quarters. To be sure, a benefit to weak states does not automatically equate to a benefit to the populations of those states. A political order that is weak vis-à-vis external powers may easily be tyrannical vis-à-vis the internal population, in whole or in part.[27] The postcolonial state has long since lost its heroic image, and in parts of the world, has failed abysmally to fulfill basic governance functions, amounting to little more than a vehicle for corruption, ethnic favoritism, repression, and worse.[28] And yet, the image of powerful states chomping at the bit to bestow beneficence, but held back by international legal constraints, does not seem compelling, either. Certainly, there are many opportunities for beneficence, not currently bestowed, that could be realized without breaching such constraints and at a far lesser cost all around. The history of intervention thus far provides little reassurance that the world's poor and weak stand to gain from the removal of legal obstacles to non-Security Council-approved impositions by strong states upon weak ones.

## V. Human Rights as a Shield, or a Sword?

Contrary to what is often imagined, the insistence on respect for the existing legal prerogatives of weak states is not at odds with vigorous human rights advocacy. It disallows only a small range of external responses to human rights violations, and such responses not only are infrequent, but tend to occur only when human rights concerns dovetail with other, less wholesome political aims. This latter tendency should not be seen as altogether disqualifying the responses–doing good only when it serves an ulterior purpose is better than not doing good at all—but it should

[26] *See* Joaquin Tacsan, *The Dynamics of International Law in Conflict Resolution* (Boston, MA: Martinus Nijhoff, 1992).

[27] This essential theme is well explored in Leslie Green, "Internal Minorities and Their Rights," in Will Kymlicka ed., *The Rights of Cultural Minorities* (Oxford: Clarendon Press, 1995), 257.

[28] *See, e.g.,* Robert H. Jackson, *Quasi-States: Sovereignty, International Relations, and the Third World* (Cambridge: Cambridge University Press, 1990).

prompt questions about whether the intervener's political will and judgment are such as to render an ameliorative long-term outcome more likely than a detrimental one. The historical record is mixed and contestable; the point to be made here is simply that the harsh realities of sovereignty in action should be measured against other harsh realities, rather than against an idealized image of "civilization to the rescue."

Genuine human rights policies are mostly policies that powerful states undertake against allies, clients, and other states that can be influenced by the withholding of benefits, often at some geostrategic or economic cost to the withholding state. Human rights policies thus represent a moral brake on the single-minded pursuit of geostrategic and economic interests. These policies can have ameliorative effects without impinging on the legal rights of the target state.

By contrast, the invocation of human rights rhetoric against geostrategic rivals, over which the invoking state has little peaceful leverage, needs to be seen in a different light.[29] Of course, there is no need to remain silent about rivals' abuses, nor to refrain from highlighting those abuses in efforts to weaken the political standing of the rival regime (though this may easily be perceived as a cynical tactic). However, the moralization of geostrategic rivalries is often a partisan effort that factions favoring confrontation employ to discredit alternative policies of accommodation. To the extent that it becomes a justification for taking measures that exacerbate interstate conflict, such moralization of the conflict potentially comes at the cost of further deterioration of those conditions of human existence that the human rights movement exists to ameliorate.

Thus, while there are episodic tensions between human rights advocacy and a pluralistic conception of the international rule of law, these tensions are not systematic and tend to be overstated. Indeed, great-power disregard for a pluralistic international rule of law is likely to discourage rival and weaker states from adopting human rights obligations, whereas it was no accident that the Soviet Bloc's adoption of the human rights provisions of the Helsinki Final Act, widely credited for helping to sow the seeds of East-Central European political transformation[30]—came in the context of geostrategic accommodation.

Not long ago, the rhetoric of human rights operated primarily as a shield, not a sword. It was a language of resistance to power, not a language for the exercise

[29] There may be circumstances in which de-escalation of tensions can usefully be conditioned on human rights improvements in a rival state, but such tactics may also pose risks to humanitarian interests. Even the archetypical measure of this nature, the 1974 Jackson-Vanik Amendment that tied U.S. trade concessions to Soviet relaxation of barriers to Jewish emigration, may have been less successful than is widely believed. Benjamin Nathans, "The Wild Desire to Leave: On Soviet Jewry," *Nation*, Nov. 10, 2010.

[30] *See, e.g.*, Daniel C. Thomas, *The Helsinki Effect: International Norms, Human Rights, and the Demise of Communism* (Princeton, NJ: Princeton Univ. Press, 2001).

of power. As such, human rights rhetoric could afford to be bold, sweeping, and imprecise, even in its legal formulations. The state—its interests and its values—would inevitably be well-represented, both in political fora and in court. Human rights advocates could concentrate on rousing consciences to affirm the dignity of human beings menaced by the power of the state, without much regard to an overall balance of jurisprudential (let alone policy) considerations; there was no real danger of excess in promoting dignity-oriented constraint on state action. Therefore, human rights scholars frequently set for themselves the goal of substantiating the broadest and deepest claims of the human rights movement and nay-saying scholars often confronted moralistic criticism of their efforts.

Such an attitude is maladaptive to the current period, in which human rights are invoked to justify exercises of power, ranging from prosecutions of former officials of adverse states to bombings, invasions, and occupations. It is in this light that one must critically examine the prospect of transnational prosecution of state actors—often characterized as the great international legal advance of the past two decades.[31] While such prosecutions are frequently touted as a peaceful alternative to military measures, a generalization of this practice actually augurs the erosion of constraints on the use of force. In partisan hands, legal proceedings can be transmogrified into festivals of self-righteousness, orchestrated not only to pillory disfavored political causes but also to reveal the fecklessness of those who counsel restraint and compromise in the face of a certified evil. In addition to hardening positions (akin to the insistence that one "never negotiate with terrorists"), attributions of criminality to adverse regimes tend to place enforcement demands on international institutions that such institutions characteristically cannot bear, opening the door to unilateral exertions that can be rationalized as implementation of universal principles.

## VI. The Way Forward

This book has two principal goals. One is to construct a unifying account of sovereign equality's manifestations in international law, from foundational doctrines to specific norms governing matters such as armed intervention and extraterritorial criminal prosecution. The other is to defend this principle—though certainly not every one of its applications—as a morally sound response to persistent and profound disagreement within the international community as to the requirements of legitimate and just internal public order. The book will make a moral argument for a pluralism of special kind, distinct from pluralisms that other theorists have accepted or (perhaps more importantly) rejected—a pluralism that is not deaf to

[31] *See, e.g.*, Kenneth Anderson, "The Rise of International Criminal Law: Intended and Unintended Consequences," 20 *Euro. J. Int'l L.* 331, 331 (2009).

cries for justice and humanitarianism and yet that remains, in certain respects, counterintuitively harsh.

Chapters 2 through 4 explore the basics of the sovereign equality framework and its justification. Chapter 2 introduces the peculiarities of the ethical questions facing (a) those proposing reforms to the international legal order, (b) those responsible for interpreting international legal standards, and (c) those having to decide whether moral imperatives justify breaching existing legal standards in a given instance. Chapter 3 gives an overview of the practical operation of the sovereign equality principle in the United Nations Charter-based order. Chapter 4 articulates a defense of the sovereign equality regime's pluralism on the basis of the need for a global order to accommodate endemic moral disagreement.

Chapters 5 through 7 elaborate the sovereign equality framework's application to some of the more vexing practical problems in public international law. Chapter 5 addresses the competing considerations involved in assessing unauthorized humanitarian intervention. Chapter 6 discusses the role of non-intervention norms in the international system's responses to crises of authority within states, including both secessionist efforts and unconstitutional changes of government. Chapter 7 probes the limits of international criminal justice, focusing on doctrines of international law that constrain domestic-court prosecutions of foreign-state officials for human rights violations.

Chapter 8 renders some concluding observations. It stresses the need to resist the temptations of a more straightforwardly moralistic approach to global order, affirming the moral value of unromantic legal doctrines that correspond to the requirements of an unromantic global reality.

# 2

# The Project of International Legal Order

## Introduction

Until very recently, contemporary normative political theory has given little systematic attention to the distinctive problems of international legal order.[1] There is, of course, no shortage of literature in normative theory devoted both to human rights and to "ethics and international affairs." Theorists of human rights have typically sought, however, to derive universally applicable standards of internal public order from first principles, without much regard to the implications for the international system of the empirical reality of conflicting political moralities.[2] Theorists of "ethics and international affairs"[3] have been more concerned to develop moral standards

[1] Some recent books point out and seek to remedy this deficit. *See* Samantha Besson & John Tasioulas eds., *The Philosophy of International Law* (Oxford Univ. Press, 2010); Larry May & Zachary Hoskins, eds., *International Criminal Law and Philosophy* (Cambridge Univ. Press, 2010); Allen Buchanan, *Justice, Legitimacy and Self-Determination: Moral Foundations for International Law* (Oxford Univ. Press, 2004). Less systematic, but significant, recent efforts to bring normative political theory to bear on the foundations of the international legal system include Terry Nardin, "Theorizing the International Rule of Law,"34 *Rev. Int'l Stud.* 385 (2008); Martti Koskenniemi, "Constitutionalism as Mindset: Reflections on Kantian Themes About International Law and Globalization," 8 *Theoretical Inquiries in Law* 9 (2007); Steven R. Ratner, "Is International Law Impartial?" 11 *Legal Theory* 39 (2005); David Held, "Law of States, Law of Peoples: Three Models of Sovereignty," 8 *Legal Theory* 18 (2002).

[2] Much literature has, of course, addressed the philosophical validity of the cultural relativist challenge to the assertion of universally applicable moral rights, but less has focused on evaluating institutional responses to the fact of moral discord. Important exceptions are Michael Walzer's brief defense of non-intervention doctrine in *Just and Unjust Wars* (New York: Basic Books, Inc., 1977) and his more elaborate response to critics of that defense, Walzer, "The Moral Standing of States," 9 *Phil. & Pub. Aff.* 209 (1980). *See also* Terry Nardin, *Law, Morality, and the Relations of States* (Princeton, N.J.: Princeton Univ. Press, 1983); Robert Jackson, *The Global Covenant: Human Conduct in a World of States* (Oxford: Oxford Univ. Press, 2000); Charles R. Beitz, Michael W. Doyle & Will Kymlicka, "Symposium: Walzer and the Moral Standing of States," 23 *Ethics & Int'l Aff.* 319 (2009).

[3] *See, e.g.,* Terry Nardin & David R. Mapel, eds., *Traditions of International Ethics* (Cambridge Univ. Press, 1992).

for a given state's external behavior in discrete subject areas (e.g., the criteria of "just war")[4] than to formulate a legal framework for coexistence and cooperation among non-like-minded states.[5]

Even John Rawls's pathbreaking late work on a liberal *ethos* of relations with non-liberal political communities did not purport to provide a blueprint for an international public order; whatever implications Rawls expected his "law of peoples" to have for international law, he understood his enterprise as the development of moral rather than strictly legal standards, recognizing that the latter would need to take account of practical considerations beyond the scope of his project.[6] It is one project to develop guidelines for unilateral action in the absence of a positive legal order, and quite another to prescribe reforms to the standards and processes that govern an existing (even if only partially efficacious) multilateral order, or to establish thresholds for unilateral ad hoc flouting of applicable positive norms that impede morally desirable action in particular instances.

Literature in ethics and international affairs often purports to evaluate and to challenge existing norms of international law. Yet very little of that literature grapples with the challenges that face makers and interpreters of international law amid existing global conditions of disparate interests and values, nor does much literature address whether and to what extent fidelity to existing international law—an accommodation among bearers of disparate interests and values—should restrain actors from acting on first-order moral considerations.[7]

Most of the ethics and international affairs literature offers moral considerations to govern decision-making that is essentially unilateral. There are at least four peculiar characteristics of the typical approach. First, the vantage point is that of a powerful, liberal country. Second, the theorist, at least implicitly, places herself in the shoes of those actually governing that country, rather than those establishing an authoritative framework for future exercises of power by unknown and untrusted officials; by eliding the gap between standard-setting and implementation, the theorist circumvents the practical concern that the qualities of judgment used to generate normative standards will be lacking in those responsible for implementing these standards. Third, the scene upon which the theorist arrives lacks existing legal norms and institutions; he or she is writing on a *tabula rasa*, without having to decide how to deal with such agreements and obligations as have been previously

[4] Walzer's *Just and Unjust Wars* is, of course, a classic in this respect.

[5] A noteworthy exception is Terry Nardin, *Law, Morality, and the Relations of States* (Princeton, N.J.: Princeton Univ. Press, 1983).

[6] John Rawls, *The Law of Peoples* (Cambridge, Mass: Harvard University Press, 1999).

[7] *See* note 2 above.

established. Fourth, the theorist undertakes the task of designing standards for his country's international conduct that are hypothetically acceptable to (because objectively fair to) hypothesized "reasonable" others, but that need not garner actual agreement from "unreasonable" participants—whose interests, values, and capacities for beneficial or harmful conduct are a fact of international life.[8]

This characterization is not intended to denigrate the theoretical work done in the field of ethics and international affairs, much of which is thoughtful and valuable. It is to say, however, that most of that theoretical work bears only indirectly on the ethical questions facing those proposing reforms to the international legal order, those responsible for interpreting international legal standards, and those having to decide whether moral imperatives justify breaching existing legal standards in a given instance. Just as a theory of justice, however inspired, can play only a limited role in generating a domestic constitutional jurisprudence, so, too, a theory of ethics and international affairs does not directly suggest guidelines for public international law.

In order to serve its essential functions, a legal order must have, in the eyes of a system's efficacious actors, a legitimacy that withstands disagreement among those actors about the substantive justness of outcomes. The project succeeds to the extent that actors comply with the law because it is the law, whether out of a sense of the system's legitimacy or out of a concern that others' perceptions of the system's legitimacy will lead, directly or indirectly, to costs for noncompliance.[9] A broad-based legitimacy amid diverse interests and values requires that all parts of the community settle for legal norms that fall short of fully realizing both their preferences and their principles. The need for accommodation, in the form of legal order, thus provides reasons for actors to commit themselves to forbear from much of what they might regard themselves to be morally justified in doing (or even, these considerations aside, morally obligated to do).

Absent an appreciation of this distinction between acts that are substantively just and ones that are internationally legitimate, the normative discourse on international behavior can become sharply skewed. Human rights advocates, as much as champions of national interests, are prone to a thin "multilateralism" that reflects a preference for working through international institutions, but little commitment to the international rule of law as such. Thus, they tend to perceive as morally binding, not international law per se (which represents an accommodation among bearers of competing interests and values), but only such norms of international law as comport with their own interpretation of substantive justice. If international law is

[8] The archetype here is John Rawls, *The Law of Peoples*, *supra*.

[9] That said, a fixation on compliance may lead to neglect of important indirect effects of international law. *See* Robert Howse & Ruti Teitel, "Beyond Compliance: Rethinking Why International Law Really Matters," 1 *Global Pol'y* 127 (2010).

valued for nothing beyond its contribution to the pursuit of a particular conception of substantive justice, then norms and doctrines that block the most direct path to that end appear as obstacles to be circumvented, not limits to be respected.

Martti Koskenniemi captures the sensibility as follows:

> [T]he advocates of deformalization now claim that their moral norms enjoy a special character that enables them to transgress the preferences of single individuals, clans, or nations. The force of their norms lies, they maintain, in the peculiar universality of those norms that result from their having been derived . . . from reason *tout court*. Because reason (in contrast to preference) is universal, these commands enjoy universal validity. . . . I can rest confident that I know what principles apply not only to me and my group but to any person or any group. If I engage in contacts with them, I need not face them as equals. I need not be open to their preferences because I already know that mine are universally valid . . . . [T]he object of my encounter can only be the transformation of the way they see the world, having them accept my principles, too (because they are not really "mine," but universally good).[10]

In international affairs, however, states (and "peoples") animated by conflicting conceptions of justice need to arrive at a working arrangement whereby each forbears from aggressive unilateral measures in service of its own moral position. The need to keep faith with the terms of accommodation—including accommodation with those who disagree about justice—undergirds commitment to the international rule of law.[11]

Koskenniemi, adverting to Kant's writings on international politics, asserts the wrongfulness of the 2003 Iraq War in the following terms:

> [T]he "illegality" of the war would become a key point in the worldwide opposition to it. Why? Because although it was carried out in the name of "freedom," it violated the key (Kantian) sense of freedom as self-determination and autonomy. The special scandal of the war did not lie in the fact that its justifications turned out to be lies and that, even if they had been true, they might not have made a persuasive case for war. The scandal was

[10] Martti Koskenniemi, *The Gentle Civilizer of Nations: The Rise and Fall of International Law 1870–1960* (Cambridge: Cambridge Univ. Press, 2001), at 489–90 (criticizing Rawls).

[11] As the book insists throughout, this conception of the international rule of law is not at odds with vigorous human rights advocacy. It disallows only a small range of external responses to human rights violations. Such responses not only are infrequent but rarely are undertaken for reasons primarily driven by human rights concerns.

> the cynical manner in which *the process to war brushed aside any need to treat other people as free, autonomous, and deserving an equal hearing in the common vocabulary of the law of peace under the United Nations Charter.*[12]

Thus, Koskenniemi finds wrongfulness in the refusal of the Bush administration to abide disagreement in the international community, quite independent of the substantive merits of the administration's case for war.

Nonetheless, if one accepts *arguendo* the substantive merits of the Bush administration's position, the persuasiveness of Koskenniemi's procedural objection is not self-evident. What is needed is a systematic account of the moral status of an accommodation with those who are wrong about justice—including with those whose claim to represent "the self-determination and autonomy" of other political communities is clouded by recourse to authoritarian and repressive internal practices.

What is largely missing from the discourse is the international political morality of the principled deal. This deal is not an amoral compact among wealth- and power-maximizing entities, but nor is it an "overlapping consensus" among bearers of diverse but "reasonable" worldviews. Rather, the deal is a combination of overlapping consensus and compromise, with respect to both material interests and moral principles. It is founded upon a mix of political morality, policy, and politics. A drafter of such a deal must propose, in good faith, terms for respectful accommodation among such bearers of disparate interests and values as one has decided—based on a calculation of the human costs and benefits of toleration and confrontation—to include in the scheme. An interpreter of such a deal must employ an interpretive method that keeps faith with those terms. And finally, an implementer must determine when, if ever, the deal should be breached in service of a greater good.

## I. Moral and Practical Considerations in the Crafting of Legal Standards

Although one might easily theorize from first principles a far superior design of the global system, with nothing resembling states as currently configured, a practical discussion of reform of global order can scarcely start elsewhere than from the political entities that are based on existing territorial units. Current territorial arrangements are, of course, morally arbitrary artifacts of past impositions, frozen by the doctrine of *uti possidetis juris* as of the inception of the current peace and security order. To be sure, one might muse about a wholesale redrawing of territorial

[12] Koskenniemi, "Constitutionalism as Mindset," *supra*, at 27 (emphasis added).

boundaries so as more plausibly to match local feelings of communal identification.[13] However, affective communities have no natural territorial coherence, and imposition of such coherence could be accomplished only by grotesque means. Although the international order might develop principled criteria for altering existing boundaries and creating new states in unusual circumstances, there is little alternative to a strong presumption in favor of the territorial status quo, with the hope (if not necessarily the expectation) that collectivities encompassing the permanent populations of existing territories regard themselves, or will come to regard themselves, as "nations" to an extent sufficient to accomplish the political tasks assigned to states in the global order.[14]

Similarly, in negotiating the terms of international cooperation, there is no practical alternative to beginning from the premise that governments exercising "effective control through internal processes" are the primary interlocutors. Such regimes are presumed to speak authoritatively for their political communities in the international order, exercising rights and incurring obligations on those communities' behalf.[15] Criteria may be developed for rejecting particular existing governmental apparatuses as patently unrepresentative of the territorially based political communities, but to begin a conversation about reshaping the international order without taking account of the presumption would be to reimagine the world rather than to seek to reform it.

In the international arena, despite a growing body of international law that bears on the internal character of domestic regimes, there persist sharply conflicting conceptions of what counts as legitimate and just internal public order. While states increasingly undertake legal obligations as to matters once regarded as "essentially within the domestic jurisdiction,"[16] and in particular contexts commit to abiding by decisions of supranational institutions, there remains an inner core of state prerogatives on which the international order itself is predicated. For all of its deepening complexity, international law remains a pluralistic enterprise, primarily rooted in the consent of individual states, that acknowledges and affirmatively protects states' presumptive monopoly on public order within their respective territories.

As will be argued at length below, there is substantial moral ground for attributing to discrete political communities, in certain respects and within certain limits, a right to be wrong about justice. This principle of self-determination entails a concomitant obligation of outsiders to respect collective enterprises of which they

[13] *See, e.g.,* Makau Wa Mutua, "Why Redraw the Map of Africa: A Legal and Moral Inquiry," 16 *Michigan J. Int'l L.* 1113 (1995).

[14] For the moral role played by nationhood, see David Miller, *On Nationality* (Oxford Univ. Press, 1995).

[15] *See* Brad R. Roth, *Governmental Illegitimacy in International Law* (Oxford Univ. Press, 1999).

[16] U.N. Charter, art. 2(7).

are not a part. However, the boundaries of the international legal order's pluralism need to be considerably broader than any first-order moral consideration, such as self-determination, alone would dictate. In addition to encompassing a multiplicity of values, the international community encompasses a multiplicity of interests. The international legal order must both, as a matter of policy, constrain cross-border exercises of power by presumptively untrustworthy actors and, as a matter of politics, maintain broad-based support in a diverse international community. The contours of a legal right to self-determination and of the associated right to non-intervention need to reflect, in addition to the political community's moral interest in immunity from even enlightened coercive interference in its internal affairs, the community's moral interest in immunity from an undue risk of self-interested, arrogant, or sophomoric interference. Thus, principle, policy, and politics can jointly be invoked in support of legal prerogatives traditionally attributed to the state.

At the core of the defense of international law's constraint on the pursuit of substantive justice is the phenomenon of moral disagreement. The most basic truth about the significance of positive law is expressed in Jeremy Waldron's simple statement: "There are many of us, and we disagree about justice."[17] As Waldron's work emphasizes, the need for a binding positive legal order at the domestic level stems as much from moral vehemence as from willful self-interestedness. This is no less true at the international level.

It is hardly remarkable that in any human society, law functions as an indispensable instrument of coordination and mutual restraint among constituent elements prone to conflicts of interest. But often neglected is the extent to which positive law—emanating from the "sovereign" authority of states, whether individually or collectively—operates as a response to conflicts rooted in *moral* disagreement. No society, domestic or international, can afford to allow its members to pursue justice, as they severally understand it, to the limit of their individual capacities. As Waldron points out:

> the Rule of Law is not simply the principle that an official or citizens should apply and obey the law even when it disserves their own interests. It is the principle that an official or citizen should do this even when the law is—in their confident opinion—unjust, morally wrong, or misguided as a matter of policy. For the enactment of the measure in question is evidence of a view concerning its justice, morality, or desirability which is different from their own; *someone* must have been in favor of the law or thought it a good idea. In other words, the law's existence, together with the individual's own

[17] Jeremy Waldron, *The Dignity of Legislation* (Cambridge Univ. Press, 1999), at 36; *see generally* Waldron, *Law and Disagreement* (Oxford: Clarendon Press, 1999).

> opinion, is evidence of *moral disagreement* in the community on the underlying issue. The official's failure to implement the law because it is unjust, or the citizen's doing something other than what the law requires because that would be *more* just, is tantamount to abandoning the very idea of law—the very idea of the community taking a position on an issue on which its members disagree.[18]

Justice, however objective a phenomenon it may be, appears in various and clashing ways to the minds of any society's members, who are no less prone to conflict when acting in a spirit of righteousness than when pursuing unprincipled ends. It is this basic truth that led Kant, typically identified with the primacy of individual conscience, to call for compliance with—indeed, absolute obedience to[19]—the norms of a successfully established political order. Whereas James Madison famously ventured that "[i]f men were angels, no government would be necessary,"[20] Kant was more perceptive:

> Even if we imagine men to be ever so good natured and righteous before a public lawful state of society is established, individual men, nations, and states can never be certain that they are secure against violence from one another, because each will have his own right to do what *seems just and good to him*, entirely independent of the opinion of the others.[21]

A domestic legal order solves this problem through the centralization of legislative, adjudicative, and executive authority: a centralization predicated on a notional commonality—however often illusory or imposed—of core interests and values within the political unit. The international legal order, however, is predicated on a much less robust perceived commonality of interests and values. While the latter order establishes positive legal obligations through treaty negotiations and norm-generating customary practice, it lacks processes for nonconsensual legislation, leaving it with community-wide norms of a least-common-denominator character. Moreover, the international order largely lacks centralized mechanisms for the

[18] Jeremy Waldron, *The Dignity of Legislation*, at 37.

[19] *See* Immanuel Kant, "On the Common Saying: 'This May Be True in Theory But It Does Not Apply in Practice,'" in *Kant's Political Writings*, ed. Hans Reiss, trans. H.B. Nisbet (Cambridge: Cambridge Univ. Press, 1970), 61 at 81.

[20] James Madison, "The Federalist No. 51," in Michael Kammen, ed., *The Origins of the American Constitution: A Documentary History* (New York: Penguin Books, 1986), 202 at 203.

[21] Immanuel Kant, *The Metaphysical Elements of Justice*, trans. John Ladd (Indianapolis: Bobbs-Merrill, 1965), sec. 44, at 76, quoted in Jeremy Waldron, "Special Ties and Natural Duties," *Phil. & Pub. Aff.* 22 (1993), 3, 4–5, 14–15. Waldron's work has built substantially on the observation that Kant attributed the perils of the state of nature not to selfishness but to moral vehemence.

adjudication and enforcement of international legal norms. There is frequently no international court with jurisdiction over an alleged transgression, and even more frequently, no international body with the authority to compel compliance or to impose penalties for noncompliance. A territorial state's consent is most often a requisite not only to a norm's recognition[22] but also to its implementation.[23]

The crucial question is whether, absent a state's consent to the implementation, within its territory, of norms recognized to be binding on that state, other states—whether individually, in an established "regional arrangement,"[24] or in an ad hoc "coalition of the willing"[25]—may find within international law a license to engage in extraterritorial application and enforcement of those norms: in other words, ***a right of self-help***. The problem, of course, is that self-help reintroduces the dangers that positive legal orders are meant to counter. Each state "will have [its] own right to do what seems just and good" —and internationally lawful— "to [it], entirely independent of the opinion of the others."

International law represents—not exclusively, to be sure, but vitally—an accommodation among entities prone to conflict rooted, not only in competing interests, but also in systematic and profound disagreement about justice. Political conflict's much-lamented intractability is largely owing to its moral component; contestants are least willing to back down from positions taken as a matter of principle. Although human beings rarely disagree about the most fundamental moral principles in the abstract (e.g., "murder is wrong"), they all too frequently disagree about the application of those moral principles to unmediated struggles over the terms of public order (e.g., "one person's terrorist is another's freedom fighter"). While the specific configurations of contemporary international conflict can be ascribed to historical

[22] The basic theme of lawmaking in the international system is that states are presumed to be free and equal and thus bound only to obligations traceable in some way to their own will. Thus, international lawmaking is, in the most general sense, a matter of state "consent." However, this consent may be express, implied, or merely imputed on the basis of some method that has achieved the acceptance of the international community of states as a whole. States need not individually and affirmatively will the obligations that bind them, though states that "persistently object" to norms in formation cannot, without some extraordinary justification, be said to become bound to those norms, even where the objection fails to impede the norm's crystallization as part of customary international law.

[23] Apart from the special powers entrusted to the United Nations Security Council under Chapter VII of the Charter, no state or intergovernmental organization has—or even claims—law enforcement authority within the territory of a foreign state. *See, e.g.*, Restatement (Third) of Foreign Relations Law of the United States § 432(2) (1987) ("A state's law enforcement officers may exercise their functions in the territory of another state only with the consent of the other state, given by duly authorized officials of that state."); *see also* G.A. Res. 46/182 (1991) (acknowledging that humanitarian operations within a state's territory require the state's consent).

[24] *See* U.N. Charter, arts. 52–53.

[25] *See Coalitions of the Willing: Avantgarde or Threat?* Christian Calliess, Georg Nolte & Peter-Tobias Stoll, eds. (Munich: Carl Heymanns Verlag GmbH, 2007).

contingencies of the "Westphalian" state system, the animating tendency toward moral disagreement is endemic to the human condition.

In the absence of commonalities of substantive moral principle, participants in the international community need to find common ground on a different plane. The imperative to honor agreements—and other forms of accommodation on which others are led to rely—henceforth becomes a duty, owed to the community, to maintain an expectation of compliance with established institutions.[26]

The point is not that considerations of extraordinary injustice, even unilaterally conceived, may never override the duty to honor one's formal commitments. It is that positive obligations may be morally binding even where they demand forbearance from the single-minded pursuit of one's unilateral moral ends. Whatever the exceptions, they do not swallow the rule.

Thus, however paradoxical it may seem, restraint on the pursuit of justice is not only central to the mission of existing international law, but also central to any sound theory of international political morality that pertains to the development of international legal institutions. Unilateral impositions, deriving from a particular, empowered conception of universal morality, are more likely to be the problem than the solution. What Prosper Weil stated a quarter-century ago remains valid today:

> At a time when international society needs more than ever a normative order capable of ensuring the peaceful coexistence, and cooperation in diversity, of equal and equally sovereign entities, the waning of voluntarism in favor of the ascendancy of some, neutrality in favor of ideology, positivity in favor of ill-defined values might well destabilize the whole international normative system and turn it into an instrument that can no longer serve its purpose.[27]

[26] Moreover, "honor" itself is not without moral significance, as it reflects integrity and respect for the other. One honors agreements made with the unjust, mostly because it is irresponsible to do otherwise when morally important interests depend on maintaining one's own and others' ability to trade on the convention of agreement in similar future contexts but also because treachery, even when employed against actors who are themselves immoral, incurs a moral taint.

[27] Prosper Weil, "Towards Relative Normativity in International Law?" 77 *Am. J. Int'l L.* 413, 423 (1983); *cf.* Alfred Rubin, "Actio Popularis, Jus Cogens and Offenses Erga Omnes?," 35 *New Eng. L. Rev.* 265, 280 (2001) ("To ignore the problems of 'standing' or to assert that the rules already evident in international practice and codified in the positive law of the United Nations Charter do not apply in the case of some selected atrocities by some selected villains (but not to others), or that lawyers' and judges' views of 'law' can overrule the political decisions of the leaders of the various communities that compose the international community today, is much more than can be accepted by anybody truly concerned with peace and justice.")

In lamenting the lack of systematic theorizing about international legal order, Allen Buchanan has observed as follows:

> [I]t is often said that humanitarian intervention is justified only to stop gross and large-scale violations of the most fundamental human rights, in particular the right against genocide, not to stop "lesser" human rights violations. What remains obscure is whether this constrained view on intervention is (1) grounded on a belief that a wider range of interventions is in principle morally justifiable, tempered by an appreciation of the fallibility and abuse that a less constrained rule would risk, (2) a concession to feasibility (on the assumption that states would not agree to a more permissive rule), (3) an implication of a particular theoretical tenet about the moral right of self-determination, according to which this right provides a fundamental moral barrier to intervention, or (4) a combination of all the preceding. Only a self-consciously systematic approach—an attempt to develop a moral theory of international law that distinguishes between basic moral principles and practical prescriptions responsive to the constraints of feasibility—can sort these matters out.[28]

Buchanan is surely correct that clarification is necessary, but the promise of a "sorting out" is misleading. Where one takes unilateral ad hoc decisions in a legal vacuum, one treats considerations of moral justification separately from those of feasibility and diplomacy; once one articulates a persuasive moral standard under which one's own measures are properly subsumed, one can move on to the discrete practical questions of whether one's well-intentioned measures will miscarry or whether they will so anger others as to produce bad overall consequences. The crafting of legal norms, however, entails additional moral responsibilities.

First, whereas the above-hypothesized proponent of a moral norm will also determine its application, and so can trust that the norm's application will be marked by the same judgment and integrity brought to bear on its articulation, the proponent of a legal norm must take care that the norm not license the kinds of decisions that tend, for systematic reasons, to be made badly. Legal standards are designed to impose accountability on not-fully-trusted implementers; a rule-of-law *ethos* militates against broadly licensing "totality-of-the-circumstances" judgments, since such judgments, even if potentially the most sound ones, also have potential to be radically unsound.

Second, in authoring standards for a "basic structure" of international legal order, one must take appropriate account of the moral interest in peaceful coexistence and cooperation among bearers of conflicting conceptions of legitimate and just

[28] Buchanan, *supra*, at 29.

public order. This moral interest should not be confused with any supposed moral duty to respect non-like-minded human beings' capacity to exercise reason on matters of political morality,[29] nor with a supposed moral duty to accept as valid for culturally different societies such home-grown ordering principles as are minimally "decent."[30] One might, indeed, accept the proposition that a single-minded effort to eradicate unjust public order everywhere would be morally desirable if it could be undertaken at an acceptable human cost. But insofar as the projected human costs of forsaking peaceful coexistence and cooperation render such an effort morally irresponsible, a designer of international legal order must offer good-faith terms for respectful accommodation among such polities as one has decided—based on a calculation of the human costs and benefits of toleration and confrontation—to include.

Poor and weak states—typically natural resource-exporting, dependent on foreign capital, and historically dominated from abroad—have long perceived systematic contradictions between their interests and those of the rich and powerful states. Although many Western observers nowadays dismiss Third World governments' complaints of neocolonialism and neoimperialism as willful distractions from more proximate causes of local problems, distrust of the more powerful states' intentions continues to be widely and strongly felt among inhabitants of the weaker states. Thus, there remains substantial popular backing within these states for insistence on maintaining sovereign equality as the bedrock principle of any scheme of international cooperation.

A legal order endures only if it reconciles the long-term policy interests of its participants, strong and weak. Since the strong often have the option to proceed by extortion or direct action rather than by accommodation, whereas the weak are willing to concede much in return for the guaranteed security of what little is left to them, the strong have disproportionate bargaining power in setting the legal rules. At the same time, the strong have reason to prefer orderly processes and clear baselines to the chaos and costliness of ad hoc exertions, and whatever their strength, the strong have much to fear from the desperate and the humiliated among the weak.

This commonality of interest between weak and strong states, as well among rival strong states, grounds an accommodation that presumptively bars any actor, however righteous, from disregarding an inner core of prerogatives and inviolabilities attendant to equal membership in the community of states. Only an exceptional

[29] Such an argument might arise as an extrapolation—albeit probably not a very good one—from Jeremy Waldron's respect-based argument against judicial usurpation of the political participation rights of those who might not be trusted to reason correctly about substantive rights. *See* Jeremy Waldron, *Law and Disagreement* (Oxford: Clarendon Press, 1999), at 250–51. Though inspired in part by Waldron's focus on disagreement about justice, I do not accept the proposition that equal respect for persons requires allowing the supporters of substantive injustice an equal say in political decisions.

[30] *See* Rawls, *The Law of Peoples*, *supra*, at 59–61.

process, established by the community of states itself and requiring an extraordinary concurrence of opinion, authorizes an override of the system's default rules.

Consequently, in the crafting of international legal standards, moral and pragmatic rationales are intertwined. The resulting proposal will contain elements of both overlapping consensus and compromise among bearers of differing conceptions of just public order. Once this *modus vivendi* achieves acceptance,[31] fidelity to it, even at the expense of optimally just outcomes, will henceforth be a presumptive moral obligation for all parties. Therefore—however paradoxically—a stricture that requires objective injustice to be left undisturbed may nonetheless be a product of moral, rather than "merely" practical, considerations.

In sum, substantive justice and the rule of law represent distinct moral values that, while often in harmony, are sometimes in tension. The rule of law, presupposing human societies beset by both conflict of interest and moral disagreement, establishes rigidities designed to promote reliability and accountability in the exercise of power. Where legal constraint lacks sufficient rigidity to withstand the pressing demands of substantive justice, the strong are unleashed to pursue substantive justice as they understand it.

To be sure, there are times when rigidities are rightly overridden, when unleashing those in a position to take decisive action is a risk worth taking. But one need not accept the conservative claim that "hard cases make bad law" to notice that "extreme cases generate bad dicta." Extrapolation from the extreme case has come to pervade present-day rhetoric associated with international criminal justice and with pro-democratic and humanitarian intervention, potentially leading in future cases to unbalanced assessments of competing considerations. The extreme case—for example, Nazi Germany or the Rwandan genocide—is invoked for the supposed lesson that inhibiting legal doctrines (e.g., *nullum crimen sine lege*, functional immunity, or the stricture against unilateral armed intervention) must give way generally to the vindication of humanitarian principles (often given a legal gloss by reference to *jus cogens* or some other juridical trump).

Yet there is little reason to accept an image of wealthy and powerful states that are ready, willing, and able to bestow beneficence upon beleaguered foreign populations but thwarted by the legal prerogatives of poor and weak foreign states.[32]

[31] The distinction between modus vivendi and overlapping consensus is a major theme of the work of John Rawls. *See* John Rawls, *Political Liberalism* (New York.: Columbia Univ. Press, 1992), at 144–50.

[32] Even the 1994 Rwandan genocide, the case often presented as illustrative of the moral bankruptcy of the sovereign equality regime, fails on close examination to demonstrate anything of the sort. As will be noted below, the failure to intervene was owing to a lack of willingness, not a lack of legal license, and when French forces finally did intervene, both the motivations and the results were equivocal at best. Although too little intervention is plausibly a greater problem than too much, it in no way follows that a broader license for intervention would yield more of the right kind of intervention

Those possessed of the capacity to engage unilaterally in supposed implementation of universal principles are both untrusted and untrustworthy. Constraints on unilateral exercises of power are thus salutary, even where they impede the capacity to pursue of what appear to be morally grounded purposes.

## II. Moral and Practical Considerations in Adjudication of International Law

### A. POSITIVISM, NATURALISM, AND THE SOURCES OF INTERNATIONAL LAW

In legal philosophy, the school of thought most frequently associated with the understanding of law as a response to moral disagreement is that of legal positivism. As Bruno Simma and Andreas Paulus put it, "It is precisely this need to get our legal message through to other people, especially representatives of states who might not share our individual moral or religious sensibilities, that constitutes one of the main reasons for the adoption of a positivist view of international law."[33] Positivism thus stresses the role of formal sources of legal authority that are manifestly accorded acceptance in the international community of states. Law must "preserve a balance between its transformative force, which does not accept reality as it is, and its roots in social reality."[34] Accordingly, if adjudicators, as delegates of the legal order, "exceed the discretion inherent in the delegation, they act *ultra vires* and are prone to lose not only their legal authority but also their practical influence."[35]

Legal positivism, in the words of its premier twentieth-century exponent, H.L.A. Hart, entails:

> the contention that there is no necessary connection between law and morals, or law as it is and ought to be, [and]
>
> the contention that the analysis (or the study of the meaning) of legal concepts is (a) worth pursuing and (b) to be distinguished from historical inquiries into the causes or origins of laws, from sociological inquiries into the relation of law and other social phenomena, and from the criticism or

in the right places. Meanwhile, if disposed to save as many lives as possible in less developed countries, wealthy states have far more reliably effective options at their disposal, none of which involve any breach of the core prerogatives of weak states.

33 Bruno Simma & Andreas L. Paulus, "The Responsibility of Individuals for Human Rights Abuses in Internal Conflicts: A Positivist View," 93 *Am. J. Int'l L.* 302, 303 (1999).

34 *Id.* at 307.

35 *Id.* at 305.

> appraisal of law whether in terms of morals, social aims, "functions," or otherwise.[36]

Positivism does not entail other contentions frequently associated with it, such as that law is essentially a command backed by a threat (a view famously held by nineteenth-century positivists such as John Austin), nor

> the contention that a legal system is a "closed logical system" in which correct legal decisions can be deduced by logical means from predetermined legal rules without reference to social aims, policies, [or] moral standards.[37]

Hart's positivism teaches that a developed legal system is based on a union of two types of rules: primary rules, specifying obligatory conduct; and secondary rules, specifying the methods by which primary rules are authoritatively recognized, adjudicated, and from time to time changed.[38] A set of secondary rules that achieves general acceptance in a society is ***constitutive*** of that society's governing authority. The legal validity of a putative primary rule is determined according to whether that rule is derived in accordance with the secondary rules.

As applied to international law, positivism entails a focus on acknowledged sources of law in the international community. The traditional starting point for discussion of sources of international law is the 1945 Statute of International Court of Justice (an amended version of the 1920 Statute of the Permanent Court of International Justice), Article 38(1) of which specifies the following sources to be applied by that Court:

> (a) international conventions, whether general or particular, establishing rules expressly recognized by the contesting states;
> (b) international custom, as evidence of a general practice accepted as law;
> (c) the general principles of law recognized by civilized nations;
> (d) subject to the provisions of Article 59 [providing that an ICJ decision has no binding force except between the parties and in respect of that particular case], judicial decisions and the teachings of the most highly qualified publicists of the various nations, as subsidiary means for the determination of the rules of law.[39]

[36] H.L.A. Hart, "Positivism and the Separation of Law and Morals," 71 *Harv. L. Rev.* 593, 601–02 n.25 (1958).

[37] *Ibid.*

[38] H.L.A. Hart, *The Concept of Law* (Oxford: Clarendon Press, 1961), pp. 77–96.

[39] Statute of the International Court of Justice, 59 Stat. 1055, U.N.T.S. 993 (1945). All member states of the United Nations are parties to the Statute by operation of Article 93 of the U.N. Charter.

Although Hart perceived the international legal order to lack a rule of recognition, Gennady Danilenko, a leading voice of unreconstructed positivism in international law, characterized this article as the constitution of the international community, "the rule according to which [international] law is created and developed."[40]

Article 38(1) has spawned innumerable controversies, many of which rage within the bounds of positivism. It is hardly clear that this list of sources is generally accepted as exhaustive today, nor that states originally intended the Article (which is obviously constitutive of the competence of a particular judicial institution) as anything more than declaratory of the progress, to that point, of a still-developing consensus on sources. Moreover, the provisions themselves—most notably, those regarding custom and general principles—are subject to widely varying interpretations. Yet it is hard to imagine a legal argument in the international system that does not at least make implicit reference to this list, and that does not appeal in some fashion to the notion of state consent (express, implied-in-fact, or imputed) that pervades the listed categories.

Positivism asserts that a legal system is essentially a set of rules derived from social facts, rather than principles derived from moral truth or policies derived from the preferences of those with the power to implement them.[41] But what counts as a legal "rule" is not so clear. Ronald Dworkin famously attributed to Hart the view that legal rules are limited to all-or-nothing propositions, either determinative or not in a given case, to the exclusion of legal "principles," which have "weight" in decision-making, but which do not "set out legal consequences that follow automatically when the conditions" of their applicability are met.[42] On this reading of Hart, controversies falling within the "core" of rules have determinate legal outcomes, whereas the resolution of issues falling outside the core—in shadowy, or "penumbral" areas—requires a judge to invoke supplemental considerations that are moral and political, not legal, in nature.[43] On that account, in cases where the applicable "rules" are insufficient to determine the outcome, the legal system typically authorizes judges to decide cases according to their "discretion," in a strong

[40] Gennady M. Danilenko, *Law-Making in the International Community* (Norwell, Mass.: Kluwer Academic Publishers, 1993), pp. 14–15, borrowing from H. Moser, *The International Society as a Legal Community* (1980), pp. 15–16.

[41] By way of contrast, *see, e.g.*, Ronald A. Dworkin, *Law's Empire* (Cambridge, Mass.: Harvard Univ. Press, 1986); Dworkin, *Taking Rights Seriously* (Cambridge, Mass.: Harvard Univ. Press, 1977); Lon Fuller, *The Morality of Law* (New Haven, Conn.: Yale Univ. Press, rev'd ed. 1969); Fuller, "Positivism and Fidelity to Law: A Reply to Professor Hart," 71 *Harv. L. Rev.* 630 (1958).

[42] Ronald Dworkin, "The Model of Rules [I],"35 *U. Chi. L. Rev.* 14, 25 (1967).

[43] *See id.* at 17; *see also* Hart, "Positivism and the Separation of Law and Morals," *supra*, 71 *Harv. L. Rev.* at 607, 614.

sense of that term; such a decision, though it henceforth carries the force of law, is not properly thought to be determined by law.

If positivism amounts to this proposition, its weaknesses are manifest, whether in the domestic or the international context. A core/penumbra distinction, separating the realm of "juridical science" from the realm of purely moral or political judgment, is unpersuasive. Even seemingly "easy" cases cannot be accounted for in so mechanical a manner as the model of all-or-nothing rules would suggest. Matters apparently within the "core" of one rule (and thus subject to purely legalistic adjudication) can often be shown to be equally within the "core" of another rule suggesting the opposite outcome. In these cases, no third rule can be found to determine mechanically which of the two applicable rules ought to be the basis of adjudication. Moreover, purportedly authoritative rules at times seem infinitely malleable, so as to make available a plausible *post hoc* rationalization of any desired outcome. Thus, the penumbra would seem to overwhelm the core.

Yet juridical opinion typically manifests an ethic of constraint; the availability of a semantically plausible legal rationalization does not, as the more extreme legal realists would predict, suffice to guarantee a legal judgment favoring the outcome desired on political or moral grounds. It is hardly plausible that such constraint reveals sheer lack of creativity on the part of the jurist.

It is more plausible, as Dworkin suggests, that principles and purposes are embedded within legal systems, and that in taking on the role of interpreter of a system's norms, a jurist takes on an obligation to temper her quest for substantive justice with concern for perpetuating the system's "integrity."[44] This means that a great many legal decisions are neither mechanically derivable from the legal system's putative sources of authority nor simply unhinged from them; rather, they result from jurists' efforts to construe the existing legal source material in such a manner as to make the output "the best it can be,"[45] which for Dworkin means construing the law to reflect the most coherent and beneficent account that can be given for the system's overall record.

Many positivists, including Hart himself,[46] have responded to Dworkin's challenge by denying that positivistic "rules" exclude the kinds of standards that have weight rather than all-or-nothing applicability, and by accepting that the legal validity of some such standards may derive from their moral content rather than

[44] As Dworkin points out, a naturalist jurist must sometimes uphold one party's "right to a consistent application of the public order" notwithstanding the other party's "right to a better public order." Ronald A. Dworkin, "'Natural' Law Revisited," 34 *U. Fla. L. Rev.* 165, 186 (1982).

[45] Ronald Dworkin, *Law's Empire* (Cambridge, Mass.: Harvard Univ. Press, 1986), at 411.

[46] In 1994, a new edition of Hart's *The Concept of Law* was posthumously published, with a "Postscript" that responded to Dworkin's critique.

their social source.[47] But these concessions render the distinction between "inclusive legal positivism" and Dworkin's attenuated version of natural law (so classified because it overtly makes "law as it is" depend to an extent on "law as it ought to be") rather abstruse, and of far greater interest in the realm of analytical jurisprudence ("what is law?") than in the realm of normative jurisprudence ("what ought legal actors to do?").

While formal sources of international law are a necessary starting point in any analysis of applicable norms in the international order, they are not the end of the analysis. As Mary Ellen O'Connell rightly contends, there is a need to consider "legal doctrine in light of the law's purposes and the polity's underlying principles."[48] Nuanced forms of positivism, in international as well as domestic law, have gone a long way to accommodate this longstanding concern,[49] just as nuanced natural-law approaches acknowledge that social facts very substantially constrain the project of legal interpretation.[50] It has thus become unclear whether the "positivist" label any longer clearly identifies an adjudicative method that is consequentially distinct from the most nuanced versions of "natural law" jurisprudence.[51]

The consequential questions, rather, concern the nature of the purposes and principles attributed to the legal order. Law is not reducible to rules that can be "found" as a matter of fact; legal interpretation is a purposive project. The real debate centers on which purposes—and especially, ***whose*** purposes—properly animate the project. In particular, the most pertinent controversies concern the appropriate weight to be accorded to the purposes and principles associated with the international order's default position: state sovereignty.

[47] *See* John Gardner, "Legal Positivism: 5½ Myths," 46 *Amer. J. Jurisp.* 199, 201 (2001) (on "inclusive" legal positivism).

[48] Mary Ellen O'Connell, "New International Legal Process," 93 *Am. J. Int'l. L.* 334, 336 (1999) (citing the canonical work of Henry M. Hart, Jr. and Albert Sacks).

[49] Simma and Paulus express this accommodation as follows:

> Both custom and general principles cannot simply be reduced to instances of state will. So-called soft law is an important device for the attribution of meaning to rules and for the perception of legal change. Moral and political considerations are not alien to law but part of it. However, formal sources remain the core of international legal discourse. Without them, there is no "law properly so-called." Only when linked to formal sources recognized as binding by the international community does law serve the decision maker in the search for a balance between idealism and realism, common values and ideological neutrality, apology and utopia.

Simma and Paulus, *supra*, at 307–08.

[50] *See* Philip Soper, "In Defense of Classical Natural Law Theory: Why Unjust Law is No Law at All," 20 *Canadian J. L. & Jurisp.* 201, 205 (2007); Ronald A. Dworkin, "'Natural' Law Revisited," *supra*, at 169; *see generally* Dworkin, *Law's Empire*, *supra*.

[51] John Gardner characterizes the differences as "normatively inert." Gardner, *supra*, at 202.

## B. THE JURIDICAL ROLE

Those who urge that international legal obligations be found to have a wider scope often assail opponents for their "formalism," their "mechanical" approach to the recognition of emergent norms of international law. One does well to recall in this regard Hart's observation that

> frequently what is stigmatized as "mechanical" . . . is a determined choice made indeed in light of a social aim but of a conservative social aim. Certainly many of the [United States] Supreme Court decisions at the turn of the century which have been so stigmatized represent clear choices in the penumbral area to give effect to a policy of a conservative type.[52]

What are being "conserved" by analogous conservative jurisprudence in the international system are, of course, principles and purposes associated with sovereignty. Adherence to traditional doctrines of sources reflects not an abject formalism, but a respect for aims that underpin state acceptance of and participation in the international legal system. One disregards these aims at the cost of losing what authority inheres in the role of interpreter of norms that states themselves acknowledge as binding.

It is this very role that Martti Koskenniemi (of all people) once disparaged in a critique of Theodor Meron's work on customary human rights norms.[53] According to Koskenniemi, Meron's search for "irreproachable legal methods" to demonstrate the existence of humanitarian norms in customary law is misbegotten. The traditional test for the existence of custom—conforming practice, combined with a manifest sense of legal obligation (*opinio juris*) —is, we are told, "relatively useless."

The first ground that Koskenniemi offers for this contention is the familiar observation that "the interpretation of 'state behavior' or 'state will' is not an automatic operation but involves the choice and use of conceptual matrices that are controversial and that usually allow one to argue either way."[54] This is a fatal objection only if "the choice and use of conceptual matrices" is something that, because not "automatically" determined by a legal rule, is entirely exogenous to a distinctively legal analysis. But a rejection of the cruder conception of positivism, as explained above, opens the door to a broader conception of the juridical enterprise, one that sees the

[52] Hart, "Positivism and the Separation of Law and Morals," *supra*, at 611.

[53] Martti Koskenniemi, "The Pull of the Mainstream," 88 *Mich. L. Rev.* 1946 (1990), reviewing Theodor Meron, *Human Rights and Humanitarian Norms as Customary Law* (Oxford: Clarendon Press, 1989).

[54] Koskenniemi, "The Pull of the Mainstream," *supra*, at 1952.

current state of the law as a complex of principles and purposes that can, as a whole, be furthered well or badly.[55]

Koskenniemi's second, and "more fundamental," ground for asserting the uselessness of source doctrine is that "it is really our certainty that genocide or torture is illegal that allows us to understand state behavior and to accept or reject its legal message, not state behavior itself that allows us to understand that these practices are prohibited by law." Indeed, to submit evidence of state practice and *opinio juris* not only "adds little or nothing to our reasons for adopting" the legal conclusion, but further "contains the harmful implication that it is *only* because this evidence is available that we can justifiably reach our conclusion."[56]

This assertion is ill-conceived (not to mention, difficult to reconcile with positions that Koskenniemi has subsequently articulated). To be sure, our certainty that genocide or torture *ought to be* illegal prompts us to read state behavior in a way that favors a finding that states have, by their conduct, acknowledged the existence of a legal prohibition. We are disposed, for example, to impose coherence on source material that can well be characterized as chaotic, in the process dismissing as "outliers" instances of conduct that contradict our thesis while enhancing the prominence of instances of conduct that support it. But insofar as we are committed to upholding standards of juridical inquiry, we must be prepared to reach the conclusion, however regretfully, that our hopes for the law are thus far frustrated by the reality.

This would be by no means to say that atrocities are somehow less morally wrong than we had thought, or that political pressure should not be mobilized to induce states to restrain their conduct. It would rather be to say that the additional source of pressure that we had hoped to bring to bear—respect for international legal obligation—cannot properly be employed in this particular instance, and that any attempt to do so here promises to impair the usefulness of that source of pressure in other instances where its prospects are more promising.

Koskenniemi elsewhere argued at length (again, during a phase of career in which his project was to expose international law's weaknesses rather than its strengths) that source doctrines are failed efforts to surmount the contradiction inherent in invoking the will of states to bind states against their will, the contradiction between a positivistic "concreteness" that threatens to validate whatever states actually do and a naturalistic "normativity" that presumes to subject states to the jurist's abstract sense of justice.[57] He then concluded that, in seeking to ground

[55] *See, e.g.,* Dworkin, "'Natural' Law Revisited," *supra.*

[56] Koskenniemi, "The Pull of the Mainstream," *supra,* at 1952–53.

[57] Koskenniemi, *From Apology to Utopia: The Structure of International Legal Argument* (Helsinki: Lakimiesliiton Kustannus, 1989), pp. 264–341.

states' obligations in their actual conduct, international legal argumentation ends up reducing either to apologism or utopianism.

Even assuming that the contradiction between concreteness and normativity is, at the level of high theory, insurmountable, this critical thesis at best accounts for the extent to which international law fails to have any real effect on international politics. Yet international law is not the crashing failure that, on that account, it ought to be: state actors do not consistently dismiss non-apologistic juridical opinions as utopian. Whether putative "sources of law" can be theoretically justified is, in the final analysis, less important than whether significant actors act as though they matter; the same can be said of any constitutional doctrine that restrains the exercise of power domestically.

Taken to the extreme, the critical account would cast international law (indeed, all law) as mere politics in disguise. But this is an elemental error ascribable to all variants of extreme legal realism. To say that law is inseparable from politics is not to say that it is reducible to ordinary political activity. Legal discourse, as opposed to moral and ordinary political discourse, plays a distinctive role in politics; stripped of the defining characteristics of that role, it performs no political function at all, neither apologistic nor utopian, neither legitimating nor constraining. And legal discourse is not capable of legitimating unless it simultaneously constrains. The very reach for the legitimacy that compliance with public law confers (whether in the international or domestic context) brings with it the cost of accepting constraint, and the violation of broadly accepted interpretations of legal constraint has the cost (albeit frequently a bearable cost) of undermining that legitimacy.[58]

## C. THE NATURE OF PUBLIC LAW

The term "public law" refers to law that regulates the exercise of public power. Although in many crucial respects domestic public law is not a model for international public law, the two share some essential characteristics. Most obviously, domestic public law does not fit the Austinian paradigm of command backed by threat, so dearly missed by those who question international law's status as "real law"; indeed, the very existence of domestic public law suggests a system that recognizes no Austinian "uncommanded commander," but that regards public authority itself as constituted by a body of law. The task of public law is to bring to heel precisely those who most directly control the means of coercion; its perceived legitimacy is its only weapon. It is therefore worth a short digression to examine how domestic public law operates.

[58] It was for this reason that E.P. Thompson famously characterized the rule of law as an "unqualified human good." E.P. Thompson, *Whigs and Hunters* (New York: Pantheon, 1975), at 258–69.

Where it is efficacious, public law embodies a broadly acknowledged framework for the legitimate exercise of power, from which can be deduced procedural and substantive limitations on power's legitimate exercise.[59] That framework consists of an agreement, express or tacit, among politically potent elements of the society on what shall constitute a valid collective decision. Exercises of public power that usurp the agreement (whether by piecemeal violation or by outright *coup d'etat*) are understood to justify resistance in appropriate measure.

A constitutionalist order—an order predicated on public law—is achieved and maintained where a society's politically relevant actors share a commitment to established principles and institutions of government. Those in power recognize that they may exercise their power only within the established competences of their offices. Those out of power recognize that they must obey the final decision of those officeholders duly authorized to render it. All understand their interests to favor sacrificing short-term objectives for the sake of maintaining long-term agreement on matters including, but not limited to, the rules of political contestation. A change in perceptions of long-term interests, however, can undermine this mutual disposition to forsake immediate ends, thereby bringing on a constitutional crisis.

The constitutional arrangement is structured in each case on the basis of the views and interests of those factions strong enough to have leverage in the political bargaining. The constitutional arrangement need not encompass every element of the political community, nor need its content have a liberal or democratic character. Some factions may reject the legitimacy of the constitutional order and thereby regard themselves as being in unmediated conflict with it; from their perspective, there is little to distinguish constitutionalism from absolutism, and indeed, their rejection of the constitution may subject them to emergency powers with absolutist characteristics.

In addressing disputes that arise under the constitutional framework, those who undertake a juridical role take on an obligation of "neutrality" in the following senses. First, they are obligated to be neutral with respect to the persons and political factions occupying the offices, the competences of which are at issue; for example, in the United States in 1974, Republican Supreme Court justices appointed by President Richard M. Nixon were obligated to doom the Nixon presidency by ruling against Nixon's exorbitant claim of executive authority to withhold evidence from the courts.[60] Second, in their interpretation of enabling statutes or constitutional provisions, jurists must not adopt a strictly partisan reading of legal norms established or tacitly preserved by agreement among factions, but must take seriously the elements of consensus and compromise underlying those norms. To simply

[59] I previously gave this as the definition of constitutionalism in "Evaluating Democratic Progress: A Normative Theoretical Approach," 9 *Ethics & Int'l Aff.* 55, 73 (1995).

[60] United States v. Nixon, 418 U.S. 683 (1974).

flout those elements for the sake of a partisan cause—even a just cause—is illegitimate in the juridical role and threatens the undoing of the framework that forestalls unmediated conflict in the society.[61]

None of this supposes neutrality in any grand sense, and where jurists make exaggerated claims of neutrality, critical theorists are correct to accuse them of obfuscating ideological preferences and power relations. Legal reasoning is a purposive enterprise. But the jurist's purposes must include fidelity to a conception of the authoritative framework that is consistent with continuing broad (though not necessarily universal) acceptance of that framework's legitimacy. To eschew that purpose in the quest for a more perfect justice is a violation of juridical responsibility unless the matter is so grave as to justify hazarding a constitutional crisis, with all of its potentially severe costs to all concerned.

Although the structure of the international legal system is very different from domestic constitutional structures, it is similarly the product of a combination of consensus and compromise among actors with differing values and interests. State actors, although concerned to maintain control over the scope of their obligations, concede that they are bound to abide by norms traceable, through source doctrines, to their own consent; a significant (though frequently not decisive) consideration in their policymaking is preservation of their reputation for abiding by such norms. The international system calls on states to restrain their pursuit of short-term unilateral objectives in the name of a long-term regime that confers mutual benefit. The system's efficacy depends on maintenance of its legitimacy in the eyes of diverse actors.

The role of international jurist carries with it responsibilities analogous to that of the domestic constitutional jurist. Those responsibilities are essentially political in nature; they reflect an ethical division of labor dictated by political imperatives. To violate these responsibilities in the name of the greater good of humanity, while undoubtedly justifiable in the most extraordinary circumstances, is to risk debasing the discourse of international legal obligation, damaging its legitimacy and hence impairing its efficacy.

[61] I regularly tell my students that I regard the existence of poverty in the United States—a consequence of decisions made or permitted by governmental authority—to be a deprivation of liberty without due process of law. I am prepared to defend this textual interpretation as being no less semantically plausible than many of the textual interpretations that have come to be well accepted in constitutional doctrine. But to adjudicate constitutional questions on this basis would be an untenable exercise of the judicial role, at least at the present historical moment. The same might not be true if social-democratic policies were at some point to become a matter of enduring bipartisan consensus in the United States.

## III. Moral Obligations to Comply with Existing International Law

### A. THE OBLIGATION TO OBEY LAW AS SUCH

Much of the point of the present book is to argue that state actors have a presumptive obligation to comply (and that individuals have a presumptive obligation to seek their states' compliance) with norms of international law, even where considerations of substantive justice might recommend to contrary. In order for that issue even to arise, however, one must first confront the objection that even in the domestic context, there is no moral ground for claims of political obligation.

According to "philosophical anarchism,"[62] obedience to even the most plausibly legitimate political authorities "remains as much in need of justification as disobedience."[63] Such philosophical anarchism might, according to Allen Buchanan, "not unreasonably" be presented as "the dominant philosophical view."[64]

The first thing to note about philosophical anarchism is that it does not deny that there are most often good reasons to comply with the law, some of which may be by-products of the very fact that putative norm is established as law. A leading proponent of this view, A. John Simmons, notes that "the existence of a legal order leads people to have certain expectations concerning how others will act. Where, say, disobedience frustrates plans based upon such expectations, there is a *reason* for obedience . . . ."[65] For example, in jurisdictions where driving on the right is the established norm, "disobedience endangers both self and others."

Indeed, the main point of philosophical anarchism is to contest patriotism rather than order. As Simmons puts it:

> We will normally have good reasons for obeying the law, and for supporting some types of governments of which our own may be one. But the reasons we have for obeying the law will be the same reasons we have for obeying the law when we are in foreign countries. And if we have reason to support our government it will be the *same* reason we have for supporting any other similar government. Thus, the conclusion that most of us have no political obligations does lead to maintaining that we are not *specially*

[62] *See* Robert Paul Wolff, *In Defense of Anarchism* (New York: Harper & Row, 1970), at 18–19; A. John Simmons, *Moral Principles and Political Obligations* (Princeton, N.J.: Princeton Univ. Press, 1979), at 194–95.

[63] Simmons, *supra,* at 200.

[64] Allen Buchanan, "Democracy and Commitment to International Law," 34 *Georgia Journal of International & Comparative Law* 305, 309 (2006).

[65] Simmons, *supra,* at 193–94.

> bound to obey *our* law or to support our government, simply because they are ours (or because of what their being ours entails). Insofar as we believe ourselves to be tied in some special way to our country of residence, most of us are mistaken.[66]

Chapter 4 below will offer grounds for rejecting philosophical anarchism's dismissal of patriotic duty, but one need not confront this problem to deal with the question of obligation to obey international law, for international law does not claim the kind of special loyalty that philosophical anarchists are keen to refute. Indeed, philosophical anarchists go a long way in explaining the moral bases of compliance precisely in the absence of such special loyalty.

Thus, R.P. Wolff observes the following:

> [I]f I am on a sinking ship and the captain is giving orders for manning the lifeboats, and if everyone else is obeying the captain *because he is the captain,* I may decide that under the circumstances I had better do what he says, since the confusion caused by disobeying him would be generally harmful. But insofar as I make such a decision, I am not *obeying his command*; that is, I am not acknowledging him as having authority over me. I would make the same decision, for exactly the same reasons, if one of the passengers had started to issue "orders" and had, in the confusion, come to be obeyed.[67]

For all of Wolff's insistence, it is not clear why in this instance the label of "authority" should be denied to the commands of the captain, or indeed, to the commands of the charismatic passenger. One obeys the commands because the existing pattern of obedience yields a beneficent efficacy, to which one might usefully add or from which one might counterproductively detract. Moreover, the effectively coordinated participants are collectively producing a "non-excludable public good." Inasmuch as one shares a common fate with the other participants and stands to share in the benefit of the collective project (as opposed, say, to being an occupant of a nearby vessel who comes aboard to confer supererogatory assistance), it would be blameworthy to shirk the responsibility of participating ***on precisely the efficacious***—if, perhaps, objectively suboptimal—***terms*** set by the charismatic passenger. The duty to comply with the commands of the charismatic passenger would even withstand manifest unfairness in the passenger's dictates, if resistance were to pose a sufficient detriment to a dynamic of collective compliance indispensable to the project of saving the ship.

[66] *Id.* at 194; see also Wolff, *supra,* at 18–19.

[67] Wolff, *supra,* at 15–16.

Substantial "content-independent reasons to comply"[68] with law can be built on this foundation, whether or not one characterizes those justifications in terms of "authority." Hobbes notoriously regarded efficacy as both the necessary and sufficient condition of both legitimacy and obligation,[69] but one need not take so extreme a position. More modestly, Rawls, following Kant, ascribed to individuals "a natural duty . . . to support and to comply with just institutions that exist and apply to us," and further qualified the justness proviso to stipulate only that the institutions be "as just as it is reasonable to expect in the circumstances."[70] Simmons questions Rawls's attempt to find in "applicability" a basis for special duties to support one's own state, but he does not deny the existence of *prima facie* moral reasons to support an efficacious and generally beneficent political order wherever one is found.[71]

## B. THE OBLIGATION TO OBEY INTERNATIONAL LAW AS SUCH

In a provocative essay, Eric A. Posner has called into question whether international law, as such, is ever morally binding, and thus whether breaches of existing legal norms should be evaluated entirely on the basis of prudential considerations. He concludes as follows:

> It can be useful for international-law scholars to point out that an act of the United States or some other country "violates international law" as long as we understand what this phrase means. It means that the United States is not acting consistently with a treaty or a customary international-law norm, and as a result the expectations of other states might be disappointed (or not), and these states might retaliate (or not), or adjust their expectations in ways that may not be to the advantage of the United States. These are all reasons not to violate international law, but they are prudential reasons, and they are reasons to be taken into account even when international law is not at issue. The phrase does not mean that the United States has a moral obligation to bring its behavior within the requirements of the treaty or

[68] Buchanan, "Democracy and Commitment to International Law," *supra*, at 311.

[69] *See, e.g.*, Thomas Hobbes, *Leviathan: Parts I and II* (Indianapolis: Bobbs-Merrill Co., 1958), at 152 (pt. II, ch. 18) (characterizing civil conflict over political legitimacy as the *summum malum*).

[70] John Rawls, *A Theory of Justice* (Cambridge, MA, Harvard University Press, 1971), at 115; *see also* Immanuel Kant, *The Metaphysical Elements of Justice*, trans. J Ladd (Indianapolis, Bobbs-Merrill, 1965), § 42, at 71 ("If you are so situated as to be unavoidably side by side with others, you ought to abandon the state of nature and enter, with all others, a juridical state of affairs . . . ."); *see generally* Jeremy Waldron, "Special Ties and Natural Duties," 22 *Phil. & Pub. Aff.* 3, 4–5, 14–15 (1993).

[71] Simmons, *supra*, at 143–56.

customary international-law norm, or that its citizens or leaders have a moral obligation to cause the United States to do this.[72]

Although Posner's is a realist perspective, many moralists display a parallel resistance to regarding international law as a source of moral obligation; the latter selectively regard particular positive norms (especially human rights norms) as a reflection of moral duties binding on independent grounds (just as Posner regards particular positive norms as supported by prudential considerations) but do not ascribe moral significance to positive norms that impede, rather than further, their moralistic designs. Thus, whatever may be thought of Posner's politics,[73] his skepticism is hardly parochial.[74]

Posner's contention rests essentially on two assertions. The first is that the supposed consensual basis of international legal norms is illusory.[75] The second is that the international legal order is inefficacious.[76]

The illusoriness of consent is a familiar point, though Posner's version of it is less familiar. Posner emphasizes the difficulty of establishing a moral obligation on the part of individual citizens—the sole bearers, he believes, of moral personality—to

[72] Eric A. Posner, "Do States Have a Moral Obligation to Obey International Law?" 55 *Stanford L. Rev.* 1901, 1919 (2003). In arguing against international law's advocates, Posner's article tends to conflate support for obedience to existing legal standards with support for expansion of international legal commitments. International law's advocates contend, he says, "that if states entered treaties with more precise and stronger obligations, gave up more sovereign powers to independent international institutions, used transparent and fair procedures when negotiating treaties, and eschewed unilateralism and bilateralism for multilateralism, then a greater level of international cooperation would be achieved than is currently observed." Ibid. Support for obedience to existing legal standards, however, in no way depends on, or commits one to, this optimistic view.

[73] Posner is generally associated with unilateralist thinking within the George W. Bush administration and has come to the defense of the highly controversial positions on international humanitarian law developed by John Yoo and other Justice Department officials. *See* Eric A. Posner & Adrian Vermeule, "A 'Torture' Memo and Its Tortuous Critics," *Wall St. J.*, July 6, 2004; Posner & Vermeule, "Should Coercive Interrogation Be Legal?" 104 *Mich. L. Rev.* 671 (2006).

[74] In response to Posner's line of argumentation, Allen Buchanan not only declines to defend the proposition that states have a moral obligation to comply with international law as such, but also affirms that "states do not have content-independent reasons to comply with international laws generally (just as individuals do not have content-independent reasons to comply with domestic laws generally)." Allen Buchanan, "Democracy and Commitment to International Law," 34 *Georgia J. Int'l & Comp. L.* 305, 311 (2006). Buchanan accepts only that "states may have content-independent reasons to comply with the norms of some international legal institutions," in situations such as "where the institution performs a valuable coordinating function by providing credible information to states, or supplies more accurate or impartial assessments regarding compliance with human rights treaties than states could achieve on their own." *Id.* at 311–12.

[75] Posner, *supra*, at 1905, 1907.

[76] Posner, *supra*, at 1914.

shoulder the burden of a past government's commitment. He complains that unlike shareholders, who are free "not to join the corporation if they prefer to avoid the corporation's liabilities," citizens cannot avoid the supposed obligation, even if they had been powerless under the political system that undertook the commitment or had not yet been born.[77]

But as E.H. Carr wryly observed, the idea of a state as a "group person" with moral responsibilities "seems to present more difficulty to the philosopher than to the ordinary man."

> The question whether the Belgian Guarantee Treaty of 1839 imposed an obligation on Great Britain to assist Belgium in 1914 raised both legal and moral issues. But it cannot be intelligently discussed except by assuming that the obligation rested neither personally on Palmerston who signed the treaty of 1839, nor personally on Asquith and Grey who had to decide the issue in 1914, neither on all individual Englishmen alive in 1839, nor on all individual Englishmen alive in 1914, but on that fictitious group-person "Great Britain," which was capable of moral or immoral behaviour in honouring or dishonouring an obligation.[78]

Posner's objection is predicated on a kind of moral individualism that only the most radical libertarians embrace, and that therefore likely "proves too much" even for Posner's own purposes, which are not of that nature.

A sounder critique of international norms' basis in consent would emphasize the methodological finesses by which consent is imputed to states, the power imbalances that mark international negotiation processes, or the problematic relationship between a government's consent and the collective will of the underlying political community. All of these constitute facially plausible objections.

These objections are troubling, however, only if a moral obligation can be predicated on nothing short of a genuine voluntary undertaking. However artificial, what passes for "consent" is the common theme of the international legal system's "secondary rules" (to use H.L.A. Hart's term for those rules that govern the recognition, legislation, and adjudication of the "primary rules" regulating conduct).[79] These secondary rules are established and accepted within a system that brings a modicum of decent regulation to what otherwise would be a severely chaotic state of affairs, with bad consequences not only for governments but also for their constituents, jointly and severally. Just as Rawls, following Kant, ascribed to individuals "a natural duty . . . to support and to comply with just institutions that exist and apply

[77] Posner, *supra*, at 1905, 1907.

[78] E.H. Carr, *The Twenty Years' Crisis* [1940] (New York: Harper & Row, Pubs., 1964), at 150.

[79] HLA Hart, *The Concept of Law* (Oxford, Clarendon Press, 1961), 91–96.

us,"[80] so, too, one can attribute to collectivities and their constituents a natural duty to support and comply with international institutions that, even if not "just" in any thoroughgoing sense, facilitate coordination and militate against predation to a greater extent than any available alternative. Moreover, while the "consent" that the system's secondary rules represent is concededly far too thin to be a self-sufficient source of moral obligation, the secondary rules, in deferring to the internal processes of territorial political communities, at least draw on such vehicles for stakeholder participation as are available. In the absence of a more legitimate and just alternative system that might feasibly be implemented, there is a fully plausible obligation to uphold rather than to undermine the existing international legal order.

This rationale presupposes, of course, that Posner's second objection cannot be sustained. If, as an empirical matter, international law does not meaningfully contribute to peaceful coexistence and cooperation, then it cannot be morally binding.

Although admitting that state behavior most frequently conforms to the standards of international law, Posner concludes that it does so principally for reasons of convenience and confluence of interests, not because the standards have the authority of law. International law does not, according to his empirical assessment, prevail upon states to do what they are disinclined to do.[81]

Many scholars have sought at length to demonstrate the shortcomings of this empirical assertion.[82] Although one cannot safely rest on Louis Henkin's exuberant claim that "almost all nations observe almost all principles of international law and almost all of their obligations almost all of the time,"[83] international law has a discernible influence on the very factors—material interests and the availability of coercion—that skeptics imagine to govern state behavior.[84] Indeed, in most of the fields of activity that international law regulates, states' stake in the stability of the regulatory regime clearly exceeds their stake in the outcome of any given episode. Powerful states regularly yield to weak ones on matters such as diplomatic immunity,

[80] Rawls, *A Theory of Justice*, supra, at 115; Kant, *The Metaphysical Elements of Justice, supra*, § 42, at 71.

[81] Posner, *supra*, at 1914.

[82] *See, e.g.*, Mary Ellen O'Connell, *The Power and Purpose of International Law: Insights from the Theory and Practice of Enforcement* (Oxford Univ. Press, 2008), at 105–28; David Golove, "Leaving Customary International Law Where It Is: Goldsmith and Posner's The Limits of International Law," 34 *Ga. J. Int'l & Comp. L.* 333 (2006), Peter Spiro, "A Negative Proof of International Law," 34 *Ga. J. Int'l & Comp. L.* 445 (2006); Robert Hockett, "The Limits of Their World," 90 *Minn. L. Rev.* 1720 (2005–06); Detlev F. Vagts, "International Relations Looks at Customary International Law: A Traditionalist's Defence," 15 *Euro. J. Int'l L.* 1031 (2004); *see also* Howse & Teitel, *supra.*

[83] Louis Henkin, *How Nations Behave* (New York: Columbia Univ. Press, 2d ed. 1979), at 58.

[84] "The importance of international law does not rest on the willingness of states to abide by its principles to the detriment of their interests, but in the fact that they so often judge it in their interests to conform to it." Hedley Bull, *The Anarchical Society: A Study of Order in World Politics* (New York: Columbia Univ. Press, 1977), at 140.

air space regulation, and the inviolability of flagged vessels on the high seas; they obey the law because it is the law, even where they have a short-term interest and a sense of righteousness that weigh against compliance.[85] It is only in respect of matters perceived to be of central importance to state actors' interests and values—which, of course, happen to be the high-profile matters that capture public attention—that the alternative of violating the law even arises as a live issue. And even in those subject areas—human rights; self-determination; peace and security; and armed conflict, in particular—international law is far from irrelevant to outcomes.

A world without international law would be a world without the baselines that are partly constitutive of international actors' very understanding of the issues at stake.[86] To speak of a state is already to have in mind a package of legal attributes, rights, and responsibilities; a world without these could be imagined, but it would require rethinking much that is currently taken for granted, and pondering measures that are currently almost never considered.

It is true that breaches are relatively frequent in those few areas of international law (e.g., the use of force and human rights) that seek to govern situations in which parties have enough of a stake in their momentary ends to risk destabilizing long-term accommodations. Yet even here, as Hedley Bull has noted, "where a violation takes place the offending state usually goes out of its way to demonstrate that it still considers itself (and other states) bound by the rule in question."[87] Not only is there, as Bull states, "acceptance of the need to provide an explanation,"[88] but there is also

[85] For example, when U.S. forces in Panama in the aftermath of the 1989 invasion searched the Nicaraguan ambassador's residence and confiscated weapons, the U.S. Embassy expressed "regrets" and returned the arms, notwithstanding President Bush's expressed skepticism about "why the diplomat had weapons 'up to his eyeballs' in his house." *See, e.g.*, Thomas L. Friedman, "After Noriega; U.S. Admits Error in Searching Home of Managua Envoy," *N.Y. Times*, Dec. 31, 1989, available at <http://www.nytimes.com/1989/12/31/world/after-noriega-us-admits-error-in-searching-home-of-managua-envoy.html?pagewanted=all>; *see also* Paul Kerr, "U.S. Stops Then Releases Shipment of N. Korean Missiles," *Arms Control Today*, Jan./Feb. 2003, available at <http://www.armscontrol.org/act/2003_01-02/yemen_janfeb03> (in 2003, after U.S. forces seized a ship carrying a shipment of missiles from North Korea to Yemen, the United States "said it lacked the necessary legal authority to seize the cargo and decided to allow the shipment to be delivered," even though Yemen had previously promised to desist from acquiring weapons from North Korea).

[86] It is important not to exaggerate in this regard. Contrary to what is occasionally suggested, international legal norms will never be constitutive of international relations in the way that the rules of chess are constitutive of chess playing. If a chess player violates any of the core rules of chess (as opposed to the peripheral rules, such as "touch-move," that typically govern chess competitions), not only is she no longer playing chess, she is no longer doing *anything at all*. The core rules alone confer meaning on a chess move; one cannot win a chess game by violating the rules, because the violation destroys the basis upon which winning is cognizable. But this is clearly not true of international politics, where violation can bring material benefits.

[87] Bull, *supra*, at 138.

[88] *Ibid.*

acceptance of a common reference point for the evaluation of such explanations.[89] Thus, in instances of violation, there is a commonly recognized basis for mobilizing opposition to the breaching acts. Breach entails a real, even if not a decisive, cost. A world in which this were not the case would be a very different, and even far more troubled, world.

The best evidence for international law's efficacy may be only indirectly observable. It is instructive, for example, that Israelis and Palestinians of virtually all stripes, for all of the parochialism that frequently characterizes their respective positions regarding the conflict, find themselves impelled to justify their positions to external audiences by reference to norms of the international legal order. Even when they dismiss that order as rank idealism, they often find themselves invoking one of its norms in the next breath. They do this, it stands to reason, because the legal validity *vel non* of their positions, even though not determinative of outcomes, is not politically irrelevant.

Although Posner and his frequent co-author Jack L. Goldsmith have sought (quite controversially) to denigrate invocations of legal norms as "cheap talk,"[90] their primary aim is to deny the rhetoric's relevance to the speaker's motivation to comply with international norms. They contend that such talk is costless and that failure to engage in it would gratuitously "convey information that the speaker is not cooperative."[91] Putting aside the question of whether rhetorical acceptance of legal constraint is as costless as the authors assert,[92] those authors do not deny the need to appeal to internationally efficacious political constituencies that are motivated by moral considerations,[93] denying only that such constituencies regard international law as relevant to those considerations.[94] In making the latter assertion (for which they cite little evidence), the authors fail to recognize that international law frequently furnishes the only ostensibly impartial baseline by which external constituencies can judge the moral merits of competing claims that are otherwise steeped in hopelessly parochial fixations (e.g., biblical claims to Judea and Samaria or the legacy for the Serb nation of the 1389 Battle of Kosovo Polje).

In the absence of commonalities of short-term material interest and substantive moral principle, efficacious actors need to find common ground on a different plane. A shared sense of honor fills this need, transcending differences of material and moral ends through a common commitment to keep faith with whatever accommodations are concluded. Of course, considerations of justice, even unilaterally

[89] *See* O'Connell, *Power and Purpose, supra,* at 169.

[90] Jack L. Goldsmith & Eric A. Posner, "Moral and Legal Rhetoric in International Relations: A Rational Choice Perspective," 31 *J. Legal Stud.* S115 (2002).

[91] *Id.* at S124.

[92] *See, e.g.,* O'Connell, *Power and Purpose, supra,* at 125–26.

[93] Goldsmith & Posner, at S136.

[94] *Id.* at S131.

conceived, may override this commitment in particular cases,[95] but they do not automatically do so. Those considerations must be set against both the practical need to maintain the ability to trade on one's word in similar future contexts and the moral obligation not to undermine the institution that sustains system-wide reliance on formal promises. (Moreover, there is something deeply unvirtuous about treachery, even when employed against actors who are themselves immoral.)

International law is thus capable of generating moral obligations. Such obligations may be binding not only where they demand compromise of material interests, but also where they demand forbearance from the single-minded pursuit of one's unilateral moral ends.[96]

## C. OVERCOMING THE PRESUMPTION: MORAL JUSTIFICATIONS FOR BREACH

> When Robin Cook, the British foreign secretary, told Secretary of State Madeleine Albright that he had "problems with our lawyers" over using force against Yugoslavia without Security Council approval, Secretary Albright responded: "Get new lawyers."[97]

Internationally lawful conduct cannot be said to represent the entire universe of policy options open to states that are guided by sound principles of political morality. Moral, as well as practical, exigencies unquestionably arise.

This is true, of course, in private life as well. Where individuals feel the need to break domestic law in the service of some higher purpose, it is often not open to them to argue that their conduct falls within a legally recognized "necessity" defense, nor that they are acting in the name of a proposed new norm under which their act would be lawful. Individuals can admit that what they did was unlawful and should remain unlawful, while still insisting that their higher purpose justified their actions

[95] In such cases, it is important that the norm be breached in the name of an alternative norm that most of the international community could plausibly embrace. Chapter 5 expands on this argument in regard to the NATO intervention to prevent the Serb campaign of "ethnic cleansing" in Kosovo.

[96] Michael Reisman argues that because the international legal system is partially inefficacious, vindication of certain—i.e, human rights-oriented—norms requires reliance on extralegal modes of enforcement. W. Michael Reisman, "Unilateral Actions and the Transformations of the World Constitutive Process: The Special Problem of Humanitarian Intervention," 11 *Euro. J. Int'l L.* 3, 14–17 (2000). His argument begs the question, though, of whether sovereignty-oriented obstacles to lawful implementation represent the system's dysfunction rather than its deliberate adoption of a particular balance of considerations that Reisman finds objectionable. If the latter is true, extralegal enforcement, whatever its other merits, cannot be regarded as a vindication of the legal order.

[97] Michael J. Glennon, "How War Left the Law Behind," *N.Y. Times*, Nov. 21, 2002.

in moral terms. Thus, for example, one might commit fraud to pay for a loved one's life-saving operation, or one might commit trespass and vandalism at a military facility to help mobilize opposition to an unjust war.

Governmental breaches of public law, however, represent a different phenomenon. Individual lawbreaking does not ordinarily destabilize legal order as such; most domestic legal systems have abundant resources at their disposal to compel compliance with law, so that even a successful instance of open flouting of the law does not have serious consequences for the survival of the breached norm or of the system of norms. Public law, however, whether domestic or international, purports to bind the very entities that possess the lion's share of coercive power. Manifest vindications of legality in the face of determined official willfulness are relatively infrequent. Public law thus relies heavily for its efficacy on a broadly shared perception of its bindingness. Desuetude is a theoretical possibility for all norms, but it is a real and ever-present danger for public law norms.

In the international legal system in particular, violation is a potential step toward the vitiation of a norm and possibly even of the entire relevant scheme of norms. An international peace and security norm that gives way "only" in the face of an empowered righteousness not only is jeopardized as a norm but also brings into question the vitality of the system of norms, or at least that part of the system that pertains to the subject area.[98] As elaborated further in Chapter 5, a successful open flouting of such a norm communicates the message that the international law of peace and security is understood by officials to be an inadequate guide to a state's responsibilities in a dangerous world. The normative force of that area of international law can scarcely endure repeated authoritative expressions of that message.

For foundational norms of the international legal order to fulfill their essential functions, they must at least be uniformly acknowledged to impose on states the need to provide a legal explanation for questionable actions. Typically, the state in question will construe the apparent breach as falling within a narrow, controverted but plausibly emerging, exception to a norm. This type of explanation has the effect of affirming the continued applicability of legal considerations even to dire circumstances. The explanation provides the opportunity for the international community to respond in concert by insisting on or modifying a previous understanding of the law, but even where the response is divided, the international system will have succeeded in characterizing even the most grievous choices as presenting a legal question. The lack of clear guidance from the international community on a particular controversial question will thus not have the effect of abandoning the field to empowered moralism.

[98] *See, e.g.,* Michael J. Glennon, *Limits of Law, Prerogatives of Power: Interventionism After Kosovo* (New York: Hampshire, 2001).

## Conclusion

A moral theory of international law needs to address not merely global justice in the abstract but the decisions facing (a) those proposing reforms to the international legal order, (b) those responsible for interpreting international legal standards, and (c) those having to decide whether moral imperatives justify breaching existing legal standards in a given instance. Absent an appreciation of the institutional considerations affecting a decentralized order that encompasses a multiplicity of interests and values, the normative discourse can become badly skewed. The result may be to undermine the perceived legitimacy of institutional constraints on untrusted and untrustworthy powers who, through unilateral invocations of universal principles, seek license to impose justice as they see it.

A drafter of legal reforms must aim to construct a framework for peaceful and respectful cooperation that can be accepted as legitimate, if not by all, at least by all seriously potent elements of an existing political community. In order to satisfy the objective need for accommodation, bearers of diverse interests and values must be prevailed upon to accept outcomes that systematically fall short of fully realizing not only their preferences but also their principles. An efficacious accommodation supplies moral reasons—in the form of the human costs associated with the breakdown of accommodation—for actors to commit themselves to forbear from much of what they might otherwise regard themselves to be morally justified in doing. It is through this lens, rather than by contrast to an ideal of global justice, that the sovereign equality framework can properly be evaluated.

# 3

# The International Law of Sovereign Equality

## Introduction

The international legal order's foundational principle is known, somewhat misleadingly, as "sovereign equality." The term might appear as an expression of naiveté, given that so many states in the international order are, as Robert Jackson puts it, mere "quasi-states": their statehood is "primarily juridical," for while they "have been internationally enfranchised and possess the same external rights and responsibilities as all other sovereign states," they are "deficient in the political will, institutional authority, and organized power to protect human rights or provide socioeconomic welfare."[1] The term might alternatively appear as a political demand of poorer and weaker states, as against substantive power imbalances in the international arena or as against treaty-based departures from equal status in particular international institutions (such as international financial institutions, the nuclear non-proliferation scheme, or the United Nations security order itself).[2]

But sovereign equality in the present context serves neither as an observation about empirical conditions nor as a political slogan, but as a reference to a core set of entitlements that the international legal order attributes equally to all states. These entitlements are expressed in the United Nations Charter as a whole,[3] and in

[1] Robert H. Jackson, *Quasi-States: Sovereignty, International Relations, and the Third World* (Cambridge: Cambridge University Press, 1990), at 21.

[2] *See* Colin Warbrick, "The Principle of Sovereign Equality," in Vaughan Lowe & Colin Warbrick, eds., *The United Nations and the Principles of International Law: Essays in Memory of Michael Akehurst* (New York: Routledge, 1994), 204.

[3] *See, e.g.,* Djura Ninčić, *The Problem of Sovereignty in the Charter and in the Practice of the United Nations* (The Hague: Martinus Hijhoff, 1970).

purportedly authoritative elaborations of Charter principles, including most prominently the 1970 Friendly Relations Declaration.[4]

Although the predication of international order on respect for the sovereignty of each member entity is traceable (at least notionally) to the 1648 Peace of Westphalia—a point frequently highlighted by those seeking to portray the notion as outmoded—the legal implications of this sovereignty have varied markedly from era to era. Except insofar as the Peace of Westphalia is associated with the notion that rightful governance incarnates a will imputable to the community inhabiting the governed territory rather than to a foreign emperor, the essential premises of the contemporary state-based legal order can scarcely be characterized as a throwback to 1648.

The current understanding of sovereign equality is owing in part to the 1945 United Nations Charter, which exalts the concept,[5] but even more to the geopolitical realities of the period from the late 1950s to the late 1980s. As Western and Socialist blocs turned from open confrontation to espousal of "containment" and "peaceful coexistence" (respectively), and as a Non-Aligned bloc emerged from decolonization to assert distinctive interests and values in the name of a "Third World," the United Nations system became a platform for accommodation among international actors who recognized few common principles of legitimate and just internal public order.

The resulting normative formula stresses the individual state's capacity to resist dictatorial interference in its internal affairs. While by no means excluding international legal norms that bind states in the conduct of their internal affairs, sovereign equality nonetheless poses substantial barriers both to the recognition and to the implementation of such norms. These barriers represent, not a mere inconvenience or a failure of political will, but integral aspects of the international legal order.

Sovereign equality, so understood, has all the while drawn moral and political criticism from nearly every quarter—from liberal cosmopolitans, from conservative realists, from neoconservative unilateralists, and from advocates for groups marginalized by the international system. The changed material and ideational conditions of the early twenty-first century have further called into question the continued viability of sovereign equality as the foundational principle of the international legal order. Long-term structural changes inevitably will—and indeed, should—result in modifications to normative constructs developed in a bygone era.

[4] Declaration on Principles of International Law Concerning Friendly Relations and Co-operation Among States in Accordance with the Charter of the United Nations [hereinafter "Friendly Relations Declaration"], G.A. Res. 2625 (1970). For analyses of the Declaration's components and assessments of its legal significance, *see generally* Lowe & Warbrick, *supra*.

[5] U.N. Charter, art. 2, ¶ 1.

Nonetheless, calls for sweeping reform need to confront an accurate unifying account and a properly qualified moral and political defense of the existing legal framework. It is by no means clear that the core elements of that pluralistic framework are outmoded or dysfunctional.

What is clear beyond cavil is that state sovereignty, far from being a status that conceptually precedes international legal order, is itself a creature of that order. The international system does not merely acknowledge sovereignty, but operates to preserve it (against forcible and other coercive intervention in internal affairs) and even to create it (in the processes of decolonization and in the recognition of new states). Sovereignty is thus necessarily transformed and qualified. Much as the individual in Rousseau's social contract trades his "natural liberty, which is bounded only by the strength of the individual," for "civil liberty, which is limited by the general will,"[6] the terms of sovereignty are altered by the state's incorporation into the international community.

Indeed, sovereign equality is a semantically inept term, since it demands a reciprocal renunciation of the same unlimited authority that it nominally invokes. In affirming and bolstering only such assertions of state prerogative as are consistent with the international system's animating purposes, that system necessarily qualifies the nature and scope of state prerogative. States can no longer claim, in the name of sovereignty, a freedom to behave in ways that contradict the very purposes for which the international community respects and protects sovereignty.

Under the United Nations Charter's conception of international legal order, respect for states' sovereign equality represents the practical implementation of "the principle of equal rights and self-determination" of the political communities that states encompass.[7] Logically, then, nonderogable limitations on states' freedom of action extend to certain matters of internal governance, the prohibition of genocide being the most obvious. Within the discourse of international law, "sovereignty" functions metaphorically, as an expressive reminder of certain legal presumptions favoring the independence of the system's units, rather than literally, as an indicator of a status beyond the reach of law.

It is here that the real questions begin. Contrary to what is sometimes suggested, the relevant clash is not over whether a shared social project animates international law but over the content of that project.[8]

[6] Jean-Jacques Rousseau, "The Social Contract," in Rousseau, *The Social Contract and Discourses*, trans. G.D.H. Cole (Toronto: J.M. Dent & Sons Ltd., 1973), 163 at p. 178 (bk. I, ch. 8).

[7] Chapter I of the U.N. Charter provides that "in pursuit of the Purposes stated in Article 1," which include "to develop friendly relations among nations based on respect for the principle of equal rights and self-determination of peoples," the "Organization and its Members . . . shall act in accordance with . . . the principle of the sovereign equality of all its Members." U.N. Charter, arts. 1(2), 2(1).

[8] Dominic Zaum distinguishes a "pluralist or 'Vattellian' international society" from a "solidarist or 'Grotian' conception" of a community interest. Dominik Zaum, *The Sovereignty Paradox: The Norms*

If one imputes to international law an inherent purpose to establish a universal justice that transcends the boundaries of territorial communities, the presumed state prerogatives unquestionably impede the global advance of legality. Those who understand the project of international legality in this way, therefore, typically portray sovereignty as the unconquered domain: a realm of lawlessness that must recede for international law to advance.[9] An alternative rhetorical move, still in keeping with this "transcendent justice" approach, is a persuasive redefinition of sovereignty that strips it of elements resistant to the grand design. Thus, a state's sovereignty is simply identified with, and reduced to, the state's responsibility to fulfill legal obligations.[10]

Yet one can posit, *contra* this "transcendent justice" approach, an alternative jurisprudence of "bounded pluralism," reflecting an assessment that the international community will, for the foreseeable future, continue to be marked by a substantial divergence of interests and values.[11] This is not to say that the international community lacks shared purposes; it is to say that those shared purposes include the establishment of peaceful and respectful relations among the among holders of a substantial range of conflicting material and moral positions.

In this view, the foundations of the international legal system reflect persistent, though bounded, disagreement within its membership as to what constitutes a legitimate and just internal public order. While the boundaries of the system's pluralism have narrowed progressively in the course of the United Nations era—excluding conquest and genocide from the outset, colonialism and *apartheid* in the

*and Politics of International Statebuilding* (Oxford Univ. Press, 2007), at 10. Zaum acknowledges that the conceptions are merely "ideal types" and not mutually exclusive in practice, but inasmuch as he associates legal positivism and non-intervention exclusively with the former, he sets up a dichotomy that needs to be problematized.

[9] Critics of the expanding scope and competence of international legal institutions, of course, similarly characterize sovereignty and international legality as rivals. *See, e.g.*, Jeremy A. Rabkin, *The Case for Sovereignty: Why the World Should Welcome American Independence* (Washington, D.C.: AEI Press, 2004); John R. Bolton, *How Barack Obama Is Endangering Our National Sovereignty* (New York: Encounter Books, 2010).

[10] *See, e.g.*, Abram Chayes & Antonia Handler Chayes, *The New Sovereignty: Compliance with International Regulatory Agreements* (Cambridge, Mass.: Harvard Univ. Press, 1995), at 27; Francis M. Deng, et al., *Sovereignty as Responsibility: Conflict Management in Africa* (Washington, DC: Brookings Institution, 1996) at 32–33; Helen Stacy, "Relational Sovereignty," 55 *Stanford L. Rev.* 2029, 2044–46 (2003).

[11] Gerry Simpson has elaborated a similar contrast between "Charter liberalism," as he (controvertibly) terms the pluralist vision associated with the Charter, and the "liberal anti-pluralism" of a set of leading U.S.-based international law scholars (i.e., Thomas M. Franck, Anne-Marie Slaughter, W. Michael Reisman and Fernando Tesón). Gerry Simpson, "Two Liberalisms,"12 *Euro. J. Int'l L.* 537 (2001). For related defenses of sovereign prerogative grounded in a qualified pluralism, *see* Jean L. Cohen, "Whose Sovereignty? Empire Versus International Law," 18:3 *Ethics & Int'l Aff.* 1 (2004); Benedict Kingsbury, "Sovereignty and Inequality," 9 *Euro. J. Int'l L.* 599 (1998).

1960s and '70s, and "ethnic cleansing" and peculiarly unpopular and violent seizures of state power in the 1990s—accommodation of diversity in modes of internal political organization remains a durable theme of the international order. This accommodation of diversity underlies the international system's commitment to preserve states' territorial integrity and political independence, often at the expense of other values.[12]

International legal processes militate against powerful states' penchant for invoking universal principles to rationalize unilateral (and typically self-serving) impositions upon weak states. If the operating principle of international legality is understood to be "bounded pluralism" rather than "transcendent justice," sovereignty-oriented constraints on the establishment and implementation of international norms appear as a fundamental premise of, rather than a mere impediment to, the project of international legality.

Sovereign equality is an unromantic foundational principle, designed for an unromantic social reality. For its moral and pragmatic justifications to be evaluated, the conception of international order that it embodies must be fully understood.

## I. The Many Meanings of Sovereignty

Since the end of the Cold War era, there has been a proliferation of scholarly works devoted to state sovereignty, most of them either approvingly announcing the phenomenon's decline, demise, or transformation,[13] or else calling into question whether the phenomenon ever existed or mattered in the first place.[14] A countervailing (though much smaller) set of works, presenting the diminution of

[12] *See* Thomas M. Franck, "Is Justice Relevant to the International Legal System?" 64 *Notre Dame L.J.* 645, 655, 662 (1989).

[13] *See, e.g.*, Deng, et al., *Sovereignty as Responsibility, supra* (arguing that sovereign prerogative can no longer validly be asserted by states delinquent in their fundamental responsibilities to their citizens); Chayes & Chayes, *The New Sovereignty, supra* (arguing for a reconceptualization of sovereignty as, not freedom to act independently, but standing to participate in international regulatory regimes); Stacy, "Relational Sovereignty," *supra* (calling for sovereignty to be redefined in terms of "care by government for its citizens" and responsible regulation of "citizens' interactions with the international community").

[14] *See, e.g.*, Stephen D. Krasner, *Sovereignty: Organized Hypocrisy* (Princeton, NJ : Princeton Univ. Press, 1999) (noting that as a result of "the absence of authoritative institutions and power asymmetries," principles associated with sovereignty are often not reflected in practice); Louis Henkin, "Human Rights and State 'Sovereignty,'" 25 *Georgia J. Int'l & Comp. L.* 31 (1995/96) (asserting that "'sovereignty' is a mistake, indeed a mistake built upon mistakes, which has barnacled an unfortunate mythology").

sovereignty as a threat to important values, proposes policies aimed at bolstering or restoring the phenomenon.[15]

Although this literature appears on its face to address sovereignty as a unitary topic, it encompasses widely variant understandings of the core concept. Often, these variant understandings bear on wholly separate areas of inquiry.

Any definition of sovereignty presupposes a set of practical questions to which the concept is thought to pertain. In general, the term "sovereign" denotes a source of ultimate authority, as opposed to authority that is shared with another institution or subordinated to systemic norms and enforcement mechanisms. But as applied, sovereignty may refer to a range of distinct phenomena, including, *inter alia*: (1) a state's empirical capacity, as measured by the tools of social science, to control its internal affairs, or to determine its own internal or external policies without regard to the preferences of external actors; (2) a domestic policymaking imperative to maintain or establish or restore a state's unilateral control over this or that realm of activity; (3) the source, within a given domestic system of governmental norms, of the last word on public order (and above all, on what counts as the legitimate use of force) in a state's territory; (4) the normative attributes of full membership in an international system premised on the "sovereign equality of states." All of these usages pertain to different (though interrelating) conversations, and any conflation of them will lead immediately to confusion.[16]

## A. SOVEREIGNTY AS AN EMPIRICAL CONDITION

Sovereignty is frequently associated with one or more empirical capacities, such as a state's ability "to control movements across its own borders," and to pursue "national policy agendas."[17] Thus, it is typically asserted that transboundary flows—whether of goods, services, migrants, criminals, terrorists, effluents, or communicable diseases—render individual state decision-making increasingly futile, and in this sense reduce a state's sovereignty. In addition, sovereignty is to said to be "violated when external actors influence or determine domestic authority

[15] *See, e.g.,* Jeremy Rabkin, *Why Sovereignty Matters* (Washington, D.C.: AEI Press, 1998) (arguing that the United States has allowed too much national policy to be decided through international channels and proposing a reassertion of American sovereignty).

[16] Other authors, of course, have developed related, but somewhat different ways of sorting out the diverse conceptions of sovereignty. *See, e.g.,* Krasner, *supra*, at 9–25 (distinguishing four types of sovereignty: "domestic," "interdependence," "international legal," and "Westphalian"); Jackson, *Quasi-States*, *supra*, at 26–31 (distinguishing "negative" from "positive" sovereignty).

[17] Krasner, *supra*, at 13 (defining "interdependence sovereignty").

structures," even if that external "infiltration of domestic authority structures" is invited by the state's rulers.[18]

Although empirical capacity is conceptually separate from legal entitlement, any treatment of international juridical sovereignty must confront the objection that globalization's diminution of states' empirical capacities has attenuated the relevance of the "Westphalian" juridical model. As the dynamics of the international markets impinge ever more on the capacity of states to regulate economic life, and as projects of governance increasingly confront challenges—from global warming to avian flu—to which geographical boundaries have little relevance, reaffirmations of state sovereignty's significance may appear archaic, or at least as distractions from the real challenges of the twenty-first century. Moreover, the emphasis on states as the predominant bearers of legal personality in the international order may be thought to be behind the times, as non-state actors increasingly have a direct impact on international affairs, unmediated by any state. Many human communities, associations, and allegiances operate across or without any respect to borders. Accordingly, a state-centric model for the coordination and regulation of global activity may appear to be both structurally and functionally out of keeping with the realities and thus moribund.

To be sure, legal structures represent long-term accommodations among efficacious actors, and while they outlast short-term fluctuations in efficacy, they cannot long endure if they are utterly disconnected from empirical realities. It is possible that a continued diminution of states' empirical capacity to exercise unilateral control over many areas of activity will eventually erode the state-based premises of the international legal order, occasioning a transformation in efficacious actors' conceptualizations of the terms of their interaction. But meanwhile, neither the diminishing efficacy of unilateral regulation nor the expansion of the influence of international organizations and non-state actors directly entails a change in statehood's legal attributes, because those core attributes do not presuppose a fixity of states' empirical capacities.

A concern for juridical sovereignty in no way disparages the importance, empirical or normative, of international and transnational patterns of cooperation and governance. The present discussion does not assume that state authority is (or ever was) unrivaled in influence over economic, social, and cultural life, domestically or internationally (though claims for the diminution of state influence are often overstated),[19] nor does it reflect nostalgia for a halcyon day when states could

[18] *Id.* at 20 (defining "Westphalian sovereignty"). Krasner thus devotes two of his four categories to questions of empirical capacity.

[19] As Krasner states, "It is nowhere near as self-evident as many observers have suggested that the international environment at the end of the twentieth century has reached unprecedented levels of openness that are placing new and unique strains on states." Krasner, *supra*, at 13. Moreover, "Increases

exercise power without regard to external influences or international norms (though democracy is inevitably debased insofar as discrete political communities lack the capacity to influence the conditions of a common social life).[20] Thus, with respect to the present inquiry, the objection to an overall fixation on states has little on which to "bite."

It is nonetheless worth noting that exclusive concentration on change in global affairs tends to obscure how much has remained the same. However much modern life is affected by global interconnectedness, it is the rare person who is well positioned to escape ruination in the event that his or her state experiences a collapse of territorial order. As long as territorial order remains crucial to human well-being, the question of the last word on what counts as public order in a given territory will remain a vital topic of inquiry.[21]

## B. SOVEREIGNTY AS A POLICY IMPERATIVE

The rhetoric of sovereignty is frequently invoked in arguments against certain modes of international cooperation and, in particular, against the undertaking of international legal obligations. In the words of John H. Jackson, "when someone argues that the United States should not accept a treaty because that treaty infringes upon U.S. sovereignty, what the person most often means is that he or she believes a certain set of decisions should be made, as a matter of good governmental policy, at the nation-state (U.S.) level, and not at the international level."[22]

Much of the rhetoric mobilized against international legal undertakings is overheated. Contrary to the commonplace framing of the issue as "state sovereignty

in transnational flows have not made states impotent with regard to pursuing national policies." Ibid. *See also* Robert Jackson, "Sovereignty and its Presuppositions: Before 9/11 and After," 55 *Pol. Stud.* 297 (2007) (arguing that disparagement of the contemporary significance of the state is largely unwarranted).

[20] *See, e.g.*, Michael Goodhart, "Europe's Democratic Deficits through the Looking Glass: The European Union as a Challenge for Democracy," 5 *Persp. on Pol.* 567, 571 (2007) (arguing for the centrality of territorial sovereignty to "democracy's meaning, justification, and legitimacy").

[21] Max Weber famously spoke of the state as the institution "that (successfully) claims the *monopoly of the legitimate use of physical force* within a given territory." Max Weber, "Politics as a Vocation," *in From Max Weber: Essays in Sociology* (H.H. Gerth & C. Wright Mills eds. & trans., 1958), 77 at 78. From a juridical standpoint, however, it is more accurate to say that the monopoly pertains to the authorization, not to the actual use, of force. For example, the central authorities may authorize subordinate governmental units or private contractors to exercise policing functions, may allow private persons to use force in circumstances of self-defense or necessity, or may consent to the introduction of foreign forces for specified purposes.

[22] John H. Jackson, "Sovereignty-Modern: A New Approach to an Outdated Concept," 97 *Am. J. Int'l L.* 782, 790 (2003).

*versus* international law,"[23] there is no inconsistency between a proliferation of international legal norms and regulatory processes and a retention of the core juridical elements of state sovereignty. Except in exceptional cases, exercises of the participating states' sovereign authority are what create those norms and processes. States do not diminish their sovereignty by binding themselves to international legal obligations, even in respect of internal public order. Just as individual freedom is not ordinarily identified with an absence of contractual obligations, but rather with the capacity to enter into contracts, juridical sovereignty is not properly defined as an absence of legal obligation. Moreover, as will be elaborated below, just as an individual who enters into a modern personal service contract is not thereby reduced to peonage status, so, too, a state that binds itself to a legal obligation nonetheless retains the last word on public order in its territory, and thus, without some dramatic further step, retains a residual authority even in respect of the subject matter of the obligation.

This is not to deny either the significance of international legal regimes or the potential merits of campaigns to resist joining them. International legal commitments frequently entail a substantial "democratic deficit," as such commitments tend to transfer decision-making authority out of the hands of officials accessible and accountable to processes of local political participation. Different interest groups and ideological factions will invoke such concerns, depending on whose ox is being gored. What from one perspective is a solution to a collection action problem or a hedge against local processes' short-term vulnerability to demagoguery is, from another perspective, a strategy by bearers of parochial interests or values to remove authority over local issues to more favorable and less publicly accountable fora. Where treaties renounce protectionist economic measures and safeguard foreign investment, they draw objection from one quarter; where they defend individual liberties against constraints responsive to local social mores, they draw objection from a different quarter.

The costs to local democracy and national interests may be particularly serious for poor and weak states, which typically have little leverage in establishing the terms to which they are to be bound.[24] As a practical matter, a poor state may be able

[23] *See, e.g.*, Henry Schermers, "Different Aspects of Sovereignty," in Gerard Kreijen et al., eds., *State, Sovereignty, and International Governance* 185 (2002), at 192 ("[U]nder international law the sovereignty of States must be reduced.").

[24] As a one-time World Bank official observed in the heyday of efforts to craft a New International Economic Order (NIEO),

> The basic question today... is not whether the poor nations are in a grossly unfavorable position in the present order. They are, and they will continue to be, unless they can negotiate a new world order. The basic question really is whether they have the necessary bargaining power to arrange any fundamental changes in the present political, economic, and social balance of power in the world.

to do little more with its sovereign authority than to conclude humiliating deals that impose debilitating constraints on its economic decision-making.[25] Background conditions, which may be direct or indirect effects of historical injustices, may prompt those exercising a state's sovereign authority to perceive such a deal as the lesser evil. Of course, that rationale may be mistaken, or worse, a smokescreen to obscure a government's promotion of private economic interests (of government officials themselves, or of their core constituents within the political community) at the expense of the common weal. All of this is to say that a state's sovereign authority may thus be of diminished practical value in a particular context, and that on some occasions, a state's sovereign authority may be sold out by a leadership that is unduly influenced or corrupted by foreign interests.

The present discussion does not seek to ignore or to minimize such problems but rather to bracket them. Even in the worst case, what is being lost is not sovereignty in the juridical sense, and to lose the latter, on top of everything else, would be worse still.

## C. SOVEREIGNTY AND DOMESTIC LEGALITY

The domestic-juridical sense of "sovereignty" evokes an anti-constitutionalist doctrine, originating in the works of Jean Bodin and Thomas Hobbes,[26] that identifies an uncommanded commander, above the law, as the ultimate source of domestic authority. According to Hobbes, "The sovereign of a commonwealth, be it an assembly or one man, is not subject to the civil laws."[27] He further explained:

> It is true that sovereigns are all subject to the laws of nature, because such laws be divine and cannot by any man or commonwealth be abrogated.

M. Ul Haq, "The Third World and the International Economic Order" (Overseas Development Council Development Paper #22, 1976), at 10, quoted in Burns Weston, "The Charter of Economic Rights and Duties of States and the Deprivation of Foreign-Owned Wealth," 75 *Am. J. Int'l L.* 437, 457 n.93 (1981).

[25] *See, e.g.*, Antony Anghie, *Imperialism, Sovereignty and the Making of International Law* (Cambridge Univ. Press, 2004), at 196–244.

[26] Jean Bodin, *Six Books of the Commonwealth* [1576], trans. M.J. Tooley (Oxford: Basil Blackwell, 1955); Thomas Hobbes, *Leviathan: Parts I and II* [1651] (Indianapolis: Bobbs-Merrill Co., 1958).

[27] Hobbes, *supra*, at 211 [ch. 26]:

> For having power to make and repeal laws, he may, when he pleaseth, free himself from that subjection by repealing those laws that trouble him, and making of new; and consequently he was free before. For he is free that can be free when he will: nor is it possible for any person to be bound to himself, because he that can bind can release; and therefore he that is bound to himself only is not bound.

*See also* Hugo Grotius, *De Jure Belli ac Pacis* (1625), Bk. I, Pt. 7 ("That power is called sovereign, whose actions are not subject to the controul of any other power, so as to be annulled at the pleasure of any other human will.").

> But to those laws which the sovereign himself – that is, which the commonwealth—maketh, he is not subject. For to be subject to laws is to be to be subject to the commonwealth—that is, to the sovereign representative – that is, to himself which is not subjection, but freedom from the laws. Which error, because it setteth the laws above the sovereign, setteth also a judge above him, and a power to punish him; which is to make a new sovereign; and again for the same reason a third to punish the second; and so continually without end, to the confusion and dissolution of the commonwealth.[28]

This approach regards all separation of powers as anathema, "[f]or what is it to divide the power of a commonwealth, but to dissolve it; for powers divided mutually destroy each other."[29]

As originally advocated, the uncommanded-commander doctrine scarcely has any remaining defenders. The alternative doctrine—the outlines of which can be seen as early as the sixteenth-century writings of Bodin's ideological opponent, François Hotman[30]—regards sovereignty as *constituted* by legal norms, whether embodied in communal traditions or in a foundational document. On this constitutive account (which need not entail liberal or democratic principles), sovereignty belongs to the political community as a whole. One identifies authentic articulations of sovereign will by reference to a legal framework that the community's efficacious actors widely acknowledge as the touchstone of legitimacy. Even a quasi-absolute dynastic monarch cannot stand above the customary law on which his rule is founded. A modern constitutional framework confers authority on the dictates of specified persons at specified times within specified ranges of competence[31]; being the source of governmental authority, it serves also as a limitation on power's legitimate exercise. As the neo-Bodinian Carl Schmitt disapprovingly observed, modern constitutionalism conceptualizes the state as "nothing else than the legal order itself. . . . The highest competence cannot be traceable to a person or

[28] Hobbes, *supra*, at 254–55 [ch. 29].

[29] *Id.* at 255 [ch. 29]. Hobbes ridiculed the idea of divided powers as "beholding to some of those that, making profession of the laws, endeavour to make them depend upon their own learning, and not upon the legislative power." *Id.*

[30] François Hotman, "Francogallia" [1574], in Julian H. Franklin, ed., *Constitutionalism and Resistance in the Sixteenth Century* (New York: Western Publishing Co., Inc., 1969) 53, 90–91 (French kings had historically been and, therefore by custom were, "bound by definite laws and compacts").

[31] *See* H.L.A. Hart, "Positivism and the Separation of Law and Morals," 71 *Harv. L. Rev.* 593, 603 (1958) ("nothing which legislators do makes law unless they comply with fundamental accepted rules specifying the essential lawmaking procedures").

to a sociopsychological power complex but only to the sovereign order in the unity of the system of norms."[32]

In ordinary times, this latter account of governmental authority dominates the jurisprudential discourse. Nonetheless, perceptions of a grave threat to public order raise questions about ultimate authority that a constitutionalist approach may not satisfactorily resolve. The Constitution, it is often said, "is not a suicide pact,"[33] but either explicitly or implicitly acknowledges a residuum of discretionary authority, inherent in sovereignty, to suspend constitutional norms in the face of existential threats to the constitutional order itself. On this theory, even where the Constitution authentically reflects the political community's will, its static interpretation of that will cannot be a complete guide to action in subsequently arising exigent circumstances, the details of which can never be fully foreseen.

As further developed in Schmitt's Weimar-era work, the insights of Bodin and Hobbes, obscured in normal times, become salient at the moment of "the exception."[34] According to Schmitt, "the authority to suspend valid law—be it in general or in a specific case—is . . . the actual mark of sovereignty."[35] Schmitt's ultimate point is that sovereignty can never be fully subsumed within a constitutional order. Enemies of the constitutional order (*pouvoir constitué*) can, after all, overthrow it in the name of the latent will of the political community (*pouvoir constituant*), and their claim that will be deemed vindicated if their revolution is efficacious.[36] So, too, argues Schmitt, can allies of the Constitution, in the name of their own interpretation of the political community's latent will (as reflected, but only imperfectly embodied, in the constitutional design), suspend temporarily those aspects of the constitutional order that impede the fight for its very survival, or indeed transform the constitutional order in the name of serving its higher purposes.[37]

To be sure, Schmitt's early critique of what might be called "reductionist constitutionalism" has disquieting implications, and Schmitt's subsequent apologism for the Third Reich provides little reassurance about the uses to which his foundational

[32] Carl Schmitt, *Political Theology: Four Chapters on the Concept of Sovereignty* [1922], trans. George Schwab (Cambridge, Mass.: The MIT Press, 1985), 19.

[33] This phrase, though surely not all of the uses to which it has been put, can be traced to Justice Jackson's dissent in *Terminiello v. City of Chicago*, 337 U.S. 1, 37 (1949).

[34] Schmitt, *supra*, at 5.

[35] Schmitt, *supra*, at 9.

[36] "Successful revolution sooner or later begets its own legality." Stanley A. de Smith, *Constitutional and Administrative Law* (London: Penguin Books, 3rd ed. 1977), at 66–67.

[37] *See generally* George Schwab, *The Challenge of the Exception*, 2d ed. (New York: Greenwood Press 1989).

insight might be put. Oren Gross and Fionnuala Ní Aoláin explain the perniciousness of Schmitt's solution to the existential threat conundrum as follows:

> The dictator's unlimited powers are exercisable in the context of the extreme case – i.e., the exception. However, the only logical outcome of Schmitt's collapsing together the power to decide the existence of the exception and the breadth of counter-emergency powers to be used in order to bring the exception to a conclusion, and depositing them both in the hands of one person – the sovereign dictator – is that the dictator's unlimited powers are never turned off.[38]

But whatever normative objections might be posed against Schmitt's suggested response to existential threats to the constitutional order,[39] the underlying conceptual scheme is harder to refute and indeed is not without liberal pedigree.

Not even John Locke, best known as the enemy of "rule by extemporary arbitrary decree,"[40] asserted that sovereign authority could be reduced to legal norms. Rather, Locke acknowledged a residual prerogative power that allowed the executive to violate legal norms in name of a unilaterally held conception of the underlying purposes of the legal order:

> This power to act according to discretion, for the public good, without the prescription of the law, ***and sometimes even against it***, is that which is

[38] Oren Gross & Fionnuala Ní Aoláin, *Law in Times of Crisis: Emergency Powers in Theory and Practice* (Cambridge: Cambridge Univ. Press, 2006), at 165.

[39] Since September 11, 2001, echoes of Schmitt can be heard in arguments for an expanded interpretation of emergency powers. *See* Jay S. Bybee, assistant attorney general, "Memorandum for Alberto R. Gonzales, Counsel to the President, Re: Standards of Conduct for Interrogation under 18 U.S.C. §§ 2340–2340A," August 1, 2002 ("Bybee Memo"), at 36–39 (asserting for the U.S. president an inherent authority to disregard statutes that interfere with the discharge of national security responsibilities). However, Schmitt's theory of "exception" arose from the political circumstances in Weimer Germany, where the constitution's enemies were well-represented in governmental institutions, portending deadlock and paralysis of those institutions in the face of the threat. Whatever other challenges the U.S. may be said to have faced after the events of September 11, ordinary institutional processes were quite unimpaired in their capacity to respond. Not all emergencies are "exceptional," in the Schmittian sense.

[40] John Locke, *Second Treatise of Government* (1690), ch. 11, sec. 136 ("The legislative, or supreme authority, cannot assume to its self a power to rule by extemporary arbitrary decrees, but is bound to dispense justice, and decide the rights of the subject by promulgated standing laws, and known authorized judges; for the law of nature being unwritten, and so no where to be found but in the minds of men, they who through passion or interest shall miscite, or misapply it, cannot so easily be convinced of their mistake where there is no established judge; and so it serves not, as it ought, to determine the rights, and fence the properties of those that live under it, especially where every one is judge, interpreter, and executioner of it too, and that in his own case . . .").

> called prerogative: for since in some governments the lawmaking power is not always in being, and is usually too numerous, and so too slow, for the dispatch requisite to execution; and because also it is impossible to foresee, and so by laws to provide for, all accidents and necessities that may concern the public, or to make such laws as will do no harm, if they are executed with an inflexible rigour, on all occasions, and upon all persons that may come in their way; therefore there is a latitude left to the executive power, to do many things of choice which the laws do not prescribe.[41]

Terry Nardin charges that "Schmitt's 'decisionism' misunderstands sovereignty, which is not *de facto* power but rather the authority to enact law that is itself constituted and regulated by law."[42] Yet the choice that Nardin poses, between legal authority and mere "*de facto* power," is a false one: as Weber pointed out, authority may derive not exclusively from law but also from other sources, such as tradition or charisma.[43] Even Schmitt's positivist opponents understood authority's ultimate source to be extralegal; positivism ascribes legal validity to exercises of power by reference to the given legal order's foundational norm (i.e., Kelsen's *Grundnorm* or Hart's set of "secondary rules"), but holds the authoritativeness of that foundational norm to be a political, not a legal, question. Schmitt's innovation was to assert a crucial role for extralegal authority—as conceptualized variously by "a militaristic bureaucracy, a self-governing body controlled by the spirit of commercialism, or a radical party organization"—not merely in the founding or overthrow of a legal order, but also in the preservation of such an order in times of crisis.[44]

While tangential to the question of sovereign equality in the international order, the domestic-juridical sense of sovereignty speaks to the nature of the state authority that the international order recognizes and protects. Paradoxically, the international rule of law establishes space for exercises of state authority that may or may not comport with domestic legality. A state, *qua* territorial political community, bears an underlying capacity (*pouvoir constituant*) to suspend, to modify, or to overthrow constituted governmental order (*pouvoir constitué*). The international system, for the purpose of respecting states' rights, obligations, powers, and immunities, is obliged to discern what counts as an authoritative exercise of that capacity. Historically, effectiveness in securing the acquiescence of the territorial population,

[41] Locke, *supra*, ch. 14, para. 160 (emphasis added), on prerogative power. *See also* Clement Fatovic, "Emergency Action as Jurisprudential Miracle: Liberalism's Political Theology of Prerogative," 6 *Persp. on Pol.* 487, 491–94 (Sept. 2008) (comparing and contrasting Locke and Schmitt on this point).

[42] Terry Nardin, "Theorising the International Rule of Law," *Rev. Int'l Stud.* 34 (2008), 385, 396.

[43] Max Weber, *Economy and Society*, eds. Guenther Roth & Clause Wittich (Berkeley: Univ. of California Press, 1978), vol 1, at 215.

[44] Schmitt, *supra*, at 9–10.

rather than consistency with preexisting constitutional norms, has been the criterion of international acknowledgment of valid exercises of state authority. Violations of domestic law thus may be recognized as valid exercises of sovereignty for purposes of international law.[45]

## D. SOVEREIGNTY AND INTERNATIONAL LEGALITY: THE SOVEREIGN EQUALITY REGIME

The term "sovereign equality of states" appropriately captures the paradox and tension inherent in a complex, contested, and not strictly hierarchical relationship between international and internal legal orders. The sovereign equality of states is best understood to establish three strong but not irrebuttable legal presumptions: (1) a state is presumed to be obligated only to the extent of its actual or constructive consent; (2) a state's obligations, while fully binding internationally on the state as a corporative entity, are presumed to have legal effect within the state only to the extent that domestic law has incorporated them; and (3) the inviolability of a state's territorial integrity and political independence, as against the threat or use of force or "extreme economic or political coercion," is presumed to withstand even the state's violation of international legal norms. Thus, however paradoxically, international law demands respect for state prerogative, even at the risk of impeding, not only the establishment of new legal norms but also the implementation of existing ones.

Notwithstanding the challenges it poses to norm implementation, the international order's respect for sovereignty in no way precludes judgmental scrutiny of, or international ostracism for, internal practices. Because international obligations on matters of internal public order and international strictures on (even righteous) cross-border exercises of power operate on separate legal planes, one can concede the inviolability of illiberal systems of internal public order without withholding judgment on the duly incurred legal obligations—let alone the moral duties—that states owe to their own nationals. Even to the extent that such inviolability renders international standards of internal public order effectively non-compulsory, it renders them no less obligatory.

[45] Although treaty law allows that a state's consent may be vitiated if it "has been expressed in violation of a provision of its internal law regarding competence to conclude treaties" and "that violation was manifest and concerned a rule of its internal law of fundamental importance," Vienna Convention on the Law of Treaties, 1155 U.N.T.S. 331 (opened for signature, 1969), art. 46(1), such "manifest" violation presupposes that the provision (and the constitutional order of which it forms a part) has not been overtly and effectively supplanted. Note also that "[a]ctions which are criminal under the local law can still have been done officially and therefore give rise to immunity *ratione materiae*." Regina v. Bow Street Metropolitan Stipendiary Magistrate (*Pinochet III*), 1 AC 147, 203 (H.L. 1999) (U.K.) (lead opinion of Lord Browne-Wilkinson).

Moreover, the barriers that the acknowledged sovereign prerogatives pose to international regulation of internal public order are somewhat less formidable than they may initially appear. International norm-formation is in many respects only superficially consensual: states can become bound to customary international human rights norms collectively and implicitly, as a result of their acquiescence in (largely rhetorical) patterns of practice. Although "persistent objection" would in principle exempt a state from an emergent norm's coverage, there is no way to "opt out" after the customary norm is deemed to have been fully established (even if the state in question came into being only after the norm's formation). Moreover, certain norms, such as the prohibition of genocide, are so fundamental that "the international community of States as a whole" is said to have recognized them as "peremptory" norms (*jus cogens*), subject neither to persistent objection nor to "derogation" (i.e., justification or excuse for nonperformance).[46]

In addition, although international obligations are ordinarily addressed to states and not to individuals, certain norms (most prominently, the core standards of the humanitarian laws of war) are understood to entail individual criminal (as well as civil) liability, even where they are unreflected in or contradicted by the domestic legal order in force at the time and place of the offending act's commission. Notwithstanding extensive jurisdictional limitations, personal and functional immunities, and safeguards against retroactive criminalization of conduct, individuals—including state officials carrying out putatively official functions—may under certain conditions be prosecuted in Security Council-authorized ad hoc international criminal tribunals, in the newly created International Criminal Court, or in foreign state courts asserting extraterritorial jurisdiction.

Finally, the Security Council (operating on the basis of 9 out of 15 affirmative votes, absent a veto from one of the five Permanent Members) has unreviewable discretion under Chapter VII of the Charter to find even purely internal crises (such as Somalia in 1992) a threat to international peace, and pursuant to that finding, to authorize coercive measures, both short of and including the use of military force.[47]

[46] *See* Vienna Convention on the Law of Treaties, *supra*, art. 53.

[47] Allen Buchanan considers it "ironic that those who have rejected the proposal for a liberal coalition to make decisions concerning the use of force almost invariably say that the Security Council is the only legitimate venue for making such decisions, given that the permanent member veto is a clear (and, one might add, morally arbitrary) violation of the principle of the 'equality of states.'" Allen Buchanan, "Democracy and Commitment to International Law," 34 *Ga. J. Int'l & Comp. L.* 305, 316 n.11 (2006). But there is no inconsistency. Any collective authority to override a given state's sovereign prerogatives represents an exception to the "equality of states" in the relevant sense, and any voting rule that raises the threshold for the exercise of that extraordinary authority bolsters sovereign equality. The present allocation of vetoes is, of course, unprincipled, but in requiring the assent of important states not aligned with the Western bloc, it serves in practice as a bulwark of sovereign equality (for better or for worse).

Although a nexus, however tenuous, to external effects was formerly a rhetorical requisite to the use of this power,[48] the Security Council is now clearly understood to have authority—and indeed, the "responsibility"—to invoke its extraordinary powers where "national authorities are manifestly failing to protect their populations from genocide, war crimes, ethnic cleansing, and crimes against humanity."[49] Furthermore, in certain instances in which the Security Council has issued no such authorization, forcible responses to perceived threats of imminent humanitarian catastrophe have proceeded without international condemnation and even have received, in the cases of interventions by the Economic Community of West African States (ECOWAS) in Liberia and Sierra Leone, a *post hoc* Security Council imprimatur.[50]

Thus, the international system's deference to sovereign prerogative is by no means absolute. Still, nonconsensual norms, individual legal accountability for state-sponsored conduct in breach of international obligations, and coercive intervention to enforce breached obligations are exceptional, not routine. Efforts to extend, let alone to generalize, these exceptions occasion principled confrontations between those committed to maintaining, and those committed to transcending, the pluralistic framework of the international legal order.

## II. The Persistence of "Antiquated" Sovereignty Within International Law

The complexities of the relationship between state sovereignty and international legality are such that even the most seemingly commonsensical disparagements of sovereign prerogative require qualification. For example, one highly respected commentator, in order to shift the focus of sovereignty discourse to more "modern" usages of the term, seeks to shake free of discredited usages as follows:

> Broadly, one could see the "antiquated" definition of "sovereignty" that should be "relegated" as something like the notion of a nation-state's supreme absolute power and authority over its subjects and territory, unfettered by any higher law or rule (except perhaps ethical or religious standards) unless

[48] *See* U.N. Charter, arts. 39, 41, and 42.

[49] G.A. Res. 60/1 (2005) (adopted without a vote), ¶ 139; S.C. Res. 1674 (2006) (reaffirming same).

[50] U.N. Doc. S/22133 (1991) (Security Council statement commending ECOWAS efforts "to restore peace and normalcy in Liberia"); S.C. Res. 788 (1992) (imposing an arms embargo against Liberian factions resisting ECOWAS); S.C. Res. 1132 (1997) (imposing an arms embargo against the Sierra Leonean *de facto* government in support of ECOWAS military efforts to restore the elected government).

> the nation-state consents in an individual and meaningful way. It could be characterized as the nation-state's power to violate virgins, chop off heads, arbitrarily confiscate property, torture citizens, and engage in all sorts of other excessive and inappropriate actions.
>
> Today, no sensible person would agree that this antiquated version of sovereignty exists. A multitude of treaties and customary international law norms impose international legal constraints (at the least) that circumscribe extreme forms of arbitrary actions even against a sovereign's own citizens.[51]

This statement is unexceptionable, so long as one highlights the generality of the commentator's purpose in offering it. The particulars, however, are less straightforward than they appear. The quoted passage (as I shall refer to it hereafter)[52] obscures complexities that pertain to each aspect of the relationship between sovereignty and international legality.

## A. THE RECOGNIZED SOURCES OF LAW

The first sentence of the passage suggests that a state is bound by "higher" law even where it does not consent "in an individual and meaningful way."[53] Perhaps this means simply to reaffirm that states can become bound to customary international human rights norms collectively and implicitly, as a result of their acquiescence in (largely rhetorical) patterns of practice. But "higher" may leave the impression that the applicable norms are rooted in something other than, and therefore can be interpreted without regard to, manifestations of the will of the lawmaking community of states. A norm against violating virgins might be uncontroversially derived from such manifestations (surely, no state has persistently objected that it has such a prerogative), but the same cannot be said of a norm against arbitrarily confiscating property, especially with respect to a common understanding of what counts as arbitrariness in this field.

The burden falls on one who asserts the existence of the legal obligation to adduce the state practice and *opinio juris* that establish the customary norm—or, in

[51] John H. Jackson, *supra*, at 790.

[52] Hopefully, Professor Jackson will forgive my exploitation of this quotation. He clearly intended it not as a rigorous account of this subject matter, but as a throw-away reference to a subject other than the one he wished to examine in detail. I have seized on this quotation only because it so well reflects a conventional wisdom that tends to be unquestioningly accepted, but that is misleading as to the details of the relationship between state sovereignty and international legality. Since the critique that follows is not directed against Professor Jackson's main point, the text deliberately avoids associating him by name with the criticized passage.

[53] Jackson, *supra*, at 790.

the alternative, to survey a cross-section of the world's legal systems to establish a general principle of law recognized by the community of nations.[54] Moreover, even a norm discerned by these methods would not bind an outlier state that has persistently objected, except upon an additional showing that "the international community of States as a whole" recognizes the norm as a "peremptory" one (*jus cogens*) "from which no derogation is permitted."[55]

In determinations of whether a purported norm counts as international law, sovereignty plays a dual role. In one respect, it is simply a residuum: generally speaking, states are free to the extent that no legal obligation is affirmatively established.[56] In the second respect, it represents the considerations that underlie the burden of proof in a law-finding process that inevitably contains a teleological component. The primary methodological problem in ascertaining the existence of a legal norm is not one of "research design" but of foundational principle: disputes that purport to turn on the strength of the adduced evidence are most frequently, in reality, disputes about the nature and strength of the presumption that states remain juridically free to act as they choose. Thus, a jurist's conclusion may, in effect, turn on whether he or she ascribes to the project of international legality a telos of "transcendent justice" or of "bounded pluralism."

## B. THE INTERFACE BETWEEN THE INTERNATIONAL AND DOMESTIC LEGAL SYSTEMS

The earlier-quoted passage goes beyond positing that all states are legally obligated not "to violate virgins, chop off heads, arbitrarily confiscate property, torture citizens, and engage in all sorts of other excessive and inappropriate actions."[57] Rather, it disputes the "nation-state's supreme absolute power"[58]—meaning, in this context, its legal authority rather than its empirical capacity—to commit that parade of horribles.

[54] *See* Statute of the International Court of Justice, 1945 I.C.J. Acts & Docs. art. 38(1)(c) (empowering the Court to apply "general principles of law recognized by civilized nations"). The more modern "community of nations" language is found in the ICCPR, *supra*, art. 15(2).

[55] *Jus cogens* refers to a "peremptory" norm, "accepted and recognized by the international community of States as a whole as a norm from which no derogation is permitted." Vienna Convention on the Law of Treaties, *supra*, art. 53.

[56] S.S. "Lotus" (France v. Turkey), 1927 P.C.I.J. (ser. A) No. 10, at 18–19 (Sept. 7). The precise nature of the presumption is actually more complicated and controvertible: as occurred in the *Lotus* case itself, sovereignty as presumed freedom may clash with sovereignty as presumed exclusivity of territorial control. *See Arrest Warrant of April 11, 2000 (Democratic Republic of the Congo v. Belgium (Yerodia))*, 2002 I.C.J. 1 (Feb. 14), separate opinion of President Guillaume, paras. 13–16.

[57] John H. Jackson, *supra*, at 790.

[58] *Id.*

This denial of sovereign authority might be taken to imply that international law contains something akin to the United States Constitution's Supremacy Clause,[59] which legally nullifies all state-level exertions of authority that transgress federal constitutional norms, and which forms part of a structure providing for the justiciability, in both federal and state courts, of the validity of state acts under the federal constitution.[60] The international legal system, however, contains no such operating principles.

The international system and domestic systems operate on different legal planes, and their interconnections are highly differentiated and complex. It is true that a state "may not invoke the provisions of its internal law as justification for its failure to perform" its international legal obligations.[61] Yet states' adoption of international obligations does not entail renunciation of the ultimate authority to violate those obligations for the sake of what they deem, unilaterally, to be the national interest, thereby incurring whatever sanctions the international community may duly inflict upon the state.

As Louis Henkin starkly put it, "International law . . . recognizes the power—though not the right—to break a treaty and abide the international consequences."[62] This comports with the Bodinian conception of sovereignty: a prince is bound by the covenants he undertakes, yet retains the unchallengeable authority to contravene them when, in his unilateral judgment, "they cease to satisfy the claims of justice."[63] Sovereignty thus does not negate the existence of a legal obligation but rather consists, above all, in retention of the capacity to act in breach of the obligation at whatever cost this might entail. Thus, Schmitt's maxim, "sovereign is he who decides on the exception,"[64] however questionable as a claim that a single such official or body must or ought to exist within any particular domestic legal regime, is accurately descriptive of a territorial political community's sovereignty on the international plane. Schmitt goes so far as to say that "[i]f individual states no longer have the power to declare the exception, . . . then they no longer enjoy the status of states."[65]

The international system does possess mechanisms by which states, and even non-state actors, may pursue remedies for breaches of international obligations. These mechanisms, however, are limited by the principle of sovereign consent. The doctrine of foreign sovereign immunity reflects the presumption that no

[59] U.S. Const., art. VI, cl. 2.

[60] *See, e.g.*, Gibbons v. Ogden, 22 U.S. 1, 30–31 (1824).

[61] Vienna Convention on the Law of Treaties, art. 27. The provision applies expressly to treaty obligations, but the same principle applies to customary obligations.

[62] Louis Henkin, *Foreign Affairs and the Constitution* 168 (Mineola, NY, Foundation Press, 1972).

[63] Bodin, *supra*, at 30.

[64] Schmitt, *supra*, at 5.

[65] *Id.* at 11.

self-respecting state will allow its inherently governmental (as opposed to its purely commercial) conduct to be subjected to judgment in the courts of a coequal state. "It has become an established rule that between two equals, one cannot exercise sovereign will or power over the other, '*Par in parem non habet imperium.*'"[66]

States do consent to the jurisdiction of international judicial and quasi-judicial bodies, but only selectively, and even then sometimes in a highly qualified manner. Thus, for example, even those states parties to the ICCPR that "recognize[] the competence" of the Human Rights Committee to consider adverse "communications," either from states under the optional Article 41 procedure or from individuals under the First Optional Protocol, do not appear to be legally bound to comply with the Committee's "views."[67] Although it surely does not acknowledge the state as the authoritative interpreter of its own obligations, even with respect to internal public order, the international legal system does not ordinarily obligate the state to yield the last word to a particular institution that it may consider biased against its interests and values. The result is that the power of authoritative interpretation is often diffused throughout the community of states as a whole and is, therefore, difficult to bring cohesively to bear.

Of course, international law condemns violative acts and establishes obligations of reparation. Even within its own plane, however, it cannot treat transgressive state acts as simply null and void. Such acts, however wrongful, successfully create certain legal facts that the international system is bound to acknowledge. Indeed, notwithstanding a transgression, "it would be a breach of international law for a court of one State to address an order to another State, or to annul an act of another State."[68]

For example, even if, as the quoted passage asserts, a state's "arbitrary confiscation" of a complainant's real property breaches an international legal obligation, it does not follow that international law recognizes the continued validity of the complainant's title to that property. Even though the state may owe reparation, it likely has the unilateral authority, as part of its "permanent sovereignty . . . over . . . natural

[66] Sompong Sucharitkul, "Immunities of Foreign States Before National Authorities," 149 *Recueil Des Cours* 87, 117 (1977); *but see* Lee M. Caplan, "State Immunity, Human Rights, and Jus Cogens: A Critique of the Normative Hierarchy Theory," 97 *Am. J. Int'l L.* 741, 745–65 (2003) (arguing provocatively that this is essentially a rule of comity, rather than of international law, and should therefore give way in respect of "most, if not all, activity that constitutes human rights offenses").

[67] *See* ICCPR, *supra,* arts. 41–42; Optional Protocol to the International Covenant on Civil and Political Rights, *opened for signature* Dec. 19, 1966, 999 U.N.T.S. 302. The Committee has lately asserted that its determinations in Optional Protocol cases are "authoritative," General Comment 33, UN Doc. CCPR/C/GC/33 (5 Nov. 2008), ¶13, but it is unclear that states parties will accept that interpretation.

[68] Michael Akehurst, "Jurisdiction in International Law," 46 *Brit. Y.B. Int'l L.* 145, 250 (1972–73).

resources," to determine the ownership of any real property in its territory.[69] Although courts take a variety approaches to claims brought in response to foreign expropriations—sometimes deferring to foreign "acts of state" and sometimes not—a "court which refuses to recognize a foreign expropriation does not really seek to annul the expropriation (despite unfortunate language treating the expropriation as invalid); it merely holds, in effect, that the expropriation has no effect in the State of the forum, so that the original owner of the property can recover it when it is brought into the State of the forum."[70]

Far more importantly, where domestic systems authorize, as they frequently do, acts that breach international obligations, individuals—including even the highest officials—who act pursuant to such authorization must be presumed to do so within the scope of the state's ultimate authority over public order in its territory. These individuals cannot be held personally liable in the international system unless states have renounced—expressly or tacitly, as in the case of the treaty-based and customary law of war crimes—not only the practices themselves but also the legal capacity to authorize them.[71]

Functional immunity (immunity *ratione materiae*) presumptively bars legal action against foreign individuals for acts committed within their own national territory under their state's official authority.[72] Functional immunity serves as a corollary to state immunity, so as not to allow the use of prosecutions and lawsuits against officials to circumvent the immunities attaching to the state itself. Inasmuch as immunity *ratione materiae* exists for the state's, rather than the agent's, benefit, it is both broader and narrower in its coverage than the defense of *nullum crimen sine*

[69] *See* G.A. Res. 1803 (XVII) (1962) (acknowledging the principle of "permanent sovereignty over natural resources"); Charter of Economic Rights and Duties of States, G.A. Res. 3281 (XXIX) (1974) (120–6-10), art. 2(2)(c) ("Each State has the right [to] nationalize, expropriate, or transfer ownership of foreign property, in which appropriate case compensation should be paid" as determined according to "the domestic law of nationalizing State" unless otherwise "freely and mutually agreed"; the domestic law provision drew the objection of capital-exporting states).

[70] Akehurst, *supra*, at 250. This issue, though somewhat esoteric, has some practical significance in regard to United States efforts to penalize persons, of whatever nationality, who may "traffic" in properties confiscated by the Cuban Government. *See* 22 U.S.C. § 6091 (2000) (codifying section 401 of the Cuban Liberty and Democratic Solidarity (LIBERTAD) Act of 1996).

[71] "He who violates the laws of war cannot obtain immunity while acting in pursuance of the authority of the state if the state in authorizing action moves outside its competence under international law." *Judicial Decisions: International Military Tribunal (Nuremberg), Judgment and Sentences*, 41 *Am. J. Int'l L.* 172, 221 (1947). However, these attributions of individual liability for participation in state acts typically occur where "the acts were *crimes* against international law, so it is doubtful whether they apply to breaches of international law which are not crimes against international law." Akehurst, *supra*, at 243.

[72] Dapo Akande, "International Law Immunities and the International Criminal Court," 98 *Am. J. Int'l L.* 407, 412–13 (2004); *accord*, Akehurst, *supra*, at 240–44 (treating such immunity as a special and international obligatory version of the "act of state" doctrine).

*lege*: broader, in that it applies even to those acts, committed under color of official capacity, that are crimes under the law of the agent's state[73]; narrower, in that the state (perhaps following regime change) can decide *post hoc* to waive the defense, thereby leaving the agent "hung out to dry."[74]

Yet, given the state's presumptive last word on public order in the territory, functional immunity is a personal defense that reflects the operation of the nonretroactivity principle in the criminal context, and of choice-of-law principles in the civil context. Thus, Antonio Cassese construes immunity *ratione materiae* as not a procedural bar to jurisdiction but a "substantive defence," available to "any *de jure* or de facto State agent" performing official acts, establishing that the "violation is not legally imputable to [the agent] but to his state."[75] On that rationale, whereas a state can always waive the immunity *ratione personae* of its diplomatic representatives (which shields them from having to answer even for private wrongs so long as they hold their positions), a state can expressly or constructively waive its agents' immunity *ratione materiae* for specified acts only in advance of their commission.[76]

The significance of this principle to the United States and its nationals is manifest. In the domestic law of the United States, any effect of customary international law (under the rubric of "federal common law") is displaced by a "controlling executive or legislative act."[77] The status of treaties is more complex. Those bearing most

[73] *See, e.g., Pinochet III, supra,* at 203.

[74] "These immunities belong not to the individual but to the state in question. They exist in order to protect the sovereignty of that state from interference by other states. They can, of course, . . . be waived by the state in question." *Pinochet III, supra,* at 265 (opinion of Lord Saville).

[75] Antonio Cassese, *International Criminal Law* (Oxford Univ. Press, 2003), at 266; *accord* Akande, *supra,* at 412–15; *see also* Anne-Marie Slaughter, "Defining the Limits: Universal Jurisdiction and National Courts," in Stephen Macedo ed., *Universal Jurisdiction: National Courts and the Prosecution of Serious Crimes Under International Law* 168, 175–76 (Philadelphia, PA: Univ. of Pennsylvania Press, 2004) (stating that breaches of international obligation are ordinarily attributed to the state alone and that *nullum crimen sine lege* can be "read to mean that international law must have prohibited the act as committed by an individual rather than by a state"). Although U.S. courts in Alien Tort Statute decisions have given relatively little express attention to state agents' presumptive immunities *ratione materiae,* the Supreme Court's recent tightening of the standards for such civil suits may effectively satisfy the concern. Sosa v. Alvarez-Machain, 124 S. Ct. 2739, 2769 (2004) (implying that such suits can prevail against only state policies "so bad that those who enforce them become enemies of the human race").

[76] *See Pinochet III,* supra, 1 A.C. at 204–05 (lead opinion of Lord Browne-Wilkinson, finding that the coming into force of the Torture Convention, with its grant of universal jurisdiction over official acts of torture, is what conclusively removes torture from the recognized scope of official authority and permits prosecution of acts occurring from that time forward).

[77] The Paquete Habana, 175 U.S. 677, 700 (1900); Garcia-Mir v. Meese, 788 F.2d 1446, 1453–55 (11th Cir. 1986), *cert. denied sub nom.,* Ferrer-Mazorra v. Meese, 479 U.S. 889 (1986). For an instructive summary of the limited status of international law in U.S. law, *see* Committee of United States Citizens Living in Nicaragua v. Reagan, 859 F.2d 929, 935–39 (D.C. Cir. 1988).

centrally on public order, such as the United Nations Charter and the International Covenant on Civil and Political Rights (ICCPR), are considered "non-self-executing"; they bind the United States on the international plane, but they have no direct effect on internal legal obligations.[78]

"Self-executing" treaties have internal legal effects, but subsequent federal legislation prevails over these to the full extent of any contradiction.[79] Moreover, the treaty interpretations that prevail are those of United States courts, not international or foreign courts,[80] and even express doctrine favors judicial acceptance of Executive Branch interpretations.[81] In practice, United States courts have, at the Executive's behest, adopted some notably improbable interpretations of treaty standards. For example, the Supreme Court has held, contrary to virtually all international juridical opinion, that the Drug Enforcement Agency's abduction of a Mexican national from his country, over Mexico's objection, to stand trial in the United States did not violate the United States-Mexico extradition treaty,[82] and that the duty of non-refoulement, contained in legislation purporting fully to implement a treaty obligation, did not apply to the return of refugees to the country of their persecution where the refugees were intercepted on the high seas.[83]

Thus, the commonplace assertion in U.S. textbooks that international law is "part of our law"[84] is highly misleading. International law's incorporation into United States law is strictly subordinated to domestic sources of authority.

As a policy matter, one may wish to denounce United States resistance to the direct internal effect of international law as parochial and outmoded. Yet authority and policy are two separate questions. The United States has the sovereign authority to resist that direct effect, regardless of whether it ought to exercise that authority. So, too, does every other state. To the extent that governmental conduct, albeit in breach of international legal obligations, is internally authoritative, an external legal system has a presumptive (albeit paradoxical) duty under international law to acknowledge it as the last word on public order in the territory.

[78] *See* Medellin v. Texas, 128 S. Ct. 1346, 1356 (2008) ("while treaties 'may comprise international commitments . . . they are not domestic law unless Congress has either enacted implementing statutes or the treaty itself conveys an intention that it be 'self-executing' and is ratified on these terms.'") (citation omitted); Buell v. Mitchell, 274 F.3d 337, 372 (6th Cir. 2001) (stating that even if the ICCPR or the Charter of the Organization of American States "were to ban the imposition of the death penalty, neither is binding on federal courts," as these treaties are "non-self-executing").

[79] The Head Money Cases, 112 U.S. 580, 598–99 (1884).

[80] Sanchez-Llamas v. Oregon, 548 U.S. 331 (2006).

[81] Sumitomo Shoji America, Inc. v. Avagliano, 457 U.S. 176, 184–85 (1982) ("Although not conclusive, the meaning attributed to treaty provisions by the Government agencies charged with their negotiation and enforcement is entitled to great weight.").

[82] United States v. Alvarez-Machain, 504 U.S. 655, 669–70 (1992).

[83] Sale v. Haitian Centers. Council, Inc., 509 U.S. 155, 187 (1993).

[84] The oft-repeated line comes from The Paquete Habana, 175 U.S. 677, 700 (1900).

Thus, contrary to the implications of the earlier quoted passage, the nation-state does indeed possess the ultimate authority, even though not the right, to "engage in all sorts of... excessive and inappropriate actions."[85] World federalism may or may not be a worthy policy goal, but it is not the current juridical reality. The open juridical questions concern the scope of exceptions to the basic rule that international law has only such direct internal effects as domestic law establishes, exceptions as to which "transcendent justice" and "bounded pluralist" approaches may generate conflicting answers.

## C. THE FUNDAMENTAL STRICTURE AGAINST COERCIVE INTERVENTION

The quoted passage denies the state's "supreme absolute power and authority over its subjects and territory."[86] But apart from the special powers entrusted to the United Nations Security Council under Chapter VII of the Charter, no state or intergovernmental organization has—or even claims—law enforcement authority within the territory of a foreign state.[87] The state's monopoly over the authorization of the use of force in its territory, the inner core of sovereignty, withstands its failures to uphold international obligations.

Consequently, although no aspect of state conduct toward its own nationals may now be considered outside the scope of international obligation and scrutiny, implementation of human rights obligations is still subject to the control of sovereign states.[88] Human rights instruments have not included intrusive implementation mechanisms, and no such mechanisms can be inferred from general international law. At least presumptively, activities within the state, undertaken by foreigners to secure the state's compliance with human rights norms, remain subject to state consent.[89]

[85] John H. Jackson, *supra*, at 790.

[86] *Id.*

[87] "A state's law enforcement officers may exercise their functions in the territory of another state only with the consent of the other state, given by duly authorized officials of that state." Restatement (Third) of Foreign Relations Law of the United States § 432(2) (1987); *see also* 1 *Oppenheim's International Law* (Sir Robert Jennings & Sir Arthur Watts eds., 9th ed.) (Essex, U.K.: Longman Higher Education, 1992) § 119, at 387–88 ("It is... a breach of international law for a state without permission to send its agents into the territory of another state to apprehend persons accused of having committed a crime.").

[88] It is worthwhile to recall that Bodin himself conceived of sovereignty not as the absence of obligation, but as the absence of any higher authority to impose compliance. *See* Bodin, *supra*, at 29–31. The fact that states nowadays undertake wide-ranging obligations regarding internal practices in no way dilutes sovereignty, so conceived.

[89] *See* G.A. Res. 46/182 (1991) (acknowledging that humanitarian operations within a state's territory require the state's consent). Third World states have collectively insisted, at least rhetorically,

Furthermore, absent Chapter VII-based resolutions of the United Nations Security Council, foreign states and intergovernmental organizations may lawfully employ only limited measures to exert pressure on human rights violators. The most straightforward stricture is the prohibition on the use of force against the territorial integrity or political independence of states, contained in Article 2(4) of the United Nations Charter.[90] As the International Court of Justice made clear in the *Nicaragua* case, allegations of human rights abuse cannot be invoked to justify armed efforts, direct or by proxy, to destabilize a government.[91]

Economic coercion and political interference directed toward regime change also consistently receive a frosty reception in resolutions of the United Nations General Assembly and other intergovernmental groups,[92] although the rules

on maintaining this principle, stressing "that humanitarian assistance should be conducted in full respect of the sovereignty, territorial integrity, and political independence of host countries, and should be initiated in response to a request or with the approval of these States." *Declaration of the South Summit* para. 54, Group of Seventy-Seven at the U.N. (Apr. 10–14, 2000), *available at* <http://www.g77.org/main/docs/Declaration_G77Summit.doc>. *See generally Declaration on the Inadmissibility of Intervention and Interference in the Internal Affairs of States*, G.A. Res. 36/103 (1981) (passed 120–22-6, over the dissenting votes of Western states) (asserting a duty "to refrain from any economic, political or military activity in the territory of another State without its consent").

[90] U.N. Charter, art. 2(4).

[91] Military and Paramilitary Activities (Nicaragua v. United States), 1986 I.C.J. 14, 134–35 (June 27), paras. 267–68. The *Nicaragua* decision confirmed the legal significance of the rhetoric quoted in an earlier note:

> No State or group of States has the right to intervene, directly or indirectly, for any reason whatever, in the internal or external affairs of any other State.
>
> ....
>
> Every State has an inalienable right to choose its political, economic, social and cultural systems, without interference in any form by another State.

*Friendly Relations Declaration, supra*, at 123.

The 133-member "G-77" bloc of developing countries recently reaffirmed its commitment to this principle in inflexible terms:

> We reaffirm that every State has the inalienable right to choose political, economic, social and cultural systems of its own, without interference in any form by other States.
>
> ....
>
> We stress the need to maintain a clear distinction between humanitarian assistance and other activities of the United Nations. We reject the so-called "right" of humanitarian intervention, which has no legal basis in the United Nations Charter or in the general principles of international law.

*Declaration of the South Summit, supra*, at paras. 49, 54.

[92] "No State may use or encourage the use of economic, political or any other type of measures to coerce another State in order to obtain from it the subordination of the exercise of its sovereign rights and to secure from it advantages of any kind." *Friendly Relations Declaration, supra*, at 123; *see also* G.A. Res. 58/198 (2004) (125–1-37) (urging elimination of using "unilateral coercive economic measures against developing countries that are not authorized by relevant organs of the United Nations or are inconsistent with the principles of international law as set forth in the Charter of the United Nations and that contravene the basic principles of the multilateral trading system"); G.A. Res. 45/151 (1990)

pertaining to these measures are far less clear. Some unilateral sanctions—such as suspensions of aid and trade and withdrawal of diplomatic relations—fall within the scope of a sanctioning state's own sovereign prerogatives, whereas others, such as secondary boycotts (i.e., coercive interference with the target state's economic relations with third states) and covert funding of opposition political groups, would seem to cross the line into presumptively unlawful intervention.

Opinion appears to be divided on whether such non-forcible coercive acts could be justified as countermeasures—proportionate reprisals against the legal rights of states—in response to violations of human rights obligations owed the international community.[93] The lesser-developed countries have long feared that licensing such measures would invite neocolonialism in the guise of human rights enforcement. The 1996 version of the International Law Commission's Draft Articles on State Responsibility included an express prohibition on the use, as a countermeasure, of "extreme economic or political coercion designed to endanger the territorial integrity or political independence of the State which has committed the internationally wrongful act."[94] The final version, submitted to the General Assembly for its consideration in 2001,[95] omitted this clause but retained restrictions to more or less the same effect.[96]

(111–29-11) (appealing to all states "to abstain from financing or providing . . . overt or covert support for political parties or groups"). For expressions of opposition to concrete measures, see G.A. Res. 58/7 (2003) (adopted 179–3-2) (repudiating the United States' secondary boycott against Cuba); *Economic Coercive Measures Against Panama*, Latin Am. Econ. Sys. Doc. No. 271 (Mar. 29, 1988) (repudiating U.S. economic sanctions imposed following the removal of President Eric Arturo Delvalle), excerpted in *United States Economic Measures Against Cuba* (Michael Krinsky & David Golove eds., Massena, N.Y.: Aletheia Press, 1993), at 286, 286–87.

[93] *See Report of the Secretary-General on Economic Measures as a Means of Political or Economic Coercion against Developing Countries*, G.A. Res. 44/125, U.N. GAOR, 44th Sess., Supp. No. 49, at para. 23, U.N. Doc. A/44/510 (1989) (indicating division of opinion on whether any exception could be made for measures in furtherance of human rights compliance); *Declaration of the South Summit*, *supra*, at para. 48 (rejecting all "forms of coercive economic measures, including unilateral sanctions against developing countries," without mentioning any exception for countermeasures against human rights violators). Given the lack of any effort to erect a collective apparatus for determining when such countermeasures would be appropriate and for policing their proportionality, there is ample reason to question whether human rights-based justifications of otherwise unlawful measures have achieved international acceptance.

[94] *1996 ILC Articles on State Responsibility*, *supra*, at art. 50(b).

[95] *Report of the International Law Commission, Draft Articles on Responsibility of States for Internationally Wrongful Acts*, U.N. GAOR, 56th Sess., Supp. No. 10, at 43, U.N. Doc. A/56/10 (2001) [hereinafter *2001 ILC Articles on State Responsibility*]. ILC Special Rapporteur James Crawford noted that "'either the countermeasures are disproportionate, in which case they are excluded by the principle of proportionality, or they are not, in which case they will necessarily be a response to extreme wrongdoing causing injuries which have not been redressed.'" David J. Bederman, *Counterintuiting Countermeasures*, 96 *Am. J. Int'l L.* 817, 831 (2002).

[96] *2001 ILC Articles on State Responsibility*, *supra*, at art. 49 ("An injured State may only take countermeasures . . . in order to induce [the wrongdoing] State to comply with its obligations . . . .");

Thus, however paradoxically, human rights norms are, as a matter of legal presumption, obligatory but not compulsory. States are, at once, legally bound by obligations and legally protected from the very coercion that may be required to assure their compliance. Human rights norms do not, in and of themselves, vitiate the legal constraints on the application of power across territorial boundaries. Frustrated by such legal constraints, W. Michael Reisman has complained that "[b]ecause rights without remedies are not rights at all, prohibiting the unilateral vindication of clear violations of rights when multilateral possibilities do not obtain is virtually to terminate those rights."[97] As Reisman himself acknowledges, however, routine circumvention of those constraints would erode the underpinnings of the system that makes those rights possible.[98]

Thus, sovereignty's relationship to international law is far more nuanced than is generally supposed. In all three areas surveyed—the recognized sources of law, the interface between the international and domestic legal systems, and the fundamental stricture against coercive intervention—sovereign prerogative amounts to a set of legal presumptions. To say that these are presumptions is to say that any or all of them may be rebuttable; the basic rules admit of many exceptions, some clearly established and others arguable. But even if one aims ultimately for the exception to swallow the rule—the "transcendent justice" approach—it is important for analytical purposes not to misidentify the exception as the rule.

## III. Self-Determination and Non-Intervention

The central normative idea underpinning the existing sovereign equality framework is the right of "peoples" to self-determination. "All peoples have the right to self-determination; by virtue of that right they freely determine their political status and freely pursue their economic, social and cultural development."[99] Yet contrary to

*id.* at art. 51 ("Countermeasures must be commensurate with the injury suffered . . . ."). Moreover, Article 54, in allowing for responses by "[a]ny State other than an injured State" to breaches of those obligations recognized in Article 48 as being "owed to the international community as a whole," mentions only "lawful measures," rather than countermeasures.

[97] W. Michael Reisman, "Sovereignty and Human Rights in Contemporary International Law," 84 *Am. J. Int'l L.* 866, 875 (1990).

[98] W. Michael Reisman, "Why Regime Change Is (Almost Always) a Bad Idea," 98 *Am. J. Int'l L.* 516, 516–17 (2004) ("Our international legal system is scarcely imaginable without" territorial communities having the right to govern themselves "without interference"; "state sovereignty prevails in all but the most egregious instances of widespread human rights violations.").

[99] *Declaration on the Granting of Independence to Colonial Countries and Peoples*, GA Res 1514 (XV) (1960) (89–0-9), ¶ 2. The Security Council reaffirmed the statement in SC Res 183 (1963), ¶ 4, and the language is repeated verbatim in Common Article 1 of the 1966 Human Rights Covenants. *International Covenant on Civil and Political Rights* (opened for signature Dec. 19, 1966), art. 1, 999

common belief and a torrent of wishful scholarly rhetoric, the authoritative interpretation of the self-determination right that emerges from United Nations pronouncement and practice reduces almost entirely to a prohibition on coercive interference in the internal affairs of existing states. The right's bearers are territorially defined political communities—conforming to the recognized borders of either existing states or overseas colonial territories—not ethno-national groups or other affective communities.[100] Those accredited to assert the right in the name of its bearers earn their standing by achieving not popular approval by democratic means but popular acquiescence by whatever means (with the exception of undue interference from abroad). The right can be summarized, with much irony but little exaggeration, as a right of territorial populations to be ruled by their own thugs and to fight their civil wars in peace.

## A. POPULAR SOVEREIGNTY AND EFFECTIVE CONTROL

For the purposes of international law, sovereignty belongs not to any governmental apparatus, but to "the state" in the abstract. Sovereignty is a legal attribute of a territorially bounded political community enjoying full membership in the international system. Recognized exercises of sovereignty are acts legally attributed to the will of the designated territory's permanent population as a whole. From international law's external standpoint, sovereignty itself lies not in a given constitutional

U.N.T.S. 171, 171[hereinafter ICCPR]; *International Covenant on Economic, Social and Cultural Rights,* (opened for signature Dec. 19, 1966), art. 1, 993 U.N.T.S. 3, 3. Moreover, one of the enumerated purposes of the United Nations is to "develop friendly relations based on respect for the principle of equal rights and self-determination of peoples," UN Charter, art. 1(2), and the Charter itself speaks in the name of "We the Peoples of the United Nations," *id.*, preamble.

[100] See Chapter 6. Although the definition of the term "people" for the purposes of the self-determination right is not so limited in principle, the international community has never authoritatively designated a bearer of this right outside of the context of colonialism and its vestiges. Even "indigenous peoples," the subnational groups to which the self-determination right might most naturally apply, were long denied this status. *See Convention Concerning Indigenous and Tribal Peoples in Independent Countries* (ILO No. 169), 72 ILO Official Bulletin 59, entered into force 5 Sept 1991, art. 1(3) ("The use of the term 'peoples' in this Convention shall not be construed as having any implications as regards the rights which may attach to the term under international law"). The 2007 United Nations *Declaration on the Rights of Indigenous Peoples,* UN Doc A/61.L.67 (12 Sept. 2007) (143–4-11), passed over dissenting votes of the United States, Canada, Australia, and New Zealand, finally ascribed to indigenous peoples the right to self-determination, nominally including the right to "freely determine their political status," *id.*, art. 3, but pointedly excluding any impairment of existing states' "territorial integrity or political unity," *id.*, art. 46. This qualification apparently assuaged African states that had theretofore insisted that the "principle of self-determination applies only to peoples under colonial and/or foreign occupation." African Group, *Draft Aide Memoire on United Nations Declaration on the Rights* of Indigenous Peoples, 9 Nov. 2006, at <http://www.ipacc.org.za/uploads/docs/Africanaidememoire.pdf>.

order (*pouvoir constitué*), but in the underlying constituency (*pouvoir constituant*) whose will to accept or repudiate that order must somehow be discerned.

Nonetheless, a governmental apparatus exercising "effective control through internal processes" has presumptive standing to assert rights, incur obligations, and confer immunities on behalf of the sovereign entity. According to the system's prevalent wisdom, empirical investigation to ascertain public opinion in a foreign state is most often impracticable, "popular will" itself is a complex and normatively loaded concept, and any imposition from abroad of procedures calculated to measure "popular will" is presumptuous at best and a usurpation at worst.[101] The Friendly Relations Declaration accordingly transforms the language of the right of peoples to self-determination into the right of states to non-intervention: "Every State has an inalienable right to choose its political, economic, social and cultural systems, without interference in any form by another State."[102]

Lacking shared normative criteria for governmental legitimacy, the international community has most frequently taken popular acquiescence as an indicator of—or proxy for—sovereign will, provided only that such acquiescence be secured without undue external interference.[103] There thus follows a presumptive duty on the part of each of the entities bearing equal juridical status to respect the outcome of political processes—that is to say, civil wars, insurrections, and coups no less than free and fair elections—internal to the others.

Decolonization was the crucial impetus to this insistence on non-intervention.[104] The new states were determined to assert in the most extravagant terms the ***absolute*** inadmissibility of ***any form*** of foreign interference, ***for any reason whatsoever***, with

[101] *See generally* Roth, *Governmental Illegitimacy*, above, at 136–49, 160–71, 253–364.

[102] Friendly Relations Declaration, above. The document elaborates as follows:

> No State or group of States has the right to intervene, directly or indirectly, for any reason whatever, in the internal or external affairs of any other State. Consequently, armed intervention and all other forms of interference or attempted threats against the personality of the State or against its political, economic and cultural elements, are in violation of international law.
>
> No State may use or encourage the use of economic, political or any other type of measures to coerce another State in order to obtain from it the subordination of the exercise of its sovereign rights and to secure from it advantages of any kind. Also, no State shall organize, assist, foment, finance, incite or tolerate subversive, terrorist or armed activities directed towards the violent overthrow of the regime of another State, or interfere in civil strife in another State.

[103] *See* Roth, *Governmental Illegitimacy*, above, at 136–49, 160–71, 253–364.

[104] Michael Walzer's 1980 exaltation of the self-determination right as the collective right on which all individual rights depend was, if a bit overly exuberant, consistent with the spirit of the times:

> [T]he distinction of state rights and individual rights is simplistic and wrongheaded. Against foreigners, individuals have a right to a state of their own. Against state officials, they have a right to political and civil liberty. Without the first of these rights, the second is meaningless: as individuals need a home, so rights require a location.

Walzer, "The Moral Standing of States," 9 *Phil. & Pub. Aff.* 209, 228 (1980).

the right of their political communities—now presumptively represented, like the rest, by a ruling apparatus in effective control—to determine their own systems of internal public order.[105] Self-determination, by light of this notion, entails a people's right to maintain its cohesion by whatever means it (or the effective authority that speaks on its behalf) sees fit, and to resist all efforts (including advocacy of any conception of internal rights not harmonious with the state's purposes) to subvert its unity and independence.

In order to fully appreciate the point, one must understand the anxiety about neocolonialism (often manipulated for partisan advantage, of course) that played so central a role in the era's politics. In the words of Ghana's founding president and Third World icon Kwame Nkrumah, the colonial power that grants independence:

> [b]y its very next act ... seeks without grace to neutralize this same independence by fomenting discontent and disunity; and finally, by arrogant ingratiation and wheedling it attempts to disinherit the people and constitute itself their conscience and their will, if not their voice and their arm. Political decisions, just as they were before independence was won, lose their reference to the welfare of the people, and serve once again the well-being and security of the erstwhile colonial power and the clique of self-centered politicians.[106]

The new African states faced danger, Nkrumah believed, from internal forces seeking "to promote those political ties by which a colonialist country binds its [former] colonies to itself with the primary object of furthering her economic advantage." The colonial power's local clients are "the political wolf masquerading in sheep's clothing"; "like a wasting disease they seek from the inside to infest, corrupt, pervert and thwart the aspirations of the people."[107] Thus, the imperative of self-determination could be construed as hardly antithetical to, but actually a justification of, repressive dictatorship.

[105] *See especially* the contested Declaration on the Inadmissibility of Intervention and Interference in the Internal Affairs of States, GA Res 36/103 (1981) [hereinafter "1981 Non-Intervention Declaration"], passed 120–22-6 over the opposition of many Western liberal states, which asserted, *inter alia*, "[t]he duty of a State to refrain from the exploitation and the distortion of human rights issues as a means of interference in the internal affairs of States." *See also* Friendly Relations Declaration, *supra*; Declaration on the Inadmissibility of Intervention in the Domestic Affairs of States and the Protection of Their Independence and Sovereignty, GA Res 2131 (XX) (1965) (109–0-1).

[106] Kwame Nkrumah, *Consciencism: Philosophy and Ideology for Decolonization* [1964] (Monthly Review Press, 1970), at 101–02.

[107] Ibid.

The non-intervention norm was most famously elaborated by the International Court of Justice in condemning U.S. military support for Nicaraguan "contra" insurgents.[108] The Court reached beyond the pleadings to address the claim of the U.S. Congress that the Government of Nicaragua had breached "solemn commitments to the Nicaraguan people, the United States, and the Organization of American States" regarding the character of its internal public order. The Court examined "whether there is anything in the conduct of Nicaragua which might legally warrant counter-measures by the United States." The Court pointed out that even had there been a legal commitment (which there had not been) and standing on the part of the United States to enforce the commitment unilaterally on behalf of the OAS (which there would not have been), the United States "could hardly make use for [that] purpose of methods which the Organization could not use itself; in particular, it could not be authorized to use force in that event. Of its nature, ***a commitment like this is one of a category which, if violated, cannot justify the use of force against a sovereign State.***"[109]

The Court went on to note that to hold a state's adherence to any particular governmental doctrine a violation of customary international law "would make nonsense of the ***fundamental principle of State sovereignty, on which the whole of international law rests,*** and the freedom of choice of the political, social, economic and cultural system of a State."[110] The Court further pointed out that the Friendly Relations Declaration and related documents "envisage the relations among States having different political, economic and social systems on the basis of coexistence among their various ideologies; the United States not only voiced no objection to their adoption, but took an active part in bringing it about."[111]

This imperative of non-intervention has not been interpreted to presuppose stable foreign regimes but rather has generally been taken—at least until recently—to apply all the more strongly in conditions of instability and civil war. Throughout most of the history of the United Nations system, internal armed conflict was widely perceived, not as an anomaly or as evidence of "state failure," but as a legitimate way for questions of public order to be worked out within states. Most governments through most of that period, after all, traced their origins more or less directly to a *coup d'état*, insurrection, or decisive civil war. The warring factions typically succeeded in presenting internal armed conflicts (often inaccurately) as struggles between ideologically motivated factions for standing to speak for the undivided population, rather than as ethno-nationalist bloodletting or as the simple thuggery

[108] *Military and Paramilitary Activities* (Nicaragua v. United States), 1986 ICJ 14 (27 June), ¶¶ 257–68.

[109] *Id.* at ¶ 262 (emphasis added).

[110] *Id.* at ¶ 263 (emphasis added).

[111] *Id.* at ¶ 264.

of armed gangs. Since foreign intervention has generally been assumed to be predatory, and to be perceived internally as such, even a tyrannical government would figure to be a more authentic representative of the polity's interests and views than foreign powers announcing benevolent intentions. Thus, the decision of the bulk of the population to acquiesce, however grudgingly, in the winning faction's project of public order has been taken as a decision to have that faction speak for the political community in international affairs.

In recent years, these assumptions about political life have eroded considerably, and for good reason. Nonetheless, as will be detailed in Chapter 6, effective governments have been denied legal standing only in rare instances—as following coups against overwhelming winners of internationally sponsored elections in Haiti in 1991 and Sierra Leone in 1997—where popular repudiation of the effective regime has been so manifest as to be perceived in common across the international community's spectrum of political, ideological, and cultural perspectives. Pluralism remains the rule, and exceptions must meet a high threshold of justification.

## B. PEOPLES AND TERRITORIAL UNITS

Cultural and ethnic affinities do not establish political communities for the purposes of international law. Apart from the peculiar context of the struggle to eradicate the international system's original sin, Western European colonial domination of overseas territories, the self-determination right has operated in support of the territorial integrity and non-fragmentation of existing states—conceptualized as consummations of the self-determination of their territorial populations—at the expense of the secessionist aspirations of territorial subcommunities.[112]

It is no accident that the most vociferous advocates of the right to self-determination, the new states emerging from decolonization, were also the most determined to limit its application. The new states perceived most keenly their vulnerability to territorial fragmentation and to threats to their political independence posed by neocolonialist penetration. Just as the long-established states were concerned to contain secessionism, so too were new states just as eager to close the door on the recognition of new "peoples" within established self-determination units.

The General Assembly's increasingly aggressive approach to self-determination beginning in the 1960s thus coincided with a stream of maximalist articulations of

[112] The 1981 Non-Intervention Declaration, *supra*, emphasized, *inter alia*, "[t]he duty of a state to refrain from the promotion, encouragement, or support, direct or indirect, of rebellious or secessionist activities within other States, *under any pretext whatsoever*, or any action which seems to disrupt the unity or to undermine or subvert the political order of other States." Annex, art. 2(f) (emphasis added).

the non-intervention norm. The Friendly Relations Declaration "squares the circle" in an instructive way. It follows its elaboration of the right to self-determination with the following "safeguard clause":

> Nothing in the foregoing paragraphs shall be construed as authorizing or encouraging any action which would dismember or impair, totally or in part, the territorial integrity or political unity of sovereign and independent States *conducting themselves in compliance with the principle of equal rights and self-determination of peoples as described above and thus possessed of a government representing the whole people belonging to the territory without distinction as to race, creed or colour.*[113]

Subsequent iterations have broadened the last clause of the qualifier to speak of "a government representing the whole people . . . without distinction of any kind."[114]

This supple and nuanced provision is best read, in light of its historical and political context, to reflect the animating principles of a global legal order marked by pronounced ideological pluralism (in 1970, it should be remembered, only a minority of states espoused liberal-democratic political principles) and extraordinary deference to states' choices of "political, economic, social, and cultural systems" (including, on the basis of sovereign equality, one-party regimes that tolerate no organized opposition). The above italicized qualification to the imperatives of territorial integrity and political unity seems to have been designed to function not as an ongoing operative exception to the sovereign prerogative of existing states but as a moral rationalization for singling out "colonial domination, foreign occupation and racist [i.e., *apartheid*] regimes" as special cases of derogation from the otherwise fiercely reaffirmed non-intervention norm.

In this reading, each existing state is the presumed manifestation of the self-determination of "the whole people belonging to the territory." This presumption allows the Declaration to justify attributing to the state the people's "inalienable right to choose its political, economic, social and cultural systems, without interference in any form," a choice that the state's effective government (even where objectively tyrannical) is further presumed to embody. Thus, the qualification, which appears to open a door, is best understood as an ingenious effort to keep that very door closed, while at the same time rendering a moral rationale for the disparate treatment of Western European colonialism and its vestiges.

[113] G.A. Res. 2625, above (emphasis added).

[114] *See* G.A. Res. 50/6 (1995); United Nations World Conference on Human Rights, Vienna Declaration and Programme of Action, June 25, 1993, 32 I.L.M. 1661, 1665 (1993).

Still, having articulated the principle, the fraternity of sovereign states cannot blunt its edge entirely.[115] Where a government manifestly fails to "represent the whole people belonging to the territory without distinction," as by the conduct of ethnic cleansing, the imperatives of "territorial integrity" and "political unity" lose their rationale. Arguably, being subjected to gross and systematic discrimination reveals a minority group (whether marked by ethnic or other characteristics) to be a "people" with its own right to self-determination—though no minority group in the non-colonial context has ever been authoritatively declared to be a "people."[116] More likely, patterns of extreme discrimination are now seen as justifying the international community—especially collectively, through Security Council action under Chapter VII of the Charter—in derogating from the system's ordinary respect

[115] Despite overwhelming international resistance to a right to secession outside the colonial context, self-determination continues to be presented as a right of general applicability. Thus, when India attached to its ratification of the ICCPR a declaration interpreting the right of self-determination to "apply only to the peoples under foreign domination and [not] to sovereign independent States or to a section of a people or a nation," invoking in support of this interpretation "the essence of national integrity," it drew objections from the Netherlands, France, and the Federal Republic of Germany. James Crawford, "The Right of Self-Determination in International Law: Its Development and Future," in Philip Alston. ed., *People's Rights* (Oxford Univ. Press, 2001), 7 at 28.

Some international jurists have sought to reconcile self-determination with non-fragmentation by speaking of a "right to internal self-determination." This language is, however, misleading insofar as it suggests an international legal mandate for any of the consociational devices that certain domestic systems have employed to empower subnational groups—such as territorial autonomy, representational quotas in governmental and other institutions, supermajority legislative voting rules for group-sensitive subject matter, and so on. *See, e.g.*, Ruth Lapidoth, *Autonomy: Flexible Solutions To Ethnic Conflicts* (Washington, DC, United States Institute of Peace Press, 1997). Except for "indigenous and tribal peoples" (additional victims of the Western European colonialism that represents the "original sin" for which the international system seeks to atone), subnational groups, whether or not territorially coherent, have no established standing in international law. Individuals, however, may have special rights in consideration of their group membership. *See*, e.g., ICCPR, *supra*, art. 27 (cultural rights of "persons belonging to national or ethnic, religious and linguistic minorities").

[116] Instructive on this point is the domestic court decision dealing most elaborately with the international law of self-determination, the Canadian Supreme Court's advisory opinion in *Reference re Secession of Quebec* [1998] 1 S.C.R. 217, *available at* <www.scc-csc.gc.ca/reference/rea.htm>. In deciding that the right, though applicable in the non-colonial context, did not justify unilateral secession, the court managed to sidestep the elemental question of whether the "people" entitled to self-determination was comprised of (a) the entire Quebec population, (b) the entire Quebec population minus the indigenous communities, (c) Francophone Quebecois, or (d) all Francophone Canadians. *Id.* at ¶ 125. It stressed merely that none of these groups is blocked from the meaningful exercise of self-determination, since Canada is "possessed of a government representing the whole people belonging to the territory without distinction." *Id.* at ¶ 136. *But see* Crawford, "The Right of Self-Determination," *supra*, at 59–60 (construing the court's position as consistent with "both the view that self-determination applies to peoples in the ordinary sense of the term and is not confined to the whole population of existing states, and the view that several peoples may coexist in relation to a particular territory").

for territorial integrity and political unity, as in the case of the international trusteeship that has supplanted Serbian rule over Kosovo.[117]

On the whole, an understanding of the self-determination right as it has operated in the existing international system requires a flair for the counterintuitive and the paradoxical, not to say the Orwellian. But contrary to the inferences that may be drawn by political theorists not steeped in the intricacies of international law, the right's paradoxical elements entail only a rebuttable presumption of certain core inviolabilities. The collective right does not preempt individual rights maintained against the collectivity. It operates primarily on a different plane, limiting not the content of a state's duties toward its citizens but cross-border exertions of power undertaken in the name of implementing those duties. Pluralism is not moral relativism, either in rationale or in effect.

## IV. Assertions of Normative Hierarchy in International Law

Some scholarly writings and dicta in some judicial opinions have lately construed *jus cogens* norms (which do not admit of "persistent objection" to their establishment, nor of justifications or excuses for nonperformance, and which void contrary treaty provisions) and obligations *erga omnes* (which are owed to the international community as a whole rather than to individual states on a reciprocal basis) as all-purpose trumps—"higher" norms that operate directly to overrule all legal impediments to their enforcement. This assertion of normative hierarchy has been invoked to overcome the distinction between state and individual responsibility, the limitations on extraterritorial jurisdiction, the immunity *ratione materiae* possessed by state agents generally, the immunity *ratione personae* possessed by currently serving diplomats, heads of states, and associated officials engaged in external relations,[118] and the immunity of state entities.

[117] *See* S.C. Res. 1244 (1999) (paying lip service to the sovereignty and territorial integrity of the Federal Republic of Yugoslavia while setting up an international administration to hold those norms in abeyance, at least temporarily); *see also* S.C. Res. 1160, 1199, 1203 (1998) (all invoking Chapter VII powers in addressing the Kosovo situation prior to the NATO intervention).

[118] After leaving their posts, former heads of state, heads of government, foreign ministers, and diplomats continue to be covered by the same immunity *ratione materiae* that applies to all other state agents, except that the scope of the latter immunity is enlarged to cover acts committed outside of national territory within the scope of the diplomatic role (states having consented to such immune foreign-state activity within their territories). References to "former diplomat" or "former head-of-state" immunity are misleading insofar as they seem to characterize immunity *ratione materiae* as a degraded form of immunity *ratione personae*; the two concepts should be understood as distinct. *See, e.g.,* Antonio Cassese, "When May Senior State Officials Be Tried for International Crimes?" 13 *Euro. J. Int'l L.* 853, 862–64 (2002).

This approach is indicated in frequently cited dicta from a 1998 decision of the International Criminal Tribunal for the former Yugoslavia (ICTY) in *Prosecutor v. Furundžija*. There the Trial Chamber held forth on the "particularly high status in the international normative system" of "the cluster of treaty and customary rules on torture," attributing as automatic consequences of *jus cogens* the establishment of universal criminal and civil jurisdiction and the voiding of immunities.[119]

However, nothing logically compels the step from a norm's supremacy within the international system to the international system's denial of legal recognition to all domestic authority shielding state agents from personal liability for breach.[120] As the International Law Commission has noted, "the category of international obligations admitting of no derogation is much broader than the category of obligations whose breach is necessarily an international crime."[121]

Thus far, state practice and *opinio juris* have failed to supply firm grounding for an assertion of normative hierarchy that overcomes all barriers of sovereign prerogative. Some prominent recent decisions of the International Court of Justice[122]; the European Court of Human Rights[123]; and the British House of Lords[124] have upheld immunities in contradiction to that assertion.[125] Most notably, in *Pinochet*, although

[119] *Prosecutor v. Furundžija*, Trial Chamber, Judgment of December 10, 1998, <http://www.un.org/icty/furundzija/trialc2/judgement/index.htm>, paras. 147, 155 (footnotes omitted).

[120] *See, e.g.*, Ward N. Ferdinandusse, *Direct Application of International Criminal Law in National Courts* (The Hague: T.M.C. Asser Press, 2006), at 182 (noting that a prohibition's *jus cogens* status does not imply the same status for the duty to prosecute the offense).

[121] International Law Commission, Commentary to the Draft Articles on State Responsibility (Art. 19) (1996) (*available at* <http://lcil.law.cam.ac.uk/ILCSR/rft/Sr19.rtf >), ¶ 62, at 120, quoted in Michael Byers, *Custom, Power, and the Power of Rules* (Cambridge University Press, 1999), at 184–185 n. 95.

[122] *See Case Concerning the Arrest Warrant of 11 April 2000, Democratic Republic of the Congo v. Belgium (Yerodia)*, 2002 I.C.J. Rep. 3, upholding the immunity *ratione personae* of a currently serving foreign minister from prosecution in a foreign-state court for crimes against humanity. The Court further gave dictum, albeit of doubtful significance, seeming to exempt from state agents' immunity *ratione materiae* in foreign-state courts only such crimes as are committed "in a private capacity," *id.*, para. 61, a category into which torture, by its very terms, cannot fall. For a persuasive critique of this dictum, see Marina Spinedi, "State Responsibility v. Individual Responsibility for International Crimes: *Tertium Non Datur*?" 13 *Euro. J. Int'l L.* 895 (2002).

[123] Al-Adsani v. United Kingdom, 34 E.H.R.R. 273 (2001), in which a closely divided Grand Chamber held that human rights law does not require a state court to void foreign state immunity in civil suits for torture. The dissent insisted that "the jus cogens nature of the prohibition of torture entails that a state allegedly violating it cannot invoke hierarchically lower rules (in this case, those on state immunity) to avoid the consequences of the illegality of its actions." *Id.* at 298–99.

[124] Al-Adsani v. Government of Kuwait (No. 2), 1996 I.L.R. 536, holding that state immunity precludes civil suits against foreign states for torture.

[125] As Hazel Fox has put it, state immunity "does not contradict a prohibition contained in a *jus cogens* norm but merely diverts any breach of it to a different method of settlement. Arguably, then,

the 3–2 decision of the first House of Lords panel sweepingly nullified the former Chilean dictator's immunity *ratione materiae* on the ground that torture, being a *jus cogens* violation, cannot count in international law as a state function,[126] the final judgment nullified immunity only for acts occurring after the Torture Convention came into force in 1988,[127] thus affirming that the *jus cogens* status of a standard of conduct does not, without a separate step, suffice to expose a breaching state's agent to foreign prosecutions. And surprisingly, a unanimous House of Lords panel has since held, even with respect to alleged violations of Article 1 of the Torture Convention, that immunity *ratione materiae* continues to protect foreign state agents from civil suits.[128]

Sweeping assertions of normative hierarchy tend to operate from the assumption that whereas ordinary norms of international law represent the express and implied consent of states to a coordination of interests, higher norms of international law represent a consensus (albeit more hypothesized than empirical) of an international community, including but not limited to states, on principles of fundamental justice.[129] However much validity there may be to this dichotomy, moral issues are no less susceptible to disagreement than non-moral ones; in particular, overlapping agreement among the bearers of various political moralities about the validity of norms in the abstract does not necessarily imply agreement about how these norms should be interpreted to apply in concrete cases—where the unity of the putative consensus frequently gives way to the diversity of the underlying constituent worldviews—nor about whether other applicable principles and policies may take priority over the norm in exigent circumstances. Although the logic of human rights and humanitarian law norms differs in important ways from norms that represent a mere coordination of interests (especially in transcending reciprocity), the former norms derive their legal character from similar processes, and are similarly constrained by the limits of those processes.[130]

there is no substantive content in the procedural plea of State immunity upon which a *jus cogens* mandate can bite." Hazel Fox, *The Law of State Immunity* (Oxford Univ. Press, 2002), 525.

[126] Regina v. Bow Street Metropolitan Stipendiary Magistrate (Pinochet I), 1 A.C. 61 (2000). That judgment was vacated after the disclosure of one Law Lord's ties to a human rights group participating in the litigation.

[127] *Pinochet III*, *supra*, at 204–05, opinion of Lord Browne-Wilkinson.

[128] Jones v. Ministry of the Interior of the Kingdom of Saudi Arabia, 2006 U.K.H.L. 26. For a persuasive criticism of this holding, *see* E. Steinerte & R.M.M. Wallace, "Case Report: Jones v. Ministry of the Interior of the Kingdom of Saudi Arabia," 100 *Am. J. Int'l L.* 901, 905 (2006).

[129] For a critical perspective on such claims, see Cohen, "Whose Sovereignty?" *supra*.

[130] For a skeptical overview of claims for normative hierarchy in the international system, *see* Dinah Shelton, "Normative Hierarchy in International Law," 100 *Am. J. Int'l L.* 291 (2006).

## Conclusion

The standard way of conceptualizing sovereignty's relationship to international legal obligation—that the former diminishes to the extent that the latter expands—is misconceived.

Sovereignty and obligation are not competitors; not only is the undertaking of an obligation itself a sovereign act, but the international order's very conceptualization of sovereign prerogative is premised on responsibilities of the state in respect of both external and internal conduct. But—and this is a crucial "but"—sovereignty may still be an international legal impediment to external efforts to compel implementation of a state's international legal obligation. Undertaking an obligation in regard to internal conduct is not tantamount to ceding ultimate authority over any aspect of territorial order. Except where subject to established international penal norms or to the United Nations' Security Council's extraordinary powers under Chapter VII of the Charter, sovereignty remains the last word on public order in a territory.

"Modern" sovereignty is often spoken of as circumscribed by international human rights, but if this were so, strictly speaking, the doctrine of non-intervention would be reducible to the "*Lotus* principle" that states are free insofar as no binding obligation can be established.[131] In actuality, the distinctiveness of the doctrine of non-intervention lies precisely in its availability to be asserted by human rights ***violators***.

There is a natural tendency to assume that if a party has a legal obligation and breaches it, someone somewhere in the system is licensed to use whatever means are necessary to see to it that the norm is vindicated. But this does not follow as a matter of abstract theory, nor does it follow in international legal doctrine. States, to be sure, do not have a "right" to violate international law, but they do have rights to territorial inviolability under international law that are not vitiated by garden-variety violations of international legal obligations. As noted above, a norm may be obligatory without being compulsory.[132]

Indeed, domestic authority, while subject to international law, is not—even as a matter of international law—strictly subordinate to international authority. The same act can be lawful and unlawful simultaneously: valid within the domestic legal order, but in breach of international legal obligation. There should be no paradox in the same act being lawful and unlawful simultaneously, since this happens

[131] As the famous (if somewhat misleading) maxim has it, "Restrictions on the independence of States cannot . . . be presumed." *Case of the S.S. Lotus, supra,* at 18.

[132] One might analogize this situation to the breach of a personal service contract in U.S. law. Although the breach is a wrongful act incurring liability for damages, the Thirteen Amendment excludes the remedy of an injunction compelling specific performance.

whenever domestic legislation with extraterritorial effect contradicts the law of the territorial state. The phenomenon seems counterintuitive only because, unlike the law of a foreign state, international law is erroneously imagined to be supreme over domestic law in the way that national law is ordinarily supreme over provincial law in a federal state.

In actuality, although violations of international legal obligation give rise to international legal consequences, including duties of reparation, the violative acts cannot necessarily be regarded as *ultra vires* of the authority that international law acknowledges as inherent in statehood. International law itself establishes norms—such as, *inter alia*, the absolute bar to the foreign enforcement of applicable laws within a state's territory and the presumptive immunity of state agents acting within the scope of official capacity within their national territory—that concede ultimate authority to the state within particular realms. Sovereignty's prerogatives within the international legal order thus include the power to create, in violation of legal obligation, facts with legal implications that the international order itself is bound to acknowledge.

The essence of the sovereign equality regime is the duty of coequal states to respect one another's core inviolabilities. This duty does not preclude states from giving effect to moral judgments within the confines of the discretionary aspects of their foreign policy. States may, for example, declare objectionable political figures *persona non grata*; provide peaceful refuge for militant opponents of objectionable regimes; sever diplomatic relations with, cut off economic assistance to, or effect a direct economic boycott of a state that engages in objectionable internal practices (but perhaps not a "secondary" boycott of the target state's trading partners, which, apart from its trade-law consequences, is a form of economic sabotage arguably amounting to unlawful coercion of a sovereign state). What the doctrine limits is the authority of individual (more powerful) states—themselves both untrusted and untrustworthy—to employ extraordinary measures of intrusion and compulsion in the service of their controversial moral judgments. And as noted above, even these limitations, while strongly presumptive, are subject to exceptions, both express and tacit.

Sovereign equality is an institutional response to, among other problems, persistent disagreement about what constitutes a legitimate and just territorial public order. It is the basis for respectful accommodation among territorial political communities, predicated on a "bounded pluralism" in regard to clashing political moralities. As the next chapter will discuss, such an approach to international order has much to recommend it.

# 4

# Global Pluralism and Conflicting Political Moralities

## Introduction

Over a half-century ago, J.L. Talmon traced the origins of modern totalitarianism to a tendency in political thought that was

> based on the assumption of a sole and exclusive truth in politics. It may be called political Messianism in the sense that it postulates a preordained, harmonious and perfect scheme of things, to which men are irresistibly driven, and at which they are bound to arrive.[1]

Talmon located the roots of extremism in a misguided calling to conquer contingency itself. He ascribed this catastrophic mission to an all-too-human urge "for a final resolution of all contradictions and conflicts in a state of total harmony," an "inability to face the fact that life is a perpetual and never resolved crisis."[2]

Generations later, there has come into prominence a trend in political and legal thought that exhibits the same habits of mind, though tending concretely in a reverse direction. The political messianism represented by totalitarianism embraced the state as a vehicle of social transformation and exalted exertions of political will; the new political messianism disparages the state and seeks to subordinate all exertions of political will to an everywhere-and-always-applicable body of law. The old political messianism saw the realization of freedom "only in the pursuit and attainment of an absolute collective purpose"[3]; the new political messianism sees freedom in the negation of collective purpose. The old political messianism, while exalting

[1] J.L. Talmon, *The Origins of Totalitarian Democracy* (London: Secker & Warburg, 1952), at 1–2.

[2] *Id.* at 254–55.

[3] *Id.* at 2.

human liberation and popular power, was a radical rejection of liberalism; the new political messianism is an extreme formulation of liberalism itself.

This liberal messianism is manifest in the trend among international human rights advocates to disparage the sovereign equality framework. In the post-Cold War era, many in the international law field have seen a hitherto unknown opportunity to extend the reach of settled legal principles—principles of human rights and liberal constitutionalism—into areas once dominated by the contingencies of politics.[4] For opponents of a pluralistic approach to global order, it is high time that international legal norms acquire sufficient determinacy to overcome political, ideological, and cultural resistance to their animating purposes, that these norms apply to individuals and not merely to abstract entities, and that those bound to obey law be compelled to comply.

Underlying this anti-pluralist project is a refusal to concede that radical disagreement about justice constitutes an enduring part of the human condition. This refusal is supportable insofar as it rejects a pluralism, grounded in deep respect for cultural difference, that would immunize egregious practices even from external moral judgments—as expressed, for example, in diplomatic rebukes, the suspension of assistance, or the withholding of trade. But such a culture-based pluralism is not the pluralism embodied in the sovereign equality framework. At issue is not abstention from moral judgment or even political pressure, but rather presumptive abstention from a limited set of unilateral coercive measures amounting to dictatorial interference in the internal affairs of a foreign political community. And the justification of that abstention rests not on a static model of civilizational difference, but a dynamic model of political struggle within societies, carried out by forces that reflect clashing moral visions of public order.

The anti-pluralist project fails to acknowledge the extent of human reliance on—and therefore, reasoned loyalty to—political projects that, having triumphed in local power struggles, succeed in setting the terms of social coordination for particular times and places. Such an acknowledgment would allow that the collective, not just the individual, enterprises of human beings have moral significance, and that strangers to those enterprises owe respect—in certain realms and within a certain range—even to those systems of collective ordering that they deem to be unjust.[5]

[4] Susan Marks has coined the term "liberal millenarianism" for the excesses of liberal internationalism, though she focuses on other aspects of the same phenomenon. *See* Marks, "International Law, Democracy, and the End of History" in Gregory H. Fox & Brad R. Roth eds., *Democratic Governance and International Law* (Cambridge University Press, 2000), 532–66.

[5] The theme of this discussion is inspired by Michael Walzer's landmark defense of the principle of non-intervention, "The Moral Standing of States," 9 *Phil. & Pub. Aff.* 209 (1980). The present argument, however, seeks to root the conclusion more firmly in liberal-individualist philosophical premises, as opposed to Walzer's more "communitarian" account of the presumptive "fit" between

# I. The Elusive Consensus on Universal Norms

Moral criticism of the sovereign equality framework typically cites universal norms that purportedly transcend territorial and other boundaries. Invocations of universality often contain an ambiguity about whether the norm in question is asserted to be *universally espoused* as well as *universally applicable*. The claim that a norm is universally applicable need not rest on, but frequently trades on (and would always benefit from), a claim that the standard is universally espoused. Moreover, whereas philosophical truth alone is sufficient to establish the universal applicability of moral norms, bare invocations of natural justice are a problematic basis for the assertion of universal legal norms.

Allen Buchanan makes an intuitive case for universal moral sensibilities as follows:

> [W]e should expect some congruence of moral values across societies, given the roles that morality plays in human life by coordinating behavior and providing relatively peaceful means for resolving or avoiding the more common mutually destructive conflicts that can occur wherever human beings go about the basic tasks that all human beings must perform.
>
> As Stuart Hampshire has observed, there is a lethal tension in the view that there is a fundamental diversity in basic ethical principles across societies, because for something to count as a *basic* ethical principle it must be grounded in and responsive to human interests – interests that all human beings have, rather than in the parochial interests that some human beings happen to have. By the most basic ethical principles, Hampshire means those that, if followed, help avert the worst harms to which all human beings are vulnerable, those principles adherence to which is necessary for people being able to lead decent human lives. But if this is so, then it is hard to see how different societies, so long as they are societies of human beings, could disagree entirely in their most basic ethical principles. At the very least, strong evidence of such fundamental disagreement would have to be marshaled.[6]

political communities and their governments. *See id.* at 212. It also extends the argument for the non-intervention norm to cover related norms limiting retrospective and extraterritorial prosecution.

[6] Allen Buchanan, *Justice, Legitimacy and Self-Determination: Moral Foundations for International Law* (Oxford University Press, 2004), at 109–10, citing Stuart Hampshire, *Innocence and Experience* (Cambridge, MA: Harvard University Press, 1989), 90.

Be this as it may,[7] when the focus shifts from abstraction to application, the generalizations of Buchanan and Hampshire seem far less persuasive. Assertions of universally espoused norms in real-life disputes amount to the rather curious contention that empirical discord has a solution rooted in empirical consensus. Whereas consent can, without contradiction, bind someone to standards with which she does not presently agree, the same cannot be true of consensus unless a peculiar condition holds, such as (a) the relevant community that is the referent of consensus does not include the dissident; or (b) all informed persons of good faith and sound reason can deduce from an uncontested consensus a conclusion that the dissident, for lack of one or more of these attributes, rejects.

The real problem with condition (a) is not the debater's point that the condition becomes tautological where dissidence itself suffices to expel the dissident from the relevant community. One can, without doing too much violence to the concept, redefine "consensus" as an insistent near-consensus, as in the authoritative definition of a peremptory (or *jus cogens*) norm as one "accepted and recognized by the international community of States as a whole as a norm from which no derogation is permitted."[8] More seriously problematic are efforts to redefine the lawmaking community so as to systematically exclude the non-like-minded. Thus, "global civil society" may be cited as an alternative source of lawmaking authority. "[W]orld social and decision processes" may be said to include the participation of, "[b]esides the traditional nation-state,... intergovernmental organizations, non-self-governing territories, autonomous regions, and indigenous and other peoples, as well as private entities such as multinational corporations, media, nongovernmental organizations, private armies, gangs, and individuals."[9] Absent a formally structured account of their supposed juridical authority, the views of any such actors can be invoked or ignored, as expediency dictates.[10] The "international community" can thus become

[7] One might counter with Richard Rorty's suggestion that there may be parts of the world lacking "conditions of life sufficiently risk-free to make one's difference from others inessential," such that "it would be just too risky—indeed, would often be insanely dangerous—to let one's sense of moral community stretch beyond one's family, clan, or tribe." Richard Rorty, "Human Rights, Rationality, and Sentimentality," in Obrad Savić ed., *The Politics of Human Rights* (New York: Verso, 1999), 67 at 77, 75.

[8] Vienna Convention on the Law of Treaties, *opened for signature* May 23, 1969, art. 53, 1155 U.N.T.S. 331, 352.

[9] Siegfried Wiessner & Andrew R. Willard, "Policy-Oriented Jurisprudence and Human Rights Abuses in Internal Conflict: Toward a World Public Order of Human Dignity" 93 *Am. J. Int'l L.* 316, 323 (1999); *see also* W. Michael Reisman, "Unilateral Actions and the Transformations of the World Constitutive Process: The Special Problem of Humanitarian Intervention," 11 *Euro. J. Int'l L.* 3, 13 (2000).

[10] *See* James C. Hathaway, "America, Defender of Democratic Legitimacy?" 11 *Eur. J. Int'l L.* 121, 130 (2000).

a pseudo-empirical category, membership in which is ascribed on the basis of cosmopolitan characteristics that correlate with liberal views.

The more frequent and significant problem, however, is posed by condition (b) above, which rests on the assumption that consensus on an abstract norm can be unproblematically projected forward to a determinate application. The scope of consensus is easily exaggerated. We often imagine that the matters of which we feel the most certain and to which we assign the greatest importance are matters as to which human beings share a common intuition, and that genuine differences pertain only to the peripheral questions, concerning which we can plainly perceive room for disagreement. It is not easy to accept that informed persons of good faith and sound reason can find themselves on opposite sides of violent confrontations, that they may apply characterizations such as tyranny and freedom, hero and murderer, in opposite ways.

The beginnings of wisdom about political conflict lie in recognizing that informed persons of good faith and sound reason,[11] while subscribing to familiar moral principles in the abstract, can disagree fundamentally on questions of public order, including on whether to support ruthless measures such as dictatorship, repression, and terrorism. If that is so, as this chapter will argue, a substantial incidence of harsh political methods is endemic to the human condition, even if most human beings are basically good.[12] However much of the world's illiberal coercion, force, and

[11] The criteria of the three characteristics—"informed," "good faith," and "sound reason"—are intended to be as independent of normative judgment as possible (though the criteria for empirical categories are never really free of the influence of normative perspectives). Thus, by "informed," I mean being neither ignorant of nor deceived about the basic facts of the situation, rather than being possessed of the insights about the situation that we would like for persons to have (so that they see it our way); by "good faith," I mean that they take seriously some general duty to "do right by" all other human beings (even if their conception of that duty is objectively inadequate), and genuinely believe that their support of particular measures observes that duty (even if they are objectively mistaken); by "sound reason," I mean that they process information in a fairly sophisticated and non-pathological way. The goal of this formulation is to avoid the question-begging that results from conflating principled disagreement (a descriptive characterization) with "reasonable" disagreement (a normative characterization). I cannot exclude the possibility that, for example, some Nazis fulfilled the criteria of the above categories (even though Nazism per se seems to have entailed a general repudiation of moral duties to non-Aryans). Rather than to blur the distinction, I would prefer to say that there is some objective threshold of aberrational injustice beyond which possession of the three characteristics is, for thoroughly practical reasons, irrelevant to the question of toleration (i.e., we cannot reach a morally worthwhile *modus vivendi* with such persons).

[12] It is worth recalling Jeremy Waldron's observation, noted in Chapter 2, that Kant attributed the perils of the state of nature not to selfishness but to moral vehemence. "Even if we imagine men to be ever so good natured and righteous before a public lawful state of society is established, individual men, nations, and states can never be certain that they are secure against violence from one another, because each will have his own right to do what *seems just and good to him*, entirely independent of the opinion of the others." Immanuel Kant, *The Metaphysical Elements of Justice*, trans. John Ladd (Indianapolis: Bobbs-Merrill,

violence may be attributed to viciousness or licentiousness, much would withstand even the eradication of those evils. Global conflict management thus requires a pluralistic framework.

## II. Culture-Based Pluralisms

### A. WALZER AND RAWLS

Michael Walzer and John Rawls have both famously offered pluralistic approaches to international ethics. Both approaches, in different ways, predicate international pluralism on the cultural differences thought to be reflected in political communities' varying systems of public order.

Walzer posits a "morally necessary," though rebuttable, presumption to govern relations with foreign states: "that there exists a certain 'fit' between the community and its government," such that the community is "governed in accordance with its own traditions."[13] This presumption is overcome in extreme cases, as where governments engage in "massacre or enslavement."[14] But the presumption holds in the case of "a military dictatorship and a religious 'republic,' without civil and political liberties, and brutally repressive," under which women are subjected to "their traditional religious subordination to patriarchal authority," in keeping with the locality's "political and religious culture" and the regime's "deep roots" in the community's history.[15] Walzer does not deny that a foreign community's principles of internal public order "may be wrong or badly conceived." Still, he maintains:

> [I]t is not the sign of some collective derangement or radical incapacity for a political community to produce an authoritarian regime. Indeed, the history, culture, and religion of the community may be such that authoritarian regimes come, as it were, naturally, reflecting a widely shared world view or way of life.[16]

Given a hypothetical opportunity to transform the situation by drugging the community's elites and masses with a "wondrous chemical" that "would wipe out of their minds their own political and religious culture" and turn them into Swedish-style

1965), § 44, at 76, quoted in Jeremy Waldron, "Special Ties and Natural Duties," 22 *Phil. & Pub. Aff.* 3, 4–5, 14–15 (1993).

[13] Walzer, "The Moral Standing of States," *supra*, at 212.

[14] *Id.* at 217.

[15] *Id.* at 225.

[16] *Id.* at 224–25.

social democrats, he would refuse do so on the ground that this would deprive them of "the only kind of state that they are likely to call their own."[17]

Rawls's pluralism is not nearly as broad as Walzer's, but it is every bit as deep—coming close to accepting foreigners' illiberal practices as "right for them," rather than merely as immune from coercive interference—and just as reliant on cultural difference as a justification. In regard to "decent, non-liberal peoples," Rawls posits a duty "not only to refrain from exercising political sanctions—military, economic, *or diplomatic*—to make a people change its ways," but also "to recognize these non-liberal societies as equal participating members in good standing of the Society of Peoples."[18] He stresses "the great importance of all decent peoples' maintaining their self-respect and having the respect of other liberal or decent peoples,"[19] in consideration of which an international system should not even "offer incentives for its member peoples to become more liberal."[20] Rawls does not elaborately account for the rejection of liberalism by peoples that are nonetheless "decent," but he assumes that a "people" is the kind of entity that can properly be characterized as liberal or non-liberal, and that a non-liberal people's self-respect is somehow invested in its non-liberal principles of public order. From these assumptions, and from his choice of a hypothesized Islamic republic ("Kazanistan") as his illustration of a decent non-liberal order,[21] one must deduce that Rawls, like Walzer, regards principles of public order as, at least potentially, embedded in a community's history, traditions, religion, and culture and worthy of presumptive respect on this basis.

Rawls's toleration is deep, but for just that reason, necessarily narrow. The "decent" non-liberalism that he posits reflects only such deviation from liberal norms as a liberal sensibility, straining for open-mindedness, can abide. Decency ends up as a near-liberal requirement that the non-liberal authority structure be (a) reasonably close to just (oriented toward a plausible conception of a common good and not in violation of a truncated set of core human rights) and (b) reasonably close to legitimate (participatory, even if through a merely consultative process and subject to hierarchical premises).[22] (Informed persons of good faith and sound reason are supposed to agree, it would seem, on the normative points that liberals deem most central and certain but may differ on more peripheral details.) Relations with non-decent systems of public order—outlaw states, burdened peoples, and even benevolent dictatorships—are not to be governed by the terms of reciprocity that Rawls sketches out, but are left to be governed in accordance with what amount

[17] *Id.* at 225–26.

[18] Rawls, *The Law of Peoples*, above, at 59 (emphasis added).

[19] *Id.* at 62.

[20] *Id.* at 84.

[21] *Id.* at 75–78.

[22] *See id.* at 62–82.

to standard "cosmopolitan liberal" principles—the "transcendent justice" approach, as defined above.

Since real-world decent non-liberal regimes, by Rawls's criteria, comprise almost a null set (Singapore might qualify), Rawls's *Law of Peoples* makes little practical contribution in this regard, except as an alternative, and more attractively broad-minded, rationale for the international pursuit of liberal justice.[23] In setting conditions for inclusion appropriate to an overlapping international consensus among liberal and (almost exclusively hypothetical) "decent non-liberal" communities—conditions for a deep respect—Rawls's text forgoes devising a useable platform for a real-world *modus vivendi* based on a more shallow respect among political communities.

## B. REJECTING CULTURE-BASED PLURALISM

Walzer and Rawls join many other less systematic thinkers in predicating their calls for an international pluralism on cultural difference. This emphasis has several troubling implications.[24] First, as noted above, if respect for persons is understood to demand respect for cultural characteristics as constitutive of personhood, and if the culture is understood to include principles of public order, then respect requires deep toleration of a community's coercion, force, and violence toward certain of its members, precluding even such measured responses to foreign public-order practices as condemnations or boycotts. Second, cultural difference is privileged over mere ideological difference: traditional-hierarchical non-liberalism has this special immunity, whereas revolutionary-egalitarian non-liberalism, being mere ideology, does not. Third, culture-based pluralism is naturally disposed to accept convenient claims of illiberal factions about the authoritative interpretation of cultural norms, while dismissing local liberal dissidents in non-Western societies as culturally inauthentic, thereby potentially rendering aid and comfort to repression. Fourth, the association of public-order practices with a social phenomenon as

[23] This is not to say that Rawls—or any of the more standard cosmopolitan theorists—denies the importance of the general pragmatic and humanitarian considerations that frequently weigh against cross-border impositions. It is to say that the restraints specific to Rawls's pluralism apply to interactions only with regimes that he regards as within the realm of "decency," whereas interactions with regimes that fail, for one reason or another, to meet this standard are governed by straightforward applications of liberal political morality.

[24] This discussion does not intend to engage with anthropological perspectives on culture. It addresses not culture itself but the distortive roles that invocations of cultural difference often play in a particular political and legal discourse. Those invocations tend either to demand special deference to whatever characteristics are attributed to cultural difference, on the ground such characteristics are constitutive of personhood and therefore worthy of respect as a matter of human dignity, or, on the darker side, to dismiss certain communities as immutably impervious to constructive influences.

intractable as "culture" tends to encourage ordinarily justice-minded actors to write off whole societies—and their most vulnerable members—as a lost cause.

None of these consequences seems justified on the merits. Liberalism has supporters and opponents in all parts of the world. The level of support depends on many variables, including the compatibility of liberal ideas with local traditions, but liberalism's following has gradually increased even in parts of the world where it had been thought unpromising. The success of liberal ideas seems to depend less on cultural norms than on the presence of the economic, political, and social circumstances of liberalism—conditions that produce questions to which liberalism is a plausible answer. These circumstances attend economic development. Of course, resistance to liberalism, whether from the Right (traditional-hierarchical) or the Left (revolutionary-egalitarian), remains viable in developing countries to varying extents, but it also remains viable to varying extents in the developed Western countries in which liberalism was born.

Moreover, "globalization," which actually started centuries ago, has long since done away with any possibility of hermetically sealed "cultures." Many local representatives of supposed non-Western interests and values have been either directly or indirectly Western educated, and many postcolonial ideologies would have been impossible without influences from Western thought. Efforts to reach back in time for a purer, more "authentic" approach are not traditionalist but revivalist, applying venerable ideas to conditions never imagined in, say, the days of the Qu'ran. Whatever else may be said for or against these ideas, they represent not culture as such but political ideology, with all of the accompanying variability and contestability.

A culture, as such, does not entail a distinctive conception of public order, unless the former is tendentiously defined so as to make the point tautological. Indeed, whereas territorial political communities have boundaries that more or less identify a permanent population as a fixed membership to which political judgments can somehow—whether or not by popular vote—be imputed, cultures have no established political boundaries; it is not clear who is and who is not a member, and it is impossible for a culture, even metaphorically, to take a decision.

To be sure, culture influences subjective perceptions of the essential nature of the relationship between the individual and the community. Such perceptions affect the popularity of liberal thought, and especially of the rhetoric by which liberals habitually express themselves. But it is important not to conflate the individual's relationships to three separate entities: (a) a community of attachment—whether it be a local village, a geographically coherent or dispersed ethnic group or clan, or a notional community of coreligionists living anywhere in the world—that may be regarded, subjectively or even objectively, as constitutive of the individual's identity and ends; (b) the notional political community encompassed by a state's territory, which is unlikely to be coextensive with any community "constitutive" of the individual's identity or ends; (c) the governmental apparatus that rules in the name of—and may or may not be accountable to—that notional political community.

Although some human rights issues authentically concern the relationship between the individual and a local community's traditional structures of authority (e.g., female genital mutilation and honor killings),[25] most—including the almost all of the ones that occasion proposals for extraordinary cross-border exertions of power—concern the conduct of an at least quasi-modern governmental apparatus that is usually unaccountable to, and often directly at odds with, such traditional and/or local structures.

In general, there is no reason to presume that the patterns of coercion, force, and violence being inflicted on individuals reflect the authentic ordering principles of some community to which these individuals are organically attached.[226] Indeed, the most seriously illiberal practices are less likely to be a product of coherent cultural communities than of internal clashes that exceed institutional capacities for conflict management.[27]

None of this is to deny that cultural difference is one of the main forces driving deep political disagreement. But in this regard, culture is not worthy of special standing, analytically independent of and morally privileged over garden-variety ideological difference. The proper focus is on ideological difference, irrespective of its (always-contested) relationship to cultural difference.

Beyond this, cultural difference may present practical considerations that affect human rights implementation. Liberal institutions and processes, designed for a Western setting, may produce perversely illiberal results if implanted without adaptation in a society where conditions, including but not limited to culture and tradition, are different. But this calls into question merely the familiar institutional implementations of liberal principles, not the applicability of liberal moral criteria.

[25] Of course, authenticity alone does not validate a practice. The universalist ethic demands that exercises of power, everywhere and always, be rationally justifiable from the standpoint of every individual subject to them. Local attitudes may affect that analysis but never justify suspending it. The pluralism that this book advocates entails no renunciation of moral judgment about matters of this nature.

[26] Allen Buchanan makes a similar point. *See* Buchanan, *supra,* at 179.

[27] Almost without exception, the kinds of events that have prompted calls for international criminal justice and humanitarian intervention—such as gross and systematic recourse to killings and torture—have been occasioned by a perceived urgent need to suppress internal challenges to a social order (e.g., the Latin American "dirty wars" of the 1970s and 1980s) or by a perceived dire threat from a rival community (e.g., the former Yugoslavia and Rwanda in the 1990s). Of course, suppression of freedom, denials of gender equality, oppression of homosexual persons, and cruel and unusual punishments are frequently rooted in cultural tendencies, but however often condemned as human rights violations, these illiberal practices almost never call into question a state's ultimate authority within its territory. Moreover, these latter practices tend to manifest themselves most dramatically when traditionalists within a culture feel that they are losing their grip, prompting a neotraditionalist revival that is both far harsher than the community's historical norm and of highly contested cultural authenticity (e.g., in Iran and Afghanistan).

Moreover, in any political context, local sensibilities determine what kinds of measures and arguments will be effective, and these sensibilities, of course, depend partly on cultural factors. Such sensibilities will affect strategy and tactics and may impose practical limitations on what can be achieved, but these are not matters of normative principle.

Liberal cosmopolitans are thus correct in rejecting cultural difference as a basis for a pluralistic approach to international order.[28] Yet they are wrong in rejecting global pluralism on the whole, for completely different reasons.

## III. The Moral Justification of a Non-Culture-Based Pluralism

### A. COLLECTIVE SELF-DETERMINATION AND MORAL DISAGREEMENT

The moral justification of a pluralist international order rests, in significant part, on the assertion of a collective moral right to self-determination. An argument for the collective right to self-determination can be made from premises that are fully consistent with ontological individualism, moral universalism, and political rationalism.[29] This argument emphasizes not the individual's embeddedness in a collective past but the individual's present and future dependence on collective projects that call for distinctively political decisions. On this account, justice remains subject to the boundaries of political community, not for cultural reasons, but for practical ones.

Fundamental human concerns necessitate uniquely political decisions about the nature of the good society wherein the good life is pursued. The state—as opposed to non-territorial or micro-territorial communities rooted in sentimental attachment rather than potential for order creation, and as opposed to an international community encompassing an unmanageable multiplicity of interests and

[28] *See, e.g.*, Jack Donnelly, *Universal Rights in Theory and Practice* (Ithaca, NY: Cornell Univ. Press, 1989), at 118 ("We must not be misled by complaints of the inappropriateness of 'Western' human rights made by repressive regimes whose practices have at best only the most tenuous connection to indigenous culture; communitarian rhetoric too often cloaks the depredations of corrupt and often Westernized or deracinated elites"); Fernando R. Tesón, "The Rawlsian Theory of International Law," 9 *Ethics & Int'l Aff.* 79, 98 (1995) (complaining that Rawls's later work "embraced a more relativistic, context-based conception of justice and political morality, in which rights and liberties no longer had a foundation in higher principles or liberal views of human nature").

[29] For an incisive discussion of liberalism's theoretical premises and their relationship to collective rights, *see* Chandran Kukathas, "Are There Any Cultural Rights?" in Will Kymlicka ed., *The Rights of Cultural Minorities* (Oxford Univ. Press, 1995), 228.

values—represents the only community in the name of which the ineluctably contentious decisions needed to structure social life can be effectively made and enforced. Even in states where these decisions are not made democratically—by light of even the loosest of the standards that may be derived from any of the radically conflicting available conceptions of democracy[30]—the political independence of the territorial entity preserves for its population at least the object of democratic struggle, and therefore the possibility of eventually achieving what may plausibly be described as self-government.[31] Notwithstanding the inherent messiness and frequent nastiness of the processes by which these matters are worked out internally, the impositions of intermeddlers, themselves systematically prone to self-interestedness, arrogance, or well-meaning short-sightedness, are rarely to be preferred. Human beings therefore have a morally important interest, albeit not always a paramount one, in being part of a territorial political community that maintains the last word on its internal public order.

The problem of deep political disagreement is rooted, not in the immutable cultural characteristics of holders of conflicting views, but in the nature of political life. The quest for an international justice that transcends territorial and political divisions comes to grief because that quest operates, at least implicitly, from an unrealistic premise: that informed persons of good faith and sound reason, notwithstanding such disagreements as are conceded to be inevitable among human beings, can be expected to reach an overlapping consensus on a core set of morally imperative political norms.

The quest finds encouragement in an empirical consensus that can be found to exist on abstract norms, such as those found in international human rights instruments. But such consensus too often ends up being illusory: First, apparent consensus on abstractions frequently dissolves at the level of application because in the face of concrete circumstances, adherents of competing "comprehensive doctrines,"[32] who endorsed the abstractions for differing reasons, will interpret the same abstract

[30] I have addressed radically conflicting conceptions of democracy at length elsewhere. *See, e.g.*, Brad R. Roth, *Governmental Illegitimacy in International Law, supra*, at 75–120; Brad R. Roth, "Evaluating Democratic Progress," 9 *Ethics & Int'l Aff.* 55 (1995); Brad R. Roth, "Retrieving Marx for the Human Rights Project," 17 *Leiden J. Int'l L.* 31, 52–61 (2004); Gregory H. Fox & Brad R. Roth, "Democracy and International Law," 27 *Rev. Int'l Studies* 327, 343–48 (2001).

[31] The following words of Thomas Nagel make a similar point (though ironically, Nagel was speaking of global rather than—and at the expense of—state institutions):

> Unjust and illegitimate regimes are the necessary precursors of the progress toward legitimacy and democracy, because they create the centralized power that can then be contested, and perhaps turned in other directions without being destroyed.

Thomas Nagel, "The Problem of Global Justice," 33 *Phil. & Pub. Aff.* 113, 146 (2005).

[32] This term is owing to John Rawls, *Political Liberalism* (Cambridge, MA, Harvard University Press, 1993), at xvi.

norms in conflicting ways, or assign them conflicting priorities. Second, consensus as to the presumptive wrongfulness of particular conduct often gives way to discord about under which adverse conditions the presumption is overcome; agreement as to inadmissible means typically fails to hold in the face of sufficiently grave threats to what some see as morally imperative ends.

The fact of political life that necessitates a pluralistic solution can be summarized as follows: ***Under sufficiently adverse conditions, such as extreme ethno-national or socioeconomic polarization, the interaction of these two problems—the inability to agree on a fair basic structure of public order, and the inability to exclude recourse to extraordinary means in the struggle to install or maintain a basic structure of public order that comports with one's own conception of fairness—leads informed persons of good faith and sound reason to support ruthless measures against one another.*** Where the gap between competing conceptions of fairness is sufficiently great and the perceived moral stakes of political conflict sufficiently high, efforts to forge a mutually acceptable institutional solution will fail, prompting recourse to an unmediated clash of social forces. The result is a principled recourse to measures, such as dictatorship, repression, and terrorism, that would be rejected in the abstract.

This unhappy tendency is not something that is true of some discrete, culturally different, "them." It is true of "us." For reasons that will be elaborated below, political contestation, even when driven by wisdom and good intentions, is universally a "contact sport" that, under the right (or more properly, the wrong) social conditions, will lead to harshly incompatible moral stands on vital issues.

The main current of contemporary liberal thought—reflected in Rawls's *Political Liberalism*[33]—seeks to establish that a basic constitutional framework can be specified independent of a collective adoption, not simply of a particular "comprehensive doctrine of human flourishing," but of a particular accommodation among some such doctrines to the disparagement or exclusion of others. This variant of liberal theory resists regarding the basic structure as a site of ineluctable conflict among bearers of common-good-oriented but mutually incompatible worldviews, which conflict will necessarily result in, if not outright victory for bearers of one conception, a bargain reflective of the comparative political leverage of the factions, with some factions disadvantaged and others excluded altogether. Rather, the theory imagines, as an achievable ideal, a basic structure that reflects an overlapping consensus among all "reasonable" worldviews.

This notion has spawned a debate far beyond the scope of the present work. Suffice it to say here, though, that the losers in this formula would scarcely accept the "persuasive redefinition" of reasonableness that Rawls devised to effect their delegitimation—and not for lack of knowledge, intelligence, or public spiritedness.

[33] Rawls, *Political Liberalism, supra.*

Informed persons of good faith and sound reason will inevitably struggle over the terms of the basic structure.

This inevitable struggle does not, in itself, necessarily augur severe strife or harsh measures. Constitutional compromises often secure social peace, not because they are universally fair or engender universal satisfaction, but because no faction that is sufficiently efficacious to destabilize the institutional framework has sufficient motive to do so, based on a comparative assessment of the attendant risks and benefits. Moreover, even where the constitutional order's specifications are in tension with international standards, the very context of social peace will likely persuade international agencies and jurists to find the deviations to fall within a "margin of appreciation."

Nonetheless, in polities sharply polarized on socioeconomic, ethno-national, or other bases, efficacious factions who regard their material interests and moral principles as unfairly subordinated or marginalized may have insufficient motive to remain loyal to the prevailing processes of decision. The potential for an unmediated clash of social forces augurs decisions, of both government and opposition, to employ harsh means against what appear, by light of their particular projects of public order, as threats to the community's vital interests.

In such cases, genuine advocates of plausible conceptions of fairness can be found on both sides.[34] For example, the Chilean coup of 1973, the Salvadoran and Nicaraguan internal armed conflicts of the 1980s, and the attempted Venezuelan coup of 2002—all conflicts rooted in socioeconomic polarization—sharply divided the respective societies, including their liberal-democratic elements. Ethnic polarization is, if anything, even more likely to pit sincerely held but clashing conceptions of fairness against one another in conflicts that are beyond the capacity of institutions to contain.[35]

A duty not to intervene in a foreign political community's internal conflict, so far as that duty extends, is a duty to respect patterns of coercion, and even violence,

[34] This is made no less true by the fact that key actors on one or both sides might properly be classified as "thugs." Indeed, it is no less true where demagogues are responsible for having exacerbated the polarization, for the fact that the ***other*** side is in the grip of demagoguery presents genuine dilemmas for one's own side. Once convinced that the other side observes no limits, one can easily become convinced of the dire need for ruthless measures. One's reactive ruthlessness, in turn, may perversely serve to vindicate the fears initially conjured by the demagogues, so that both sides are trapped in a logic of escalating violence.

[35] The Israeli-Palestinian conflict, though not an "internal" conflict in the ordinary sense, comes to mind as an example of a violent confrontation as to which liberal internationalists from all over the world have taken up different sides, in vitriolic opposition even to one another.Any use of illustrative examples has the serious pitfall that readers, depending on their own substantive political principles, will perceive different conflicts differently. Rest assured that the author has very strong loyalties of his own in regard to each of the conflicts cited here; the concession that informed persons of good faith and sound reason could support the opposite side of each is rather a grudging one.

within a collectivity of which one is not a member. It is not akin to a duty to allow individuals peacefully to pursue their own good in their own way. Nor is it a matter of minding one's own business; the human costs of such conflicts are manifestly the business of all humanity. Rather, the duty of outsiders is to appreciate, in their assessment of the propriety of imposing their own will, the unshared collective stake that members of a given political community have in the outcomes of decisions about the fundamental direction of social life in the territory. Outsiders do not have standing to be partisans in another community's conflict; yet, their assessments of distant crises, apart from being prone to sophomoric oversimplification and deliberate manipulation, tend disproportionately to reflect the perspectives of those conflict participants with whom they personally most closely identify. The duty to refrain from coercive interference, while overcome in some class of unambiguously catastrophic cases, properly withstands the strong and wholesome moral intuition to take on others' causes as one's own.

Thus, the international order's pluralism should never be confused with the "gorgeous mosaic"[36] pluralism of the liberal imagination, in which an overarching unity as to "the right" renders inoffensive, and even enriching, the persistence of differences over "the good." As long as radical disagreement about justice remains part of the human condition, an international pluralism, even in its ideal form, will at moments be a tense and almost unbearably ugly pluralism, an accommodation among political communities dominated by incompatible positions on matters of justice and injustice, freedom and tyranny, and—ultimately—life and death.

## B. THE MORAL SIGNIFICANCE OF THE STATE

### *1. Deontological Liberalism and the Moral Devaluation of the State*

What I have called the "transcendent justice" approach to the international legal order strains against traditional limitations on the reach of international law and international institutions. Its justifications for doing so are based on a denial that the state is an entity—or a project—worthy of special deference. Reacting against the discredited anthropomorphic conceptualizations of the state that are characteristic of traditional approaches to international law, this approach embraces the opposite extreme, seeking to reduce the state *qua* political community to the sum of the individuals who make it up, and the state *qua* ruling apparatus to a resource-allocation and dispute-resolution mechanism at the disposal of those individuals.

[36] Former New York Governor Mario Cuomo and former New York City Mayor David Dinkins used this term to describe New York's cultural diversity. Calvin Sims, "To Save Money, City Hall Considers Cutting Parades," *N.Y. Times*, Apr. 7, 1992, at B5.

This moral devaluation of the state is largely traceable to the deontological, or neutralist, variant of contemporary liberal political thought.[37] Deontological liberalism gives categorical priority to the imperative of respect for the human subject as a rational chooser of its own ends. This approach contrasts with teleological approaches to liberal political morality that seek to maximize the realization of criteria of social well-being, whether such criteria reflect aggregated subjective preferences (utilitarianism) or an authoritative conception of the good life (perfectionism). Deontological liberalism is the leading secular basis for regarding rights as inherent in the human person; whereas utilitarian and perfectionist liberals (as well as those who reject liberalism's individualistic ontological premises) may assert moral grounds on which political institutions ought to create liberal legal rights, deontologists consider that liberal rights have an independent "existence" as a matter of deduction from first principles, and that the role of political institutions regarding such rights is, at best, to recognize and to implement them.[38]

Deontological liberalism has direct implications for the appropriate role of politics in social life and thus for moral status of the state. Deontologists divide the universe of moral issues into two realms: matters of "the right" and matters of "the good." "The right" is understood to include questions of justice, in the peculiar sense of fairness in weighing the legitimately competing claims of end-choosing human subjects; it is associated with a standard list of liberal rights that are deemed to be universally applicable and neutrally protective of end-choosing subjects. "The good" is understood to include questions of the nature of the good life and the proper objects of human striving, answers to which must be derived from one of many competing "comprehensive doctrines of human flourishing"; as these doctrines are deemed to be hopelessly controversial, the conflicting versions of "the good" that they generate are subordinated to a transcendent conception of "the right."[39]

[37] The starting point for discussions of "deontology" in contemporary political theory is John Rawls, *A Theory of Justice* (Cambridge, Mass.: Harvard Univ. Press, 1971), at 30. The associated issues have been extensively debated. *See, e.g.*, Michael Sandel, *Liberalism and the Limits of Justice* (New York: Cambridge Univ. Press, 1982); William Galston, *Liberal Purposes* (New York: Cambridge Univ. Press, 1991); Ronald Beiner, *What's the Matter with Liberalism?* (Berkeley: Univ. of California Press, 1992); George Sher, *Beyond Neutrality: Perfectionism and Politics* (New York: Cambridge Univ. Press, 1997). An excellent summary of the issues is contained in Will Kymlicka, *Liberalism, Community, and Culture* (New York: Oxford Univ. Press, 1989), at 9–99.

[38] Although Rawls is a crucial figure in the development of this deontological approach to human rights, his own work after *A Theory of Justice* developed in a divergent direction. The natural-law overtones of the early work were replaced by much more contingent formulations, especially as applied expressly to international political morality. *See* Rawls, *The Law of Peoples* (Cambridge, Mass.: Harvard Univ. Press, 1999). As a result, Rawls-inspired anti-pluralists have found themselves sharply at odds with their mentor. *See, e.g.*, Tesón, "The Rawlsian Theory of International Law," *supra.*

[39] *See, e.g.*, Ronald A. Dworkin, *A Matter of Principle* (Cambridge, Mass.: Harvard Univ. Press, 1985), 181–204, (controvertibly) defining liberalism in neutralist terms. Dworkin contrasts liberalism

The result is moral absolutism as to "the right" and moral subjectivism as to "the good."[40]

All liberal political thought seeks to demystify the state—to debunk, as Fernando Tesón puts it, the "Hegelian myth" of the state's existence as an organic entity[41] and to condition the state's authority on rational justification from the standpoint of every individual subject to it.[42] The deontological version, however, goes beyond this to deny that the collective enterprise may legitimately aim to transform the ends of its participants. This brand of liberalism does not envisage the mission of political life as the breaking down of diverse interests to forge a common good; rather, it imagines the common good to consist precisely in making society safe for the pursuit of diverse interests.[43]

The liberal belief in "limited government" thus takes on a dual meaning: it is not merely that governmental organs should be subject to substantive and procedural limitations (i.e., individual legal rights and institutional checks and balances) to prevent all exercise of absolute and arbitrary power, but that the mission of governance itself should be narrowed to resolution of a limited set of "collective action problems" that individuals and voluntary associations are structurally incapable of solving, such as the provision of dispute adjudication, law enforcement, national defense, economic infrastructure, and other "neutrally" justified public goods. This is to say, not that deontological liberalism rejects an activist (or even a sharply redistributive) state, but that it confines the activism of the state to "neutral" pursuits that do not encroach upon the individuality of the human person *qua* rational end-chooser.[44]

with the view that "the treatment government owes citizens is at least partly determined by some conception of the good life," a view he associates with both "American conservatism and various forms of socialism or Marxism." *Id.* at 192. Although a "perfectionist liberal" school has arisen to take issue with this neutralist approach to liberalism, *see, e.g.*, Galston, *Liberal Purposes, supra*; Sher, *Beyond Neutrality, supra*, Left-leaning theorists have been slow to acknowledge a distinctive conception of the good, repelled as they are by the thought of even so abstract a kinship to conservatism, and disposed as they are to the limitless appreciation of "difference."

[40] Deontologists typically deny that their neutrality is rooted in skepticism, asserting rather that even objectively valid judgments about the good life can produce "the good" only when the individuals in question voluntarily embrace them. *See* Kymlicka, *supra*, at 12.

[41] Fernando Tesón, *Humanitarian Intervention: An Inquiry into Law and Morality* (Ardsley-on-Hudson, N.Y.: Transnational Publishers, 1988).

[42] I owe this formulation to Jeremy Waldron.

[43] This approach to political life has special resonance in the United States, having been eloquently articulated by James Madison in *Federalist 10* (1787), reproduced in Michael Kammen ed., *The Origins of the American Constitution* (New York: Penguin Books, 1986), 145–52.

[44] "[T]he capabilities citizens need to function as equals in civil society count as neutral goods for purposes of justice not because everyone finds these capabilities equally valuable, but because reasonable people can recognize that these form a legitimate basis for making moral claims on one another." Elizabeth S. Anderson, "What is the Point of Equality?" 109 *Ethics* 287, 330 (1999). Note, however,

Compulsion is deemed unjust where predicated on grounds that presuppose a state-preferred conception of the good.

A potential implication of the deontological scheme is that politics has no legitimate role in determinations of either the right or the good. Just as questions of the good are to be decided in a realm below politics—by the independent determinations of individuals, alone or in freely chosen association—questions of the right are to be decided in a realm above politics, by deduction from first principles.

Logic does not compel this move. The deontological scheme, per se, concerns the substantive grounds, not the procedural rules, for determinations about justice; it may thus serve solely to inform participants in a properly rambunctious and open-ended political process, rather than to justify imposing authority from outside that process. However, the assertion that "the right" is independent of, rather than dependent on, a necessarily controversial judgment about "the good" suggests an objectivity and a universality of "the right" that weigh against deference to political processes in this realm. The deontological approach naturally encourages, even if it does not formally justify, the disparagement of politics. The widespread popularity of judicial review of legislation among deontological liberals confirms this tendency.[45]

If justice is universal (at least in its "fundamentals"), rather than the product of a decision at a particular time and place, and if the good life is purely a matter of individual prerogative, then the enterprise of politics is appropriately confined to a limited and subordinate set of purposes. The project of the state, it follows, is of limited and subordinate moral significance, as is the positive law that derives from that project.[46]

In the twenty-first century, this unromantic view of the state has a special appeal. The strong state is widely associated with totalitarian experiments, ethno-nationalist warfare, arbitrary traditional hierarchies, the imposition of the religious and cultural preferences of the politically powerful upon the rest, and a failure of universal concern for human beings as such. Freedom has never been so widely conceptualized as freedom from the state, and more generally as freedom to opt out of all relationships and roles not attributable to voluntary consent. Globalization has loosened the bonds of place and called into question the efficacy of national policymaking in all realms, from economy to culture. Persistent and intensifying immigration trends

that this statement assumes it to be possible to make a "neutral" assessment of "what capabilities citizens need to function as equals in civil society."

[45] For an atypical deontological approach that embraces politics (and rejects judicial review), see Jeremy Waldron, *Law and Disagreement* (Oxford University Press, 1999).

[46] Once again, such a conclusion assumes away, or at least judges unworthy of moral regard, the prevalence of fundamental disagreement about justice. Positive law serves as a working resolution of that disagreement for a particular time and place. *See* Jeremy Waldron, *The Dignity of Legislation* (Cambridge University Press, 1999).

have rendered at once unfeasible and dysfunctional the strong sense of national identity that once derived from common ethnicity and common religious and cultural values.

The philosophical roots of the moral devaluation of the state lie in an overreaction to the fetishization of local community and culture. In properly denying that the dignity of a human being can be reduced to the dignity of his or her assigned role in a corporative entity, and that his or her interests can be lightly sacrificed in the name of the supposed health of the social whole, many liberals (often inspired by, though not necessarily well educated in, the deontological approach) go so far as to exalt the prerogatives of the individual at the expense of the collective enterprises that are calculated to secure the conditions of individual flourishing. The result is akin to the dogmatism that, in the name of freedom, champions the associational right of individual workers to resist membership in labor unions, to the detriment of the workers as a whole.

Notwithstanding the need to affirm the individual as the ultimate referent of moral value, many human ends can be pursued only by means of compulsory collective decisions. Consequently, respect for individuals frequently requires respect for the decisions of the collectivities of which they are a part. This is often true even where the decisions in question can reasonably be characterized as unjust (as to both their substance and the processes by which they were taken), especially if one allows that assessments of "the right" cannot be isolated from the wide-ranging clash of ideas about "the good."

### *2. Compulsory Collective Decisions and the Conditions of Human Flourishing*

Liberalism justifiably seeks to empower individuals to pursue their own conceptions of the good life, but such pursuits—indeed, even such conceptions—do not arise in a vacuum. Most human pursuits are not even imaginable without a context generated by highly contingent social processes. (To take a random example, an individual can scarcely aspire to become a cellist in a symphony orchestra in the absence of complex processes that bring forth fellow musicians, composers, instrument makers, orchestra halls, and much more.) One's capacity to engage in particular pursuits depends largely on which public goods (some tangible, like highways; and some intangible, like tolerance) that one's society has decided to produce and which to forsake. The production of those public goods, in turn, largely depends—directly and indirectly—on exercises of the coercive power of the state. The characteristic liberal celebration of freedom of choice frequently obscures the complexity of freedom's relationship to coercion and the centrality of state power to the liberal project.

In particular, liberals frequently fail (again, more by disposition than by deduction) to recognize that increasing the choices of the well positioned—that is to say, those possessed of material resources, marketable skills, and so on—can empower them to opt out of relationships beneficial to the less well positioned.

(For example: Landowners who are set free to engage in mechanized export agriculture may throw sharecroppers off of their land, simultaneously producing unemployment and increasing the local price of food; the opportunity for urban-based businesses and residents to relocate to the suburbs may deplete a city's tax base and its core of civic participants, leading to dilapidation and despair; the option to send the most motivated and talented pupils to private schools may deprive the public schools of their sources of dynamism and morale, as well as of their political base of influential and engaged parents.) The result is that the least well off find their essential life choices diminished by what appears, at first glance, to be an increase in societal freedom. The creation and maintenance of the conditions of genuinely meaningful choice (a category that eludes value-neutral specification) for the greater part of the society may require that the choices of the strong be coercively constrained.

Moreover, the civic institutions that provide the context for meaningful choices can be sustained only in the presence of civic virtue. Not even administrative and market mechanisms elaborately designed to make "ambition counteract ambition" can withstand a general breakdown of public spiritedness and personal rectitude.[47] The needed civic virtue can arguably be eroded by the ready availability of opportunities for instant gratification (everything from promiscuity, gambling, and drugs to rampant consumerism) and by the free expression of antisocial ideas (such as speech that incites hatred and discrimination against ethnic minorities, pornographic images that demean or objectify women, and music that romanticizes or normalizes criminal gang activity). The requisites of civic virtue can be seen in different ways in different places at different times, and reasonable minds will often differ as to whether repression limits or furthers the empowerment of individuals to make meaningful choices.

By no means does deontological liberalism altogether neglect the need to subject individuals to compulsory collective decisions. Indeed, all variants of liberalism take as their project the remaking of state coercion as a component of "ordered liberty."

Deontological liberalism nonetheless asserts that "ordered liberty" can be specified independent of a collective adoption of a comprehensive doctrine of human flourishing (or collective adoption of a particular accommodation among some such doctrines to the exclusion of others), and therefore that universal rights can fully transcend the decisions of particular political communities about the nature of

[47] *See, e.g.,* Charles Taylor, "Cross -Purposes: The Liberal-Communitarian Debate," in Nancy L. Rosenblum ed., *Liberalism and the Moral Life* (Cambridge, Mass.: Harvard University Press, 1989), 159–82 (arguing that "republican solidarity underpins freedom").

the good society wherein the good life is pursued.[48] By all accounts, individual pursuit of the good life requires the existence of certain nondivisible public goods, the creation of which is burdened by collective action problems (e.g., the temptation to be a free rider), the solution to which frequently requires collective decisions authorizing coercive implementation. Deontological liberals believe that such collective decisions can be limited to those that can be justified "neutrally," without reference to a contentious conception of "the good"; since human equality entails, from the deontological perspective, equal prerogative of each individual to pursue his or her own conception of the good life (subject only to the condition of compossibility), justice entails freedom from all "non-neutral" compulsion.

This model assumes, though, that public goods are a relatively marginal and exceptional ingredient in the pursuit of the good life, and thus that there is no real need for collective decisions about the ends that individuals ought to pursue. Although deontological liberals are frequently in the forefront of egalitarian economic redistribution, their preferred device of social coordination remains the market—wherein social decisions, even if coercive in their own way, arise from an aggregation of individual preferences, thereby maintaining neutrality.[49] Individuals are imagined to pursue the good life, not as participants in official institutions, but either alone or in associations freely chosen from time to time.

But what if the barring of collective decisions in certain realms leads necessarily to an atomization that precludes pursuit of many plausible conceptions of the good? What if the requirement of neutrality on matters of "the good" debilitates the state from serving as the instrument of a needed social transformation? What if the suppression of distracting and corrupting influences is indispensable to the creation and maintenance of the institutions on which the good life for many heavily depends? What if the very existence of a common social endeavor, quite independent of this endeavor's specification, is crucial to the cohesiveness of the community and therefore to the structures that sustain the crucial life options of its members?

Such theses and their policy implications will inevitably be controversial on their merits, but there is no obvious incompatibility between such positions and essential liberal premises about the nature of political life. The state's task in effectuating core freedoms can thus legitimately be imagined not as the acknowledgment and implementation of an abstractly deducible set of rights, but as the making of hard political choices that determine the content of rights in a particular society.

If "the right" is dependent on a contingent, political conclusion about "the good" (or if it is fairly controvertible for other reasons, such as internal ambiguities and tensions), then its valid specifications will vary from political community to political

[48] For a related line of criticism, pointing out that liberalism encompasses rival freedoms, see John Gray, *Two Faces of Liberalism* (New York: The New Press, 2000), at 69–104.

[49] *See, e.g.,* Dworkin, *A Matter of Principle, supra,* at 181–204.

community and from time to time, though not limitlessly. "Justice" will still be a transcendent value, but it will have to be reconceived as entailing creation of the appropriate conditions for the individual pursuit, on an acceptably equal basis, of those ends that a collectivity has reasonably decided ought to be pursued.

This is not an illiberal standard, but rather one that takes seriously the self-determination of peoples as extending to fundamental choices of political, economic, social, and cultural systems (as provided for in numerous authoritative international instruments),[50] notwithstanding the ontological primacy of the individual and the universality of certain basic principles of human equality. This standard allows that the collective capacity to make fundamental decisions—and to have outside actors acknowledge their status as governing law—has a moral value independent of the justice or injustice of the decisions themselves (albeit a moral value that may be trumped where that capacity is egregiously abused). It is a standard that assigns to statecraft, and therefore to positive law, a moral standing that deontological liberalism tends to repudiate.

Moreover, whereas the deontology-inspired human rights camp concedes the permissibility of harsh measures only in direct defense of universal, abstractly deduced rights of the individual, the foregoing approach allows that such measures may reasonably be entertained in defense of a political program that embodies a debatable and contested conception of human flourishing. Bearers of differing substantive conceptions of a just public order—even those operating from common premises about human dignity—can be expected to disagree radically on the permissibility of uses of coercion and force in particular contexts. States tasked with creating and preserving the social conditions that underlie valued ways of life will take such measures as they deem exigent to protect a favorable—or to block an unfavorable—process of social transformation. Those loyal to the project, including informed persons of good faith and sound reason, can be expected to participate in these repressive measures pursuant to the prerogatives and dictates of (domestically) lawful authority.

Although an appreciation of this plurality of political projects in no way precludes strong censure of such measures (or the ends that animate them), it weighs strongly against the anti-pluralist invocation of universal standards to nullify, retrospectively or extraterritorially, the legal authority underlying them. Such extravagant assertions

[50] *See, e.g.,* Declaration on Principles of International Law Concerning Friendly Relations and Co-operation among States in Accordance with the Charter of the United Nations, G.A. Res. 2625 (XXV) (1970) (adopted without a vote) ("Every State has an inalienable right to choose its political, economic, social and cultural systems, without interference in any form by another State."); International Covenant on Civil and Political Rights, 999 U.N.T.S. 171 (1967), Art. 1(1) ("All peoples have the right to self-determination. By virtue of that right they freely determine their political status and freely pursue their economic, social and cultural development.").

of universalism ignore the role that political projects, in all of their contingency, play in securing the bases of human flourishing.

### 3. *Proliferating Rights, Clashing Duties, and Political Decisions*

The "right-good distinction" is not the only source of deontological liberalism's deprecation of the moral status of political decisions. Deontological liberalism further tends to posit a set of categorical priorities among universal human interests, emphasizing interests that depend on holding the state at bay (i.e., negative rights connected to negative state duties, such as freedom from arbitrary arrest or from censorship) over interests that depend for their fulfillment on the vigorous exercise of state power to create the needed social conditions (i.e., negative and affirmative rights connected to affirmative state duties, such as protection from crime and subversion or provision of adequate food, shelter, health care, and education). Even those deontological liberals most committed to the latter set of interests rule out furthering them in ways that compromise the former set.[51] It is not clear that these categorical priorities can be justified.

At the core of the human rights movement is the quest to bring about the conditions of a dignified human existence. Human rights thus entail not merely duties to avoid violating human dignity by discrete and direct acts of violence, but further duties affirmatively to protect the right-bearer from violence and from analogous inflictions with similarly dehumanizing effects. Beyond those lie duties to take all necessary measures to secure for all right-bearers (within the limits of what is materially feasible) the conditions that permit human potentialities to be realized. The proliferation of internationally certified human rights—now encompassing "first-generation" civil and political rights well beyond inviolability of the physical integrity of the person, "second-generation" economic and social rights, and "third-generation" collective rights to the minimal conditions of societal flourishing—represents a series of efforts to correct for the manifest inadequacy of simple negative imperatives.

It is currently fashionable to argue, given the patent abuse of arguments to the contrary by tyrannical regimes, that there are no systematic clashes among the internationally recognized rights. But unless one has a deep-seated (and suprarational) faith in a morally ordered universe in which all virtues are mutually reinforcing, it can hardly be denied that the question of their clash is an empirical one in every given instance, and that reasonable minds will differ on priorities. The argument would not be that civil and political rights interfere with economic and social rights

[51] Rawls thus famously posits a "lexical" priority of his first principle of justice (civil and political liberty) over his second principle (equity of distribution). Rawls, *A Theory of Justice, supra*, at 60–65, 302–03. He does, however, condition that priority on the satisfaction of basic material needs. *Id.* at 542–43.

as a general matter (the straw position that is typically posed for refutation), but rather that in a given instance, respect for certain negative rights will unjustifiably block the fulfillment of other vital human interests that can equally be expressed in the language of rights.[52]

The deontological error lies in the dismissing of contingency. The more holistically rights claims address human dignity, the more inexorably and expansively do they appropriate the space of politics.[53] Invocation of the term "human rights" altogether fails to preempt political contestation, because competing views of how to prioritize and how to accomplish the posited ends constitute the very core of politics.[54] The application of universal principles in real-life situations requires decisions, which political entities are in the position of having to make. These decisions, embodied in positive law, provisionally resolve the question of justice for the purposes of that political community at that time.

One can, and should, second-guess those decisions, even from afar. But to treat them as morally insignificant is a serious error. It is this error that the anti-pluralist sensibility embodies. The error lies not in affirming that there are right answers to questions of justice, nor in denouncing collectivities and individuals who have gotten these answers wrong. It lies rather in treating collectivities as though they have no right to arrive at their own answers, and individuals as though they have no right to implement the answers their collectivities arrive at, unless those answers are deemed—in hindsight or from a distant perspective—to be the right ones. International law's traditional limitations on coercive intervention in the internal affairs of states and on retrospective and extraterritorial prosecutions are rooted, not in moral relativism or skepticism, nor in the sacrifice of the individual to the collective, but in a moral appreciation of the role of collectivities in the lives of individuals.

[52] As will be noted below, fulfillment of human rights is an outcome gauged by the condition of the right-bearer, and ought not to be confused with a very different kind of "deontological" concern having to do with the moral quality of the agent's acts per se; if the duty to respect rights has categorical priority over the duty to protect or to ensure them, it is for some reason other than concern for human rights as such.

[53] Ronald Beiner explores the consequences of this reality for "rights talk" in *What's the Matter with Liberalism?* (Berkeley: University of California Press, 1992), at 80–97.

[54] According to Steven Lukes, "the real test of a belief in human rights comes when the goals of the struggle or strategy come into conflict with the defence of rights claims." Steven Lukes, *Moral Conflict and Politics* (Oxford Univ. Press, 1991), at 188. This view of human rights is widely held, but it rests on a highly questionable proposition: that "the defence of rights claims" is qualitatively different from, and therefore capable of taking categorical priority over, "the goals of a struggle or strategy." Of course, where "the goals of a struggle or strategy" represent a particularist interest or an idiosyncratic conception of the common good that can be counterposed to genuine universal principles, the proposition appears sound. It would be appalling, on any account, to assert as a moral precept: "My parochial end justifies any means that maximizes the likelihood of that end's fulfillment." The difficult questions, however, arise where the satisfaction of one set of vital human interests can occur only at the expense of another set of vital human interests.

## C. PLURALISM AT THE FAR END: POLITICAL CONFLICT AND THE PHYSICAL INTEGRITY OF THE PERSON

The foregoing discussion argues generally against the invocation of universal rights to nullify sovereign prerogative and positive law. It may seem not to pertain, however, to rights involving the physical integrity of the person, which are precisely the ones that underlie the most familiar recent developments in international criminal law and humanitarian intervention. On the surface, these rights appear to represent something approaching an empirical consensus (at least in the sense that no one dares openly to disavow them), thereby grounding standards of criminal responsibility that are independent of the variables of political order. The supposed consensus appears to render actors chargeable with knowledge of the existence, validity, and applicability of these standards, whatever the political context. However robust its pluralism, a decent international order must be committed to ensuring respect for human dignity, and violation of the physical integrity of the person is, it would seem, incompatible with such respect.

There is much to be conceded to this view. First, gross and systematic violations of the integrity of the person, of such a nature as to reflect ends that are incompatible with respect for human dignity (e.g., violence manifestly disproportionate to any plausible beneficent objective or directed against a particular racial, ethnic, or religious community), contradict the very basis upon which an international order that respects sovereignty considerations is most compellingly justified. To proclaim, for example, "Hutu Power" (the ideology of the Rwandan *genocidaires*) as an admissible answer to the question of public order would be a grotesque parody of the pro-sovereignty argument advanced above.[55] Second, as a matter of positive international law, many standards regarding physical integrity of the person provide directly for individual criminal responsibility—in some instances, even without a threshold finding of a pattern of gross violation. Such criminal responsibility attaches irrespective of domestic law or superior orders, and sometimes irrespective of otherwise-applicable immunities and limitations on extraterritorial jurisdiction. Thus, the standards regarding physical integrity of the person unquestionably have some special claim to universality.

Nonetheless, it warrants noticing that when abstract propositions are applied to concrete conditions of violent conflict, a meaningful universality of standards is far less empirically evident. Participants in unmediated social conflict are consequentialists, almost by necessity; political actors are expected to take responsibility, not exclusively for their own acts, but for the outcomes that befall their constituents.[56]

[55] For a chilling account, see Philip Gourevitch, *We Wish to Inform You that Tomorrow We Will be Killed with Our Families: Stories from Rwanda* (New York: Picador USA, 1998).

[56] Of course, not all instrumentalism qualifies as consequentialism; conflict participants may undertake violence in the service of their own cause without any regard to the moral worth of those

In such contexts, the cause of human dignity frequently appears to demand the violation of the rights of some as a means to protect or establish the rights of others. If there is a "universal" intuition on this topic, it would seem to be that while many acts can be presumptively condemned as heinous, no acts are absolutely excluded where the most vital moral interests are perceived to be at stake.

The truth of this proposition is manifest in the general complacency of Western populations, statesmen, and even scholars about the deliberate incineration of hundreds of thousands of innocent people in Hamburg, Dresden, Tokyo, Hiroshima, and Nagasaki. Even those who condemn the firebombings and atomic bombings generally feel compelled to engage seriously with the empirical question of whether these measures were necessary to prevent far worse harms.[57] Moreover, even condemnation of the acts seldom crosses the line to vilification of the actors; the scope for good-faith disagreement militates against attributing criminality to those who were in the unenviable position of having to make the decisions. (Of course, whereas "civilized" folk may incinerate innocent civilians for weighty reasons, it is easily assumed from a distance that "other" folk commit analogous acts for frivolous reasons.)

The increased stringency of *jus in bello* norms since World War II should not be taken to indicate any generalized transcendence of ruthlessness. International law continues to bar only those tactics anticipated to be unnecessary to legitimate military objectives,[58] and conflicting assessments of necessity continue to reflect the

upon whom their violence falls. It should not be assumed, however, that this is the case whenever conflict participants depart from deontological strictures, as there are frequently serious (whether or not erroneous) arguments that it is a morally imperative to do what appears necessary to avert even greater human costs. Moreover, that conflict participants may fail to observe a strict impartiality about harms to civilians—that they may give higher priority to the protection of those civilians to whom they bear special ties and special duties—does not reduce their conduct to sheer instrumentalism.

[57] *See, e.g.*, Walzer, *Just and Unjust Wars*, *supra*, at 251–68. Moreover, the International Court of Justice has been unwilling to rule out the legality of the use of nuclear weapons in the case of a dire threat to a state's survival. *Advisory Opinion on Legality of the Threat or Use of Nuclear Weapons*, 1996 ICJ 226 (8 July), ¶¶ 95–97.

[58] This general tendency is reflected in the limitation of criminal liability for collateral infliction of civilian losses to cases in which such losses figure to be "clearly excessive in relation to the concrete and direct overall military advantage anticipated." *Statute of the International Criminal Court*, art 8(2)(b)(iv). Meanwhile, many gruesome but useful military tactics remain unprohibited. Such tactics include, shockingly, the use of white phosphorus in combat against enemy troops. *See* "U.S. Forces Used 'Chemical Weapon' in Iraq," *Indep.*, November 16, 2005, *available at* <http://news.independent.co.uk/world/americas/article327379.ece>; Scott Shane, "Defense of Phosphorus Use Turns Into Damage Control," *N.Y. Times*, November 21, 2005, A1. Article 35(2) of Additional Protocol I to the Geneva Conventions, June 8, 1977, 1125 U.N.T.S. 3 (to which the United States is not a party, but which it acknowledges as including many provisions that embody customary international law), prohibits employing "weapons, projectiles and material and methods of warfare of a nature to cause superfluous injury or unnecessary suffering," but this provision arguably does not preclude use of incendiary chemicals against fortified structures occupied by combatants.

parties' differential access to military technology.[59] And indeed, the international community itself has, in the name of a greater good, authorized crippling economic sanctions even where their consequences have been known to be lethal to large numbers of innocents, including (especially) children.[60]

This is not to say that sadism, venality, bigotry, and a plethora of other human vices do not play a major role in the perpetration of atrocious practices around the world. But the typical focus on these human vices distracts from the role that principled persons often play on both sides of violent conflicts. Even where leaders are cynical demagogues, their demagoguery operates precisely by mobilizing the moral dispositions of constituents in support of decisive action. And while many of the worst atrocities are committed, by thugs recruited for this purpose, in at least partial secrecy from those constituents—an implicit acknowledgment that they go beyond what even a wartime sensibility can abide—this is often because the constituents prefer not to know (and know that they prefer not to know) the details of what is done in pursuit of ends they endorse.[61]

Participants on both sides of conflicts typically fight in the name of ends associated with human dignity. The daily sufferings of those denied the requisites of a dignified existence are frequently seen to justify "bringing home the cost" of those sufferings to the comfortable and influential.[62] The security of the many is just as

[59] It is telling that although "terrorism" is sweepingly condemned, the term continues to lack an authoritative definition, as one part of the international community has sought to exempt military action by states, and another part has sought to exempt asymmetrical resistance to "colonial domination, alien occupation, and racist regimes." *See, e.g.*, Alex Schmid, "Terrorism—The Definitional Problem," 37 *Case W. Res. J. Int'l L.* 375, 388 (2005); Jan Petman, "The Problem of Evil and International Law," in Jarna Petman & Jan Klabbers eds., *Nordic Cosmopolitanism: Essays in International Law for Martti Koskenniemi* (Martinus Nijhoff Publishers/Brill Academic Publishers: Leiden, 2003), at 111–40.

[60] *See, e.g.*, Richard Garfield, "Health and Well-Being in Iraq: Sanctions and the Impact of the Oil-for-Food Program," 11 *Transnat'l L. & Contemp. Probs.* 277 (2001); Roger Normand & Christophe Wilcke, "Human Rights, Sanctions, and Terrorist Threats: The United Nations Sanctions Against Iraq," 11 *Transnat'l L. & Contemp. Probs.* 299 (2001).

[61] The truth of this observation hides in plain sight. The Reagan administration's conduct of the Cold War, after all, is associated in the public mind with "moral clarity," rather than with that administration's underwriting of armed factions whose ruthlessness (indeed, brutality) was known beyond cavil, such as the Salvadoran armed forces, the Nicaraguan *contras*, the Angolan UNITA rebels, Cambodian anti-Vietnamese insurgents operationally (as well as formally) conjoined to the genocidal Khmer Rouge, and the various unsavory factions battling Soviet troops in Afghanistan. Whether the end justified the means in any or all of these cases is beyond the scope of this discussion; what matters is that a great many informed persons of good faith and sound reason thought so. And among those who thought otherwise, some proclaimed solidarity with opposing factions themselves known to employ ruthless means. Still others, while eschewing ruthless means in all of these cases, have accepted them, however reluctantly, in other cases.

[62] Lukes asserts that "[i]t is vital to keep alive the sense, among politicians and citizens alike, that deception, betrayal, and worse, when they are committed for the public good, violate morally important principles and commit uncancelled wrongs." Lukes, *Moral Conflict and Politics*, *supra*, at 196–97.

frequently seen to depend upon the infliction of immobilizing fear upon the potentially treacherous few. Acts understood to be presumptively wrongful are widely accepted as valid in deterrent retaliation for similar or analogous wrongs supposedly committed by the other side.[63] Once convinced that the other side observes no limits, partisans are frequently open to adopting measures that they normally would reprehend.

These rationales are not pathologies of the depraved; they are routinely articulated by informed persons of good faith and sound reason. Moreover, denunciations of that whole class of rationales too often emanate from the comfortable sidelines. Where societies experience a breakdown of shared normative premises and institutional processes, partisan considerations take on an urgency not fully anticipated in the calm of the remote assembly chamber or seminar room. That an outside observer roundly condemns, however ingenuously, others' transgressions in defense of their perceived vital interests is little evidence that the observer would exercise forbearance if similarly situated. What appears "disproportionate" to someone else's cause, however just, frequently appears exigent in the service of one's own. These discomforting realities are, arguably, just as "universal" as the abstract affirmations of the international standards in question.

He deems Marxism to be incompatible with this position, on the ground that it, "one-sidedly rules out or ignores, in the assessment of human action and character, all that it holds out to be irrelevant to the project of human emancipation." *Id.* at 208–09. A Marxian response would be that "bourgeois morality," by normalizing the violence associated with the operation and maintenance of the bourgeois order, and by identifying as exceptional the violent response occasioned by that very order's contradictions, functions "ideologically" to distort the moral picture. The latter violence it identifies as "wrongs," whereas the former, however incommensurable the associated human costs, it classifies as "mere" harms, inflicted without bad will. (An example is the "double-effect" rule often said to govern the problem of collateral damage in warfare.) The pain of the victims-in-focus obscures the pain of a great many more victims hidden, as it were, in plain sight. Roth, "Retrieving Marx for the Human Rights Project," *supra*, at 44–51.

[63] Notwithstanding international efforts to prohibit belligerent reprisals against civilians, Additional Protocol I to the Geneva Conventions, 8 June 1977, 1125 UNTS 3, arts. 51–55. the major liberal war-fighting powers have refused to renounce them, see Eyal Benvenisti, "Human Dignity in Combat: The Duty to Spare Enemy Civilians," 39 *Israel L. Rev.* 81, 103 n.84 (2006) (discussing the reservations of Britain and France to Additional Protocol I). The U.S. representative to the 1977 Geneva Protocol negotiations stated the objection as follows: "It is unreasonable to think that massive and continuing attacks directed against a nation's civilian population could be absorbed without a response in kind. By denying the possibility of response and not offering any workable substitute, Art. 51 [of the First Additional Protocol] is unrealistic and cannot be expected to withstand the test of future conflicts." Report of George H. Aldrich, excerpted at 72 *Am. J. Int'l L.* 405, 406 (1978); *see also* the reservations to Article 51 appended to the Additional Protocol I ratification instruments of the United Kingdom,<http://www.icrc.org/Web/eng/siteeng0.nsf/iwpList166/A06D567EA584477CC1256B66005B94B8>, and of France, <http://www.icrc.org/web/fre/sitefre0.nsf/htmlall/5fzhxv?opendocument>.

## D. PATRIOTISM AND THE DUTY TO UPHOLD A COMMUNITY'S POLITICAL INDEPENDENCE

It remains to speak to the moral significance of patriotic duty. Patriotism denotes loyalty to a political community, most typically one whose membership encompasses, at least notionally, the permanent territorial population without distinction.[64] Patriotism, like sovereignty, is open to an array of conflicting interpretations. A typical finesse in confronting the concept is to present two polar versions: the first so sharply provocative as to be patently unreasonable, and the second so harmonized with liberal-universalist political morality as to be denuded of any normative significance. In fact, many commonplace invocations of patriotism are patently unreasonable in that they assign little moral worth to foreigners (or to citizens who show inordinate concern for foreigners).[65] At the same time, many orthodox liberal universalists sincerely regard themselves, by virtue of being public spirited and having a deep emotional connection to their country's history and symbols, as patriots. If, however, patriotism poses any distinctive intellectual challenges, these must emanate from a conception that falls into neither of these categories.

Universalism does not preclude an ethical division of labor. Efficacy considerations alone dictate that individuals concentrate the bulk of their affirmative efforts to enrich the lives of others on those to whom they bear special ties rather than

[64] "Nationalism" today most frequently refers to something very different: an ethno-nationalism that problematizes the fit between state boundaries and community membership—rooting duties of loyalty in a common race, language, culture, or creed—and asserting privileges accordingly. The international legal system attributes "nationality" to individuals on the basis of connections to a territorial state and predicates sovereign prerogatives on the equal rights of each of the "peoples" that territorial states respectively represent.

[65] Some such invocations can be seen in "war on terrorism" rhetoric. The September 11 attacks inevitably reminded Americans of their common identity and destiny as a people. The victims, after all, had been targeted solely for inhabiting buildings that the attackers identified as symbols of America. Yet in their shared outrage, Americans seemed divided between those who regarded the attacks as an affront primarily to the humanity of the victims (to whom they felt a special bond as Americans) and those who regarded the attacks as an affront primarily to the nation. Whereas the former demanded only to bring individual perpetrators to justice and to restore safety, and assessed proposals for the use of force in light of those ends alone, the latter demanded further to reassert a national potency that the attacks, by their sheer audacity, were perceived to have called into question.

Attributing America's vulnerability to its having inspired insufficient fear (a somewhat doubtful assessment of the sociology of suicidal fanaticism), this latter view assigned an independent value to uses of force as demonstrations of might and resolve. Even beyond that, it found redemption in inflicting retribution on those perceived to have manifested disrespect for (even if they had not actually attacked) the United States and in flouting restraints that it associated with a treacherous or feckless solicitude for those manifesting such disrespect. (One is tempted to surmise that certain individuals, forced to endure disrespect in their own lives, derive a vicarious sense of vindication from identifying with an entity, in which they notionally participate, that displays the capacity to extract expressions of respect from the recalcitrant.) This view may qualify as "patriotism" of a sort, but rejecting it can hardly be characterized as "unpatriotic."

diffusing them impartially across humanity as a whole. Beyond that, efficacious social action requires collectivities that are empowered to decide on and to coordinate social projects; for "us" to take action, there must first be an "us" to whom the decisions pertain and who bear special responsibility for following through on those decisions, irrespective of individual opinions and preferences, because those decisions have been validly taken in the name of the collectivity. Moreover, universalist political morality posits goals that presuppose a determinate scope of application; boundaries are inherent in the effort to secure for all the opportunity to live in a community that treats each member with equal concern and that palpably belongs to all of its members in equal measure. Because distinct communities have moral standing from even a universalist perspective, universalists acknowledge that in the event of irreconcilable conflict between communities, when "no just accommodation of both sides' legitimate interests is possible[,] . . . universal morality would not require [liberals] to abandon or betray their own communities."[66]

Insofar as patriotism poses a challenge to liberal-universalist political morality, it does so by asserting that loyalty to a political community's distinctive interests or distinctive values should override, at least to some significant extent, universalist ethical imperatives.[67] Such a challenge must assert either (a) that the citizen is bound to side with her own political community in conflicts with others, even (at least to some extent) where it is objectively in the wrong; or (b) that the citizen is bound to further a particular conception of justice that reflects the political community's distinctive character or traditions, even (at least to some extent) where a conception of justice foreign to its character or traditions is objectively superior.

The collective moral right to self-determination, as elaborated and defended above, does not entail a general acceptance of either of these assertions (nor does it necessarily reject them). It does suggest, however, that where foreign exertions jeopardize a political community's capacity to defend its interests or to arrive at decisions in keeping with the distinctive values of its members, the imperative to maintain that capacity—inasmuch as this is itself a matter of objective moral right—justifies coming to the defense of that community's sovereign prerogatives, even where those prerogatives have been exercised unjustly. This conclusion is predicated not on a rejection of universalist morality, but on a paradox that arises

[66] Stephen Nathanson, " In Defense of Moderate Patriotism," 99 *Ethics* 535, 541 (1989).

[67] *Compare id.* at 535 (elaborating a patriotism consistent with universalist premises), *with* Alasdair MacIntyre, "Is Patriotism a Virtue?," in Ronald Beiner ed., *Theorizing Citizenship* 209 (1995) (elaborating a patriotism sharply at odds with universalism).

within universalist morality. It is in the nature of moral rights to demarcate an inviolable space (however limited) within which the right-bearer, whether individual or collective, is free to exercise discretion, even if immorally.[68] "Our country . . . right or wrong,"[69] is, in this very limited application, consistent with objective right.

Thus, there may be a patriotic duty to help prevent foreign political communities from improperly dictating to or intervening within one's own community, even where there is a simultaneous duty to work for an internal remedy to the injustice of which the foreigners complain.[70] Similarly, an oppositionist, even if justified in working to install a foreign-inspired system of public order (on the ground that it is morally superior to anything rooted in local traditions), may have a patriotic duty not to accept inappropriate kinds or degrees of foreign assistance for these efforts. Once again, however, these duties are only presumptive; where state misconduct is so extreme as to defeat the purposes for which the community's political independence is duly valued, the duties are vitiated. (Of course, it does not follow that even such gross misconduct will suffice to eradicate perceptions of patriotic duty.)

This take on patriotism, like the collective right to self-determination from which it derives, is a matter of peculiar significance to poor and weak states. It speaks to reasons that even tyrannized inhabitants of such states have to resist foreign-initiated projects of "regime change." Whatever moral justification there may be for supporting one's own state's violations of other states' territorial integrity and political independence will have to be sought elsewhere.

[68] *See* Jeremy Waldron, *Liberal Rights: Collected Papers, 1981–1991* (Cambridge Univ. Press, 1993), at 63–64.

[69] Viet Dinh, "Nationalism in the Age of Terror," 56 *Fla. L. Rev.* 867, 877 (2004) (quoting Commodore Stephen Decatur, Toast at a Dinner in Norfolk, Virginia (Apr. 1816), in Alexander Slidell Mackenzie, *Life of Stephen Decatur* 295, 295 (1848)).

[70] While the United States does not often find its sovereignty genuinely threatened, U.S. reservations to human rights treaties provide a fittingly mundane illustration. American international lawyers routinely advocate the withdrawal of these reservations on the ground that they license unjust practices. Those same lawyers may nonetheless object to foreign efforts to treat the reservations as nullities (on the strained theory that the reservations are not only inconsistent with the treaties' object and purpose, but also severable from the rest of the ratified instrument). The United States cannot properly be held accountable to obligations, however righteous, from which it has expressly withheld its consent. There is no inconsistency in insisting on respect for treaty reservations that one deems to be unjust. While patriotism has nothing to do with the merits of the point, it does, perhaps, place a special (if relatively trivial) onus on U.S. lawyers to stand up for the point in international fora.

## IV. Moral Disagreement as the Foundation of a Pluralist Global Order

### A. THE MORAL IMPLICATIONS OF DISAGREEMENT

Observations about deep political disagreement do not alone suffice to justify a pluralistic global order. The mere fact of intractable disagreement about the moral quality of political acts does not make the conduct in question any less wrongful (let alone any less harmful to its victims), and no moral immunities automatically attach to having thoughtful and decent reasons for acting on an egregious conception of justice. But the observation does have important implications for the design of a morally responsible approach to political difference.

First, as an empirical matter, the circumstances of global pluralism are intractable. At any given moment, various of the world's territorial political communities are destined to be dominated, at least for the short to medium term, by incompatible conceptions of political morality.

Second, a good-faith accommodation among bearers of incompatible conceptions of internal public order is both empirically possible and moral respectable. Perpetrators and supporters of ruthless measures are not, *ipso facto*, treacherous scoundrels.

Third, there is a practical peril in allowing the governments of powerful states (or particular constituencies within such states) selectively to attribute criminality to certain foreign officials. With so rich a potential target list, governments are most likely to designate as outlaws those whom they oppose for partisan reasons, notwithstanding that those designated may not be any worse, morally speaking, than other foreign officials whom those governments may support or tolerate.

Fourth, there is a practical peril in conditioning an end to political conflict on prosecutions of those who perpetrated ruthless acts, insofar as a substantial sector of the populace regarded those acts as necessary expedients in the service of an honorable cause. Where complicity for the ruthless measures runs all the way down to the grass roots, prosecutions are likely to impede efforts to secure the cooperation of important constituencies.

Fifth, there is a practical peril in seeking to cast into outlawry foes whom one cannot wish away, and with whom one must reach some kind of working arrangement. Ronald Reagan's "Evil Empire" rhetoric was rendered harmless by fortuitous subsequent events, but in general, such rhetoric is counterproductive, above all because it raises the political cost of selling the needed working arrangement to one's own constituents.

Sixth, it is morally dubious to affix the stain of criminality for acts that most individuals, in truly analogous circumstances, would find themselves, even on the basis of considered moral judgment, committing or supporting. Criminality properly implies not mere moral wrongfulness but also some element of deviance.

If deep political disagreement is endemic rather than aberrational, efforts to manage political conflict must accept a certain modesty of mission. As will be discussed at length in Chapter 7, a moralistic campaign to eradicate political ruthlessness will likely lead either to disillusionment or, far worse, to the licensing of a ruthlessness to end all ruthlessness. Attributions of outlawry to adverse regimes, in addition to hardening positions counterproductively (akin to the insistence that one "never negotiate with terrorists"), tend to place enforcement demands on international institutions that such institutions characteristically cannot bear, opening the door to unilateral exertions that can be rationalized as implementation of universal principles. Transnational criminal proceedings against foreign state actors, if directed at non-aberrational conduct, not only will be skewed by a political selectivity of prosecution, but may degenerate into festivals of self-righteousness, orchestrated not only to designate scapegoats for international dissensus, but also to reveal the fecklessness of those who counsel restraint and compromise in the face of a certified evil.[71]

A responsible approach to global order, therefore, is a pluralist approach. A commitment to pluralism in no way implies agnosticism about the wrongfulness of the other's conduct, nor need it assert that the conduct, albeit wrong "for us," may be right "for them." Rather, pluralism (or more precisely, a qualified or "bounded" pluralism) accords to the other, within a system of reciprocity, certain basic prerogatives and inviolabilities that withstand the other's wrongful, but non-aberrant, conduct.

Fidelity to such a system of respectful accommodation is a moral duty, insofar as that system is reasonably efficacious, compared with the foreseeable alternative, in preventing uncontrolled international conflict, limiting predation (often carried out in the name of humanitarianism) against poor and weak states, and providing the basis for international cooperation on matters of significant human concern. That fidelity also reflects a humility and restraint becoming of an outsider who lacks a stake appropriate to participation in an internal struggle. Even the best-intentioned

[71] If my scholarship in this area can be said to have an immediate political purpose, it is to expose the latent kinship of certain human rights advocates with the neoconservatives, whose practical positions they rarely embrace. *But see* Fernando Tesón, "Ending Tyranny in Iraq," 19 *Eth. & Int'l Aff.* 1 (2005) (defending the 2003 Iraq invasion on human rights grounds); W. Michael Reisman, "Unilateral Actions," *supra* (generally advocating the unilateral coercive implementation of the norms of a supposed human-rights-based international order).In my view, a substantial element of human rights advocacy has lost its way, departing from the path that leads more reliably to peace. In generating demands that exceed the institutional capacities of the international system, the quest for a transcendent justice leads to a fork in the road, where one path leads to frustration and disillusionment and the other to alliance with the neo-conservatives—who are, in essence, liberal internationalists who have become disillusioned with the constraints of both broad multilateralism and deontological ethics. What I offer is a moral argument for adherence to international legal constraint that is unavailable to those who see international law merely as an instrument of transcendent justice.

outsiders face certain moral pitfalls. Our lack of familiarity and stake allows us (a) to make judgments based on limited information, often packaged for us by partisans in the conflict; (b) to make judgments, supposedly in the interest of the whole, where our objectivity has been contaminated by identification with certain sectors of a foreign society at the expense of others; and (c) to make judgments that leave others to bear the consequences of our decisions long after we have lost interest and moved on. Beyond this, as a matter of dignity, participants in a struggle over the basic direction of their own society should not, presumptively, have to suffer the coercive interference of those who will not have to live with the resulting conditions. (In principle, of course, deference should be reserved for those who speak authentically for the society, but this is typically what the conflict is *about*.)

## B. THE POLICY JUSTIFICATION OF A NON-CULTURE-BASED PLURALISM

The boundaries of the international legal order's pluralism are considerably broader than the collective moral right to self-determination alone would dictate. These boundaries additionally reflect both the system's policy goal of constraining cross-border exercises of power by presumptively untrustworthy actors and its political need for broad-based support in a diverse international community.

In addition to encompassing a multiplicity of values, the international community encompasses a multiplicity of interests. Moreover, poor and weak states, and substantial constituencies within them, tend to perceive systematic contradictions between their interests and those of the rich and powerful states. Their distrust, rooted in a history of exploitation perpetrated under the guise of a "civilizing mission," lies at the foundation of the sovereign equality principle.

Furthermore, external impositions—affected, as they predictably are, by self-interest and arrogance—cannot lightly be presumed to be salutary. As will be discussed in regard to armed humanitarian intervention in Chapter 5, rich and powerful countries are seldom willing to invest substantial blood and treasure for moral objectives alone. At best, armed interventions occur in locations (e.g., in Kosovo rather than in far more devastated African regions)[72] and in ways (e.g., by aerial bombardment of civilian infrastructure rather than ground-troop confrontation of génocidaires)[73] that reflect political rather than moral priorities. At worst,

[72] *See* Richard B. Bilder, "Kosovo and the 'New Interventionism': Promise or Peril?," 9 *J. Transnat'l L. & Pol'y* 153 (1999).

[73] *See, e.g.*, Paolo Benvenuti, "The ICTY Prosecutor and the Review of the NATO Bombing Campaign Against the Federal Republic of Yugoslavia," 12 *Eur. J. Int'l L.* 503 (2001) (criticizing the targeting employed in the North Atlantic Treaty Organization (NATO) bombing campaign against Yugoslavia).

the interests motivating the external investment may distort the mission's goals (as has been alleged in the case of France's Opération Turquoise in Rwanda)[74] or may call for cut-rate and irresolute methods that leave the situation worse than it was before the intervention (as may have been true of the later phases of the United States mission in Somalia and as may turn out to be true in Afghanistan). Even if too little intervention is now objectively a greater overall problem than too much intervention, it does not follow that a broader licensing of intervention would occasion more of the right measures in the right places.

A pluralistic global order thus serves to protect the poor and weak states from the divergent interests, as well as from the overbearing values of the rich and strong states. It is, and is reasonably, an ordering principle of "the deal" that the international system embodies. The boundaries of the international order's pluralism nonetheless remain variable, and relative convergences in both values and interests over time have led to the broadening of exceptions to sovereign prerogative, such *as jus cogens*, universal jurisdiction, and humanitarian intervention.[75] Yet this pluralism continues to withstand the demands of many a moralistic project.

Why should an overwhelmingly strong power, confident in its righteousness, be concerned to keep faith with this "deal"? Why should it respect the sovereign prerogatives of states that hold no moral high ground and that can be effectively manhandled? The question is all the more pressing when the strong power finds itself faced not merely with obstacles to its interests and affronts to its values, but with dire security threats from non-state actors, heedless of all legal order, whom other states may brazenly refuse to acknowledge as common enemies.

As suggested in Chapter 2, a legal order endures only if it reconciles the long-term policy interests of its participants, strong and weak. Since the strong often have the option to proceed by extortion or direct action rather than by accommodation, whereas the weak are willing to concede much in return for the guaranteed security of what little is left to them, the strong have disproportionate bargaining power in setting the legal rules. At the same time, the strong have reason to prefer orderly processes and clear baselines to the chaos and costliness of ad hoc exertions, and whatever their strength, the strong have much to fear from the desperate and the humiliated among the weak. The strong should thus resist the temptation, once they have negotiated a legal order that provides avenues by which most of their goals can be achieved, to have their cake and eat it too—to insist that the terms of the deal are binding on the weak, but reserve to themselves (and by extension, to all

[74] *See* Philip Gourevitch, *We Wish to Inform You That Tomorrow We Will Be Killed with Our Families: Stories from Rwanda* 157–61 (1998).

[75] The present chapter is devoted to explaining what kinds of lines need to be drawn, without articulating positions on precisely where the lines should be drawn. Chapters 5, 6, and 7 speak to the latter in greater detail.

others with the power to get away with it) the prerogative to do as they see fit. And this is no less true where the strong perceive their cause to be righteous.

In the long run, international peace cannot be predicated on the privilege of the momentarily strong to pursue forcibly their unilateral determinations of what is just in any given instance. Wagers on the continued impotence of others are bad long-term bets.

## C. THE LEGAL TERMS OF A BOUNDED PLURALISM

As elaborated in Chapter 3, sovereignty represents the political community's retention of ultimate authority within the territory, notwithstanding international legal obligations pertaining to the exercise of that authority.[76] Although local authorities' failures to implement obligations are breaches that require remedies and license appropriately limited countermeasures,[77] breaches do not license external forces to take action within the territory without the consent of local authorities, and local officials may be immune from personal liability in foreign courts for breaches committed within the scope of state authority. States do not typically renounce the capacity to put themselves out of compliance with international law; indeed, internal law may provide for a decision to override the dictates of international obligations, temporarily or permanently, based on a residual unilateral capacity to find the existence of emergency conditions or a fundamental change in circumstances, whether or not such findings preclude wrongfulness as a matter of international law. States anticipate that disagreements about norms will manifest themselves in contingencies, the details of which cannot be fully anticipated in the course of legal standard-setting. Without some assurance of the maintenance of the core legal capacity to resist impositions, states would be chilled in their willingness to subscribe to international obligations.

The international system licenses proportionate sanctions against states for adopting internal practices that breach obligations, but only in relatively rare cases—not ordinary human rights violations, but aberrant atrocities—are states deemed to have renounced, not only the practices themselves but also the legal

[76] "International law . . . recognizes the power—though not the right—to break a treaty and abide the international consequences." Louis Henkin, *Foreign Affairs and the Constitution* (Mineola, NY, Foundation Press, 1972), 168.

[77] These limitations are spelled out in Articles 49 to 54 of the Articles on State Responsibility promulgated in 2001 by the International Law Commission. Report of the International Law Commission, *Draft Articles on Responsibility of States for Internationally Wrongful Acts*, U.N. GAOR, 56th Sess., Supp. No. 10, at 43, U.N. Doc. A/56/10 (2001).

capacity to authorize them.[78] In still rarer cases will the international system approve recourse to armed intervention, either expressly through Security Council authorization under Chapter VII or tacitly through acquiescence in unauthorized actions to forestall imminent humanitarian catastrophe.

Advocates of a "transcendent justice" approach to international legal order find such negation of sovereign prerogative to be far too rare. And to a significant extent, they may be correct. The justification of the existing sovereign equality framework operates from the assumption that internal political conflict represents, in the largest number of cases, struggle among competing factions seeking, however ruthlessly, to apply their principled conceptions of public order to governance of the undivided whole. Yet internal political conflict has turned out, on too many occasions, to be a cover for something else: unlimited violence unleashed against civilian populations, either for reasons of ethno-nationalist ideology (e.g., Rwanda, the former Yugoslavia) or as a by-product of efforts by wholly unprincipled armed gangs to usurp control of economic activity and natural resources (e.g., Somalia, Liberia, Sierra Leone). Although the existing system has an available mechanism to address internal humanitarian crises as to which diverse elements of the international community can agree on the equities and the response—Chapter VII—and although the system's failures to intervene are far less attributable to legal strictures than to an unwillingness of the powerful to invest blood and treasure in purely humanitarian pursuits, the inflexibilities of the existing system are genuinely problematic. Moreover, improved mechanisms of international criminal justice are needed to deny impunity to perpetrators of acts that, notwithstanding the color of state authority, are beyond the pale of any plausible good-faith conception of public order.

Nonetheless, it is important not to move, from a conceptually narrow (if empirically altogether too ample) class of cases in which the equities are starkly clear, to a sweeping rejection of strictures on the pursuit of moralistic causes. Whether or not (as conservative lawyers tend to say) "hard cases make bad law," extreme cases surely invite bad "dicta" (i.e., broad elaborations of principle unnecessary to the outcome of the particular case). Although discrete reforms to the current system are needed, the system's underlying principles are sound. A broad licensing of cross-border exercises of power is less likely to further global justice than to open the door to arrogant (let alone self-interested) impositions, and to undermine the institutional basis for

[78] *See, e.g.,* "Judicial Decisions: International Military Tribunal (Nuremberg), Judgment and Sentences," 41 *Am. J. Int'l L.* 172, 221 (1947) ("He who violates the laws of war cannot obtain immunity while acting in pursuance of the authority of the state if the state in authorizing action moves outside its competence under international law."). Although attributions of international criminal responsibility are no longer limited by the Nuremberg Tribunal's requirement of a nexus to interstate warfare, the threshold for the international criminalization of state acts remains higher for purely internal conduct.

cooperation among the non-like-minded. The precise scope of exceptions to sovereign prerogative may properly be debated, but the exceptions should not be allowed to swallow the rule.

## Conclusion

If liberalism has one great superiority over rival political philosophies, it is that liberalism does not presuppose—as have Rousseau, the communists, fascists, and religious fundamentalists alike—that the answers to questions of public morality would be intuitively obvious, but for the distortions introduced by partisan interests. In a healthy community, these non-liberals have believed, there is almost unanimous agreement regarding what constitutes the common good.

Liberalism, by contrast, rejects this notion. Deontological liberals may seek to make an exception for "justice" as they understand it. But if, as has been contended above, justice ultimately depends on a broader view of the common good, and what constitutes the common good is inevitably contested even where partisan interests do not distort deliberation, then questions of justice are equally contestable in good faith.

The pursuit of peace is, on the whole, well served by an international legal framework that, rather than embracing a particular vision of a just public order, embodies a respectful accommodation among conflicting visions. That accommodation includes, to be sure, elements of overlapping moral consensus, but that consensus should not be overestimated.

The affirmation of the legitimacy of moral diversity in the international arena is not, as some would charge, a surrender to moral skepticism or relativism. It is, rather, a sound application of the most essential liberal premises about morality, in light of a sober recognition of the limitations of moral absolutes in international politics.

Notwithstanding international law's dramatic expansion into areas once considered matters of exclusive domestic jurisdiction, respect for sovereign prerogative continues to be a central feature of the international legal system, limiting both the establishment of binding obligations and the means by which established obligations can be enforced. The inviolability of self-governing political communities stands as a foundational principle of international order. This principle appears inconvenient when the decisions that emerge from these communities seem to be, and perhaps objectively are, unjust ones. Nonetheless, fundamental disagreements about justice are an enduring feature of the human condition, and they necessitate a pluralistic solution. In certain respects and within certain limits, collectivities must be said to have a right to be wrong about justice, and outsiders must be called on to respect collective enterprises of which they are not a part. Moreover, a broad license for powerful states to impose solutions on less powerful ones in the name of universal justice is not an especially promising alternative.

Although exceptions to respect for sovereign prerogative have properly prevailed in many instances, the exceptions should not be permitted to swallow the rule. A respectful and orderly relationship among bearers of conflicting conceptions of just public order provides the only firm basis for international peace and cooperation. It also provides the basis upon which human beings—situated, as they are, in political communities—have the best chance to accomplish their ends.

# 5

# Reconciling the Non-Intervention Norm with the "Responsibility to Protect"

## Introduction

With the global geopolitical and ideological balance of the Cold War era fast receding into distant memory, new issues arise for the continued vitality of international legal constraints on the use of force. The lack of a global competitor to the United States in the security realm, and of a global alternative to liberal internationalism in the ideological realm, has changed perceptions of the role of the peace and security system—especially among Western states, nongovernmental organizations (NGOs), and intellectuals, and especially with respect to internal armed conflict. The perceived need to accommodate rival conceptions of public order has given way, in many quarters, to a perceived opportunity to harness the unchallenged military power of the Western Allies to the pursuit of a predominant conception of justice. This development constitutes a potential challenge to the foundations of the international legal system—above all, to the norm against forcible intervention in the international affairs of states, absent Security Council authorization.

The challenge to the non-intervention norm is widely associated with a new conceptual framework, initiated by the "norm entrepreneurs" of the Canadian Government-sponsored International Commission on Intervention and State Sovereignty (ICISS) and eventually adopted in part by the United Nations order itself, known as "The Responsibility to Protect," or "R2P." The 2001 ICISS Report construed the United Nations Charter as effecting a "re-characterization" of traditional sovereignty, "from *sovereignty as control* to *sovereignty as responsibility* in both internal functions and external duties."[1] The significance of this assertion does not lie in the idea that sovereignty entails responsibilities; as discussed above, sovereignty

[1] International Commission on Intervention and State Sovereignty, *The Responsibility to Protect* (December 2001) [hereinafter ICISS Report], § 2.14, *available at* <http://www.iciss.ca/pdf/Commission-Report.pdf>.

has long been understood to belong not to governmental apparatuses, but to the territorial populations whose will and interests those apparatuses are presumed to represent "without distinction." But whereas a more conventional interpretation of the United Nations Charter passively assumes sovereignty as responsibility while actively upholding sovereignty as control, the ICISS Report denies sovereignty's claims to the last word on how those responsibilities are fulfilled. The Report's innovation was to propose explicit recourse for external actors where bearers of sovereignty are deemed to have defaulted on their internal responsibilities.

Even as conceived by ICISS, however, R2P does not amount to the radical reordering that one might imagine. The ICISS Report itself concedes much to the non-intervention norm:

> 4.11 The starting point, here as elsewhere, should be the principle of non-intervention. . . . Most internal political or civil disagreements, even conflicts, within states do not require coercive intervention by external powers. The non-interference rule not only protects states and governments: it also protects peoples and cultures, enabling societies to maintain the religious, ethnic, and civilizational differences that they cherish.
>
> 4.12 . . . Intervention in the domestic affairs of states is often harmful. It can destabilize the order of states, while fanning ethnic or civil strife. ***When internal forces seeking to oppose a state believe that they can generate outside support by mounting campaigns of violence, the internal order of all states is potentially compromised.*** The rule against intervention in internal affairs encourages states to solve their own internal problems and prevent these from spilling over into a threat to international peace and security.[2]

The Report's provisions for extraordinary recourse pertain only to "exceptional circumstances" in which "all order within a state has broken down or when civil conflict and repression are so violent that civilians are threatened with massacre, genocide or ethnic cleansing on a large scale."[3] In such circumstances, the Report calls for "military intervention for human protection," to be governed by the following criteria: "right authority, just cause, right intention, last resort, proportional means and reasonable prospects."[4]

Insofar as "right authority" is interpreted in accordance with the United Nations Charter scheme, R2P amounts to nothing more than an affirmation of a well-established pattern of practice. Although a literal reading of Chapter VII does not confer authority on the Security Council to respond with coercive measures to crises fully contained within the borders of a single state, the Security Council

[2] ICISS Report, *supra,* §§ 4.11, 4.12 (emphasis added).

[3] *Id.* at § 4.13.

[4] *Id.* at § 4.16.

repeatedly did just this from the early 1990s onward, justifying itself by ever more implausible references to remote trans-boundary consequences and to the "sui generis" nature of the particular crisis. In its 2005 invocation of the R2P theme, the United Nations General Assembly obviated the need for such elaborate rationalizations, acknowledging that the Security Council's extraordinary authority extends to circumstances where "national authorities are manifestly failing to protect their populations from genocide, war crimes, ethnic cleansing, and crimes against humanity."[5]

Where the General Assembly most conspicuously did not follow ICISS was in respect of the latter's suggestion of flexibility about what might constitute "right authority" in "circumstances when the Security Council fails to discharge what this Commission would regard as its responsibility to protect, in a conscience-shocking situation crying out for action."[6] This leaves the fundamental question as it has long been: in the absence of Security Council authorization, can forcible intervention lawfully be undertaken on humanitarian grounds?

The question of unilateral or narrow-multilateral humanitarian intervention has long occupied scholars of both international law and international political morality. The issue arose most significantly in the wake of the 79-day 1999 bombing campaign that the North American Treaty Organization (NATO) undertook, without Security Council authorization, against the Federal Republic of Yugoslavia (FRY) in response to the Kosovo crisis.

The humanitarian intervention question poses a dilemma for legal scholars and advocates committed to holding the great powers accountable in their foreign policies to the strictures of the international peace and security order. The keenly felt need to resolve the tension between those strictures and the perceived demands of humanitarianism has occasioned recourse to dubious jurisprudential devices for squaring the circle. These jurisprudential devices, even though often invoked without ulterior motive, tend effectively to license systematic disregard of legal restraints on the use of force, with troubling long-range consequences. Yet a more stable resolution of the tension has proved elusive for various reasons, not least among them that moralistic appeals run aground on the shoals of moral disagreement.

## I. The Challenge to the Premises of the Charter Peace and Security System

The international law of peace and security, as established in the United Nations Charter and in the interpretive practices of states and intergovernmental

[5] G.A. Res. 60/1 (2005) (adopted without a vote), ¶ 139; S.C. Res. 1674 (2006) (reaffirming same).

[6] ICISS Report, *supra*, at § 6.37.

organizations, embodies not simply a set of rules consented to by the effective leaderships of sovereign states, but also a set of principles and policies premised on a collective moral and political vision that has developed continuously over the history of the Charter system. To assert this is not to deny but rather to explain the significance—and even, in many instances, the rigidity—of the rules governing the use of force. These rules designedly preclude unilateral efforts to pursue a particular conception of justice within states at the expense of peace among states.[7]

Having developed over a period in which the international system encompassed widely divergent conceptions of internal political order, the Charter system manifests a commitment to pluralism as a principled basis for peaceful and respectful international relations. That pluralism draws upon aspects of liberal political thought, but it is not in all respects a liberal pluralism.[8] Appeals to a higher principle that mistake Charter pluralism for a liberal conception of international justice produce a skewed account of the values and priorities of the international system.

The relationship of Charter pluralism to liberalism can be summarized in three points. First, the Charter follows modern international law generally in imagining, in the style of liberal social contract theory, international society as arising out of a hypothesized state of nature, with the units of that society being regarded as juridically equal and at perfect liberty unless and until bound by their own consent. Second, and importantly, although the units of the system are states rather than individuals, states are presumed to be the manifestations of the self-determination of the populations (*qua* political communities, or "peoples") that they territorially encompass[9]; state actors, in turn, derive their international

[7] As Thomas M. Franck put it,

> [W]hen contemplating military intervention, the United Nations (U.N.) usually has preferred not to differentiate between just and unjust reasons to intervene. Instead, the nations have favored treating all states as autonomous entities entitled to be left alone, and doing so on grounds of maintaining international peace and order, rather than advancing justice.

Franck, "Is Justice Relevant to the International Legal System?" 64 *Notre Dame L.J.* 645, 655 (1989). Franck drew from such observations, and more generally from the system's designation of states rather than individuals as the primary units of analysis, the conclusion that justice is "not among the indicators of legitimacy in the international system." *Id.* at 662. This conclusion is (or at least was in 1989) correct insofar as the liberal conception, or any particular substantive conception, of justice is concerned; it is misleading to the extent that it implies a straightforwardly amoral order.

[8] Gerry Simpson has elaborated a contrast between "Charter liberalism," the pluralist vision associated with the Charter, and the "anti-pluralist liberalism" of a set of leading U.S.-based international law scholars (i.e., Thomas M. Franck, Anne-Marie Slaughter, W. Michael Reisman, and Fernando Teson). Simpson, "Two Liberalisms," 12 *Euro. J. Int'l L.* 537 (2001). His exposition, while generally astute, overstates liberalism's proclivity to accommodate competing sets of political values and therefore identifies Charter pluralism too closely with liberalism.

[9] *See Declaration on Principles of International Law Concerning Friendly Relations and Co-operation among States in Accordance with the Charter of the United Nations* [hereinafter *Friendly Relations*

authority not from their own power and will, but from a presumption that they serve as agents of the collectivities that they purport to represent. But third, and even more importantly, notwithstanding the Charter's exhortations regarding "human rights and fundamental freedoms," the aforementioned presumptions are not necessarily rebuttable in accordance with liberal political principles. Internal processes are typically accorded deference, even where those processes may offend liberal principles.[10]

The Charter's pluralism is superficially liberal in that it is tolerant, but its tolerance exceeds the bounds of any cognizably liberal pluralism. In brief, the dominant strain of contemporary liberalism is tolerant of errant conceptions of the proper objects of human striving ("the good") but not of the implementation of errant conceptions of justice ("the right").[11] An alternative within liberalism is to tolerate injustice, but only within freely formed associations that maintain an unhindered opportunity for their associates to exit.[12] The Charter's pluralism has no such limits. Although it excludes certain deviant governing arrangements—Axis-era fascism from the start; and "alien, colonial, and racist" regimes later on[13]—it otherwise represents an accommodation among radically differing conceptions of justice.

*Declaration*], G.A. Res. 2625 (XXV) (1970) (adopted without a vote), affirming as an imperative "the territorial integrity [and] political unity of sovereign and independent States conducting themselves in compliance with the principle of equal rights and self-determination of peoples . . . and thus possessed of a government representing the whole people belonging to the territory without distinction as to race, creed or colour."

[10] For an in-depth study of the circumstances under which holders of territorial control have and have not been accorded standing to assert rights, incur obligations, and authorize acts on behalf of political units in the international system, see Brad R. Roth, *Governmental Illegitimacy in International Law* (Oxford: Oxford University Press, 1999).

[11] *See* John Rawls, *A Theory of Justice* (Cambridge, Mass.: Harvard University Press, 1971), at. 447–48. Rawls's later work on political morality in international relations, *The Law of Peoples* (Cambridge, Mass.: Harvard University Press, 1999), adopts a broader pluralism than extrapolation from his earlier, domestic-oriented work might have suggested (though still not coextensive with the pluralism of the U.N. Charter), and as such has been criticized by some liberals as a departure from fundamental liberal principles. *See, e.g.*, Fernando Teson, "The Rawlsian Theory of International Law," 9 *Ethics & Int'l Aff.* 79, 98 (1995) (complaining that Rawls's later work "embraced a more relativistic, context-based conception of justice and political morality, in which rights and liberties no longer had a foundation in higher principles or liberal views of human nature . . . .").

[12] Excellent on this point is Chandran Kukathas, "Are There Any Cultural Rights?" in Will Kymlicka ed., *The Rights of Minority Cultures* (Oxford: Oxford University Press, 1995), 228.

[13] *See Friendly Relations Declaration, supra* ("subjection of peoples to alien subjugation, domination and exploitation . . . is contrary to the Charter"); *Declaration on the Inadmissibility of Intervention and Interference in the Internal Affairs of States*, G.A. Res. 36/103 (1981) (120-22-6) (non-intervention norms shall not "prejudice in any manner the right to self-determination, freedom and independence of peoples under colonial domination, foreign occupation or racist regimes . . . .").

It combines overlapping consensus with *modus vivendi*, a least-common-denominator morality with a prudential policy of compromise.[14]

Prior to the post-1989 advent of unipolarity in the international system, the moral and political vision underlying the international law of peace and security enjoyed widespread support in the international community, even as the rules themselves were breached with some frequency. Large majorities in the United Nations General Assembly and in other intergovernmental organizations could be counted on to condemn armed invasions and other interferences in the internal affairs of states.[15] Even the perpetrators typically defended their actions in ways that expressly or tacitly reaffirmed the validity of the rules[16]; the occasional departures from such norm-affirming rhetoric, such as the superpowers' articulations of the Brezhnev and Reagan "Doctrines," met with strong collective censure in international fora and did not persist.[17]

Underlying this normative stability (and the paradox of its coexistence with political instability) were two characteristic premises that dominated Cold War-era thinking about internal armed conflict. The first was the geopolitical premise that external intervention, irrespective of its announced intentions and of the direness of the conditions on the ground, was presumptively predatory. The essential grounds for this premise predated and survived the Cold War, but the structure of that confrontation reinforced them. The technology of all-out warfare having rendered direct clashes between the superpowers all but unthinkable, superpower competition had been deflected to the periphery, taking the form of a struggle between the First and Second Worlds for influence in the "Third." By the late 1950s, the two rival

[14] The contrast between "overlapping consensus" and "*modus vivendi*" derives from John Rawls, *Political Liberalism* (New York: Columbia University Press, 1993), at. 144–50.

[15] U.N. General Assembly responses to interventions by Western, Socialist, and Non-Aligned states include G.A. Res. 44/240 (1989) (75-20-40) (characterizing the U.S. invasion of Panama as "a flagrant violation of international law"); G.A. Res. ES-6/2 (1980) (104-18-18) (emergency session resolution demanding an "immediate, unconditional, and total" Soviet withdrawal from Afghanistan); G.A. Res. 2793 (XXVI) (1971) (104-11-10) (responding to Indian intervention in East Pakistan by calling "upon the Governments of India and Pakistan to take forthwith all measures for an immediate cease-fire and withdrawal of their armed forces on the territory of the other to their own side of the India-Pakistan borders").

[16] Perhaps the most instructive example is the elaborate Soviet effort to characterize its 1956 invasion of Hungary as a result of invitation by the legitimate government. *See* J.A. Szikszoy, *The Legal Aspects of the Hungarian Question* (Ambilly-Annemasse, France: Imprimerie "Les Presses de Savoie," 1963) (meticulously rebutting the Soviet contention).

[17] Tellingly, the United States did not advance Reagan Doctrine principles in defending the *Nicaragua* case before the International Court of Justice. The Court nonetheless reached beyond the pleadings to address arguments "advanced solely in a political context," admonishing against any principle of "ideological intervention." *Military and Paramilitary Activities (Nicaragua v. United States)*, Merits, 1986 I.C.J. 14, 134–35, ¶¶ 266–68 (June 27, 1986).

blocs had nominally committed themselves to "peaceful coexistence," while a third, "Non-Aligned" bloc of mostly poorer and weaker states had emerged, seeking to make real the promises of territorial integrity, political independence, and sovereign equality to which the stronger states, shopping for allegiance, paid lip service.

In this context, transgression of non-intervention norms was viewed simultaneously as East-West escalation and as Northern encroachment upon the South (even if actually committed by regional actors) and was in no event perceived as motivated by noble purposes.[18] Moreover, since intervention on one side would almost inevitably draw counterintervention, it could be expected to exacerbate rather than to ameliorate internal conflicts, in the process further empowering and emboldening rather than suppressing human rights abusers. Intervention by either of the rival blocs thus routinely excited the opposition, not only of the other and of the Non-Aligned, but also of intergovernmental and nongovernmental bodies concerned with peace, order, and humanitarianism.

The second relevant premise concerned the essential nature of internal conflict. Internal armed conflict was widely perceived, not as an anomaly or as evidence of "state failure," but as a legitimate way for questions of public order to be worked out within states. Internal wars typically succeeded in presenting themselves as struggles between ideologically motivated factions for standing to speak for the undivided population, rather than as ethno-nationalist bloodletting or as the simple thuggery of armed gangs.[19] After all, during this period, most governments in the world traced their origins more or less directly to a *coup d'etat*, insurrection, or decisive civil war. The image of civil war implicit in international discourse was that of, in effect, a trial by ordeal, in which a winning faction—absent unlawful assistance from a foreign power—demonstrated its worthiness of representing a given political community by achieving and maintaining effective control, i.e., acquiescence of the bulk of the populace in that faction's project of public order.[20]

This premise represented not a repudiation of the moralistic principle of popular sovereignty, but rather an application of that very principle in the absence of shared

[18] The international reaction to the 1978–79 Vietnamese invasion of Pol Pot's Democratic Kampuchea is the most striking illustration of the strength of this presumption. *See* G.A. Res. 34/22 (1979) (91-21-29) (demanding an "immediate withdrawal" of Vietnamese forces). A similar reaction greeted the 1983 ouster of thuggish and locally despised putschists in Grenada by armed forces of the United States with the participation of the Organization of Eastern Caribbean States. *See* G.A. Res. 38/7 (1983) (108-9-27) (denouncing the invasion as a "flagrant violation of international law").

[19] There is no doubt that the latter frequently masqueraded as the former, often for the sake of procuring weapons and other assistance from the rival blocs. Somali dictator Mohammed Siad Barre and Angolan rebel leader Jonas Savimbi are two notorious examples of leaders who shifted ideological affectations, as convenient, to enlist foreign support for essentially nonideological agendas.

[20] *See generally* Roth, *Governmental Illegitimacy in International Law*, *supra*, at 136–49, 160–71, 253–364 (detailing the history of that era's practice and pronouncements on civil wars, recognition contests, and political participation).

assumptions about popular sovereignty's substantive and procedural requisites. The conventional wisdom held that empirical investigation to ascertain public opinion in a foreign state was most often impracticable; that "popular will" itself was a complex and normatively loaded concept; and that any imposition from abroad of procedures calculated to measure "popular will" was presumptuous at best, and a usurpation at worst.[21]

This wisdom was reinforced by the very nature of the Cold War, which presented itself to the world as not merely a clash of powers but a clash of universal creeds. Liberal democracy and revolutionary socialism represented two complete and opposing conceptions of public order struggling for adherence within all nations. Moreover, the intensity of the struggle allowed for the paradoxical rationalization, on both sides, of dictatorial, repressive, and even terroristic means to "democratic" ends. Expressions of principled outrage at such means could easily be dismissed as—and indeed, frequently amounted to—partisan propaganda.

As a matter of both policy and principle, then, the perceived international interest in internal conflict in the Cold War era was more (a) that foreign powers not obtain undue advantage and (b) that the winner be determined by authentically internal means than (c) that the armed conflict be halted or even (d) that human rights abuses be curtailed. That order of priorities reflected, at least in part, both direct and indirect effects of the global geopolitical and ideological confrontation.

The turn of the 1990s brought the end of both the geopolitical and the ideological standoff. First, the United States emerged as the sole superpower. As a result, non-humanitarian motivations for U.S. intervention were diminished (though not necessarily eliminated). Moreover, any U.S.-led interventions would be far less likely to occasion counterintervention by a rival power, and thus far less likely to result in an escalation of internal conflict.

Second, liberal-democratic values, even if not achieving unquestioned international acceptance,[22] no longer faced a competing set of values pretending to universal applicability.[23] This development not only reduced the extent of international

[21] *See* ibid.

[22] *See* Thomas M. Franck, "The Emerging Right to Democratic Governance," 86 *Am. J. Int'l L.* 46 (1992) (the seminal work heralding a shift in international legal norms toward a "democratic entitlement"); Gregory H. Fox & Brad R. Roth eds., *Democratic Governance and International Law* (Cambridge: Cambridge University Press, 2000) (compendium of conflicting assessments of whether and to what extent such a shift has taken place).

[23] To be sure, the radical Islamist fringe currently represents such a set of values to the extent that it exhorts universal conversion to Islam and *jihad* against infidels. In general, however, "mainstream" Islamism, especially as advocated by state actors, demands recognition of Islamic exceptionalism rather seeking a transformation in the ordering principles of non-Muslim countries or regions. Furthermore, even within countries with large Muslim populations, its political claims typically are not asserted in the name of the latent will of the non-Muslim population.

dissensus on matters of internal order but also altered the reigning paradigm of internal conflict. The prior image had been of factions struggling to apply competing conceptions of public order to governance of the undivided whole, with the opposing regular and irregular armed forces as the primary targets and with the ruthlessness of the fighting mitigated, at least to some degree, by competition for the "hearts and minds" of broad sectors of the population. The new images—reflecting to some extent a change in perception alone, and to some extent a change in reality—were of, on the one hand, unlimited violence aimed at civilian populations directly, inspired by narrowly parochial, ethno-nationalist ideologies reminiscent of the long-repudiated Axis-era fascism (e.g., in Rwanda and parts of the former Yugoslavia); and of, on the other hand, efforts by wholly unprincipled armed gangs to usurp control of economic activity and natural resources (e.g., in Liberia, Somalia, and Sierra Leone).

These shifts in the geostrategic situation and in the paradigm of internal conflict were reflected in the actions of the international community. The Security Council, no longer subject to structurally overdetermined deadlock in cases involving internal affairs, began to characterize even unambiguously domestic humanitarian crises as threats to international peace and security, signaling at least a potential for the authorization, under Charter Articles 41 and 42, of coercive measures. In a few such cases—such as Somalia, Haiti, Rwanda, and Albania—the Security Council proceeded to authorize the use of force.[24] Even more tellingly, the Security Council provided unambiguous *post hoc* endorsements to unauthorized armed interventions by the Nigerian-led Economic Community of West African States (ECOWAS) in Liberia and Sierra Leone.[25] Moreover, the international community acquiesced in United States and allied intervention to secure a *de facto* Kurdish autonomous entity in Northern Iraq, an intervention nominally predicated on a Security Council resolution that did no more than "insist that Iraq allow immediate access by international humanitarian organizations" to victims of internal war and repression.[26]

Nonetheless, the extent of the change in the international community's stance toward internal conflict must not be exaggerated. States have, both individually and collectively, been highly reluctant to generalize from the cases that have so far presented themselves. Although, with the advent of R2P, the Security Council has now abandoned the practice of characterizing (less and less persuasively) situations

[24] S.C. Res. 794 (1992), 814 (1993) (Somalia); S.C. Res. 929 (1994) (Rwanda); S.C. Res. 940 (Haiti); S.C. Res. 1101 (1997) (Albania).

[25] U.N. Doc. S/22133 (1991) (Security Council statement commending ECOWAS efforts "to restore peace and normalcy in Liberia"); S.C. Res. 788 (1992) (imposing an arms embargo against Liberian factions resisting ECOWAS); S.C. Res. 1132 (1997) (imposing an arms embargo against the Sierra Leonean *de facto* government in support of ECOWAS military efforts to restore the elected government).

[26] S.C. Res. 688 (1991).

leading to the authorization of intrusive measures as *sui generis*,[27] there has been no move in United Nations bodies toward an express modification of use-of-force rules to allow for humanitarian intervention without Security Council authorization. Moreover, changed perspectives are far more evident among the wealthier and more powerful states (and, of course, among journalists, intellectuals, and NGOs based in those countries); notwithstanding the African Union's general affirmation in its 2000 Constitutive Act of its own right "to intervene in a Member State pursuant to a decision of the Assembly in respect of grave circumstances, namely: war crimes, genocide and crimes against humanity,"[28] the 133 states members of the G-77 contemporaneously reaffirmed their adherence to the earlier vision of the international peace and security order.[29]

The end of bipolarity in the military and ideological realms has not altered the essential premises to which most of the world's state actors adhere, and thus has not produced a visibly dramatic revision of a legal order established by consent. Yet the dominance of the United States in the military realm and the preeminence of liberal-democratic principles in the ideological realm have caused many statespersons, activists, and scholars in the West—and above all in the United States, with its strong traditions of both unilateral action and universalist justification—to question the legitimacy of that order's continued constraints on humanitarian intervention. Constituencies once wedded to those constraints as a matter of both policy and morality now increasingly seek to circumvent them and look to international law scholars for aid and comfort. And increasingly, international law scholars have obliged, though in sharply differing ways.

[27] *See, e.g.*, S.C. Res. 940 (1994), *supra* (characterizing the authorization of force in Haiti as "an exceptional response" to the "extraordinary nature" and "unique character of the present situation").

[28] Constitutive Act of the African Union (11 July 2000), art. 4(h), *available at* <http://www.africa-union.org/root/au/aboutau/constitutive_act_en.htm#top>. This is stated as a "Principle," but no specifics on its implementation are elaborated.

[29] Group of 77 South Summit Declaration (April 2000),<http://www.g77.org/summit/Declaration_G77Summit.htm>, ¶¶ 49, 54:

> 49. . . . We reaffirm that every State has the inalienable right to choose political, economic, social and cultural systems of its own, without interference in any form by other States.
>
> . . . .
>
> 54. We stress the need to maintain a clear distinction between humanitarian assistance and other activities of the United Nations. We reject the so-called "right" of humanitarian intervention, which has no legal basis in the United Nations Charter or in the general principles of international law. . . . Furthermore, we stress that humanitarian assistance should be conducted in full respect of the sovereignty, territorial integrity, and political independence of host countries, and should be initiated in response to a request or with the approval of these States.

*See also* ¶ 48 ("rejecting [all] forms of coercive economic measures, including unilateral sanctions against developing countries," without mentioning any exception for countermeasures against human rights violators).

## II. Rationalizing the Use of Force Outside the Charter Framework: Three Jurisprudential Approaches

At the core of the humanitarian intervention conundrum is the complexity of the relationship between international legality and substantive justice. The legal restraints that humanitarians so frequently find inconvenient stem primarily, not from the legacy of the Cold War, but from the more durable and useful tendency of the international system to reflect and to respect a plurality of views on fundamental questions of political order. As discussed at length above, the international legal order is by nature an accommodation among peoples who persistently disagree about justice. The recent diminution of fundamental differences among participants in the international system, while very real, can all too easily be exaggerated in the service of methodological approaches that either assume away fundamental differences or else delegitimate them.

Scholarly reaction to the Kosovo campaign, undertaken by the North Atlantic Treaty Organization (NATO) in 1999 against the Federal Republic of Yugoslavia (FRY) without United Nations Security Council authorization, provides illustrations of the problematic tendencies. Although the incompatibility of the action with any sound positivistic reading of international law is typically (though not always) acknowledged, the propriety of the action has nonetheless been widely (though by no means universally) affirmed. These affirmations have fallen principally into two, diametrically opposed jurisprudential categories. Though so different, both categories entail modes of justification that, taken to their logical conclusions, fatally undermine either the legal substance or the political influence, respectively, of the international law of peace and security. Neither approach successfully preserves international law as a basis for criticizing—let alone restraining—future exercises of military power that may be undertaken in the name of purportedly "humanitarian" goals.

The central debate pits adherents of "policy-oriented jurisprudence," who deny the separation of law from the moral purposes of actors with whom they identify, against those whom I shall call "moralistic positivists," who insist on that separation but who consciously choose moral over legal duties. The former would reinterpret international law to license humanitarian intervention quite broadly, whereas the latter would, having interpreted international law to preclude humanitarian intervention, advocate violating international law on an *ad hoc* basis in the service of the greater good.[30]

[30] These conflicting tendencies reproduce, in significant respects, the classic debate between Lon Fuller and H.L.A. Hart over the appropriateness of prosecuting, in postwar West Germany, a Gestapo informant whose actions, when committed, had comported with the applicable positive enactments of the Third Reich. Fuller, understanding law as a purposive process, considered the prosecution consistent with legality, whereas Hart, regarding law as a system of rules, deemed the prosecution unlawful,

What both approaches centrally share is disregard for the need to accommodate those who disagree with the dominant view of what count as morally compelling causes. Although this disregard is expressed in the name of international law itself, with reference to human rights norms, it nonetheless (however paradoxically) undermines the foundations of the international legal order.

A preferable third approach is to try to derive substantive criteria and authorization procedures for humanitarian intervention from a common ground of principle in the international system—not a superimposed or idealized common ground, but a common ground demonstrably immanent in the developing historical reality. These criteria and procedures would provide a basis for circumventing manifest abuse of the Security Council veto, but not for circumventing the reality of moral dissensus in the international community. The resulting criteria would inevitably be far too limited and the resulting procedures far too cumbersome for many advocates of humanitarian intervention, but they would have the merit of denying open-ended legal or political licenses to the great powers, which have been known throughout history to invoke humanitarianism in support of dubious pursuits.

## A. BENDING THE LAW: POLICY-ORIENTED JURISPRUDENCE

Since the sources of international law, as traditionally conceived, furnish relatively few resources for those who would uphold the legality of the Kosovo action, it is not surprising that the most significant efforts to vindicate the action should rely on an alternative methodology. This methodology, known as "policy-oriented jurisprudence," derives from the copious work of the so-called "New Haven School"—foremost, the writings of Myres S. McDougal, Harold D. Lasswell, and W. Michael Reisman.[31] It is hard to characterize in brief the principles of this jurisprudential trend without being accused of caricaturing them, and any effort to make broad generalizations about the usefulness of the New Haven approach is beyond the scope of this essay. Nonetheless, the elements of this approach that commend it to the project of justifying what otherwise appear as violations of settled norms can easily be identified.

In an effort to summarize and defend the principles of policy-oriented jurisprudence, Siegfried Wiessner and Andrew R. Willard portray law not as "a body of rules," on the one hand, nor as mere "processes of power," on the other, but rather as

yet justifiable on grounds of moral exigency. Hart, "Positivism and the Separation of Law and Morals," 71 *Harv. L. Rev.* 593, 615--21 (1958); Fuller, "Positivism and Fidelity to Law—A Reply to Professor Hart," 71 *Harv. L. Rev.* 630, 648–61 (1958).

[31] *See, e.g.,* Myres S. McDougal, Harold D. Lasswell & W. Michael Reisman, "Theories About International Law: Prologue to a Configurative Jurisprudence," 8 *Va. J. Int'l L.*, 189 (1968); McDougal, Lasswell & Reisman, "The World Constitutive Process of Authoritative Decision,"19 *J. Legal Educ.* 253 (1967).

"an ongoing process of authoritative and controlling decision" through which "members of a community seek to clarify and secure their common interest."[32] In recognition of law's character as a purposive process, policy-oriented jurisprudence has both descriptive and prescriptive components; this jurisprudence is said to provide not only "methods for tracking the development of law," but also "criteria for appraising its contribution to clarifying and securing the common interest, and procedures for improving its performance in any community."[33] Because law "is only a means to an end, not an end in itself," legality is identified with progress in "founding and maintaining *minimum public order* . . . [and] advancing toward an *optimum public order*,"[34] both of which are specified in accordance with a set of underlying values said to be broadly shared in the community.

The approach thus combines elements of positivism, realism, and naturalism, as power and morals share the stage with established expectations and authorized procedures. Although this combination is appealing at a high level of abstraction—since positivism, realism, and naturalism each seem to disclose part, but only part, of the essence of legality—it is not so clear how the pieces fit together to produce determinate conclusions about concrete problems.

First, concessions to realism, in overcoming the inflexibility of established sources of law, may tend to render short-run efficacy both the necessary and the sufficient condition of normativity. The expansion of the list of supposed "participants" in international lawmaking, while putatively reflective of the contemporary weight of non-state actors in world affairs, introduces extraordinary room for apologistic sleights of hand. The "world social and decision processes," as Wiessner and Willard describe them, include an indeterminate set of actors, to whose words and deeds are imputed lawmaking authority. "Besides the traditional nation-state," these actors may, depending on the circumstances, "include intergovernmental organizations, non-self-governing territories, autonomous regions, and indigenous and other peoples, as well as private entities such as multinational corporations, media, nongovernmental organizations, private armies, gangs, and individuals."[35] Moreover, the juridical significance accorded the acts and opinions of any of these actors is variable. "[T]he authority of institutional arrangements . . . is context-dependent, [and] is never known, with specificity, in advance of a particular problem. The authority and potential authority of each arrangement . . . must always be determined empirically in a given context."[36] Absent a formally structured account of their supposed

[32] Siegfried Wiessner & Andrew R. Willard, "Policy-Oriented Jurisprudence and Human Rights Abuses in Internal Conflict: Toward a World Public Order of Human Dignity," 93 *Am. J. Int'l L.* 316, 319–20 (1999).

[33] *Id.* at. 321.

[34] *Id.* at 324 (emphasis in original).

[35] *Id.* at 323.

[36] *Id.* at 324.

juridical authority, these various actors can be invoked or ignored, as convenience dictates, by those who have the power to create facts in disregard of the long-term accommodations that positive norms represent.[37]

Second, concessions to naturalism may tend to neglect the contested nature of justice. To speak of law as a purposive project is to beg the question of ***whose*** purposes drive the project. Any community, let alone the global community, is beset by disagreement about underlying values—if not about their validity, at least about their order of priority. Where controversial outcomes are claimed to derive from uncontroversial normative premises, this is usually a sign, not that controversy results from faulty reasoning or bad faith, but that the shared premises contain hidden ambiguities. Appeals to authoritative goals such as "minimum public order," employed to attribute to arid formalism the failure of established sources of law to support the proposed outcome, tend to obscure the real limits of consensus and the corresponding need for accommodation.

Third, the combination of strands of realism and naturalism in one jurisprudential package yields a dangerous temptation: realism and naturalism can achieve unity in the identification of the interests of the hegemonic power with the universal interest.[38] As Martti Koskenniemi has pointed out, law, if reduced to "social facts and moral ideas," becomes nothing but "a servile instrument for power (of what works) to realize its objectives (of what should work)"; "any conception of law as fixed 'rules' seems irrelevant to the extent that it is not backed by sanction and counterproductive inasmuch as it limits the choices available to those who have the means to enforce them."[39]

That the policy-oriented approach lends itself systematically to justifications for unilateral uses of force can be seen in the multicontextual writings of one of its

[37] As James C. Hathaway has noted, unilateralists can use this method to rationalize departures from state-based *opinio juris* in either direction. On the one hand, where "unilateral intervention [is] called for by the media and other non-state actors, . . . powerful states enjoy the right to interpret and act upon the prescriptions of this 'constitutive process.'" On the other hand, "if that same unofficial network suggests the need to rid the world of landmines that kill and maim thousands of innocent civilians every year, . . . powerful states ('those with the wherewithal' to act) remain the final arbiters of the result of the diffuse lawmaking conversation." Hathaway, "America, Defender of Democratic Legitimacy?" 11 *Euro. J. Int'l L.*, 121, 130 (2000).

[38] Edward Hallett Carr long ago illuminated the mischievous tendency for the great powers' publicists to identify those powers' partisan interests as the interests of the international community. Carr, *The Twenty Years' Crisis, 1919–1939: An Introduction to the Study of International Relations* [1939] (New York: Harper & Row Pubs., Inc., 1964), at 41–62.

[39] Martti Koskenniemi, "Carl Schmitt, Hans Morgenthau, and the Image of Law in International Relations," in Michael Byers ed., *The Role of Law in International Politics* (New York: Oxford Univ. Press, 2000), 17, at 32, 33, & 29, respectively.

accredited founders, Professor Reisman.[40] The following statement is strikingly illustrative of the groundwork for the positions that he has staked out over time:

> Positivist jurisprudence, which lends itself to decision-making by many of the levels of a bureaucracy, identifies lawfulness in terms of compliance with rules. The decision-maker at the pinnacle, in contrast, does not think in terms of compliance with rules, but in terms of making decisions that optimize the many policies that may be expressed in rules, but which are presented for decision in situations that are anything but routine; if they were routine, they would have been adequately dealt with by bureaucrats at lower levels of the behemoth. From the perspective of the jurist who is deploying a positivist jurisprudential frame, the decision-maker is acting unilaterally and unlawfully. Using a different and quite possibly more appropriate jurisprudential lens could lead to the opposite conclusion.[41]

A more subversive conceptualization of international legality can scarcely be imagined.[42] It is reminiscent of Jean Bodin's conception of sovereignty, in which the prince may unilaterally determine that the covenants limiting his discretion "cease to satisfy the claims of justice"[43]—a conception summed up in Carl Schmitt's famous phrase, "Sovereign is he who decides on the exception."[44] The United Nations system, of course, designates the bearer of a global power to "decide on the exception": the Security Council. Reisman's statement (which he intends as applying to

[40] *See, e.g.*, W. Michael Reisman, "Unilateral Actions and the Transformations of the World Constitutive Process: The Special Problem of Humanitarian Intervention," 11 *Euro. J. Int'l L.* 3 (2000); Reisman, "Kosovo's Antinomies," 93 *Am. J. Int'l L.* 860 (1999) (justifying the NATO bombing of Serbia); Reisman, "Sovereignty and Human Rights in Contemporary International Law," 84 *Am. J. Int'l L.* 866 (1990) (justifying the U.S. invasion of Panama); Reisman, "Coercion and Self-Determination: Construing Charter Article 2(4)," 78 *Am. J. Int'l L.* 648 (1984) (justifying the U.S. invasion of Grenada).

[41] Reisman, "Unilateral Actions," *supra*, at 5 n. 2.

[42] I cannot resist invoking here a reference to Richard Nixon's famous words about the legality of the domestic-espionage activities of his "Plumbers" unit: "When the President does it, that means it is not illegal." Michael Schudson, *Watergate in American Memory* (New York: Basic Books, 1992), at 191. Perhaps more to the point, the Iran-Contra defendants viewed constitutional limitations in just the way that Reisman's statement suggests. Their apologists tellingly lamented the prosecutions as "the criminalization of policy differences," implying that the question of whether or not to observe the Constitution presented a mere policy choice.

[43] Jean Bodin, *Six Books of the Commonwealth* [1576], trans. M.J. Tooley (Oxford: Basil Blackwell, 1955), at 30 (bk. I, ch. 8).

[44] Carl Schmitt, *Political Theology: Four Chapters on the Concept of Sovereignty* [1922], trans. George Schwab (Cambridge, Mass.: The MIT Press, 1985), at 5.

***external*** affairs) speaks volumes about his understanding of the role of the United States and its allies in the international legal system.[45]

With respect to the Kosovo action itself, Reisman, continuing the analogy to domestic law, invokes the maxim that "the Constitution is not a suicide pact."[46] The maxim itself is fair enough, but applicable only where adherence to the rule in question jeopardizes the very institutional framework that provides the basis for the rule.

In the present case, the "suicide pact" analogy is inapt. The FRY's subjugation of the Kosovar Albanians and the violent suppression of their independence movement, however offensive to collectively held values and however much denounced by the authoritative organs of the international system, did not augur the destruction of the international peace and security order. Nor has Reisman made the case that Kosovo represented narrowly exceptional circumstances of a kind not anticipated when the rules were drawn up and repeatedly reaffirmed, anticipation of which would manifestly have occasioned a legal exemption; Reisman's quarrel is with the very fact that Charter law reflects a deliberate choice to favor (at least presumptively) territorial integrity over other values. Nor was the Security Council "paralyzed," as Reisman puts it—any more than it is "paralyzed" when the United States vetoes resolutions imposing terms on itself or its allies; Chapter VII procedures establish a default position of inaction that is, by design, difficult to overcome.[47] Moreover, the appropriate remedy for "paralysis" would have been the convening of a special meeting of the General Assembly under the "Uniting for Peace" procedure,[48] an option that was eschewed—perhaps because of fear of how

[45] Reisman's statement reflects the jurisprudential understanding that legal rules are designed for untrusted implementers of underlying principles and policies but is heedless of the fact that in the international order, the United States and its allies ***are*** untrusted implementers. Of course, even untrusted implementers must have recourse to principles and policies in circumstances, unforeseen when the rules were established, in which strict application would defeat the rules' manifest purposes. But here, Reisman adopts a reading of the non-intervention norm's underlying purposes that is hardly a matter of consensus in the lawmaking community.

[46] Reisman, "Kosovo's Antinomies," *supra*, at 860–61. James Hathaway has commented adversely on Reisman's use of this oft-cited metaphor (which appears in at least two U.S. Supreme Court opinions), on the ground that its authors sought to limit individual rights in the interest of the general welfare, rather than to expand rights of unilateral action at the expense of a binding collective commitment. Hathaway, *supra*, at 127–28 & nn. 24–-25.

[47] As Reisman bluntly puts it, "Why was action undertaken without Security Council authorization? Because the authorization could not be secured." Reisman, "Kosovo's Antinomies," *supra*, at 861. Imagine such an explanation for taking unconstitutional action domestically.

[48] G.A. Res. 377 (A) (1950) (where "the Security Council, because of lack of unanimity of the permanent members, fails to exercise its primary responsibility for the maintenance of international peace and security, . . . the General Assembly shall [if requested by the Security Council on the vote of any seven members, or by a majority of the Members of the United Nations] consider the

the restoration of that device might threaten U.S. interests in other contexts, such as the Israeli-Palestinian conflict.

Reisman seeks to harmonize the Kosovo action with Article 2(4) (restricting the use of force against the territorial integrity and political independence of states) by radically reinterpreting the latter. In his view, Article 2(4) has been modified by what he terms the "contraction" of Article 2(7) (restricting external intervention in matters essentially within the domestic jurisdiction of states). This contraction, "by effectively eliminating for serious human rights violations the defense of domestic jurisdiction, removed from the sphere of 'political independence' of a state the right to violate in grave fashion and with impunity the human rights of its inhabitants." A change in one part of the Charter must, Reisman contends, occasion "appropriate adjustments in other parts."[49]

Yet Reisman ultimately attributes the Security Council's failure to do as he sees fit precisely to "profound, possibly unbridgeable divides between the permanent members" on "the international control of the essential techniques by which governments manage and control their people internally."[50] Thus, the modification of non-intervention norms that Reisman posits is aspirational; in reality, the system's failure to authorize intervention resulted not from an anomaly but from the legal need to accommodate differences of opinion. Nor are the two recalcitrant permanent members of the Security Council isolated in their non-conforming views on "the international control of the essential techniques by which governments manage and control their people internally."[51] Reisman's "reinterpretation" of the Charter repudiates not merely the rules as written, but their underlying purpose as well: international peace, based on accommodation (though not necessarily limitless accommodation) of differences about internal standards of justice.

There is, of course, considerable appeal to Reisman's position on human rights-oriented intervention in the abstract, and perhaps even greater appeal to its application in the concrete circumstances of the Kosovo action. The flaw in Reisman's abstract position, however, is significant: although states are generally agreed (or, almost as importantly, pay lip service to the proposition) that violations of treaty-based and customary rights of individuals and groups are not "essentially within the domestic jurisdiction," but rather are proper concerns of the international community as a whole, states are not generally agreed that the invocation of human rights concerns obliterates the considerations of non-intervention. Article 2(7)—and *a fortiori* Article 2(4)—continues to apply to the question of ***implementation*** of

matter immediately with a view to making appropriate recommendations to Members for collective measures . . . .").

[49] Reisman, "Kosovo's Antinomies," *supra*, at 861.

[50] *Id.* at 862.

[51] *See* Group of 77 South Summit Declaration, *supra*.

human rights obligations. The fact that states have bound themselves to certain international legal standards (without, it should be noted, accepting any explicit regime of penalties for non-compliance) need not logically entail that states have accepted to be externally compelled to comply with their obligations. These are two separate juridical steps. There is no contradiction in embracing the former while excluding the latter; indeed, Bodin's conception of sovereignty, noted earlier, suggests just this combination.[52]

To be sure, the recent practice of the international system has manifested considerable diminution of sovereign prerogative. But there is (as yet) no general principle of the sort that Reisman posits—namely, the exemption of armed redress for "serious" human rights violations from the category of "use of force against political independence." Even more gravely, the community-wide acceptance of the most basic human rights standards does not necessarily entail acceptance of the proposition that reasons of state may never justify "serious" violations (notwithstanding the treaty language limiting derogation); there remains considerable vitality to the view that if the stakes are high enough, few means are too terrible to contemplate.[53] There is little reason to believe that states—or peoples—widely accept that outsiders will have the last word on the means that they will employ to protect what they regard as vital interests. Even putting aside the anxiety about predatory intervention under humanitarian cover, there is considerable appeal in the international community for the licensing of humanitarian intervention only in cases where the Security Council, with its vast range of ideological and cultural perspectives, can come to an agreement on the equities. In other words, the system's failure to forcibly counter injustice is not, in itself, evidence that its rules frustrate its actual purposes.

Policy-oriented jurisprudence is ill disposed to accept such a conclusion. Unfortunately, the alternative it poses provides little basis for limitation of great-power impositions that invoke humanitarian concern. At its worst, the policy-oriented approach equates law with justice as interpreted by the strong.

[52] According to the authoritative interpretation of Article 2(7) contained in the U.N. General Assembly's 1970 Friendly Relations Declaration, "Every State has an inalienable right to choose its political, economic, social, and cultural systems, without interference in any form by another State," and "[n]o State or group of States has the right to intervene, directly or indirectly, for any reason whatever, in the internal or external affairs of any other State." *Friendly Relations Declaration, supra.* Despite the increasing emphasis on human rights norms, General Assembly reiterations of the non-intervention norm continue, without any indication that the inviolability of the latter norm is, as a general matter, conditioned on compliance with the former. This is not to deny that in some particularly egregious instances of human rights noncompliance, the international community has implicitly adopted such conditionality.

[53] The "*non liquet*" holding of the International Court of Justice Advisory Opinion on *Legality of the Threat or Use of Nuclear Weapons*, 1996 I.C.J. 226 (8 July 1996), ¶¶ 95–97, refusing to rule out the legality of the use of nuclear weapons in the face of dire threats, constitutes a tacit admission of this general point.

## B. BREAKING THE LAW: POSITIVISM FOR MORALISTS

"Policy-oriented jurisprudence," while neither a uniquely American phenomenon[54] nor uniquely the device of apologists for U.S. foreign policy,[55] remains a controversial mode of legal analysis, especially among those who seek to maintain a critical perspective on U.S. actions. Its leading methodological competitor, positivism, regards international law as a set of rules derivable (more or less "objectively") from accepted "sources of law." While the point is not entirely beyond cavil, positivists are generally agreed that the NATO military campaign cannot be reconciled with the strictures of the United Nations Charter.

For those positivists who are in moral and political sympathy with the Kosovo action, this legal conclusion poses a dilemma of the precise sort that policy-oriented jurisprudence tends to obviate. Positivists regard acknowledgment of such dilemmas as a healthy recognition that the universe lacks a moral order that renders all virtues mutually reinforcing; life poses situations in which even the right moral choice may have a moral cost.[56] In morally exigent circumstances, positivists would prefer to admit breaking the law in an isolated case, rather than to bend legality to the moral needs of the moment, thereby concealing the conflict of values and undermining law's restraining function.

Some positivists further hold the related, but not directly deducible, view that even where the violation of existing law is morally justified, it does not necessarily follow that the law ought to be reformed prospectively to accommodate future actions of a similar sort.[57] Although manifestations of support in the international community for the violation of an existing norm present opportunities for jurists to recharacterize the violative act as a step toward the development of an exception

[54] *See* Rosalyn Higgins, *Problems and Process: International Law and How We Use It* (New York: Oxford Univ. Press, 1994).

[55] Note, for example, the wide-ranging work of Richard Falk.

[56] *See* Hart, "Positivism and the Separation of Law and Morals," *supra*, at. 619--20.

[57] It is worth noting that the common-law defenses of necessity and excuse are both incompatible with this position. The necessity defense entails assertion of the kind of legal exception being resisted here. As one court has put it:

> In some sense, the necessity defense allows us to act as individual legislatures, amending a particular criminal provision or crafting a one-time exception to it, subject to court review, when a real legislature would formally do the same under those circumstances. For example, by allowing prisoners who escape a burning jail to claim the justification of necessity, we assume the lawmaker, confronting this problem, would have allowed for an exception to the law proscribing prison escapes.

*United States v. Schoon*, 955 F.2d 1238, 1241 (9th Cir. 1992). The excuse defense, conversely, while sheltering the actor from blame on ground of diminished agency, concedes that the act is unjustifiable and ought not to have been done. *See* Joshua Dressler, "Exegesis of the Law of Duress: Justifying the Excuse and Searching for its Proper Limits," 62 *S. Cal. L. Rev.* 1331, 1349 n. 124 (1989).

to the norm—opportunities that effectively turn international lawyers into lobbyists for changes in the practice and *opinio juris* of states and intergovernmental organizations—many jurists have declined such opportunities with respect to the Kosovo action, even while avowing the moral and political rectitude of the violation. Their concern is that a legal exception to the non-intervention norm, once created with a given humanitarian action in mind, would inevitably swallow the rule, creating an open-ended license for the unilateral use of force.[58]

Oscar Schachter articulated this concern as follows in 1991:

> Even in the absence of . . . prior [Security Council] approval, a State or group of States using force to put an end to atrocities when the necessity is evident and the humanitarian intention is clear is likely to have its action pardoned. But, I believe it highly undesirable to have a new rule allowing humanitarian intervention, for that could provide a pretext for abusive intervention. It would be better to acquiesce in a violation that is considered necessary and desirable in the particular circumstances than to adopt a principle that would open a wide gap in the barrier against unilateral use of force.[59]

The concern is a valid one, but Professor Schachter's advice fails to satisfy it. Although collective acquiescence in a violation does not alone vitiate the violated norm as a general matter, the specific "acquiescence" hypothesized here—manifesting a moral and political judgment that the violation is "necessary and desirable" —cannot help but "open a wide gap in the barrier." To reject the effort to establish a carefully delimited exception, even while affirming the necessity and desirability of the violation, exposes the whole of the non-intervention norm to discredit.

In the history of the contemporary peace and security order, the non-intervention norm has, it is true, successfully withstood widespread international acquiescence in the outcomes of purportedly "humanitarian" interventions. That acquiescence, however, has rarely been tantamount to moral or political approval of the interventions themselves, let alone to acknowledgment of armed intervention as an instrument of humanitarianism. In most cases where morally and politically desirable consequences followed from intervention, the international community perceived these consequences to have resulted from an accidental confluence of the intervenor's interests with those of the population of the target state. These happy

[58] For an elaborate exposition of this stance, see Peter Hilpold, "Humanitarian Intervention: Is There a Need for a Legal Reappraisal?" 12 *Euro. J Int'l L.* 437 (2001).

[59] Oscar Schachter, *International Law in Theory and Practice* (Boston : M. Nijhoff Pubs., 1991) at 126. For a Kosovo-occasioned assessment of Schachter's statement, see Louis Henkin, "Kosovo and the Law of 'Humanitarian Intervention,'" 93 *Am. J. Int'l L.* 824 (1999).

accidents appeared insufficiently systematic to justify reform of the non-intervention norm (just as the episodes were not so frequent or so similar in their essential characteristics as to give rise to patterns of acquiescence sufficient to indicate the emergence of a customary exception). It therefore made sense to advocate maintenance of the strict rule of non-intervention even while conferring an imprimatur on the fruits of the illegal act (e.g., recognition of the state of Bangladesh after the 1971 Indian invasion of East Pakistan, or of the government of the Central African Republic after the 1979 French removal of "Emperor" Bokassa).[60]

Acceptance of a violation of the non-intervention norm as itself "necessary and desirable" has far different implications, especially in circumstances where the essential characteristics of both the intervenor and the target situation in question can be anticipated to recur with some regularity. It is one thing to affirm that it is morally and prudentially right to disobey a just and prudent rule that has failed to take into account the characteristics of the situation at hand. It is quite another thing to affirm that it will be morally and prudentially right in the future (given that the essence of normativity lies in the like treatment of like cases) to disobey a rule that is recommended, on moral and prudential grounds, to be retained notwithstanding anticipation of the recurrence of such characteristics. The latter affirmation is inconsistent with the practical requisites of normativity in the international system.[61]

The "barrier against unilateral use of force," such as it is, does not, as Schachter's advice implies, derive from the mere existence of a restrictive legal doctrine. Strictures on the use of force—relying, as they do, not on a centralized system of sanctions but on the moral and political dispositions of constituencies in a position to restrain exercises of military power—cannot endure without being widely regarded as an integral part of a morally and prudentially compelling scheme. To insist on a set of strictures in legal doctrine while simultaneously admitting that they will, under predictable conditions, be morally or prudentially unsustainable in practice is to concede that the strictures are utopian—that is, that their obligatoriness is subject to conditions precedent and yet to be realized. Since the charge of utopianism has perpetually dogged efforts to establish the obligatory character of the international law of peace and security, it is imperative to avoid inadvertently bolstering such a charge.

[60] *See, e.g.,* G.A. Res. 2793 (XXVI) (1971) (104-11-10) (calling "upon the Governments of India and Pakistan to take forthwith all measures for an immediate cease-fire and withdrawal of their armed forces on the territory of the other to their own side of the India-Pakistan borders," thereby indirectly repudiating the Indian intervention that resulted in the establishment of Bangladesh).

[61] As Nico Krisch has put it, "Law loses much of its weight if its deviation from moral standards is openly admitted and other ways of justification are recognized." Krisch, "Legality, Morality, and the Dilemma of Humanitarian Intervention after Kosovo," 13 *Euro. J. Intl L.* 323, 327 (2002).

The problem has special salience in the political context of the U.S. penchant for unilateralism. A long-time observer of U.S. practice cannot help but find irony in Thomas Franck's description of the U.S./NATO position on Kosovo:

> Neither the U.S. Department of State nor NATO seriously attempted to justify the war in international legal terms. They clearly did not want their actions to legitimate a reversion to the pre-Charter era when states or regional organizations could claim an uncircumscribed right of unilateral recourse to military force.[62]

Given that the allied European powers are not serial violators of use-of-force norms, it is plausible that they intended, by avoiding a statement of general principle, to restrict the precedential implications of the action. But the most plausible motivation attributable to U.S. policymakers, given past practice, is just the opposite: ***to keep a free hand***. Rather than elaborating an exception that would affirm a commitment to non-intervention in all but the narrowly specified circumstances, the United States remains silent as to the scope of the implied license. By making no effort to place the action under a generally applicable normative standard, whether in the nature of *lex lata* or *lex ferenda*, the initiators of the Kosovo action effectively assert for themselves the privilege (in the literal sense of *privi-lege*) of disregarding acknowledged strictures of international law when (i.e., whenever) they think that they are in the right. Any concern for limitation of license is directed, not at promising restraint in future actions that the United States (and any allies of the moment) might want to take in some unilaterally designated "just cause," but at precluding the use of the precedent by non-approved powers.[63]

The U.S. agenda here is effectively camouflaged by its compatibility with the rhetorical approach recommended by bearers of the opposite intention. Thus, Bruno Simma seeks, in just the same manner as the U.S. State Department, to characterize Kosovo as an isolated case in which "overwhelming humanitarian necessity" justifies an *ad hoc* disregard of legal strictures:

> [T]he decisive point is that we should not change the rule simply follow our humanitarian impulses; we should not set new standards only to do

[62] Thomas M. Franck, "Lessons of Kosovo," 93 *Am J. Int'l L.* 857, 859 (1999).

[63] The problem here is not one of philosophical inconsistency; it is perfectly consistent to trust oneself, but not others, to engage in enlightened rule-breaking. The problem is a sociological one: a cooperative scheme cannot easily endure one member's overt assertion of such a prerogative. Moreover, humanitarian advocates ought to be very cautious about regarding the United States and its allies of the moment as a trusted "us" in this respect.

> the right thing in a single case. The legal issues presented by the Kosovo crisis are particularly impressive proof that hard cases make bad law.[64]

But the fact that Professor Simma renders this judgment in a distinctly non-American context is crucial. Simma describes the *Bundestag* debate of mid-October 1998 on German participation in NATO airstrikes as follows:

> [T]he international legal issues involved were discussed at great length and in considerable depth. The respect for UN Charter law demonstrated throughout the debates was remarkable. . . . [I]t was stressed by all voices in favour of such participation . . . that German agreement . . . was not to be regarded as a 'green light' for similar NATO interventions in general.[65]

In Germany (at least on Simma's account), the political legitimacy of the restraining role of the international law of peace and security is not in question.

In the United States, the opposite is true: disrespect for that body of law is long standing and bipartisan, an artifact of the U.S. role in the Cold War. So, for example, even congressional opponents of U.S. policy in Nicaragua in the mid-1980s only rarely invoked the decision of the International Court of Justice in *Nicaragua v. United States*; to do so was largely perceived in mainstream political circles as a sign of unworthiness to participate in a serious and responsible discussion of U.S. foreign policy. The dominant position among mainstream foreign policy commentators in the United States during the Cold War was that the international law addressed to the use of force had been designed for a better world than then existed.[66] This remained the conventional wisdom even after human rights became an established (and, by 1982, bipartisan) part of the mainstream foreign policy discourse; instructively, direct invocation of moral considerations (including human rights, which were then seen more in moral and domestic-law terms than in international-law terms) was more respectable than invocations of international law.

[64] Bruno Simma, "NATO, the UN, and the Use of Force: Legal Aspects," 10 *Euro. J. Int'l L.* 1, 14 (1999).

[65] *Id.* at 12–13.

[66] For a noteworthy elaboration of that view, see Jeane Kirkpatrick & Allan Gerson, "The Reagan Doctrine," in Louis Henkin ed., *Right v. Might: International Law and the Use of Force* (New York: Council on Foreign Relations, 2d ed. 1991), 19. Although the Reagan policies were highly controversial on numerous grounds, even opponents tended to accept, at least tacitly, Kirkpatrick and Gerson's proposition that the international law of peace and security was an inadequate guide to U.S. responsibilities in a dangerous world.

The end of the Cold War and the new receptiveness of the Security Council to U.S. security initiatives, starting with the 1990 response to the Iraqi invasion of Kuwait, created an opening to inject considerations of international law into U.S. foreign policy discourse on the use of force. Yet it is still only a modest opening. In this context, Simma's suggestion promises to have virtually the opposite effect as in the German context: far from highlighting the gravity of the dilemma and discouraging future departures from legality, the suggestion that properly construed international law stands in the way of, and therefore must give way to, morally exigent measures threatens again to associate the international law of peace and security as a whole with fuzzy-headed utopianism. The problem is compounded by a refusal to advocate reform of the law to accommodate action of the sort deemed necessary on this occasion; the implication is that not only existing doctrine, but the whole project of legal limitation of all actors on an equal basis, is risible.

Given the historical frequency of violations and the notorious lack of effective sanctions, international law's status as law—at least in the area of peace and security—has long hinged on a felt need to rationalize violative actions in terms of generally accepted legal categories. Hypocrisy thus plays an indispensable role as, so the saying goes, "the tribute that vice pays to virtue." In the words of Hedley Bull, "where a violation takes place[,] the offending state usually goes out of its way to demonstrate that it considers itself (and other states) bound by the rule in question."[67] That this is frequently accomplished by factual and analytic distortions merely reaffirms that states perceive that they cannot afford to portray their present and future conduct as unfettered by considerations of generally applicable legal standards. Not only is there, as Bull notes, near-universal "acceptance of the need to provide an explanation,"[68] but there is also acceptance of common doctrinal reference points for evaluation of such explanations.

Individual citizens may, for reasons of conscience, violate the civil or criminal law in morally compelling circumstances without compromising the foundations of legality in their societies. The same cannot be said of the most powerful states in international society, any more than it can be said in respect of violations of public law by the Executive in the domestic context. An affirmation of the moral and political rectitude of the Kosovo action, without advocacy of a corresponding modification in the legal doctrine governing such actions, has the effect of eroding the sociological foundation of use-of-force norms: those with the power to do what is "necessary and desirable" need no longer provide a legal explanation. This approach

[67] Hedley Bull, *The Anarchical Society* (New York: Oxford University Press, 1977), at 138.

[68] *Ibid.*

therefore does as great a long-run disservice to the international law of peace and security as does "policy-oriented jurisprudence."

## C. HUMANITARIAN INTERVENTION AND THE PROGRESSIVE DEVELOPMENT OF THE LAW

Is there room for a jurisprudential defense of interventions such as the Kosovo action? The answer turns on whether the intervention can be reconciled with the purposes that animate the international legal order—not the purposes hypothesized or confabulated by those operating from a particular vantage point or a particular conception of just political order, but the shared purposes of a wide range of actors whose frames of reference are not limited to stable, liberal-democratic societies.

The international legal order is neither a blueprint for the global advancement of liberal-democratic values nor an amoral alliance of ruling apparatuses with a common bond of mutual advantage. The United Nations Charter, the Friendly Relations Declaration, and an impressive array of other authoritative pronouncements reflect an orientation toward peace, based on accommodation among "peoples," or political communities, who share some basic moral premises but who can be expected to differ widely in their detailed interpretations of those premises. Peoples have the inalienable right of self-determination, and states, whether or not organized in accordance with liberal-democratic principles, are presumed to represent the expression of the self-determination of all those who live permanently within their boundaries.

The presumption linking state sovereignty to popular self-determination is strong but not altogether irrebuttable. "Alien, colonial, and racist" domination (i.e., illegal conquests and occupations, colonialism, and *apartheid*) and certain spectacularly bad governments (e.g., Uganda under Amin, the Central African Republic under Bokassa, Nicaragua under Somoza, Haiti under Cedras, Congo-Kinshasa under Mobutu, Sierra Leone under Koroma) and ruling arrangements (e.g., East Pakistan under Islamabad, Iraqi Kurdistan under Baghdad during the Saddam Hussein regime) have explicitly or implicitly lost the protection of the international peace and security order because they violated broadly held premises about acceptable governance and popular sovereignty. Governance is an inherently teleological concept: no culture or ideology classifies as governance the maintenance of effective control at gunpoint by thugs who abuse the population at will and perform no function that any significant part of the populace regards or could regard as beneficial. Similarly, while governments have traditionally found a myriad of dubious devices for representing themselves as manifestations of popular will—and states as manifestations of the self-determination of all those living within their boundaries—there are circumstances in which no respected system of thought furnishes the intellectual basis for such a finding.

As Adam Roberts has put it, "strictly observing non-intervention in all circumstances in defiance of all evidence of human misery . . . could itself discredit the non-intervention rule."[69] Indeed, the Kosovo operation was largely continuous with a series of other unauthorized but widely supported forcible interventions in the previous decade—i.e., the interventions of the Western allies in Northern Iraq and of the Economic Community of West African States (ECOWAS) in Liberia and Sierra Leone—undertaken for the sake of averting widely anticipated and imminent humanitarian catastrophe. The ECOWAS operations, both of which received *post hoc* Security Council approval, helped to inspire the African Union's affirmation, in its 2000 Constitutive Act, of its own right "to intervene in a Member State pursuant to a decision of the Assembly in respect of grave circumstances, namely: war crimes, genocide and crimes against humanity."[70] United Nations Secretary-General Kofi Annan thus had a substantial basis for submitting, in the Kosovo operation's aftermath, that there is a "developing international norm in favour of intervention to protect civilians from wholesale slaughter," even while cautioning that "intervention must be based on legitimate and universal principles if it is to enjoy the sustained support of the world's peoples."[71]

Yet in the absence of Security Council authorization, it remains true, as a British Foreign Office panel concluded in 1984, that "the best case that can be made in support of humanitarian intervention is that it cannot be said to be unambiguously illegal."[72] All efforts to establish an overt norm, however limited, in favor of unilateral or narrow-multilateral humanitarian intervention have been rebuffed. Most state responses to Annan's 1999 statement about an emerging norm were adverse.[73]

The 2001 ICISS Report suggested that in the absence of Security Council authorization, intervention might be legitimated in one of two alternative ways: either by a two-thirds vote of the General Assembly (acting with the "Uniting for Peace" framework), notwithstanding the General Assembly's conceded lack of legal capacity to suspend an applicable norm, or by the decision of a Charter-recognized "regional arrangement" (especially with respect to a member state, with or without

[69] Adam Roberts, "The So-Called Right of Humanitarian Intervention," *Trinity Papers*, No. 13 (2000), at 23, *available at* <www.trinity.unimelb.edu.au/publications/trinity_papers/TrinityPaper 13.pdf>.

[70] Constitutive Act of the African Union (11 July 2000), art. 4(h), *available at* <http://www.africa-union.org/root/au/aboutau/constitutive_act_en.htm#top>.

[71] *Secretary-General Presents His Annual Report to General Assembly*, U.N. Press Release Doc. SG/SM/7136, GA/9596 (20 September 1999).

[72] Roberts, "The So-Called Right," *supra*, at 23.

[73] Roberts, "The So-Called Right," *supra*, at 17 (reporting that only eight states supported this position).

*post hoc* Security Council approval),[74] notwithstanding Chapter VIII's express requirement of Security Council authorization for regional enforcement actions.[75] The version of R2P that survived the 2005 World Summit negotiations, however, in specifying the recourse where "national authorities are manifestly failing to protect their populations from genocide, war crimes, ethnic cleansing and crimes against humanity," acknowledged only the Security Council's authority to intervene.[76]

If anything, events following the Kosovo operation—especially the unauthorized (and, it is widely believed, disastrous) decision of the United States and its "coalition of the willing" to invade Iraq—have given great-power circumvention of the Security Council a bad name. Tellingly, when Gareth Evans, one of the ICISS report's principal authors, addressed the matter at a 2009 General Assembly session initiated by R2P opponents, he reaffirmed the exclusivity of the Security Council's authority: "If the Security Council behaves erratically or disappointingly on these issues, as it sometimes has in the past, the task is not to find alternatives to the Security Council, or go round it, but to make the Security Council work better."[77]

The ICISS Report itself had acknowledged that, "[a]s a matter of political reality, it would be impossible to find consensus, in the Commission's view, around any set of proposals for military intervention which acknowledged the validity of any

[74] It is frequently assumed that states can consent in advance, through treaties such as the AU Charter, to forcible intervention without U.N. Security Council authorization. *See, e.g.,* Dan Kuwali, "Protect Responsibly: The African Union's Implementation of Article 4(h) Intervention, 11 *Y.B. Int'l Humanitarian L.* 51, 86 (2008). It is not clear that this is true as a blanket proposition; a treaty purporting to validate the use of external force against an existing government acknowledged to represent the state's sovereignty would potentially run afoul of Article 103 of the U.N. Charter. *See, e.g.,* Louise Doswald-Beck, The Legal Validity of Military Intervention by Invitation of the Government, 56 *Brit. Y.B. Int'l L.* 189, 246–47 (1986) (detailing the Cypriot government's early objection to the Treaty of Guarantee that purported to authorize external intervention to enforce constitutional provisions); R. St. J. MacDonald, "International Law and the Conflict in Cyprus," 19 *Can. Y.B. Int'l L.* 3, 17 (1981) (posing the question of whether the treaty was void since a state cannot contract out sovereignty and at the same time keep it); *see also* Brad R. Roth, "The Illegality of 'Pro-Democratic' Invasion Pacts," in Gregory H. Fox and Brad R. Roth eds., *Democratic Governance and International Law* (Cambridge University Press, 2000), 328 (asserting the invalidity of a proposed treaty system that would establish the equivalent of a "Brezhnev Doctrine" for democratic states). However, the argument against such a treaty is far weaker where the treaty's object is the halting of mass atrocities rather than the prevention of unapproved internal regime change.

[75] ICISS Report, *supra,* §§ 6.29–6.35.

[76] G.A. Res. 60/1 (2005) (adopted without a vote), ¶ 139; *see also* Alex J. Bellamy, "Whither the Responsibility to Protect? Humanitarian Intervention and the 2005 World Summit," *Ethics & Int'l Aff.* 20(2006) 143.

[77] Gareth Evans, "Implementing the Responsibility to Protect," Statement to the U.N. General Assembly Informal Interactive Dialogue on the Responsibility to Protect, 23 July 2009, *available at* <http://www.un.org/ga/president/63/interactive/protect/evans.pdf>.

intervention not authorized by the Security Council or General Assembly."[78] It had nonetheless asserted that "if the Security Council fails to discharge its responsibility in conscience-shocking situations crying out for action, then it is unrealistic to expect that concerned states will rule out other means and forms of action to meet the gravity and urgency of these situations."[79] Its strategy had been to warn that if the ensuing "intervention is carried through successfully—and is seen by world public opinion to have been carried through successfully—then this may have enduringly serious consequences for the stature and credibility of the UN itself."[80]

But if part of the international community took from the Security Council's deadlock over Kosovo the lesson that the system's default rule against forcible intervention could in such cases be "legitimately" flouted,[81] the backlash against the ensuing Iraq War has served to bolster insistence, especially among weaker states, on adherence to the terms of the United Nations Charter. Meanwhile, some notable interventionist failures on the ground in the decade following the Kosovo operation—in particular, of U.S. and allied forces in Afghanistan and Iraq and of Ethiopian forces in Somalia—have bolstered the political credibility of those who doubt the efficacy of forcible intervention, whether authorized or not, in producing humanitarian success. Arguably, experience has taught that disagreement about forcible intervention, even in the face of dire conditions on the ground, should not be so quickly attributed to bad faith or fecklessness, and that there is much to recommend a default rule of non-intervention that can be overcome only by a widespread, cross-cutting consensus.

The Kosovo intervention itself was a closer case than conceded in some quarters; there were legitimate considerations on both sides.[82] To be sure, for a decade, the vast majority of Kosovars were treated as enemy aliens in their own land.[83]

[78] ICISS Report, *supra*, § 6.37.

[79] ICISS Report, *supra*, § 6.39.

[80] ICISS Report, *supra*, § 6.40.

[81] A panel of well-known experts concluded that the NATO military intervention had been "illegal but legitimate." Independent International Commission on Kosovo, *The Kosovo Report: Conflict, International Response, Lessons Learned* (Oxford Univ. Press, 2000) ("Goldstone Commission Report")" *available at* <http://www.reliefweb.int/library/documents/thekosovoreport.htm>. That language was later appropriated by supporters of the Iraq war. *See, e.g.*, Anne-Marie Slaughter, "Good Reasons for Going Around the U.N.," *N.Y. Times*, March 15, 2003.

[82] For a harsh critique of the intervention, *see, e.g.*, Danilo Zolo, "Humanitarian Militarism?" in Samantha Besson & John Tasioulas eds., *The Philosophy of International Law* (Oxford University Press, 2010), 549 at 554–58.

[83] According to the Report of the Goldstone Commission:

> The revocation of Kosovo's autonomy spawned an increase in human rights abuses and discriminatory government policies designed to Serbianize the province. These included discriminatory language policies: the closure of Albanian language newspapers, radio, and television; the closure of the Albanian Institute; and the change of street names from Albanian to Serbian. In particular, the introduction of a new Serbian curriculum for universities and

Consequently, the armed rebellion against the territorial integrity of the FRY can scarcely be seen as having been anything but provoked. Yet the worst of the FRY's preintervention abuses were occasioned by the rebellion itself (putting aside the fact that the truly massive abuses occurred ***after*** the foreign intervention commenced), and the rebellion was arguably calculated less to achieve liberation by force of its own arms than to draw foreign intervention by bringing down on the population a merciless wave of Serb retribution.[84] The international system can ill afford to reward such insurgent strategies—for their human costs no less than for the threat they pose to existing structures of state authority—though it also can ill afford to give predators a guarantee of non-interference in pillage, or to admit that the state sovereignty it was designed to protect altogether lacks moral underpinnings. And, of course, it should not be forgotten that the human cost of the NATO bombing campaign itself turned out to be substantial, with an estimated 500 civilians killed and 6000 wounded.[85]

The Security Council's failure to reach the consensus necessary to authorize the Kosovo operation can be seen in conflicting ways. Russia and China, though they blocked neither the characterization of the events in Kosovo as a threat to international peace and security nor the demands that the FRY cease and desist from its norm-offending actions in that territory,[86] strongly objected to the NATO action.[87] Consistent with the peace and security scheme's current claim to legitimacy, rather than with the temporal circumstances by which it happens to have arisen, one can

> schools . . . . ". . . [M]ore than 18,000 teachers and other staff of Albanian-language classroom facilities (. . .) were summarily dismissed when they rejected the textbooks of the uniform curricula." Thousands of Albanians were dismissed from public employment; according to the independent Kosovar Albanian Association of Trades Unions, 115,000 people out of a total 170,000 lost their jobs. . . . Legislation was also passed which made it illegal for Kosovar Albanians to buy or lease property from Serbs . . . . Above all, there were widespread human rights abuses—arbitrary arrest, torture, detention without trial. Albanians were accused of "verbal crimes" and taken to police stations for "informative talks." . . . It is said that at least one member of every Albanian family had been called to a police station, or had spent some time in jail, or was waiting for a trial.

*The Kosovo Report*, *supra* (footnotes omitted).

[84] *See, e.g.*, Alan J. Kuperman, "The Moral Hazard of Humanitarian Intervention: Lessons from the Balkans," 52 *Int'l Stud. Q.* 49 (2008).

[85] Tania Voon, "Pointing the Finger: Civilian Casualties of NATO Bombing in the Kosovo Campaign," 16 *Am. U. Int'l L. Rev.* 1083, 1085; *see also* Human Rights Watch, *Civilian Deaths in the NATO Air Campaign* (2000), *available at* <http://www.hrw.org/reports/2000/nato>; Tim Judah, *Kosovo: War and Revenge* (Yale Univ. Press, 2000), at 264.

[86] *See* S.C. Res. 1160, 1199, 1203 (1998) (all invoking Chapter VII powers in addressing the Kosovo situation).

[87] *See* U.N. Press Release Doc. SC/6659 (26 March 1999) (Russia, China, and Namibia support draft Security Council resolution, defeated 3-12-0, characterizing NATO's "unilateral use of force" as "a flagrant violation of the United Nations Charter" and demanding "an immediate cessation").

envisage the veto-possessing permanent members not as holders of a privilege, to be deployed in their own interests, but as empowered representatives of principled but otherwise underrepresented viewpoints. Given Russia's special relationship with Serbia and the parochial concerns of Russia over Chechnya and of China over Tibet and Taiwan, circumvention of the veto in this case might be justified as a means of overcoming recalcitrant wills rather than dissenting opinions. However, the Russian and Chinese governments were not truly isolated in their oppositional stance: for example, the Indian government opposed the campaign as "interfering in the internal affairs of a country," the 12-state Rio Group expressed "regret" for "the recourse to the use of force in the Balkan region in contravention of the provisions" of the Charter, and the South African government asserted that such violation of the Charter "cannot be tolerated by the international community."[88] The United States, complain though it might about the veto in the hands of others, has at times been considerably more isolated in its threatened exercises of the veto in opposition to measures directed against Israel.

Faced with Russian and Chinese opposition, the NATO powers declined to put their planned operation to the test of the opinion of the broader community of states. The "Uniting for Peace" procedure provides a mechanism for such a test. The failure to invoke it—where, as here, there would have been sufficient time for such a special meeting of the General Assembly to be convened—is surely a strike against the effort to reconcile the NATO action with the demands of international normativity.

Even a failed effort at an explicit legal justification would have been salutary. The onus to make the case would have forced proponents to draw the proposed exception narrowly, so as to minimize opposition. An overt normative crisis—a clash between adherents of absolute and qualified versions of the non-intervention norm—would have been far preferable to a creeping desuetude of substantive and procedural norms. A breach of existing law in the name of a demand for a narrow exception reaffirms law as a guide to action, rather than enabling the insidious take-away message that the law should not be allowed to get in the way of doing the right thing (as perceived by the strong).

## III. Overselling the Responsibility to Protect: The Dangers of Disparaging Constraints on Empowered Moralism

Whatever may justly be said about sovereignty-as-responsibility as a limitation on sovereignty-as-control, the international system's would-be implementers of that

[88] Heike Krieger ed., *The Kosovo Conflict and International Law: An Analytical Documentation, 1974–1999* (Cambridge Univ. Press, 2001), at 493.

limitation are both untrusted and untrustworthy. Regrettably, it has thus far proved impossible to arrive at self-executing substantive standards for humanitarian intervention—standards so specific and susceptible of objective verification as to overcome the potential for perceived or actual misuse.[89] Any formula for humanitarian intervention must thus include procedural as well as substantive requisites, and an implication of procedural requisites is the obligation to abide outcomes with which one disagrees, even at the cost of forgoing action that first-order moral principles might recommend.

The "sovereignty as responsibility" language, however, has the unfortunate consequence of encouraging the audience to condition its respect for the international order's default rules—predicated, as they are, on respect for states' sovereign prerogatives—on a unilateral assessment of whether the state in question has fulfilled its responsibilities.[90] It is no accident that Richard Haass, the U.S. State Department's Director of Policy Planning under President George W. Bush, seized upon this language in an effort to validate a bold doctrine of unilateral action—one that, to be fair, went both far beyond and far astray from anything that most R2P advocates ever suggested or approved.[91]

Moreover, both the African Union's Constitutive Act and the 2005 United Nations World Summit resolution establish as a substantive justification of intervention the state's failure to protect its population from, not only genocide and crimes against humanity (and in the United Nations version, ethnic cleansing), but also "war crimes."[92] This category presents at least three difficulties.

First, while it can be assumed that the triggering language as a whole is intended to apply only where, in the words of the ICISS Report, "all order within a state has

[89] As Ryan Goodman acknowledges, the main obstacle to the legalization of unilateral humanitarian intervention (UHI) has been the concern about use of humanitarianism as a pretext for aggression. Goodman, "Humanitarian Intervention and Pretexts for War." 100 *Am. J. Int'l L.* 107 (2006). Goodman offers an empirical case for denying that an explicit legalization of UHI would exacerbate this danger.

[90] For some reasons to prefer the older language of "humanitarian intervention," *see* Jose Alvarez, "Notes from the President: The Schizophrenias of R2P," *ASIL Newsletter* 23:3 (2007), *available at* <http://www.asil.org/newsletter/president/pres070927.html>.

[91] For a summary and evaluation of this phenomenon, see Nicholas J. Wheeler, "The Bush Doctrine: The Dangers of American Exceptionalism in a Revolutionary Age," 27:4 *Asian Perspective* 183 (2003). There were some notable R2P supporters who endorsed the Bush approach outright, *see, e.g.*, Fernando R. Teson, "Ending Tyranny in Iraq," 19 *Ethics & Int'l Aff.* 1 (2005), but others sought vociferously to distinguish the two projects, *see, e.g.*, Terry Nardin, "Humanitarian Imperialism," 19 *Ethics & Int'l Aff.* 21 (2005). For one thing, as Tom J. Farer notes, the human rights situation in Iraq, while appalling, did not amount to an emergency, and "[i]n no instance in recent history has an intervention been widely perceived as humanitarian where the supposedly triggering violations were chronic." Farer, "The Prospect for International Law and Order in the Wake of Iraq," 97 *Am. J. Int'l L.* 621, 626 (2003); Goodman, *supra*, at 133.

[92] G.A. Res. 60/1 (2005), ¶139; Constitutive Act of the African Union, *supra*, art. 4(h).

broken down or when civil conflict and repression are so violent that civilians are threatened with massacre, genocide or ethnic cleansing on a large scale,"[93] a would-be intervener could make a facially plausible case for the presence of war crimes and the threat of massacre in almost any civil war. War crimes are endemic to war, and bearers of partisan sympathies, even when perfectly sincere, tend to invoke them in convenient ways. Even the news media of liberal-democratic countries, relied on so heavily to move the consciences of political constituencies and to fact-check partisan allegations, are hardly immune to the tendency to transmit accounts—especially those sponsored by the governments of their own states—that tendentiously exaggerate atrocities or take events out of context.[94]

Second, the authoritative documents' exclusive focus on criminality may be salutary in narrowing the justifications for intervention—the ICISS Report had gone farther to include even "overwhelming natural or environmental catastrophes, where the state concerned is either unwilling or unable to cope, or call for assistance, and significant loss of life is occurring or threatened"[95]—but it subtly distorts the nature of the project. The cross-border humanitarian use of force has generally been understood as a stop-gap measure to avert impending humanitarian catastrophe, not as recourse against wrongdoing as such. If international criminal law comes to be perceived as a normative order that displaces the international law of peace and security, this portends dangerous developments in a world where violators of the former can be found in almost every conflict. The authoritative documents' emphasis on crime tends to blur the line between humanitarian intervention and criminal justice, with the possible long-term effect of undermining a non-intervention norm that is needed precisely to constrain the single-minded (and thus reckless) pursuit of justice.

Third, tying the intervention threshold to criminality rather than to the extent of humanitarian catastrophe contributes to a trend toward attributing political violence to high-level conspiracies—or "joint criminal enterprises" —rather than to social conflicts. This may not be the most productive way to understand the problem. Even where "political entrepreneurs" can be identified as conspirators behind campaigns of political violence, they ordinarily rely on substantial popular constituencies, and are ordinarily "called forth" by social conditions that afford them political opportunities (which, in the absence of one set of opportunists, might just as easily be capitalized on by another). Efforts to establish peaceful order are

[93] ICISS Report, *supra*, at § 4.13.

[94] The major U.S. media have historically done a poor job of fact-checking U.S. Government charges against foreign governments, allowing caricatures of disfavored foreign leaders to be drawn without challenge. *See, e.g.*, Jeff Cohen & Mark Cook, "How Television Sold the Panama Invasion," *Extra!* (Fairness and Accuracy in Reporting, Jan./Feb. 1990), *available at* <http://www.fair.org/index.php?page=1546>.

[95] ICISS Report, *supra*, at § 4.20.

potentially impaired by a tendency to make political violence out to be a simpler phenomenon than it is.

A further problem with the rhetoric of the "Responsibility to Protect" is that it conveys a misimpression about the role that international law plays in humanitarian intervention. In jettisoning the provocative language of a "right" of humanitarian intervention, the R2P project obscures the ineluctable reality that the legal issue reduces to just this. International law can do no more than to license intervention by willing and able powers, whereas bringing about the intervention is a matter of the political will of interested states. Indeed, the humanitarian use of force is not meaningfully a matter of legal "responsibility" at all, since an omission in this respect cannot be thought to count, nor realistically be made to count, as a breach of any state's legal obligation.[96]

Real-world humanitarian intervention depends on a confluence of interests that is highly contingent. With unintended irony, the ICISS Report understates the point as follows:

> It may not always be the case that the humanitarian motive is the only one moving the intervening state or states, even within the framework of Security Council-authorized intervention. Complete disinterestedness—the absence of any narrow self-interest at all—may be an ideal, but it is not likely always to be a reality: mixed motives, in international relations as everywhere else, are a fact of life.[97]

Although the Report demands that "[t]he primary purpose of the intervention must be to halt or avert human suffering,"[98] this proposed standard seems impossible to operationalize: individuals may have a "primary purpose," as distinct from a "secondary" one, but it is doubtful that the same can be said of the collection of actors whose participation is necessary to produce so complex a result. This standard would appear, moreover, to be intertwined with the hopelessly unrealistic requirement that like cases be treated alike—that lesser cases of atrocity not be prioritized while worse cases go unaddressed—a standard that reduces to the pernicious demand that if good cannot be done everywhere, it should not be done anywhere. In practice, supporters of humanitarian intervention will have to settle for self-interested behavior that, by happy accident, yields communal benefit.[99]

[96] This is not to disparage R2P's significance as part of an effort to develop an international political constituency for greater external involvement in internal catastrophes. R2P's greatest significance may lie outside the legal realm.

[97] ICISS Report, *supra*, § 4.35.

[98] ICISS Report, *supra*, § 4.33.

[99] Ironically, it may be that, as one pro-intervention commentator puts it, "a humanitarian intervention is more likely to succeed where an intervener has clearly defined political motives in addition to

Even if what the world needs is more intervention rather than less, licensing intervention more broadly (as by allowing circumvention of the Security Council) in no way equates to increasing the amount of the right intervention in the right places. At their best, interventions occur in places—e.g., in Kosovo, not Sudan, Congo, or Rwanda—and in ways—e.g., by aerial bombardment of economic infrastructure rather than ground-troop confrontation of *genocidaires*—that reflect political rather than moral priorities. An intervener's priorities may lead to cut-rate and irresolute methods that leave the situation worse than it was before the action was undertaken. At worst, the interests motivating the intervener's investment may distort the project's goals altogether.

Rwanda is the example most frequently invoked in opposition to the non-intervention norm, but in the actual event, what impeded a rescue of the genocide's victims was not a lack of legal authority to override the norm but a lack of political will.[100] The true lesson of Rwanda is that where the only interests in play are humanitarian ones, and where interveners figure to incur significant costs in blood or treasure, foreign powers typically lack sufficient motivation to intervene. And tellingly, when France—whose historical ties were with the perpetrators rather than the victims of the genocide—belatedly undertook to intervene (with Security Council authorization),[101] both the intentions and the outcome were highly equivocal.[102]

Some of the literature disparaging the non-intervention norm gives the impression that the legal prerogatives of weak states constitute the great impediment to the betterment of the human condition—that wealthy and powerful states are chomping at the bit to bestow beneficence, but frustrated by legal constraint. The realities demonstrate little reason to believe this. Moreover, if powerful states really are looking to do good in a universalist sense, forcible intervention is unlikely to the surest—let alone most cost-effective—humanitarian investment. The ugly realities

humanitarian ones—so long as the political motives do not overwhelm humanitarian objectives—than when the political interests are obscure or non-existent." Dan Kuwali, "Protect Responsibly: The African Union's Implementation of Article 4(h) Intervention, 11 *Y.B. Int'l Human. L.* 51, 82 (2008).

[100] As Kuwali notes, "No member of the Security Council tried to oppose intervention . . . on the grounds that the intervention violated Rwanda's sovereignty." Kuwali, *supra*, at 92.

[101] S.C. Res. 929 of 22 June 1994 (invoking Chapter VII authority).

[102] According to one source, "General Jean-Claude Lafourcade, commander of Operation Turquoise, admitted that the safe zone was intended to keep alive the Hutu government in the hope that it would deny the RPF total victory and international recognition as the rulers of Rwanda." Chris McGreal, "France's Shame?" *The Guardian*, Jan. 11, 2007, *available at* <http://www.guardian.co.uk/world/2007/jan/11/rwanda.insideafrica>. Whether or not this is true, the French intervention had the effort of facilitating the passage of genocidal Hutu militias into neighboring Congo, where their presence precipitated a series of devastating armed conflicts. For a critical account of the intervention's effects on the ground, *see* Philip Gourevitch, *We Wish to Inform You That Tomorrow We Will Be Killed with Our Families: Stories from Rwanda* (New York: Picador USA, 1998), 157–61.

that attend non-intervention in troubled states need to be compared, not to an idealized vision of "civilization to the rescue," but to the mixed picture of qualified success and colossal failure that reflects the actual experience of forcible intervention. Critics of non-intervention manifest an understandable aversion to standing idly by in the face of criminal violence; would that there were a comparable aversion to standing idly by in the face of less dramatic scourges that routinely destroy a far greater number of innocent lives, and that could be addressed with far fewer resources, with no "collateral damage," and with a far lesser likelihood of unintended adverse human consequences.

## Conclusion

Hard cases, it is frequently said, make bad law. It may be more accurate to say that hard cases expose the tensions and ambiguities underlying seemingly straightforward legal standards and force jurists to come to grips with the principles and policies embodied in those standards.

Policy-oriented jurisprudence purports to do this, but its method does not provide reassurance that the effort is faithful to the complex accommodations among competing interests and competing conceptions of justice that international law represents. Rather, the method seems all too easily to provide jurisprudential cover for empowered actors to exceed the bounds of consensus and compromise. Convenient principles and policies are imputed to the international community on the basis of evidence for which no standards of admissibility and weight have been fixed.

The alternative that I have dubbed "moralistic positivism," however, does not even rise to the normative challenge. In advocating the armed pursuit of a particular conception of international justice, it seeks neither to respect, to reinterpret, nor to reform existing legal limitations on such pursuits. In avoiding a bad legal precedent, it creates a worse political one.

The third way to address hard cases is to ascertain the extent to which principles and policies favoring an exception to an apparent rule are embedded in the established source material for the drawing of legal conclusions, and to advocate, if necessary and appropriate, an incremental extension of those principles and policies to cover the case at hand (along with any future case sharing its essential characteristics). Even where this approach acknowledges that the law is being broken on this occasion for a good cause, it manifests a regard for the subordination of empowered will to generally applicable principle, and places before the lawmaking community the question of whether the law's animating purposes justify acts of the sort undertaken. The effect is to affirm the continued applicability of legal considerations even to dire humanitarian circumstances, rather than abandoning that field to empowered moralism.

At stake is the viability of any meaningful international law of peace and security. The essence of the project entails generally applicable norms, arrived at through a process of accommodation among notionally equal juridical entities that cannot be expected to agree comprehensively on questions of justice.

Today, the unrivaled military power of the United States and the ascendancy of its articulated ideals call into question the continued vitality of such a project, as well as its continued justification on moral and policy grounds. The legal principle of sovereign equality, always limited in practical effect, may seem all the less relevant in conditions of unipolarity, where weak states confronting U.S.-led alliances have no powerful supporters to bolster their position.

It is natural for those who associate themselves with the conceptions of justice espoused by the United States and its closest allies to ask: Why defer to an accommodation made with people who are wrong about justice, and who are not strong enough to prevent or to retaliate against actions taken in the service of justice, or to invoke the precedent for their own dubious purposes?

One answer is that in the long term, international peace cannot be predicated on the privilege of the momentarily strong to pursue forcibly their unilateral determinations of what is just in any given instance. Wagers on the continued weakness of others—and especially on the continued irrelevance of their disposition to cooperate on security issues—are bad long-term bets. As the aftermath of the September 11, 2001, catastrophe has demonstrated, the security of even the great powers requires active collaboration from unlikely quarters, collaboration that cannot always be purchased or extorted.

Another answer is that the practical demands of justice are often fairly contestable and sometimes conflicting: the principle of self-determination of distinct political communities includes, for prudential and perhaps even moral reasons, the right of those communities to be wrong about justice, even in ugly ways, albeit not limitlessly. Outside impositions—affected, as they predictably are, by self-interest and arrogance—cannot be lightly presumed to be salutary. Moreover, assessments of justice from great distances are notoriously unreliable; the news media of global reach (which are heavily dominated by U.S.-based outlets) cannot be counted on to characterize the crises in question in a manner free of sophomoric oversimplification and partisan manipulation.

Instead of asking the typically American question, "What should ***we*** be allowed to do to further justice abroad?"—to which the answer might well be, "Everything we can"—one might do better to pose, as does much of the rest of the world, the question, "What should powerful foreign states be allowed to do in ***our*** troubled country in the name of furthering justice?" The answer is likely to be different.

# 6

# Secessions, Coups, and the Effective Control Doctrine

## Introduction

Although "recognition" is frequently discussed as a political or diplomatic rather than a legal matter, no task is more fundamental to the international rule of law than that of identifying both the primary units of the global order and the institutions that have standing to act in the name of those units. International law acknowledges "states" as bearers of a distinctive package of rights, obligations, powers, and immunities (i.e., "sovereignty"), and attributes to each state a "government" with the legal capacity (for the time being) to assert rights, incur obligations, exercise powers, and confer immunities on the state's behalf.[1] Where contestation arises over whether an entity has the legal properties of a state or whether a particular governmental apparatus acts validly in the state's name, legal relationships of all kinds are called into question.[2] Legal doctrines are thus needed to govern international conferral of legal status on local exercises of *de facto* authority, whether carried out in the name of new sovereign units (e.g., Kosovo and Somaliland) or of new leaderships asserting rule over existing sovereign units (e.g., new regimes coming to power by force in Madagascar and Honduras in 2009).

The international legal order's repudiation of "might makes right" in relations among states masks a critical component of that order's traditional doctrines governing what is cognizable as an exercise of state authority: an emphasis on

[1] The legal framework for the latter attribution is the theme of this author's 1999 book. *See* Brad R. Roth, *Governmental Illegitimacy in International Law* (Oxford Univ. Press, 1999).

[2] Of greatest potential significance in this context is the authority to invite foreign military forces to play a role in bolstering a particular system of public order against challenges by its rivals. *See, e.g.*, Institut de Droit International, 10th Commission: Present Problems of the Use of Force in International Law: D. Sub-Group on Intervention by Invitation (Gerhard Hafner, rapporteur) (July 25, 2007), *available at* <www.idi-iil.org/idiF/annuaireF/10th_commission_d.pdf>; Louise Doswald-Beck, "The Legal Validity of Military Intervention by Invitation of the Government," 56 *Brit. Y.B. Int'l L.* 189 (1985).

present or past patterns of effective control. Although the doctrinal schemes for recognizing states and governments are distinct and are each complex, a traditional common thread is the role played by "effective control through internal processes"—processes that may be marked by the very violence and coercion that the international order disdains to dignify in interstate relations. International legal standing has traditionally been established by victory in a trial by ordeal: a region initially integral to an existing state successfully establishes itself as an independent sovereign unit only where its secession movement creates—usually by decisive victory in an armed struggle–facts on the ground that appear irreversible; an insurgent faction successfully establishes itself as a government where it overthrows an existing constitutional structure and secures—even if at bayonet-point—widespread popular acquiescence. The international order's attribution of sovereign independence to established territorial political communities thereby has traditionally entailed (to put it most bluntly) the right of each to fight its civil war in peace and to be ruled by its own thugs. Insofar as it is perceived as little more than an imprimatur for "might makes right" at the local level, this "effective control doctrine" is manifestly offensive to a rule-of-law sensibility.

It comes as no surprise, then, that so many present-day commentators, theorists, jurists, and even diplomats view the effective control doctrine negatively and resist its implications for contemporary recognition controversies. Where local impositions appear to defy popular will or the rule of law, there is a natural inclination, consistent with the moral principles articulated in international human rights instruments and other authoritative international pronouncements, to prefer more plausibly democratic or constitutional solutions to recognition contests. In the developments of the past two decades, there is a nexus between trends in the recognition of states and those in the recognition of governments: the international community's rejection of local efforts to maintain by force the territorial integrity of the Socialist Federal Republic of Yugoslavia (SFRY), in the face of clear majorities for independence within the constitutionally established territorial subunits, is of a piece with the international community's newfound reluctance to recognize unconstitutional seizures of power from democratically elected authorities.

However, the effective control doctrine cannot so easily be jettisoned. The doctrine fills a void inherent in a decentralized legal order founded on arbitrarily drawn territorial boundaries and beset by continuing clashes of both interests and values. While a rigid application of traditional premises may produce genuinely perverse results, a radical departure from those premises would open up questions that the international system has had good reason to keep closed, and would potentially invite the kind of unconstrained external intervention in internal affairs that the international law of peace and security seeks to preclude. Disparagement of the effective control doctrine is all too easy in the absence of a "moral reading" of the doctrine,[3] one that exposes the doctrine's role in effectuating the purposes and principles of the United Nations Charter system.

The effective control doctrine is best understood, not as an amoral or tactical concession to *realpolitik*, but as a means of reconciling two fundamental principles of the international order's relationship to domestic political authority: popular sovereignty and ideological pluralism. On the one hand, the United Nations Charter is notionally a compact, not among ruling apparatuses, but among territorially based political communities; respect for existing states and governments in that framework is formally premised on the idea that these states manifest the self-determination of their whole populations without distinction, and that existing governmental structures (for the time being) authentically represent those states. On the other hand, the Charter and its official glosses "envisage the relations among States having different political, economic and social systems on the basis of coexistence among their various ideologies"[4]; the system's ideological pluralism, while not preclusive of efforts to promote human rights and democratic participation, has generally militated against any international effort to nullify the legal status of emanations from established and effective domestic authority. The effective control doctrine squares popular sovereignty with ideological pluralism by establishing a presumption—in many circumstances, an irrebuttable one—that enduring patterns of effective authority reflect underlying realities consistent with the Charter's idealization of existing states and governments.

In the past two decades, the international order's ideological pluralism has narrowed, and numerous events have highlighted, for observers across the spectrum of principled worldviews, the unreasonableness of an irrebuttable presumption that effective control manifests popular will. Given these developments, the effective control doctrine has inevitably begun to fray.

Nonetheless, facile invocations of democratic or constitutionalist values do not provide a firm foundation for substitute approaches to the recognition of states and governments. Because democracy and constitutionalism are themselves open-textured and contested concepts, their application to recognition questions has the potential to yield equally arbitrary but far less stable and predictable outcomes. Despite occasional exceptions and bursts of exuberant rhetoric about popular will

[3] As noted above, the legal philosopher Ronald Dworkin coined the term "moral reading" for an interpretation that, "all things considered, makes the community's legal record the best it can be from the point of view of political morality." Ronald Dworkin, *Law's Empire* (Cambridge, Mass.: Harvard Univ. Press, 1986), at 411.

[4] *Military and Paramilitary Activities (Nicaragua v United States)*, 1986 ICJ 14 (June 27), ¶ 264; *see, e.g.*, Declaration on Principles of International Law Concerning Friendly Relations and Co-operation Among States in Accordance with the Charter of the United Nations [hereinafter Friendly Relations Declaration], G.A. Res 2625 (1970).

and the rule of law, the effective control doctrine continues to play a crucial role in setting the international system's default position on ascriptions of the statuses of "state" and "government." Consequently, the international community's resolutions of the pressing recognition questions of the day, from the 2008 Kosovar Unilateral Declaration of Independence to the 2009 Honduran *coup d'etat*, are destined to have an ad hoc quality that will leave observers (and, of course, many partisans) unsatisfied.

# I. Effective Control and the Assessment of Secession Questions

## A. "RECOGNITION" AND INTERNATIONAL LEGAL STATUS: CONSTITUTIVE AND DECLARATORY APPROACHES

Although the conferral of international legal status on states and governments is typically discussed in the same breath with "recognition," the precise relationship between the entity's legal status and other states' recognition of the entity remains unresolved in international law. Most authorities repeat the orthodoxy that the entity's legal status is an objective matter and that the entity's reception by other states is merely "declaratory," rather than "constitutive," of that status,[5] but the reality is more complicated than such assertions suggest.

One source of confusion is that "recognition" in this context is ordinarily identified with overt gestures—such as declarations of recognition, the opening of full diplomatic relations, the issuance of certificates of recognition addressed to internal courts, or the admission of the entity (or, in the case of a putative government, the credentialing of its representatives) to an international organization for which statehood is a requirement—that are, even though ***sufficient*** indications, not ***necessary*** concomitants of a legal consciousness that the entity bears a particular status. A foreign state may acknowledge (or ***take cognizance of***) the entity's legal status, even while being unwilling to make what looks like a political statement in the entity's favor. An aggregation of such acknowledgments, reflecting the *opinio juris* of the greater part of the international community, is much more plausibly constitutive of statehood than the orthodox view concedes.[6]

[5] *See, e.g.*, Conference on Yugoslavia Arbitration Commission, Opinions on Questions Arising from the Dissolution of Yugoslavia, 31 I.L.M. 1488, 1495 (1992).

[6] According to the most celebrated publicist of recognition practice, Sir Hersch Lauterpacht (writing in 1947), the view of recognition

> approximating most closely to the practice of States and to a working juridical principle is: (a) that recognition consists in the application of a rule of international law by way of ascertaining the existence of the requisite conditions of statehood; and (b) that the fulfillment of that

Even those who deny that recognition is legally constitutive of status tend to concede its indirect legal relevance.[7] Without question, while an elaborate body of legal doctrine purports to govern status determinations, whether a territorial entity actually experiences the legal benefits of statehood turns on whether other states treat the entity as having statehood's legal attributes. As with the old riddle, "If a tree falls in a forest and no one is there to hear it, does it make a sound?" there may be little practical consequence to an objective legal status that the relevant community fails to acknowledge. It remains to be asked only whether the position adopted by states, collectively or aggregatively, can be said to govern the entity's entitlements[8] or whether, by contrast, the entitlements are so fully objective that where the bulk of

> function in the affirmative sense—and nothing else—brings into being the plenitude of the normal rights and duties which international law attaches to statehood.

Hersch Lauterpacht, *Recognition in International Law* (Cambridge Univ. Press, 1947), at 73. Thus, members of the international community (either separately or in coordination) have a duty to recognize as states those entities that qualify for the status under applicable legal criteria, but it is only their implementation of this duty that brings statehood into being. Lauterpacht expressed the point as follows:

> [T]he full international personality of rising communities . . . cannot be automatic . . . . [A]s its ascertainment requires the prior determination of fact and law, there must be *someone* to perform that task. In the absence of a preferable solution, such as the setting up of an impartial international organ to perform that function, the latter must be fulfilled by States already existing. The valid objection is not against the fact of their discharging it, but against their carrying it out as a matter of arbitrary policy as distinguished from legal duty.

*Id.* at 55.

[7] James Crawford, for example, maintains that "An entity is not a State because it is recognized; it is recognized because it is a State." James Crawford, *The Creation of States in International Law* (Oxford Univ. Press, 2d ed. 2006), at 93. He nonetheless maintains that recognition can

> have important legal and political effects. Recognition is an institution of State practice that can resolve uncertainties as to status and allow for new situations to be regularized. That an entity is recognized as a State is evidence of its status; where recognition is general, it may be practically conclusive. States, in the forum of the United Nations or elsewhere, may make declarations as to status or "recognize" entities the status of which is doubtful; depending on the degree of unanimity and other factors this may be evidence of a compelling kind.

*Id.* at 27 (footnotes omitted). However, since the presence or absence of objective criteria can be independently ascertained (and indeed, far more accurately so in the absence of the distortions introduced by diplomacy), it makes no sense to speak of recognition as providing "evidence"—let alone "practically conclusive" evidence—for an entity's fulfillment of such criteria. What recognition establishes is not some empirical truth about the entity, but rather the position that states and intergovernmental organizations take toward the entity.

[8] Crawford rejects this reasoning on the ground that in international law generally, neither individual nor collective determinations of states have definitive legal effect. Crawford, *supra*, at 20. But the notorious puzzle of the role of *opinio juris* in customary law formation is precisely this: that a legal duty is constituted, in part, by the widespread state perception of the existence of the duty. The anomaly seems no worse in the application of norms than in their formation.

the international community is seen to misapply the fixed legal criteria, states treating the entity in accordance with that collective misapplication can be said thereby to breach their legal obligations.[9]

Either view is conceptually possible, but as a practical matter, the latter view seems implausible, for at least two reasons. First, it assumes away the international community's need for authoritative judgment as to whether particular doctrinally relevant events will be permitted to affect an entity's legal status; the facts on the ground can hardly be said to speak for themselves, and yet remarkable coordination has prevailed in this area of state practice, as evidenced by the paucity of genuine recognition controversies in contrast to the plethora of intense crises of local authority. Second, the collective *opinio juris* in application to the case at hand, if clearly manifested and essentially uniform, can be construed as a refinement of accepted legal doctrine and thus as itself a lawmaking phenomenon.

Even if collective legal acknowledgment of an entity's status is ultimately constitutive, such acknowledgment is composed of the individual recognition practices of foreign ministries and intergovernmental organizations, which are bound to determine those practices in light of international law, with an error in either direction potentially entailing a breach of legal obligation. Moreover, where the international reaction is split (e.g., in respect of Kosovo) or where it is difficult to discern whether prevailing state practice reflects *opinio juris* or is purely political in character (e.g., in respect of Taiwan),[10] there is no substitute for an independent determination of whether the legal criteria of statehood have been objectively fulfilled.

## B. EFFECTIVITY AS AN ASPECT OF THE TRADITIONAL CRITERIA OF STATEHOOD

The characteristics of statehood are routinely said to be those four listed in Article 1 of the 1933 Montevideo Convention on Rights and Duties of States: "(a) a permanent population; (b) a defined territory; (c) a government; (d) the capacity to enter into relations with other states."[11] This enumeration reflects that Convention's

[9] That this is not an entirely moot question is demonstrated by Robert D. Sloane, "The Changing Face of Recognition in International Law: A Case Study of Tibet," 16 *Emory Int'l L. Rev.* 107 (2002). Sloane attributes Tibet's pre-1950 lack of international recognition wholly to the combination of Tibet's peculiarly unassertive leadership and the crassly political decisions of the very few interacting states. He contends that China's control of the territory to this day represents an illegal occupation of a Tibetan state that maintains an objective legal existence. *Id.* at 135–51.

[10] *See* Brad R. Roth, "The Entity That Dare Not Speak Its Name: Unrecognized Taiwan as a Right-Bearer in the International Legal Order," 4 *E. Asia L. Rev.* 91 (2009); Roth,"Taiwan's Nation-Building and Beijing's Anti-Secession Law: An International Law Perspective," in Chen Chi-sen, et al. ed., *Sovereignty, Constitution, and the Future of Taiwan* (Taiwan Law Society, 2006), 1.

[11] For text, see 28 *Am. J. Int'l L.* (Supp. 1934) at 75.

purpose of placing respect for the rights of states on a non-discretionary and ideologically neutral footing. The Convention sought to predicate the entity's status, not on political predilection or moral entitlement (as to which competing interests and values promised to generate endless controversy), but on whether the entity constituted an objective political unit, not subject to the law of another state, that had to be reckoned with on the basis of international law.

Article 3 thus affirms that "[t]he political existence of the state is independent of recognition by the other states," and ascribes to the state "[e]ven before recognition... the right to defend its integrity and independence, to provide for its conservation and prosperity, and consequently to organize itself as it sees fit, to legislate upon its interests, administer its services, and to define the jurisdiction and competence of its courts." The reference in Article 1 to "the capacity to enter into relations with other states" thus appears to have been intended, not as conditioning statehood on the entity's reception by other states, but as excluding entities whose international relations were confessedly subordinate to another state—i.e., units of federal states (e.g., Michigan, Tasmania) and territories that have full internal self-governance but are dependent in external affairs (e.g., "associated statehood" arrangements, such as the relationship of the Cook Islands to New Zealand).[12]

As independent criteria for statehood, "permanent population" and "defined territory" merely beg the question, since virtually all statehood claims, whether or not accepted in the international legal order, characteristically include sufficiently precise claims on behalf of a permanent population to a defined territory. What matters in the Montevideo Convention context is that the "permanent population" and "defined territory" be united by some common and distinguishing pattern of effective governance. Thus, if taken as the legal standard for international personality, the Montevideo criteria would confer sovereign rights, obligations, powers, and immunities on any territorially coherent political community found under the long-term effective control of an independent government.

However, such a standard falls far short of capturing the essence of traditional recognition practice. Many states have continued to be recognized as undivided political units notwithstanding the failure of the central government to maintain effective control over substantial parts of the national territory. Indeed, in some cases, new states were recognized without a central government ever having established effective control throughout the territory.[13] A state is more plausibly

[12] A state "has competence, within its own constitutional system, to conduct international relations... as well as the political, technical, and financial capabilities to do so." *Restatement (Third) of the Foreign Relations Law of the United States* (1987), sec. 201, comment e; *see* Christopher J. Carolan, "The 'Republic of Taiwan': A Legal-Historical Justification for a Taiwanese Declaration of Independence," 75 *NYU L. Rev.* 429, 455 & n.167 (2000).

[13] This has been true in, for example, the contexts of decolonization (*e.g.*, Democratic Republic of the Congo in 1960 and Angola in 1975) and state dissolution (*e.g.*, Croatia and Bosnia-Herzegovina in 1992).

defined, in conformity with recognition practice, not as a territorially based political community that is effectively self-governing, but as a territorially based political community that existing states collectively decide ***ought*** to be self-governing, whether based on existing, remembered, or foreseen patterns of governance within it.

Insofar the international community's deviations from the effective control requirement can be attributed to a doctrinal logic, three countervailing traditional doctrines can be identified: (1) the Stimson Doctrine, (2) the rule against "premature" recognition, and (3) the principle of self-determination of peoples as applied to the project of decolonization.

The Stimson Doctrine, so named for the early-1930s efforts of the U.S. Secretary of State to mobilize opposition to the recognition of Manchukuo, holds that a foreign state's unlawful intervention—in that case, Japan's invasion of the northern Chinese province of Manchuria in violation of the 1928 Kellogg-Briand Pact of Paris—cannot be allowed to yield a successful secession.[14] The Stimson Doctrine remains relevant to this day and has precluded almost all states from recognizing breakaway regions of Georgia (Abkhazia and South Ossetia, unlawfully sponsored by Russia),[15] Moldova (Transnistria, unlawfully sponsored by Russia),[16] Azerbaijan (Nagorno-Karabakh, unlawfully sponsored by Armenia),[17] and Cyprus (the Turkish Republic of Northern Cyprus, unlawfully sponsored by Turkey).[18]

Unlike the Stimson Doctrine, the rule against premature recognition operates even in the absence of unlawful foreign assistance to a secession movement. Rather, it asserts that premature recognition itself constitutes unlawful intervention in the internal affairs of the preexisting state.[19] The rule is premised on the state's sovereign right to use force within national boundaries to preserve its territorial integrity and

[14] *See, e.g.,* Malcolm Shaw, *International Law* (Cambridge Univ. Press, 5th ed. 2003), 390–91. *See also* International Law Commission, Articles on State Responsibility (2001), arts. 40–41 ("No State shall recognize as lawful a situation created by" a "gross or systematic failure by the responsible State to fulfil" a peremptory obligation, nor may it "render aid or assistance in maintaining that situation"); *Legal Consequences of the Construction of a Wall in the Occupied Palestinian Territory, Advisory Opinion,* 2004 ICJ Rep. 36 (July 9), Kooijmans sep. op., ¶¶ 43–44 (obligation of non-recognition of unlawful situation applies to "legal claims to territory").

[15] *See, e.g.,* Christopher J. Borgen, "The Language of Law and the Practice of Politics: Great Powers and the Rhetoric of Self-Determination in the Cases of Kosovo and South Ossetia," 10 *Chi. J. Int'l L.* 1 (2009).

[16] *See, e.g.,* Christopher J. Borgen, "Imagining Sovereignty, Managing Secession: The Legal Geography of Eurasia's 'Frozen Conflicts,'" 9 *Or. Rev. Int'l L.* 477 (2007).

[17] *See* S.C. Res. 822, 853, 874, and 884 (1993) (calling for withdrawal of Armenian troops).

[18] *See* S.C. Res. 541 (1983) (on the "invalidity" of the TRNC's declaration of independence).

[19] *See, e.g.,* Shaw, *supra,* at 383.

its right against any interference with such efforts by a foreign state.[20] The Brierly treatise explains the rule's contours as follows:

> It is impossible to determine by fixed rules the moment at which other states may justly grant recognition of a new state; it can only be said that so long as a real struggle is proceeding, recognition is premature, whilst, on the other hand, mere persistence of the old state in a struggle that has obviously become hopeless is not a sufficient cause for withholding it.[21]

Lauterpacht went a bit further to say that "the sovereignty of the mother country is a legally relevant factor so long as it not abundantly clear that the lawful government has lost all hope or abandoned all effort to reassert its dominion."[22]

But in reality, the rule is even harsher in application. As Crawford points out:

> Since 1945 no state which has been created by unilateral secession has been admitted to the United Nations against the declared wishes of the government of the predecessor state. By contrast there are many examples of failed attempts at unilateral secession, including cases where the seceding entity maintained *de facto* independence for some time.[23]

One example is the case of Eritrea, which achieved international recognition only after Ethiopia's formal relinquishment, despite far earlier establishment of the "facts on the ground."[24] Even a clear-cut military victory by secessionist forces does not seem, in practice, to yield an international acknowledgment of independence until the original state concedes the point.

While the rule against premature recognition supplants "effective control through internal processes" as the actual touchstone of status in cases of secessionary wars, it operates on the same essential logic, qualified only by a "first in time" proviso.

[20] The Declaration on the Inadmissibility of Intervention and Interference in the Internal Affairs of States, G.A. Res. 36/103 (1981) [hereinafter "1981 Non-Intervention Declaration"] (passed 120-22-6 over the opposition of many Western liberal states) emphasized, *inter alia*, "[t]he duty of a state to refrain from the promotion, encouragement, or support, direct or indirect, of rebellious or secessionist activities within other States, *under any pretext whatsoever*, or any action which seems to disrupt the unity or to undermine or subvert the political order of other States." Annex, art. 2(f) (emphasis added). Similarly, the Friendly Relations Declaration, *supra*, G.A. Res. 2625 (1970), states that "no State shall . . . interfere in civil strife in another State."

[21] J.L. Brierly, *The Law of Nations* (6th ed., C.H.M. Waldock ed., 1963), 138, quoted in David A. Ijalaye, "Was 'Biafra' At Any Time a State in International Law?," 65 *Am. J. Int'l L.* 551, 558 (1971).

[22] Lauterpacht, *supra*, at 45–46, quoted in Ijalaye, *supra*, at 558.

[23] James Crawford, "State Practice and International Law in Relation to Secession," 69 *Brit. Y.B. Int'l L.* 85, 92 (1998) (footnote omitted); *see also id.* at 116 (summarizing non-recognition practice).

[24] *Id.* at 106–07.

The "prematurity" formulation implies that the boundaries of the "internal" are independent of the boundaries of effective control, until and unless the latter somehow "mature." Sovereignty is "earned" by effective struggle, with a very strong presumption in favor of the forces that earned it first. Not only are the borders between states, however much the result of past conquests, sanctified as of the inauguration of the current peace and security order, but the territorial integrity of existing states is all but frozen, subject to modification only through an unambiguous outcome of a trial by ordeal.

The third countervailing doctrine concerns self-determination as applied to Non-Self-Governing and Trust Territories, which the United Nations Charter-based order regards as not integral to the states governing them. Chapters XI to XIII of the Charter gave imprimatur to Western powers' control over colonized territories, but predicated the legitimacy of that control on fiduciary responsibility rather than sovereign authority. By 1960, that approach had given way to the demands for an end to colonialism in all of its forms.

General Assembly Resolution 1514 (XV), issued without a dissenting vote, fatefully stated: "All peoples have the right to self-determination; by virtue of that right they freely determine their political status and freely pursue their economic, social and cultural development."[25] However indeterminate the implications of this statement may be outside of the colonial realm, the consequences for Western European "salt water colonialism" were concrete:

> Immediate steps shall be taken, in Trust and Non-Self-Governing Territories or all other territories which have not yet attained independence, to transfer all powers to the peoples of those territories, without any conditions or reservations, in accordance with their freely expressed will and desire, without any distinction as to race, creed or colour, in order to enable them to enjoy complete independence and freedom.[26]

The accompanying resolution, 1541 (XV), though framed rather innocuously as an interpretation of an obscure obligation of colonial powers under Chapter XI of the Charter to "transmit information" on "economic, social, and educational conditions" in Non-Self-Governing Territories, in effect established (over the dissenting votes of only Portugal and South Africa) the criteria for specifying the territories,

[25] Declaration on the Granting of Independence to Colonial Countries and Peoples, G.A. Res. 1514 (XV) (1960) (89-0-9), ¶ 2. The Security Council reaffirmed the statement in S.C. Res. 183 (1963), ¶ 4. The same language is repeated in other declarations and instruments, and constitutes Article 1(1) of both the International Covenant on Civil and Political Rights, 999 U.N.T.S. 171, 171(1966) [hereinafter ICCPR] and the International Covenant on Economic, Social and Cultural Rights, 993 U.N.T.S. 3, 3 (1966).

[26] G.A. Res. 1514, ¶ 5.

upon the populations of which the previous resolution had conferred an immediate right to "freely determine their political status" by opting for sovereign independence. The category included any "territory which is geographically separate and is distinct ethnically and/or culturally from the country administering it" and which is subject to "administrative, political, juridical, economic, or historical" factors that "arbitrarily place it in a position or status of subordination."[27] In purporting to interpret Chapter XI, Resolution 1541 noted that the chapter's authors "had in mind" its application to "territories which were then known to be of the colonial type."[28] Whether this articulation of principle can so easily be cabined is another matter, but the immediate applications were unambiguous.[29]

Equally unambiguous was the authoritative position on the boundaries of territorial units emerging from colonial status: "Any attempt aimed at the partial or total disruption of the national unity and the territorial integrity of a country is incompatible with the purposes and principles of the Charter of the United Nations."[30] It was no accident that the most vociferous advocates of the right to self-determination, the new states emerging from decolonization, were also the most determined to limit its application. The new states perceived most keenly their vulnerability to territorial fragmentation and to threats to their political independence posed by (real and imagined) neocolonialist penetration. Thus, even though (and indeed, partly because) the newly independent units' central authorities had not fully established effective control throughout all parts of the allocated territories,[31] the dice were

[27] G.A. Res. 1541 (XV) (1960) (69-2-21), Annex, Principles I, IV, V. The "territory and its peoples" realize self-determination in one of three ways: "(a) Emergence as a sovereign independent State; (b) Free association with an independent State; (c) Integration with an independent State." The first option is framed not only as an absolute right, but as the presumptive outcome, whereas the latter two choices are laden with requisites calculated to assure that they result from a genuine exercise of popular will. *See id.*, Principles II, VI. VII, VIII, IX.

[28] *Id.*, Principle I.

[29] Although mere General Assembly resolutions, G.A. Res. 1514 and 1541 quickly attained the status of binding international law in the eyes of United Nations organs, notwithstanding "persistent objection" from Portugal and South Africa. *See* S.C. Res. 180 and 183 (1963) ("deprecating" Portugal's noncompliance and expressly confirming G.A. Res. 1514); Advisory Opinion of 21 June 1971 on The Legal Consequences for States of the Continued Presence of South Africa in Namibia (South West Africa) notwithstanding Security Council Resolution 276 (1970), 1971 I.C.J. Reports 16, 31-32 ("A further important stage in [the development of international law subsequent to the Charter] was the Declaration on the Granting of Independence to Colonial Countries and Peoples"); Advisory Opinion of October 16, 1975, on the Western Sahara, 1975 I.C.J. Rep. 12, 31--33, paras. 55–59.

[30] G.A. Res. 1514 (XV) (1960), *supra*, ¶ 6.

[31] Many emergent states were, as Robert Jackson puts it, mere "quasi-states": their statehood was "primarily juridical," for while they "have been internationally enfranchised and possess the same external rights and responsibilities as all other sovereign states," they were "deficient in the political will, institutional authority, and organized power to protect human rights or provide socioeconomic welfare."

heavily loaded against secessionist factions (beginning with Katangese insurgents in the Democratic Republic of the Congo).[32]

The strength of the presumption in favor of territorial integrity *vis-à-vis* internal contestants was driven by much the same concern as the separate and more overtly absolute insistence on the inviolability of post-decolonization boundaries *vis-à-vis* external contestants, i.e., the principle of *uti possidetis*. As the International Court of Justice explained in 1986:

> *Uti possidetis*, as a principle which upgraded former administrative delimitations, established during the colonial period, to international frontiers, is . . . a principle of a general kind which is logically connected with this form of decolonization wherever it occurs.
>
> The territorial boundaries which have to be respected may also derive from international frontiers which previously divided a colony of one State from a colony of another, or indeed a colonial territory from the territory of an independent State, or one which was under protectorate, but had retained its international personality. There is no doubt that the obligation to respect pre-existing international frontiers in the event of a State succession derives from a general rule of international law, whether or not the rule is expressed in the formula *uti possidetis*. . . .
>
> . . . At first sight this principle conflicts outright with another one, the right of peoples to self-determination. In fact, however, the maintenance of the territorial status quo in Africa is often seen as the wisest course, to preserve what has been achieved by peoples who have struggled for their independence, and to avoid a disruption which would deprive the continent of the gains achieved by much sacrifice. ***The essential requirement of stability in order to survive, to develop and gradually to consolidate their independence in all fields, has induced African States judiciously to consent to the respecting of colonial frontiers, and to take account of it in the interpretation of the principle of self-determination of peoples.***[33]

Thus, all of the traditional rules place a premium on territorial integrity. Even where these rules are at odds with actual effectivity, they favor the legal prerogative of existing states' central authorities to reestablish by forcible means the effective

Robert H. Jackson, *Quasi-States: Sovereignty, International Relations, and the Third World* (Cambridge: Cambridge University Press, 1990), at 21.

[32] *See* Rene Lemarchand, "The Limits of Self-Determination: The Case of the Katanga Secession," 56 *Am. Pol. Sci. Rev.* 404 (1962); M. Rafiqul Islam, "Secessionist Self-Determination: Some Lessons from Katanga, Biafra and Bangladesh," 22 *J. Peace Research* 211 (1985).

[33] Frontier Dispute (Burkina Faso/Republic of Mali), Judgment of December 22, 1986, 1986I.C.J. Rep. 554, 566–67, paras. 23–25 (emphasis added).

control that local resistance has compromised. Unless secessionist forces can, unaided by inadmissible foreign intervention, prevail upon an existing state to relinquish the territory in question, the traditional rules leave little prospect—except in the case of the most unambiguous victory in a civil war (and then, it seems, only notionally)—for a new state to emerge at the expense of an existing state's territorial integrity.

## C. SELF-DETERMINATION OF PEOPLES IN NON-COLONIAL CONTEXTS

Although the anticolonial movement was greatly concerned with non-fragmentation, it could not be content to limit the applicability of self-determination to the liberation of dependent territories, if for no other reason than that vestiges of colonialism might be preserved within independent entities. Southern Rhodesia's 1965 Unilateral Declaration of Independence, for example, separated the territory from the colonial power, but did not change the reality of colonial settler domination (and was, indeed, an effort to frustrate substantive decolonization); similarly, *apartheid* in South Africa, though colonialist in nature, was the policy of a sovereign state.

Moreover, the United Nations Charter establishes self-determination as a universal principle underlying the state system: not only does the Preamble ascribe authorship of the Charter to "We the Peoples of the United Nations," but the Charter's articulated moral grounding for the legal principle of sovereign equality (Article 2(1)) is found in the underlying "purpose" of developing "friendly relations among nations based on respect for the principle of equal rights and self-determination of peoples" (Article 1(2)).[34] Thoroughgoing decolonization, based on the insistence that "[a]ll peoples have the right to self-determination" and thus a right "freely [to] determine their political status," sought to effectuate for collectivities residing in Non-Self-Governing and Trust Territories a standing presumed to be enjoyed already by the populations of established states, whatever their prevailing governmental systems.

The 1970 Friendly Relations Declaration, after recapitulating the essence of 1960 Resolutions 1514 and 1541, added the following "safeguard clause":

> Nothing in the foregoing paragraphs shall be construed as authorizing or encouraging any action which would dismember or impair, totally or in

[34] For the elaboration of the connection between sovereignty and self-determination, viewed from the standpoint of the "Non-Aligned" bloc that played a central role in Charter interpretation in the postcolonial era, see Djura Ninčić, *The Problem of Sovereignty in the Charter and in the Practice of the United Nations* (The Hague: Martinus Hijhoff, 1970).

> part, the territorial integrity or political unity of sovereign and independent States ***conducting themselves in compliance with the principle of equal rights and self-determination of peoples as described above and thus possessed of a government representing the whole people belonging to the territory without distinction as to race, creed or colour.***[35]

This was a test that Rhodesia and South Africa were intended to fail, but that garden-variety "scientific socialist" and "Bandung nationalist" one-party regimes, "representing" their populations within the terms established by their prevailing ideologies, were intended to pass.[36]

Despite overwhelming international resistance to a right to secession outside the colonial context, self-determination continues to be presented as a right of general applicability. Thus, when India attached to its ratification of the International Covenant on Civil and Political Rights (ICCPR) a declaration interpreting the right of self-determination in Article 1 to "apply only to the peoples under foreign domination and [not] to sovereign independent States or to a section of a people or a nation," invoking in support of this interpretation "the essence of national integrity," this declaration drew objections from the Netherlands, France, and the Federal Republic of Germany.[37]

However, the formulation of self-determination as a right possessed by "all peoples" raises daunting questions. It is not even clear that the statement is anything more than a disguised tautology: since the definition of "peoples" is not fixed independently of the entitlement to self-determination, it remains open to argue that a grouping is certifiable as a "people" only once it is ascertained to possess the entitlement.[38] Article 27 of the ICCPR separately covers "ethnic, religious or linguistic minorities" within existing states. Whatever academic theories may be brought to bear on the question—including considerations of, for example, religion, race, ethnicity, culture, kinship, territorial separateness or prior conquest—a "people" is in the final analysis a political community that authoritative organs of the international community acknowledge as such, and such acknowledgment has been hard to come by.

[35] G.A. Res. 2625, *supra* (emphasis added). Subsequent iterations have broadened the last clause of the qualifier to speak of "a government representing the whole people . . . without distinction of any kind." *See* G.A. Res. 50/6 (1995); United Nations World Conference on Human Rights, Vienna Declaration and Programme of Action, June 25, 1993, 32 I.L.M. 1661, 1665 (1993).

[36] *See, e.g.*, Antonio Cassese, *Self-Determination of Peoples: A Legal Reappraisal* (Cambridge University Press, 1995), 115–18 (discussing the preparatory work to the safeguard clause, which reveals concessions to non-liberal-democratic states).

[37] James Crawford, "The Right of Self-Determination in International Law: Its Development and Future," in Philip Alston ed., *People's Rights* (Oxford: Oxford Univ. Press, 2001), 7 at 28.

[38] *See, e.g.*, Timothy William Waters, "Contemplating Failure and Creating Alternatives in the Balkans: Bosnia's Peoples, Democracy, and the Shape of Self-Determination," 29 *Yale J. Int'l L.* 423, 432–35 (2004).

Even "indigenous peoples," the substate groups to which the self-determination right might most plausibly apply, were long explicitly denied this status; tellingly, the 1991 International Labor Organization Convention Concerning Indigenous and Tribal Peoples in Independent Countries insisted that "[t]he use of the term 'peoples' in this Convention shall not be construed as having any implications as regards the rights which may attach to the term under international law."[39] The 2007 United Nations Declaration on the Rights of Indigenous Peoples[40] passed over dissenting votes of the United States, Canada, Australia, and New Zealand, finally ascribed to indigenous peoples the right to self-determination, nominally including the right to "freely determine their political status,"[41] but pointedly excluding any impairment of existing states' "territorial integrity or political unity."[42] This qualification—which entails a seeming literal contradiction—apparently assuaged African states that had theretofore insisted that the "principle of self-determination applies only to peoples under colonial and/or foreign occupation."[43]

Instructive as to the ambiguity of "peoples" is the domestic court decision dealing most elaborately with the international law of self-determination, the Canadian Supreme Court's advisory opinion in *Reference re Secession of Quebec.*[44] In deciding that the right, though applicable in the non-colonial context, would not justify the unilateral secession of Quebec, the court managed to sidestep the elemental question of whether the "people" entitled to self-determination was comprised of (a) the entire Quebec population, (b) the entire Quebec population minus the indigenous communities, (c) Francophone Quebecois, or (d) all Francophone Canadians.[45] It stressed merely that none of these groups is blocked from the

[39] Convention Concerning Indigenous and Tribal Peoples in Independent Countries (ILO No. 169), 72 ILO Official Bulletin 59, entered into force Sept. 5, 1991, art. 1(3).

[40] G.A. Res. 61/295 (Sept. 12, 2007) (143-4-11).

[41] *Id.*, art. 3.

[42] *Id.*, art. 46.

[43] African Group, Draft Aide Memoire on United Nations Declaration on the Rights of Indigenous Peoples, Nov. 9, 2006 <http://www.ipacc.org.za/uploads/docs/Africanaidememoire.pdf>.

[44] Reference re Secession of Quebec, 1 S.C.R. 217 (1998), *available at* <www.scc-csc.gc.ca/reference/rea.htm>.

[45] *Id.* at ¶ 125. For an argument that "the inhabitants of Quebec" do not constitute a "people" with a right to self-determination, *see* Johan D. van der Vyver, "Self-Determination of the Peoples of Quebec under International Law," 2 *J. Transnat'l L & Policy* 1, 21 (2000). Interestingly, in 2006, the Canadian House of Commons officially recognized "that the Québécois form a nation within a united Canada," reportedly intending "nation" to be understood in a "cultural-sociological" rather than in a legal sense. CBC News, "House Passes Motion Recognizing Québécois as Nation," Nov. 27, 2006, *available at* <http://www.cbc.ca/canada/story/2006/11/27/nation-vote.html#ixzz0rcRZwjMg>. Yet there remains an evident strategic ambiguity about the precise delimitations of this "nation," an ambiguity similar to that which has plagued the Quebec sovereignty movement. (Upon losing the 1995 sovereignty referendum with 49.4 percent of the vote, Quebec Premier Jacques Parizeau made bitter remarks about non-Francophone voters that cast doubt on his movement's purportedly

meaningful exercise of self-determination, since Canada is "possessed of a government representing the whole people belonging to the territory without distinction."[46]

The most elegant reconciliation of the competing considerations lies in the withholding of recognition to any distinct "people" wherever an existing state is perceived to extend to all parts of the territorial population (including its "ethnic, religious or linguistic minorities") some minimally adequate inclusion in the benefits of governance. A "people" would thus equate to the whole population of an existing state or Non-Self-Governing or Trust Territory—an interpretation consistent with the literal terms of the Friendly Relations Declaration (which refers to "the whole people belonging to the territory"), though not those of Resolution 1541 (which refers to "the peoples of the territory")—in the absence of some extraordinary system of oppression. A *de jure* caste system—especially one, such as *apartheid,* associated with the international order's "original sin," Western colonialism—thus overcomes the presumption, vitiating both the state's claim to sovereign inviolability and its claim to encompass one self-determining people.[47]

An arguable implication of the safeguard clause's wording is that, in cases where the arbitrarily subordinated subcommunity is territorially coherent (by its nature, rather than by virtue of *Bantustans* imposed for the oppressors' purposes), such a caste system might prompt the recognition of a separate people with a right to choose its political status (i.e., an option on sovereign independence).[48] Even so, a question would remain as to whether a mere garden-variety *de facto,* rather than a

inclusionary vision of Quebec nationhood; he was, however, immediately obliged thereupon to resign.) The Parliamentary statement needs to be read alongside two previous unsuccessful constitutional reform proposals that would have recognized Quebec as a "distinct society."

[46] Reference re Secession of Quebec, *supra,* at ¶ 136. *But see* Crawford, "The Right of Self-Determination," *supra,* at 59–60 (construing the court's position as consistent with "both the view that self-determination applies to peoples in the ordinary sense of the term, and is not confined to the whole population of existing states, and the view that several peoples may coexist in relation to a particular territory"); Patrick Dumberry, "Lessons Learned from the *Quebec Secession Reference* before the Supreme Court of Canada," in Marcelo G. Kohen ed., *Secession: International Law Perspectives* (Cambridge Univ. Press, 2006),416 at 436 (court's opinion implies "juxtaposition of many" peoples within Quebec).

[47] The idea that the safeguard clause provides a formula for vitiating sovereign inviolability, without a necessary further consequence of establishing peoplehood or licensing territorial fragmentation, may be more promising. Although not accompanied by invocations of such a rationale, the absence of opposition to the 1991 U.S.-U.K. intervention in Iraqi Kurdistan (not widely discussed as unlawful, despite the absence of express legal authorization) and of strong, broad-based opposition to the 1999 NATO intervention in Kosovo (widely discussed as unlawful, but as perhaps legitimated by the international order's emerging values) might usefully be seen through this lens.

[48] *See, e.g.,* Antonio Cassese, *Self-Determination of Peoples: A Legal Reappraisal* (Cambridge Univ. Press, 1995), at 120; *but see* Malcolm N. Shaw, "Peoples, Territorialism, and Boundaries," 8 *Euro. J. Int'l L.* 478, 483 (1997), rejecting this interpretation of the "safeguard clause" on the ground, *inter alia,* that "[s]uch a major change in legal principle cannot be introduced by way of an ambiguous subordinate

neocolonial *de jure*, system of arbitrary subordination within an existing state, covering the majority of inhabitants of a discrete region, establishes a people entitled "to choose its political status."[49]

Although this non-committal interpretation of peoplehood would square the circle, many commentators prefer instead to posit some substantive understanding of the concept, even though none has been authoritatively established.[50] These commentators do not ascribe to substate groups an option on sovereign independence, but instead invoke a "right to internal self-determination" that reconciles self-determination with inviolability of territorial integrity.[51] The original authoritative instruments leave little room to read choice of "political status" as anything short of an option on sovereign independence, but since the 2007 Declaration on the Rights of Indigenous Peoples effectively reduces this language's payoff to "the right to autonomy or self-government in matters relating to [the indigenous peoples'] internal and local affairs, as well as ways and means for financing their autonomous functions,"[52] advocates of a group right to internal self-determination for ordinary ethnic, religious or linguistic minorities or historically subordinated regions can take heart.

Outside the special context of indigenous peoples, however, there is no direct international legal mandate for any of the consociational frameworks that certain domestic systems have employed to empower substate groups—a wide range of devices that includes territorial autonomy, representational quotas in governmental

clause, especially when the principle of territorial integrity has always been accepted and proclaimed as a core principle of international law . . . ."

[49] The international recognition of Bangladesh, albeit not conferred until Pakistan had conceded the point, might be taken to represent an implicit vindication of this suggestion. Although the U.N. General Assembly had responded to the 1971 Indian invasion by calling for an immediate withdrawal of forces from foreign territory, G.A. Res. 2793 (XXVI) (Dec. 7, 1971) (104-11-10), the international community accepted the new state born of India's use of force once Pakistan had been prevailed upon to acquiesce. There were, of course, other factors that might be said to render the case anomalous, such as the former state's territorial non-contiguity and seceding region's encompassing of a majority of the former state's population. For an exploration of the contrasts between this case and failed secessionist efforts, *see* Islam, *supra*, 22 *J. Peace Research* 211.

[50] *See, e.g.*, David Raič, *Statehood and the Law of Self-Determination* (Kluwer Law International, 2002) 226–307; Jane Wright, "Minority Groups, Autonomy, and Self Determination," 19 *Oxford J. Legal Studies* 605, 625–27 (1999); *but see, e.g.*, Gaetano Pentassuglia, *Minorities in International Law: An Introductory Study* (Council of Europe Publishing, 2002) 168, who insists on an "ethnically and culturally neutral, thus territorially-based notion of a 'people.'" and similarly Patrick Thornberry, 'Self-Determination, Minorities, Human Rights: A Review of International Instruments' 38 *Int'l & Comp. L. Q.* 867 (1989).

[51] *See, e.g.*, Raič, *supra*, at 226–307; Wright, *supra*, at 628–29; Allan Rosas, "Internal Self-Determination" in Christian Tomuschat ed., *Modern Law of Self-Determination* (Martinus Nijhoff, 1993), 225.

[52] G.A. Res. 61/295, *supra*, art. 4.

and other institutions, supermajority legislative voting rules for group-sensitive subject matter, and much more.[53] Thus far, particular solutions of this nature remain matters of sovereign discretion. While various efforts have been undertaken to confer international status on minority groups as such,[54] the dominant approach has been to ascribe international rights solely to individual "persons belonging to such minorities,"[55] partly so as to avert an ensuing rivalry between "national" minorities accorded group rights and "non-autochthonous" minorities denied them,[56] and partly so as to avoid endorsing cultural restrictions that an autonomous group might impose on individuals in its midst.[57]

In any event, the putative "right to internal self-determination," whatever its pedigree or merits, has no specific bearing on the question of secession. The issue remains whether international law provides for a right of secession in case of an extreme *de facto* violation of the normative expectations that undergird the existing state's right to territorial integrity. In the past, the international order's ideological pluralism, established by accord among discrete First, Second, and Third Worlds, excluded only Axis-era fascism and the vestiges of saltwater colonialism. While this pluralism has narrowed substantially in less-fraught contexts, the assertion of a more exacting set of normative requisites to the inviolability of territorial integrity, in opening a potential Pandora's Box of secessionist claims, may be incompatible with the international order's overriding imperatives of maintaining peaceful and respectful relations among states as they actually are, and of discouraging the kinds of internal conflicts that tend to exacerbate overall levels of human rights violations.

## D. NONCONSENSUAL DISSOLUTION OF FEDERAL STATES: THE BADINTER IMPROVISATION

The doctrinal framework summarized above can be said in some way to encompass (even if it might not compellingly explain) the international responses to almost all

[53] *See, e.g.,* Ruth Lapidoth, *Autonomy: Flexible Solutions To Ethnic Conflicts* (Washington, DC, United States Institute of Peace Press, 1997).

[54] *See* Shaw, "Peoples, Territorialism, and Boundaries," *supra,* at 486, citing European documents, such as the Council of Europe's 1995 Framework Convention for Protection of National Minorities, that, "while extremely cautiously formulated and accompanied by significant provisos," introduce "a territorial dimension into minority rights within the territorial framework of independent states."

[55] *See* ICCPR, *supra,* art. 27; Declaration on the Rights of Persons Belonging to National or Ethnic, Religious and Linguistic Minorities, G.A. Res. 47/135 (Dec. 18, 1992).

[56] *See, e.g.,* Sabrina P. Ramet, *The Three Yugoslavias: State-Building and Legitimation, 1918–2005* (Bloomington, Indiana: Indiana Univ. Press, 2006) at 560 (noting this distinction in Slovenian law).

[57] *See* Lovelace v. Canada, Communication No. R.6/24 (December 29,1977), U.N. Doc. Supp.No. 40 (A/36/40) at 166 (1981) (Human Rights Committee upholds under ICCPR Article 27 the right of an individual member of an indigenous band to privileges of band membership, from which her previous marriage to a non-indigenous person could not disqualify her).

secession crises that have occurred in the period of the United Nations Charter-based order. But at least one substantial outlier remains: the breakup of the Socialist Federal Republic of Yugoslavia (SFRY). Investigation of the international *opinio juris* in reaction to that development is aided by the existence of quasi-authoritative documents establishing a legal rationale: the contemporaneous judgments of the European Community's Conference on Yugoslavia Arbitration Commission, known by the name of its chair, French Constitutional Council President Robert Badinter.[58]

The Yugoslav state established after World War I maintained a continuous international legal personality until the early 1990s, despite major disruptions of its patterns of internal governance, a World War II-era Axis-sponsored *de facto* secession of an Independent State of Croatia (NDH) (more or less encompassing the territory of what is now Croatia and Bosnia-Herzegovina), and a series of socialist-era constitutional reforms that decentralized substantial governmental authority into the hands of regional administrative units bearing distinctive ethnic compositions. The SFRY was constitutionally organized as a federation—made up of six Republics, one of which (Serbia) contained two special autonomous provinces—that recognized its inhabitants as at once Yugoslav citizens, citizens of their respective territorial republics, and members of their respective ethnic groups.[59] The ruling party's monopoly on power at all levels, operating under the anti-ethno-nationalist banner of "Brotherhood and Unity," counteracted the tension arising from the imperfect fit between ethnic populations and the territorial boundaries of ethnically inspired federal units. The unraveling of one-party rule, however, prompted democratization on a republic-by-republic basis, with ethno-nationalist parties in the lead, while ethno-nationalists from Yugoslavia's largest republic and plurality ethnic group wholly or partially captured institutions at the center—most importantly, the armed forces. The government of the Republic of Serbia and most of the Serb population of other republics favored centralization of Yugoslavia, whereas other elements of the federation—often for economic and political as well as ethnic reasons—sought a transformation that would leave Yugoslavia as, at most, a confederation.

[58] Conference on Yugoslavia Arb. Comm'n, Opinions on Questions Arising from the Dissolution of Yugoslavia, Jan. 11 and July 4, 1992 [hereinafter, *Badinter Commission Opinions*], 31 I.L.M. 1488 (1992). For trenchant criticisms of the Badinter Commission opinions, *see, e.g.*, Waters, "Contemplating Failure," *supra*, 29 *Yale J. Int'l L.* at 438–44; Miodrag Jovanovic, *Constitutionalizing Secession in Federalized States: A Procedural Approach* (Utrecht: Eleven International Publishing, 2007), 83–114; Peter Radan, "Yugoslavia's Internal Borders as International Borders: A Question of Appropriateness," 33:2 E. European Q. 137 (1999); Radan, *The Break-Up of Yugoslavia and International Law* (New York: Routledge, 2002).

[59] *See* Susan L. Woodward, *Balkan Tragedy: Chaos and Dissolution after the Cold War* (Washington, DC: The Brookings Institution, 1995), at 29–41.

In late 1991, the Badinter Commission confronted the following circumstances: clear majority voter support for independence, expressed in referenda and/or legislative acts, in Slovenia, Croatia, Bosnia-Herzegovina, and Macedonia (four of Yugoslavia's six republics); effective establishment of an independent Slovenia after a very brief and decisive armed confrontation with the (Serbian-dominated) Yugoslav People's Army (JNA); an ongoing and brutal war in Croatia pitting Croatian Government forces against a combination of JNA forces and Croatian Serb irregulars; manifest militant opposition by the bulk of Bosnia's minority Serb community to the prospect of an independent Bosnian state that would assert authority over Serb inhabitants.

Faced with this situation, the Badinter Commission resolved to delegitimate further uses of force across republic boundaries. It did so, however, in a way that is difficult to reconcile with traditional doctrines.

The Commission asserted that:

> in the case of a federal-type State, which embraces communities that possess a degree of autonomy and, moreover, participate in the exercise of political power within the framework of institutions common to the Federation, the existence of the State implies that the federal organs represent the components of the Federation and wield effective power[.][60]

The Commission found, however, that:

> The composition and workings of the essential organs of the federation ... no longer meet the criteria of participation and representativeness inherent in a federal state;
>
> The recourse to force has led to armed conflict from the different elements of the federation which has caused the death of thousands of people and wrought considerable destruction within a few months. The authorities of the Federation and the Republics have shown themselves to be powerless to enforce respect for ... ceasefire agreements ....[61]

Since the very existence of the Yugoslav state presupposed functioning federal institutions, the Commission deduced, the collapse of these institutions and the recourse to force entailed nothing less than "a process of dissolution" of the Yugoslav state into its component republics.

The Yugoslav state was thereby said to be losing its international legal personality, with the six republics collectively succeeding to that personality.[62] Furthermore,

[60] Badinter Commission Opinions, *supra*, No. 1, para 1(d) (Jan. 11, 1992), 31 I.L.M. at 1495.

[61] *Id.*, No. 1, ¶ 2, 31 I.L.M. at 1496--97.

[62] *Id.*, No. 1, ¶ 3, 31 I.L.M. at 1498, 1500.

with the disappearance of central authority, the republics' territorial relations *inter se* were to be governed (even before the territories' objective emergence as states, let alone any formal external recognition) by the venerable principle of *uti possidetis*, which in the decolonization context had ascribed to the newly independent states their previous colonial boundaries.[63]

Consequently, the Commission found, the borders of the component republics represented inviolable boundaries as a matter of international law in the course of the "process of dissolution." Whatever might be said for a Bosnian Serb right to self-determination, this could not be implemented through forcible changes in the republic boundaries.[64] Bosnian Serbs might well have wondered why, if Bosnia-Herzegovina could be supported in its secession from Yugoslavia, a Bosnian Serb republic could not equally be supported in its effort to secede from Bosnia; the answer given was that Bosnia had not seceded, but had rather *succeeded* to a share, demarcated by the republic borders, of the legal personality of the dissolved Yugoslav federation.

Whatever merits might be attributed to this set of conclusions, the invocations of traditional doctrines in support of the result must be seen as a sleight of hand. The boundaries of a state's subdivisions do not ordinarily have international legal significance, nor does international law ordinarily take cognizance of the distinction between a federal and a unitary constitutional structure[65]; as the Montevideo Convention indicates, "The federal state shall constitute a sole person in the eyes of international law."[66] There is no traditional reason why a crisis of constitutional authority, even up to and including internal armed conflict, would change this. A corollary of states' "inalienable right" to choose their political systems is the right (whether carried out by established governments or by successful rebels) to overthrow their constitutions and to reconfigure internal boundaries. A federation's consensual dissolution—indeed, any partition of a state consented to by the effective authorities of all of the succeeding units—would have the effect of creating international legal personality for the new units and international boundaries between them. A nonconsensual "dissolution," however, has a more doctrinally appropriate name: civil war. Such a characterization would traditionally imply a corresponding duty of foreign states to maintain neutrality pending the outcome, and certainly a duty not to intervene against forces seeking to maintain the state's territorial integrity.[67]

[63] *Id.*, Nos. 2 and 3, 31 I.L.M. at 1498, 1500.

[64] *Id.*, Nos. 2 and 3, 31 I.L.M. at 1497–1500.

[65] For a statement of the general irrelevance—in either direction—of domestic constitutional law to the international law of secession, *see* Thornberry, *supra*, at 439– 43.

[66] Montevideo Convention, *supra*, art. 2.

[67] *See, e.g.*, Friendly Relations Declaration, *supra* ("no State shall . . . interfere in civil strife in another State"); 1981 Non-Intervention Declaration, *supra*, Annex, art. 2(f) (affirming '[t]he duty of a state to refrain from the promotion, encouragement, or support, direct or indirect, of rebellious or

The Badinter Commission's invocation of *uti possidetis* as a norm of general international law, applicable to the dissolution of central sovereign authority as well as to the withdrawal of colonial authority, is likely correct[68] but premature in application. Boundaries become inviolable as a result of a completed dissolution, not at the inception of a "process of dissolution."[69] If there is no mutual consent to dissolution, then dissolution would follow only from a decisive creation (by force, if necessary) of a stable set of new facts on the ground. But of course, such fact creation was precisely what the Commission—for perfectly plausible reasons of morality and policy—sought to preempt.

From the perspective of many Serbs, both in the "rump Yugoslavia" (Serbia and Montenegro) and in Croatia and Bosnia-Herzegovina, this outcome seemed arbitrary. The Commission sought to preclude both an armed struggle to maintain a (Serb-predominant) greater Yugoslavia, on the one hand, and international recognition of Serb-dominated entities seeking secession from newly independent states of Croatia and Bosnia, on the other, thereby thwarting the Serb ethno-national project at both ends. Meanwhile, by predicating Croatian and Bosnian independence on respect for preexisting internal boundaries amid the crisis of central authority, the Commission effectively vindicated Croat and Bosniak ethno-national projects (which the republic boundaries happened to fulfill),[70] conveniently without need of recourse to a claim that any of the groups in question constituted "peoples" with a right of external self-determination.

In the absence of a consensual dissolution, the Commission's analogy to decolonization breaks down: Not only had the colonial borders been external rather than internal, and the newly decolonized entities liberated from the colonial powers rather than from one another, but *uti possidetis* in that context had represented

secessionist activities within other States, *under any pretext whatsoever*, or any action which seems to disrupt the unity or to undermine or subvert the political order of other States" (emphasis added)); Convention on Duties and Rights of States in the Event of Civil Strife, 134 L.N.T.S. 45, entered into force May 21, 1929 (Inter-American treaty forbidding "the traffic in arms and war material, except when intended for the Government, while the belligerency of the rebels has not been recognized, in which latter case the rules of neutrality shall be applied"); Institut de Droit International, Resolution: The Principle of Non-Intervention in Civil Wars (Aug. 14, 1975) *available at* <http://www.idi-iil.org/idiE/resolutionsE/1975_wies_03_en.pdf>.

[68] Some critics have questioned whether this norm applies outside the special context of decolonization. *See* Jovanovic, *supra*, at 106.

[69] *See* Jovanovic, *supra*, at 107.

[70] It may be objected that the Republic of Bosnia and Herzegovina was not an ethno-national project and that some Serbs, especially in cosmopolitan Sarajevo, were loyal to the multi-ethnic Bosnian state. The reality is complex, as different agendas coexisted. By far the leading parties among all ethnic groups were the respective ethno-nationalist parties, and the initial alliance of Bosniak and Bosnian Croat nationalists can be interpreted as tactical (it unraveled into brutal warfare in 1993–94) rather than reflective of any transcendence of ethno-nationalism.

maintenance of the *status quo inter se* rather than, as in the Yugoslav context, a drastic shift in power relations among the emergent states' constituent groups.[71]

Of course, the traditional approach outlined above does not provide—nor purport to provide—a principled basis for governing the interaction of these constituent groups; it leaves those as matters "essentially within the domestic jurisdiction," to be worked out through internal processes, however brutal. In the case of the Yugoslav breakup, the brutality—especially, though not exclusively, on behalf of the Serb ethno-nationalist project—was already becoming manifest.

The Badinter Commission's conclusions find their authentic support, not in the application of traditional doctrine, but in a set of emerging values of the contemporary international system. As the Croatian conflict had already demonstrated, an internal war to carve out new territorial units on an ethno-national basis would entail, as an almost inevitable concomitant, the phenomenon of mass expulsions and associated atrocities that has come to be known by the failed euphemism, "ethnic cleansing." If an ethno-national project could establish an internationally recognized claim to territory by seizing and holding effective control over it, there would be a natural motivation to purge the territory of populations presumptively loyal to a rival project (and, indeed, even to encourage rivals' expulsions of one's own co-ethnics, who could then be settled in the carved-out territory, completing its demographic transformation). Whereas the international system had once accepted "population transfer" as a legitimate means of sorting out rival self-determination claims,[72] that system was now coming to understand both the end and the probable means of such transfer as "crimes against humanity."[73] The Commission's approach seemed well-calculated to stem a kind of violence, however "internal," that the international order came to perceive as beyond the pale.[74]

[71] Moreover, while the application of *uti possidetis* discourages violence ***across*** the boundary lines, it may actually encourage violence within them. *See* Radan, "Yugoslavia's Internal Borders as International Borders," *supra*, at 148 (criticizing the Badinter framework's role in validating the 1995 Croatian military offensive to reincorporate rebel Serb enclaves, in the course of which "the great majority of Serbs were expelled from Croatia").

[72] *See, e.g.*, Timothy William Waters, "Remembering Sudetenland: On the Legal Construction of Ethnic Cleansing," 47 *Va. J. Int'l L.* 63 (2006) .

[73] *See, e.g.*, Rome Statute of the International Criminal Court, Art. 7, enumerating crimes against humanity (a "widespread or systematic attack . . . against [a] civilian population"); International Criminal Tribunal for the former Yugoslavia, Blagojevic Trial Judgment, Jan. 17, 2005, ¶ 595 ("[D]isplacements within a state or across national borders, for reasons not permitted under international law, are crimes punishable under customary international law.").

[74] The Badinter Commission's conclusions led, in short order (indeed, in shorter order than their authors had hoped), to the international recognition of (and U.N. membership for) Slovenia, Croatia, and Bosnia. That speaks well for the efficacy of the work product of international jurists, but alas, it is not the end of the story.

Still, the Badinter Commission approach needs to be understood as a contrivance. The federal boundaries upon which the judgments rely derived their authority exclusively from a domestic constitution. Federally organized states do not have a different international standing from unitary ones. It is always error, for purpose of international law, to characterize a constitution as "constitutive" of statehood[75]; rather, a constitution presupposes statehood, and inherent in statehood is the authority to overthrow the constitution.[76] Moreover, the creation of a new rule

Although the international order conferred recognition on Bosnia and affirmed the legal inviolability of its boundaries, the international community mostly stood by while those same boundaries were grossly violated, and the Bosnian civilian population subjected to sustained and grotesque violence at the hands of forces heavily supplied from across the Serbian border. Indeed, in imposing an arms embargo on the whole of the former Yugoslavia that failed to distinguish aggressor from victim, the Security Council inflicted disparate disadvantage on the defenders of the supposedly sacrosanct Bosnian state, in derogation of that state's "inherent" right under Article 51 of the UN Charter to receive aid from its allies for its self-defense. *See, e.g.*, Paul C. Szasz, "Peacekeeping in Operation: A Conflict Study of Bosnia," 28 *Cornell Int'l L.J.* 685, 697 (1995).

Insofar as the legal opinions issued at the onset of the Yugoslav conflict by the Badinter Commission, or any international diplomacy set in motion by those opinions, emboldened the Bosnian Government to make a unilateral declaration of independence, over the opposition of a militant Bosnian Serb minority backed by the military power of the army of the dissolving Yugoslavia, it prompted a fatal miscalculation. *See* Szasz, *supra*, at 693 ("to the extent that these opinions encouraged the Bosnian Government to seek early independence, that step provoked the disaster . . . ."). The international community did not, as it turned out, have the courage of the Commission's convictions.

[75] It has been said that "the [c]onstitution constitutes the People who in turn constitute it." Duncan Ivison, "Pluralism and the Hobbesian Logic of Negative Constitutionalism," 47 *Political Studies* 81, 84 (1999), quoted in Zoran Oklopcic, "Constitutional (Re)Vision: Sovereign Peoples, Constituent Powers and the Formation of Constitutional Orders in the Balkans," forthcoming in *Constellations: An International Journal of Critical and Democratic Theory*. It may be that the constitutional document happens to announce—in doctrinal terms, to be "declaratory" of—the existence of a people that has not heretofore been acknowledged, and that the taking hold of the system of public order embodied in the constitution can be taken as evidence of the existence of a viable political community of the specified contours. But the governmental order that the constitution founds can be recognized as exercising sovereign powers only if it corresponds to an entity that the international community is willing to acknowledge as a bearer of sovereignty; irrespective of the actual chronology, the latter is conceptually prior.

[76] States retain their international legal personality, as well as obligations previously incurred, notwithstanding fundamental changes of governmental order. *See, e.g., Case Concerning the Gabcikovo-Nagymaros Project (Hungary/Slovakia)*, 1997 ICJ Rep. 7, 64 (Sept. 25, 1997), ¶ 104 ("profound changes of a political nature"—the collapse of communism—did not amount to a "fundamental change in circumstances" affecting treaty obligations). The political community is not understood to be re-founded when there is constitutional discontinuity; in *Gabcikovo-Nagymaros*, it is not that democratic Hungary succeeds to the international legal obligations of communist Hungary, but that the obligations incurred by Hungary's communist government are those of Hungary *tout court*. Moreover, if "[e]very State has an inalienable right to choose its political, economic, social and cultural systems, without interference in any form by another State," Friendly Relations Declaration, *supra*, this right

of international law rendering federations more vulnerable to breakup than unitary states would generate perverse incentives, very much at cross-purposes with efforts to effectuate "internal self-determination" for territorially concentrated minorities.[77]

While the Badinter Commission judgments might seem consistent with the democratic will of the Yugoslav republics' population, democracy as such can provide no general rule for such circumstances. Abstract democratic principles, even if posited as authoritative, cannot resolve the question of the democratic political community's configuration—what might be referred to, most intuitively, as the "majority of whom?" problem. The outcome of a plebiscite will depend on who gets to participate; a majority of the residents (perhaps even of the totality of pre-dislocation residents) of the territory of the Bosnian Serb Republic (which has since, ironically, itself become a federal unit) would, if allowed, breach the territorial integrity of Bosnia-Herzegovina, whereas a majority of the whole Bosnian population would disallow this result. It is unhelpful to speak of a democratic decision about the status of a delimited territory when the decision process itself presupposes the territorial delimitation.

## E. KOSOVO AND BEYOND: THE INEVITABILITY OF *AD HOC* RESPONSES TO SECESSION CRISES

The final piece of unfinished business from the break-up of the SFRY is the uncertain status of Kosovo. This has given rise to a rare major split in international recognition practice and an unprecedented reference of the question to the International Court of Justice.[78]

against interference necessarily extends to whatever changes in internal political structure may authentically be attributed to "the State."

James Crawford seems to attribute limitations on Cypriot sovereignty to that state's constitution. Crawford, *Creation of States, supra,* at 89. These, however, are properly traced not to the 1960 constitution but to the accompanying Treaty of Guarantee that purported to license external armed intervention to enforce adherence to the constitution's terms. The Cypriot government immediately thereafter contended, very plausibly, that this aspect of the treaty violated the United Nations Charter and was therefore legally ineffective. *See, e.g.,* Louise Doswald-Beck, "The Legal Validity of Military Intervention by Invitation of the Government," 56 *Brit. Y.B. Int'l L.* 189, 246–50 (1985); R. St. J. MacDonald, "International Law and the Conflict in Cyprus," 1981 *Canadian Y.B. Int'l L.* 3, 17.

[77] *See* Radan, "Yugoslavia's Internal Borders as International Borders," *supra,* at 150.

[78] G.A. Res. 63/3 (2008) (requesting Advisory Opinion); International Court of Justice, *Accordance with International Law of the Unilateral Declaration of Independence in Respect of Kosovo,* Advisory Opinion of of July 22, 2010 [hereinafter Kosovo Advisory Opinion], *available at* <http://www.icj-cij.org/docket/index.php?p1=3&p2=4&k=21&case=141&code=kos&p3=5> (holding, 10-4, that the declaration, as such, "did not violate international law," but declining to address the declaration's legal consequences).

The Badinter Commission's theory of Yugoslav dissolution characterized the SFRY as having been constituted by its six republics, not its eight administrative entities (notwithstanding the allocation to Kosovo of a seat on the eight-member SFRY State Council). Thus, Kosovo, a province endowed with autonomous status under the 1974 SFRY Constitution, was understood to be an integral part of the Republic of Serbia, and thus of a new state emerging from SFRY dissolution, the Federal Republic of Yugoslavia-Serbia and Montenegro (FRY).

The Milosevic government's 1989 withdrawal of Kosovo's autonomy and the ensuing pattern of harsh discrimination against the province's large majority of ethnic Albanians precipitated a distinct crisis by the late 1990s, as an ethnic-Albanian insurgency was met by ever more ruthless counterinsurgent efforts.[79] After the FRY rebuffed Security Council demands that it desist from its norm-offending actions in that territory,[80] and refused to accede to the comprehensive solution proposed by Western powers in the Rambouillet "accords,"[81] the Security Council deadlocked on the question of forcible imposition, setting the stage for the famously unauthorized 79-day NATO air campaign.[82] Although the Security Council never affirmed the lawfulness of the NATO intervention, it adopted that intervention's fruits in Resolution 1244, precluding the FRY's exercise of territorial control and placing Kosovo under, in effect, an international trusteeship.[83]

While authorizing a thoroughgoing transformation of the terms of public order on the ground, Resolution 1244 purported to operate without prejudice to Kosovo's status as an integral part of the FRY. "Reaffirming the commitment of all Member States to the sovereignty and territorial integrity of the Federal Republic of Yugoslavia," the Resolution, *inter alia*:

> 10. Authorizes the Secretary-General, with the assistance of relevant international organizations, to establish an international civil presence in Kosovo in order to provide an interim administration for Kosovo under which the people of Kosovo can enjoy ***substantial autonomy within the Federal Republic of Yugoslavia***, and which will provide transitional

[79] *See generally* Independent International Commission on Kosovo, *The Kosovo Report: Conflict, International Response, Lessons Learned* (Oxford Univ. Press, 2000) (the "Goldstone Commission Report").

[80] *See* S.C. Res. 1160, 1199, 1203 (1998) (all invoking Chapter VII powers in addressing the Kosovo situation).

[81] Interim Agreement for Peace and Self-Government In Kosovo, Rambouillet, France—February 23, 1999, *available at* <http://jurist.law.pitt.edu/ramb.htm> [hereinafter, Rambouillet Accords].

[82] *See* U.N. Press Release Doc. SC/6659 (March 26, 1999) (Russia, China, and Namibia support draft Security Council resolution, defeated 3-12-0, characterizing NATO's "unilateral use of force" as "a flagrant violation of the United Nations Charter" and demanding "an immediate cessation").

[83] S.C. Res. 1244 (1999).

administration while establishing and overseeing the development of provisional democratic self-governing institutions to ensure conditions for a peaceful and normal life for all inhabitants of Kosovo;

11. Decides that the main responsibilities of the international civil presence will include:

(a) Promoting the establishment, pending a final settlement, of ***substantial autonomy and self-government in Kosovo, taking full account of annex 2 and of the Rambouillet accords*** (S/1999/648);[84]

(b) Performing basic civilian administrative functions where and as long as required;

(c) Organizing and overseeing the development of provisional institutions for democratic and autonomous self-government pending a political settlement, including the holding of elections;

(d) Transferring, as these institutions are established, its administrative responsibilities while overseeing and supporting the consolidation of Kosovo's local provisional institutions and other peace-building activities;

(e) ***Facilitating a political process designed to determine Kosovo's future status,*** taking into account the Rambouillet accords (S/1999/648);

(f) In a final stage, overseeing the transfer of authority from Kosovo's provisional institutions to institutions established under a political settlement; . . . .[85]

The referenced Rambouillet accords themselves had recalled "the commitment of the international community to the sovereignty and territorial integrity of the Federal Republic of Yugoslavia" and had sought to confer on Kosovo "authority to conduct foreign relations within its areas of responsibility equivalent to the power provided to Republics under Article 7 of the Constitution of the Federal Republic

[84] Annex 2 provides, *inter alia*, for:

5. Establishment of an interim administration for Kosovo as a part of the international civil presence under which the people of Kosovo can enjoy substantial autonomy within the Federal Republic of Yugoslavia, to be decided by the Security Council of the United Nations. The interim administration to provide transitional administration while establishing and overseeing the development of provisional democratic self-governing institutions to ensure conditions for a peaceful and normal life for all inhabitants in Kosovo. . . .

8. A political process towards the establishment of an interim political framework agreement providing for substantial self-government for Kosovo, taking full account of the Rambouillet accords and the principles of sovereignty and territorial integrity of the Federal Republic of Yugoslavia and the other countries of the region, . . . .

[85] S.C. Res. 1244, *supra* (emphasis added).

of Yugoslavia."[86] Thus, although nothing in Security Council Resolution 1244 stands in the way of Kosovo independence as an outcome of negotiations, there is nothing in the Resolution that makes any affirmative contribution to a legal case for unilateral Kosovo secession from Serbia (which succeeded the FRY in this respect following the 2006 negotiated independence of Montenegro).

Absent either an agreement between Kosovar and Serbian authorities or a new Security Council consensus, the "interim" Kosovo arrangement is akin to an airplane that has clearance to take off but never to land. The unsatisfactoriness of this situation, as a matter of both policy and politics, has been widely noted and given authoritative expression in the Comprehensive Proposal for Kosovo Status Settlement authored in 2007 by the United Nations Secretary-General's Special Envoy, former Finnish President Martti Ahtisaari.[87] Such manifest unsatisfactoriness of the *status quo*, however, cannot itself constitute legal authority for a departure from existing legal norms.

For a part of the international community, Kosovo independence represents the long-awaited application of the Friendly Relations Declaration's safeguard clause to an existing state that has failed, with respect to an integral territory, to comply "with the principle of equal rights and self-determination of peoples" by maintaining "a government representing the whole people belonging to the territory without distinction."[88] Yet that failure is attributable to a past, long-repudiated government of Serbia, whereas the new Serbian political order, which has never had an opportunity to govern the territory, purports a willingness to concede the broadest autonomy to the local authorities.[89] Moreover, the precedential impact of this application of

[86] Rambouillet Accords, *supra*, preamble and ch. I, art. 1(6)(c). The document specified that the "national communities" therein recognized "shall not use their additional rights to endanger . . . the sovereignty and territorial integrity of the Federal Republic of Yugoslavia . . .," *id.*, Framework, art. 1(2). The plan also called for "an international meeting" in three years' time "to determine a mechanism for a final settlement for Kosovo, on the basis of the will of the people, opinions of relevant authorities, each Party's efforts regarding the implementation of this Agreement, and the Helsinki Final Act . . . ." *Id.*, ch. VIII, art. 1(3).

[87] Comprehensive Proposal for Kosovo Status Settlement (March 26, 2007), *available at* <http://www.unosek.org/docref/Comprehensive_proposal-english.pdf>; *see generally* Jean d'Aspremont, "Regulating Statehood: The Kosovo Status Settlement," 20 *Leiden J. Int'l L.* 649 (2007).

[88] See the Written Statement of Germany filed with the ICJ. in connection with the Kosovo Advisory Proceedings, at 34--37, *available at* <http://www.icj-cij.org/docket/files/141/15624.pdf >; *see also* Written Statements of Albania, Estonia, Poland, and Ireland, *available at* <http://www.icj-cij.org/docket/index.php?p1=3&p2=4&k=21&case=141&code=kos&p3=1>; Kosovo Advisory Opinion, *supra*, Cancado-Trindad sep. op., ¶¶ 173–81, 240; Yusuf sep. op., ¶¶ 11–12.

[89] *See*, e.g., Milan Milosevic, "Independence or Substantial Autonomy: The Serbian Proposals for Kosovo's Final Status," *World Politics Review* (Dec. 10, 2007), *available at* <http://www.worldpoliticsreview.com/articles/1422/independence-or-substantial-autonomy-the-serbian-proposals-for-kosovos-final-status>.

the safeguard clause has the potential to be highly destabilizing, and is strongly resisted by states with territorially concentrated and restive ethnic minorities.[90] There is also a potential for perverse incentives, as secessionists may be tempted to commence an armed conflict that they cannot win, thereby provoking a harsh counterinsurgent campaign that can then be cited as evidence that the state, in subjecting the local population to discriminatory predation, has vitiated its claim to territorial inviolability.[91]

Meanwhile, insofar as Kosovo authorities have established effective control on the ground, they have been able to do so only by virtue of the shield provided by Resolution 1244, which was not supposed to prejudice Serbia's political unity. Under ordinary circumstances, a secessionist local regime runs the risk that the central government will have recourse to forcible suppression in furtherance of the state's sovereign prerogative to maintain its territorial integrity. Since the Security Council has disabled Serbia's forcible response, thereby relieving the Kosovo authorities of that risk, one cannot argue that Kosovo has established statehood in accordance with the effective control doctrine.

International legal mechanisms have, up to now, simply not provided for a path to secession that is at once peaceful and nonconsensual. And yet, it scarcely seems possible nowadays even to invoke, in opposition to Kosovo statehood, the true essence of the traditional doctrinal objection: that the secessionist forces have not prevailed, by their own devices, in a trial by ordeal. Still, while 69 states had recognized Kosovo's statehood as of mid-2010,[92] the bulk of the international community could find little appeal in any legal argument for the recognition of Kosovo that did not characterize the matter as somehow *sui generis*.[93]

The ICJ's 2010 Advisory Opinion was obliging in this respect, holding "the right to separate from a State" to be "beyond the scope of the question posed by the General Assembly."[94] Conveniently, that question had read merely: "Is the unilateral declaration of independence by the Provisional Institutions of Self-Government of Kosovo in accordance with international law?"[95] The question, the Court noted,

[90] Note, for example, the Written Statements of Cyprus, Spain, and the Russian Federation filed with the ICJ in connection with the Kosovo Advisory Proceedings, *available at* <http://www.icj-cij.org/docket/index.php?p1=3&p2=4&k=21&case=141&code=kos&p3=1>.

[91] *See, e.g.*, Alan J. Kuperman, "The Moral Hazard of Humanitarian Intervention: Lessons from the Balkans," 52 *Int'l Studies Q.* 49 (2008).

[92] Benjamin Birnbaum, "Serbia Firm Against Recognition of Kosovo," *The Washington Times* (July 1, 2010).

[93] *See, e.g.*, Written Statement of Germany, *supra*, at 26–27.

[94] Kosovo Advisory Opinion, *supra*, at ¶ 83.

[95] G.A. Res. 63/3, *supra*. Serbia's formulation appears to have been a studied effort to avoid a diplomatic affront to states that had already recognized Kosovo, while at the same time to induce the Court

> does not ask about the legal consequences of that declaration. In particular, it does not ask whether or not Kosovo has achieved statehood. Nor does it ask about the validity or legal effects of the recognition of Kosovo by those States which have recognized it as an independent State.[96]

Viewed so narrowly, the question admits of an easy answer: Although the rhetoric invoked in particular cases may seem to indicate otherwise, international law is best understood to be indifferent to unilateral declarations of independence as such; it is other states' reactions to the declaration that may or may not accord with international law.[97]

As to the merits, the Court limited itself to noting that states have expressed "radically different views" on: (1) "[w]hether, outside the context of non-self-governing territories and peoples subject to alien subjugation, domination, and exploitation, the international law of self-determination of peoples confers upon part of the population of an existing State a right to separate from that state"; (2) "whether international law provides for a right of 'remedial secession' and, if so, in what circumstances"; and (3) "whether the circumstances which some participants maintained would give rise to a right of 'remedial secession' were actually present in Kosovo."[98] The effect of the Court's nondecision is to leave Kosovo's trajectory

to speak to the declaration's overall implications. That effort appears, in retrospect, to have been too clever, as the Court majority seized the opportunity to sidestep what everyone understood to be the real issue.

In order to seize that opportunity, however, the Court had to make a rather dubious move, asserting—in what amounts to a disguised tautology—that the declarant body, though established as part of the Provisional Institutions of Self-Government of Kosovo under Security Council Resolution 1244, was acting in a different (and yet somehow, not wrongfully *ultra vires*) capacity. *See* Kosovo Advisory Opinion, *supra*, at ¶¶ 102–09. Moreover, the Court's phrasing characterizes the declarants as acting "together in their capacity as representatives of the people of Kosovo outside the framework of the interim administration," *id.* at ¶ 109, though to infer any legal conclusions about Kosovar "peoplehood" on this basis would be to overread what Zoran Oklopcic properly calls "a seemingly off-the-cuff remark," Oklopcic, "Preliminary Thoughts on the Kosovo Opinion," *EJIL:Talk!* (July 26, 2010) <http://www.ejiltalk.org/preliminary-thoughts-on-the-kosovo-opinion/#more-2505>, one that may refer merely to the declarants' subjective understanding of their "capacity."

[96] Kosovo Advisory Opinion, *supra*, at ¶ 51.

[97] In the Court's words, "the scope of the principle of territorial integrity is confined to the sphere of relations between States." Kosovo Advisory Opinion, *supra*, at ¶ 80. Where unilateral declarations of independence have been authoritatively condemned as illegal, the Court explained, the illegality "stemmed not from the unilateral character of these declarations as such but from the fact that they were, or would have been, connected with the unlawful use of force or other egregious violations of norms of general international law, in particular those of a peremptory character (*jus cogens*)." *Id.* at ¶ 81.

[98] Kosovo Advisory Opinion, *supra*, at ¶ 82.

toward statehood unimpeded,[99] while simultaneously avoiding any imprimatur that might encourage emulation.

Kosovo may continue to be denied recognition by a significant part of the international community, and thus to be denied membership in intergovernmental organizations, but it has already been recognized by most of the states with which it needs to interact systematically. It thus will effectively possess the rights, obligations, powers, and immunities associated with statehood.

Other entities are less favorably situated. By a standard reading of traditional doctrine, Somaliland (as well as, perhaps, neighboring Puntland) presents a relatively strong case for recognition.[100] Whereas Kosovo must rely either on a doubtful interpretation of self-determination doctrine or on some *sui generis* quality, Somaliland appears to have long established effective control through internal processes.[101] As noted above, recognition of seceding entities is, in principle, not precluded where a central government's reunification efforts are manifestly futile for reasons other than foreign interference. Moreover, whereas the Badinter Commission's assertion of Yugoslavia's nonconsensual dissolution relied on questionable assertions about a collapse of the governmental order, Somalia has lacked an effective central authority for two decades, and represents a failure of far more than any one constitutional arrangement. And certainly, no argument can be made that respect for democratic values or popular will recommends maintaining this orderly region as an integral part of a state whose name has become synonymous with chaos.

Yet arguments from these objective factors seem unlikely to carry the day at any time in the near future. The fear of total Somali fragmentation—and even more, of the potential demonstration effects—prompts what amounts to a collective decision to ignore all doctrinal principles—*lex ferenda* as well as *lex lata*—in favor of simple expediency. The case of Somaliland, like that of Kosovo, bespeaks the ad hoc nature of the international order's solutions to the question of what constitutes a state.[102]

[99] The European Union subsequently prevailed upon Serbia to abandon further efforts to harness international mechanisms to impugn Kosovo's status. *See* "The UN Urges Direct Talks between Serbia and Kosovo," BBC, Sept. 9, 2010, *available at* <http://www.bbc.co.uk/news/world-europe-11255990>.

[100] *See, e.g.,* Aaron Kreuter, "Note: Self-Determination, Sovereignty, and the Failure of States: Somaliland and the Case for Justified Secession," 19 *Minn. J. Int'l L.* 363 (2010); Alison K. Eggers, "Note: When is a State a State? The Case for Recognition of Somaliland," 30 *B.C. Int'l & Comp. L. Rev.* 211 (2007).

[101] *See, e.g.,* Paul Reynolds, "Somaliland's 'Path to Recognition,'" BBC News, Apr. 25, 2008, *available at* <http://news.bbc.co.uk/1/hi/world/africa/7365002.stm>.

[102] Taiwan represents yet another scenario that defies doctrinal solution. I have dealt with this case at length in other writings. *See* Roth, "The Entity That Dare Not Speak Its Name," *supra*; Roth,"Taiwan's Nation-Building and Beijing's Anti-Secession Law," *supra*.

## II. Effective Control and the International Status of Coup Regimes

### A. POPULAR SOVEREIGNTY, IDEOLOGICAL PLURALISM, AND THE EFFECTIVE CONTROL DOCTRINE

As with recognition of states, there is an ambiguous relationship between what is ordinarily called "recognition of governments" and an assessment of the legal status of the institution being accorded or denied affirmation. An overt act of recognition is typically a sufficient, but not a necessary, indication of whether a governmental apparatus is thought to bear the legal capacity to assert rights, incur obligations, exercise powers, and confer immunities on behalf of the underlying sovereign entity. Although overt recognition may be withheld as an expression of political disapproval or as an effort to maintain neutrality in internal struggles, some legal obligations owed to the state in question cannot be discerned without ascertaining the government's international legal status.

As Lauterpacht noted, "[t]he problem of recognition arises . . . because the accompanying violence and the resulting period of unsettlement demand an answer to the question whether the new government claiming to represent the State is in fact the government of the country."[103] Efforts to "abolish" the practice of officially recognizing governments, such as the "Estrada Doctrine" that Mexico famously promulgated in 1930,[104] have typically amounted to a practice of automatic acknowledgment of governments exercising effective control, on the unspoken assumption that effective control has constituted—subject to a few doctrinal qualifications (in particular, rules against premature recognition and foreign-installed regimes)[105]—the internationally authoritative criterion for an apparatus's standing as the state's government.

The effective control doctrine is best described in draft documents preliminary to the 1950 passage of United Nations General Assembly Resolution 396 (V), which took a non-committal position on criteria for the credentialing delegations where "more than one authority claims to be the government entitled to represent a Member State."[106] Although the political support maintained by the Nationalist

[103] Lauterpacht, *supra*, at 98.

[104] Estrada Doctrine, 25 *Am. J. Int'l L. Supp.* (1931) at 203 (discontinuing the practice of issuing "grants of recognition, since that nation considers that such a course is an insulting practice and one which, in addition to the fact that it offends the sovereignty of other nations, implies that judgement of some sort may be passed upon the internal affairs of those nations by other governments, inasmuch as the latter assume, in effect, an attitude of criticism when they decide, favourably or unfavourably, as to the legal qualifications of foreign regimes").

[105] *See* Roth, *Governmental Illegitimacy*, *supra*, at 172–99.

[106] G.A. Res. 396 (V) (1950) ("Recognition by the United Nations of the Representation of a Member State").

Chinese government, by then limited in its reach to Taiwan, precluded the establishment of objective criteria, the rejected drafts articulated the position that came to dominate subsequent UN credentials practice (including, by 1971, practice addressed to the question of Chinese representation). One such document recommended as follows:

> where the question of representation of a Member State arises in consequence of internal processes or changes which have taken place in that State, the right of a government to represent the Member State concerned in the United Nations should be recognized if that government exercises effective control and authority over all or nearly all the national territory, and has the obedience of the bulk of the population of that territory, in such a way that this control, authority and obedience appear to be of a permanent character.[107]

Another contemporaneous document highlighted the relevance of "[t]he extent to which that authority has been established through internal processes in the Member State."[108]

The effective control doctrine is rooted in Kelsenian positivism: A new *Grundnorm* is established when "the individuals whose behavior the new order regulates actually behave, by and large, in conformity with the new order."[109]

It is often imagined that the advent of popular sovereignty rendered the effective control doctrine obsolete. Yet there is nothing new to the international order about popular sovereignty in the abstract. The time is long past when monarchical regimes were understood to be "sovereign" over, and not organic parts of, the territorial

[107] 5 GAOR, Annexes, Agenda Item 61, at 8; U.N. Doc. A/AC.38/L.21/Rev. 1 (1950), quoted in Roth, *Governmental Illegitimacy, supra*, at 258–59.

[108] 5 GAOR, Annexes, Agenda Item 61, at 8; U.N. Doc. A/AC.38/L.45 (1950), quoted in Roth, *Governmental Illegitimacy, supra*, at 259.

[109] Hans Kelsen, *General Theory of Law and State*, Anders Wedberg trans. (New York: Russell & Russell, 1961), at 118. Kelsen elaborated as follows:

> Under what circumstances does a national legal order begin to be valid? The answer, given by international law, is that a national legal order begins to be valid as soon as it has become—on the whole—efficacious; and it ceases to be valid as soon as it loses this efficacy. . . . The government brought into permanent power by a revolution or coup d'etat is, according to international law, the legitimate government of the State, whose identity is not affected by these events. Hence, according to international law, victorious revolutions or successful coups d'etat are to be interpreted as procedures by which a national legal order can be changed. Both events are, viewed in the light of international law, law-creating facts.

*Id.* at 120–21.

political communities over which they ruled.[110] The idea that sovereignty ultimately inheres in the political communities themselves, with governmental apparatuses acting as agents, is at the core of the sovereign equality envisaged in the UN Charter. The question has been and remains how to give it effect.

Popular sovereignty has traditionally been tightly interwoven with a principle of non-intervention in the internal affairs of foreign states and a rejection of any imposition of foreign views as to what constitutes the legitimate government of the state.[111] Long discredited are international compacts, such as the 1815 Holy Alliance, that pledged to restore to power ousted monarchs bearing "rightful" dynastic claims.[112] As Thomas Jefferson suggested in regard to the French Revolution, recognition of a foreign government has generally turned on the will of the subject people "substantially declared"—i.e., declared by any perceived means of articulation, above all by trends of actual obedience *vel non* to established authority.[113] Although the "Tobar Doctrine," embodied in Central American treaties in 1907 and 1923, sought to deny recognition to seizures of power that violated preexisting local constitutional norms, this arrangement was as plausibly an effort to thwart as to vindicate popular will, and suffered from the conceptual problem that legal orders themselves have extralegal origins; the experiment was shortly abandoned.[114] The international community's broad-based rejection of Cold War-era ideological legitimism—reflected in such articulations as the "Brezhnev Doctrine" (rationalizing the Soviet invasion of Czechoslovakia)[115] and the "Reagan Doctrine" (rationalizing the U.S. invasion of Grenada and support of insurgent forces in Nicaragua)[116]—reaffirmed the principle of deference to whatever internal processes find acceptance, over substantive evaluations of the pedigree or ideological merits of a governing regime.[117]

[110] *See* Maurice Cranston, "From Legitimism to Legitimacy," in Legitimacy/***Légitimité*** (Athanasios Moulakis ed.) (New York: Walter de Gruyter, 1986), 36.

[111] "Every State has an inalienable right to choose its political, economic, social and cultural systems, without interference in any form by another State." Friendly Relations Declaration, *supra.*

[112] *See* Lauterpacht, *supra,* at 103.

[113] *See* Lauterpacht, *supra,* at 125–26.

[114] *See* J. Izarry y Puente, "The Doctrines of Recognition and Intervention in Latin America," 28 *Tulane L. Rev.* 313, 317–26 (1954); Roth, *Governmental Illegitimacy, supra,* at 144–46.

[115] Pravda Article Justifying Intervention in Czechoslovakia, 7 I.L.M. 1323 (1968) (translation by Novosti, Soviet press agency) (the Soviet Union and its allies "discharg[ed] their internationalist duty toward the fraternal peoples of Czechoslovakia and defending their own socialist gains").

[116] *See* Jeane J. Kirkpatrick & Allan Gerson, "The Reagan Doctrine, Human Rights, and International Law," in *Right v. Might: International Law and the Use of Force* (Louis Henkin ed.) (New York: Council on Foreign Relations, 2d ed. 1991), 19.

[117] The ICJ's *Nicaragua* judgment reached beyond the pleadings to repudiate Reagan Doctrine-oriented justifications of U.S. efforts to undermine the Nicaraguan government. *See Military and Paramilitary Activities, supra,* ¶¶ 257–68. The Court noted that to hold a state's adherence to any particular

Popular sovereignty has, of course, also been understood as a standard to which states are bound to adhere in their internal practices. But while internal governmental practices, including modes of political participation, have long been subject to international legal obligations, a governmental apparatus's standing to act in a state's name has not generally been conditioned on compliance with such obligations.[118] To establish such conditionality would have grave consequences for the doctrine of non-intervention, as a state's government is presumed to have the legal capacity to invite forms of foreign involvement, up to and including a foreign troop presence to maintain or to restore order, that would otherwise constitute a violation of Articles 2(7) and 2(4) of the United Nations Charter.[119]

It is true that Article 21(3) of the 1948 Universal Declaration of Human Rights demanded that "the will of the people shall be the basis of the authority

governmental doctrine a violation of customary international law "would make nonsense of the *fundamental principle of State sovereignty, on which the whole of international law rests,* and the freedom of choice of the political, social, economic and cultural system of a State." Ibid, ¶ 263 (emphasis added).

[118] *See, e.g., Military and Paramilitary Activities, supra,* ¶¶ 257–68 (even had there been a violation of legally binding commitment on the part of Nicaragua to hold elections of a particular type, sovereignty norms would continue to circumscribe the range of lawful responses to such a violation).

[119] *See, e.g.,* Doswald-Beck, *supra;* Institut de Droit International, 10th Commission: Present Problems of the Use of Force in International Law: D. Sub-Group on Intervention by Invitation (Gerhard Hafner, rapporteur) (July 25, 2007), *available at* <www.idi-iil.org/idiF/annuaireF/10th_commission_d.pdf>.

A complicated question arises when insurgent forces achieve such efficacy as to achieve the status of "belligerent," thereby establishing the existence of a full fledged "civil war." Since a government's standing traditionally hinges on its maintenance of effective control through internal processes, the inability of a regime to maintain control by its own devices calls that standing into question, thereby traditionally triggering an obligation of foreign states to observe neutrality. *See* Convention on Duties and Rights of States in the Event of Civil Strife, 134 L.N.T.S. 45, entered into force May 21, 1929 (Inter-American treaty forbidding "the traffic in arms and war material, except when intended for the Government, while the belligerency of the rebels has not been recognized, n which latter case the rules of neutrality shall be applied"); Institut de Droit International, Resolution: The Principle of Non-Intervention in Civil Wars (Aug. 14, 1975) *available at* <http://www.idi-iil.org/idiE/resolutionsE/1975_wies_03_en.pdf>; Oscar Schachter, "International Law in Theory and Practice," *Academie de Droit International, Recueil des Cours,* Vol 178, pp. 160–66 (1982-V) (citing same); Rein Mullerson, "Intervention by Invitation" in *Law and Force in the New International Order* 127, 132 (Lori Fisler Damrosch & David J. Scheffer eds., San Francisco: Westview Press, 1991) ("The majority of Western authors consider that international law does not forbid the rendering of military assistance at the request of a legitimate government with the aim of restoring order in the case of internal disorders, but that it is nonetheless impermissible to interfere in a civil war, no matter which side makes the request."). Doswald-Beck regards this neutrality rule as having fallen into desuetude, Doswald-Beck, *supra,* at 251, but even if it survives formally, it tends to give way because, as a practical matter, successful insurgencies are typically beneficiaries of unlawful foreign assistance, thus triggering a right of counterintervention in favor of the government's allies. *See* Roth, *Governmental Illegitimacy, supra,* at 185–88.

of government."[120] This statement (which was not repeated in this provision's legally binding counterpart, Article 25 of the ICCPR) could, however, be read in light of ideological pluralism to express nothing more specific than the claim that almost all ruling apparatuses in recent memory have made for themselves. The United Nations Charter-based order was an accommodation based on the sovereign equality of liberal-democratic and non-liberal-democratic states, and any development of international law required the assent of the Socialist and Non-Aligned as well as Western blocs. Prior to the 1990s, there was neither a political nor legal basis in the international order for calling into question the one-party or military regime that tolerated no organized opposition, but that nonetheless predicated its legitimacy on its supposed embodiment of authentic popular will.[121]

In that context, the effective control doctrine could be seen not as a repudiation of the popular sovereignty norm, but rather as an application of it in those circumstances of ideological pluralism. Contrary to its reputation in some circles as a mere concession to *realpolitik* or as rank apologism for absolutist regimes,[122] the effective control doctrine can be interpreted to embody respect for the self-determination of diverse political communities as to which empirical investigation to ascertain public opinion is most often impracticable. Moreover, given that "popular will" itself is a complex and normatively loaded concept, any imposition from abroad of procedures calculated to appropriately measure popular will might be seen as at best presumptuous and at worst a usurpation.[123]

[120] G.A. Res. 217 (III) (1948) (48-0-8).

[121] *See generally* Roth, *Governmental Illegitimacy, supra,* at 75–120 (on "The Rise and Fall of Revolutionary-Democratic Dictatorship").

[122] *See, e.g.,* Fernando Tesón, *Humanitarian Intervention: An Inquiry into Law and Morality* (Dobbs Ferry, New York: Transnational Publishers, Inc., 1988), at 53 (arguing that non-intervention norms are attributable to an organicist "Hegelian Myth" about the moral standing of the state); W. Michael Reisman, "Sovereignty and Human Rights in Contemporary International Law," 84 *Am. J. Int'l L.* 866, 871 (1990) (excoriating the "mystical survival of a monarchical right that supposedly devolves *jure gentium* on whichever warlord seizes and holds the presidential palace").

[123] Even General Assembly resolutions on "Enhancing the effectiveness of the principle of periodic and genuine elections" have included the pointed caveat that international electoral assistance "should not call into question each State's sovereign right freely to choose and develop its political, social, economic, and cultural systems, whether or not they conform to the preferences of other States," G.A. Res. 45/150 (1990) (129-8-9), and have reaffirmed "that electoral assistance and support for the promotion of democratization are provided only at the specific request of the Member State concerned." G.A. Res. 49/190 (1995) (155-1-12). These supportive resolutions have typically been accompanied by counterpart resolutions, passed by majority over the objection of the most strongly liberal-democratic states, that reaffirm "respect for the principles of national sovereignty and non-interference in the internal affairs of States in their electoral processes," acknowledging the plurality of approaches, reserving to the domestic jurisdiction control over implementation, and criticizing unwelcome external influences on local processes. G.A. Res. 45/151 (1990) (111-29-11); G.A. Res. 49/180 (97-57-14); GA Res. 54/168 (91-59-10). *See also* Boutros Boutros-Ghali, *An Agenda for Democratization*

The case for the effective control doctrine as the most promising application of the principle of popular sovereignty is much more formidable that is commonly supposed. It is hardly clear how to respect popular will in the ordinary case other than by deferring to the apparatus to which the populace has, for whatever reason, evidently decided to render obedience.[124] Even where this decision has been made under duress, the populace may not be well served by leaving open the question of who may assert rights, incur obligations, and confer immunities in its name. Having made their peace with the unwanted regime, subjects may plausibly prefer—notwithstanding whatever internal issues remain—that the state's interests in foreign affairs be represented by an apparatus that has both the efficacy and the incentive to do so. They may plausibly wish their ruling apparatus to be able to enter into binding agreements of all kinds on their behalf. They may plausibly demand to be respected in their obedience and service to the only effective instrument of coordination that their political community possesses, and to have any retrospective prosecution of their actions in that service accord with the international standard of *nullum crimen sine lege*. And they may plausibly regard those powerful foreign states that evince interest (however purportedly "humanitarian") in their internal affairs not as rescuers, but as potential predators. Albeit paradoxical, it is far from ridiculous that popular sovereignty may amount, as a matter of practical application, to the right to be ruled by domestic thugs rather than by foreigners announcing benevolent intentions.

## B. TOWARD A DOCTRINE OF GOVERNMENTAL ILLEGITIMACY IN INTERNATIONAL LAW

### *The Haiti and Sierra Leone Cases*

In the period immediately following the end of the Cold War, however, a substantial literature developed hailing the emergence in international law of a "right to

(New York: United Nations, 1996), 1 at 3 (U.N. then-Secretary-General notes that "individual states decide if and when to begin democratization" and that the new emphasis on democratization 'does not imply a change' in the traditional principle of non-intervention).

[124] *See Mokotso v. King Moshoeshoe II* [Lesotho High Court, 1988], 90 *Int' L. Rep.* 427, 519 (Lauterpacht & Greenwood eds., 1990):

> [It has been observed] that "Legality should be achieved only if and when the people accept and approve, for in them lies political sovereignty." I respectfully observe, however, that the people may well accept without necessarily approving, as such, and the aspect of approval may in any event be difficult if not impossible to determine, except in the clearest of cases. The people make their choice in the matter. If they decide to accept the new regime, even if that decision is based on weakness or even fear, such decision may not be gainsaid. The [judge's] function in the matter... goes no further than to give effect to the will of the people. Ultimately it is the will of the people, however motivated, which creates a new legal order and the court must recognise this fact and give effect thereto.

democratic governance."[125] This literature, imputing greater determinacy and consequence to the previously open-textured right to political participation, cast aspersions on the standing of violator governments to assert, in the name of the sovereign state, rights against foreign interference in internal matters.[126] The implications of such claims for what constitutes a law-governed international response to civil strife are unclear; some (but by no means all) advocates of the "democratic entitlement" suggest the appropriateness of measures hitherto regarded as inadmissible, up to and including the use of force, to unseat "non-democratic" regimes.[127] W. Michael Reisman's defense of the 1989 U.S. invasion of Panama, which installed an apparently elected government that had been denied accession to power, contained a quintessential statement of this view:

> When [the people's] confirmed wishes are ignored by a local caudillo who either takes power himself or assigns it to a subordinate he controls, a jurist rooted in the late twentieth century can hardly say that an invasion by outside forces to remove the caudillo and install the elected government is a violation of national sovereignty . . . . [If cross-border military actions] displace the usurper and emplace the people who were freely elected, they can be characterized, in this particular regard, as a violation of sovereignty only if one uses the term anachronistically to mean the violation of some mystical survival of a monarchical right that supposedly devolves jure gentium on whichever warlord seizes and holds the presidential palace or

[125] Separate articles by Thomas Franck and Gregory Fox are now widely cited as the seminal works of this literature. *See* Thomas M. Franck, "The Emerging Right to Democratic Governance," 86 *Am. J. Int'l L.* 46 (1992); Gregory H. Fox, "The Right to Political Participation in International Law," 17 *Yale J. Int'l L.* 539 (1992). For an elaboration of contrasting positions on whether and to what extent a "democratic entitlement" is emerging in international law, *see* Gregory H. Fox & Brad R. Roth, "Democracy and International Law," 27 *Rev. of Int'l Studies* 327 (2001); *see also* Gregory H. Fox & Brad R. Roth eds., *Democratic Governance and International Law* (Cambridge University Press, 2000) (collection presenting a range of views on related questions); Susan Marks, *The Riddle of All Constitutions* (Oxford Univ. Press, 2003) (assessing the democratic quality of these developments).

[126] As Fox, *supra*, at 595, put it:

> For a non-democratic regime to claim that participatory rights violate its national sovereignty begs the question of whether that regime has legitimate authority to make such a statement. When the will of the people is the basis of the authority of government, regimes that thwart the will of the people lack legitimacy. . . . [I]f political participation is to have any meaning as an internationally enforceable right, the community of states must be empowered to prescribe standards detailing how participation is to occur and to insist that parties to the major treaties adopt these standards as law. A regime that bases its legitimacy on nothing more than the fact that it holds power exercises no "sovereign" authority to object to such prescriptions.

[127] For elaboration, see Fox & Roth, "Democracy and International Law," *supra*, at 335–38.

if the term is used in the jurisprudentially bizarre sense to mean that inanimate territory has political rights that preempt those of its inhabitants.[128]

Notwithstanding the widespread international condemnation of the Panama invasion,[129] a sea change occurred shortly thereafter. The international community authoritatively repudiated the 1991 overthrow of Haitian President Jean-Bertrand Aristide and the 1997 ouster of Sierra Leonean President Ahmad Tejan Kabbah, even though the changes in government were effectively achieved through internal processes. These international responses went far beyond a denial of "recognition," in the diplomatic or political sense of that term. Rather, the authority of the *de facto* regime was deemed to be null and void for purposes of international law, including for purposes of asserting the state's theretofore supposedly "inalienable" right against forcible intervention.[130] In the Haitian case, following a request from the government-in-exile for "swift and determined action," the Security Council ultimately authorized force "to assist the legitimate government of Haiti in the maintenance of public order,"[131] whereas in the Sierra Leone case, the Council implicitly encouraged the armed forces of the Economic Community of West African States (ECOWAS) to effectuate the Kabbah government's restoration, and subsequently "welcome[d] the fact that the military junta ha[d] been brought to an end."[132]

[128] W. Michael Reisman, "Sovereignty and Human Rights in Contemporary International Law," 84 *Am. J. Int'l L.* 866, 871 (1990). For similar views, see Lois Fielding, "Taking the Next Step in the Development of New Human Rights: The Emerging Right of Humanitarian Assistance to Restore Democracy," 5 *Duke J. Comp. & Int'l L.* 329 (1995); Malvina Halberstam, "The Copenhagen Document: Intervention in Support of Democracy," 34 *Harvard J. Int'l L.* 143 (1993); Anthony D'Amato, "The Invasion of Panama Was a Lawful Response to Tyranny," 84 *Am. J. Int'l L.* 516 (1990); *but see* Thomas M. Franck, *The Empowered Self: Law and Society in the Age of Individualism* (Oxford University Press, 2000), pp. 272–73 (asserting Security Council authority to license "military rescue of democracy," but insisting that international law does not "permit any state, or any regional organization, to take enforcement of the democratic entitlement exclusively into its own hands"). For a detailed study of the international law of collective non-recognition of governments, with a critical assessment of the claims for the emergence of a democratic entitlement as of 1999, *see* Roth, *Governmental Illegitimacy, supra.*

[129] By a vote of 75 to 20, with 40 abstentions, the U.N. General Assembly characterized the intervention as "a flagrant violation of international law and of the independence, sovereignty, and territorial integrity of States." G.A. Res. 44/240 (1989).

[130] In these cases, the Security Council deemed coups against the elected governments to be "threats to the peace." S.C. Res. 841 (1993) (unanimous vote on Haiti economic sanctions); S.C. Res. 1132 (1997) (unanimous vote on Sierra Leone arms and oil embargo). Ultimately, the Security Council authorized armed intervention in Haiti, S.C. Res. 940 (1994), and gave the forcible restoration of the Sierra Leonean President a post hoc imprimatur, UN Doc. S/PRST/1998/5 (Security Council Presidential Statement welcoming the removal of the Sierra Leonean junta); S.C. Res. 1162 (1998) (commending ECOWAS after the fact for its role in the Sierra Leonean transition). For elaboration, *see* Roth, *Governmental Illegitimacy, supra*, 366–87, 405–09.

[131] S.C. Res. 940 (1994).

[132] UN Doc. S/PRST/1998/5 (Presidential Statement).

There was, nonetheless, much reason to resist an overreading of these events: while much had changed, even more had thus far remained the same. The international repudiations, dramatic though they were, seemed to represent incremental rather than radical change. While these coups had been directed against both established constitutional orders and unambiguous electoral outcomes, the strength of the international response did not clearly rest on an attribution of decisive significance to either of these factors. The facts on the ground in each case were exceptional—including the landslide victory of the ousted president in a very recent, internationally monitored election, and the notorious brutality and demonstrable unpopularity of the forces involved in the coup—leading a vast diversity of international actors, cutting across the international system's plurality of interests and values, to perceive in common a population's manifest will to restore an ousted government.[133] Although other coups might be disfavored politically, or even regarded as breaches of binding international commitments, there was no immediate indication of a general rule that an internal seizure of effective control would be ineffective in establishing a regime's standing to exercise the state's sovereign rights in the international order.[134] The tepidness of reactions against subsequent coups—including, ironically, the 2004 ouster of Haiti's Aristide—bolstered the conclusion that the 1991–94 Haitian crisis and the 1997–98 Sierra Leonean crisis were outlier cases.

## C. THE ANTI-COUP PROCLAMATIONS OF REGIONAL ORGANIZATIONS

Nonetheless, both in Latin America and in Africa, regional organizations have begun to take progressively more adverse positions toward disruptions of existing constitutional orders. Given how strongly the non-interventionist hard line was

[133] For elaboration, see Roth, *Governmental Illegitimacy*, *supra*, at, 366–87, 405--09.

[134] Seemingly to the contrary, Jean d'Aspremont asserts that "the recognition of overthrown democratic governments is generally not questioned and the recognition of putschists [is] systematically denied." D'Aspremont, "Responsibility for Coups d'Etat in International Law," 18 *Tulane J. Int'l & Comp. L.* 451, 455–56 (2010). But d'Aspremont immediately makes clear that once "the authors of a coup d'état . . . have gained effective power," they become for legal purposes "an organ of the state," and their subsequent breaches of international legal obligation "are attributable to the state." *Id.* at 473. Thus, whatever may be said about "the systematic condemnations and sanctions against coups carried out against democratically-elected governments," d'Aspremont, "Legitimacy of Governments in the Age of Democracy," 38 *NYU J. Int'l L. & Politics* 877, 893 (2006); *but see* Mikulas Fabry, "The Right to Democracy in International Law: A Classical Liberal Reassessment," 37 *Millennium—J. Int'l Studies* 721, 735 (2009) (responses to coups "have varied not just across different organisations or countries, but also in the course of the same organisations' or countries' treatment of nominally like cases"), these political reactions do not ordinarily rise to the level of a denial of a coup regime's legal standing to represent the state for purposes of international law. D'Aspremont does not invoke any examples of international reactions matching those that followed the 1991 Haitian and 1997 Sierra Leonean coups.

previously associated with both the Organization of American States (OAS) and the Organization of African Unity (OAU, predecessor to the African Union (AU)), these developments are striking.

The OAS Charter affirms that "The solidarity of the American States and the high aims which are sought through it require the political organization of those States on the basis of the effective exercise of representative democracy."[135] The Charter nonetheless simultaneously provides that "No State or group of States has the right to intervene, directly or indirectly, for any reason whatever, in the internal or external affairs of any other State," elaborating further that the prohibition extends beyond the use of force to "any form of interference," with special reference to "coercive measures of an economic or political character."[136] Although the Charter anticipates "measures adopted for the maintenance of peace and security in accordance with existing treaties," the non-intervention norm otherwise prevails in the face of "any reason whatever," and applies "not only [to] armed force but also [to] any other form of interference or attempted threat against the personality of the State or against its political, economic, and cultural elements."[137]

In the decades leading up to the 1990s, both an increased diversity of governmental forms and ideologies in Latin America and an increase in nationalistic self-assertion as a counter to United States hegemony ensured that the non-intervention norm would predominate in OAS practice.[138] Indeed, this period's singular OAS repudiation of an existing government, the pathbreaking June 23, 1979, resolution calling for the "immediate and definitive replacement of the Somoza regime" in Nicaragua,[139] came in the context of a rebuff to a U.S. effort to interject "peacekeeping" forces against the will of an insurrectional movement that was less than a month from outright victory.[140]

However, in June 1991, the OAS General Assembly convened in Santiago, Chile, and promulgated two documents espousing representative democracy as "the form

[135] OAS Charter, 11 U.N.T.S. 3 (1948), Art. 5(d).

[136] OAS Charter, Arts. 19, 20. These points are reiterated elsewhere in the Charter to the point of redundancy. Under Article 3, "International order consists essentially of respect for the personality, sovereignty, and independence of States, and the faithful fulfillment of obligations derived from treaties and other sources of international law"; "Every State has the right to choose, without external interference, its political, economic, and social system and to organize itself in the way best suited to it, and has the duty to abstain from intervening in the affairs of another State."

[137] OAS Charter, Arts. 19, 23.

[138] The OAS General Assembly declared in 1973 that "every state has the right to adopt, with complete independence, its own system of government and economic and social organization." AG/Res. 128 (III-0/73).

[139] OEA/Ser.F/II.17, Doc. 43/79 (June 23, 1979). The 1979 resolution did not, however, unseat the Somoza Government's representative to the OAS, nor did it overtly call for member states to take measures calculated to bring down that Government.

[140] *See* Roth, *Governmental Illegitimacy in International Law*, *supra*, at 290–303.

of government of the region."[141] The first, the "Santiago Commitment to Democracy and the Renewal of the Inter-American System," assigned "special priority" to, *inter alia*, "[s]trengthening representative democracy as an expression of the legitimate and free manifestation of the will of the people," albeit "always respecting the sovereignty and independence of member states."[142] The second, entitled "Representative Democracy," more concretely mandated, "in the event of any occurrences giving rise to the sudden or irregular interruption of the democratic political institutional process or of the legitimate exercise of power by the democratically elected government in any of the Organization's member states," an immediate ad hoc meeting of Ministers of Foreign Affairs or special session of the General Assembly to take decisions "deemed appropriate, in accordance with the Charter and international law."[143]

No doubt, the Santiago documents indicated a new emphasis in the inter-American system on participatory mechanisms in the hemispheric scheme of popular sovereignty. Yet the dual emphasis on representative democracy and non-intervention norms that marks the OAS Charter and previous OAS pronouncements was merely recapitulated in these documents. The "Representative Democracy" resolution's preambular promise to promote democracy was qualified by the words "with due respect for the principle of non-intervention."[144] How much respect is "due"was, of course, the open question, but the operative provision of the resolution—authorizing a meeting "to look into the events collectively and adopt any decisions deemed appropriate"—merely begged this question by referring to the OAS Charter and international law. Not only is collective derecognition not directly proposed, but the preamble also emphasizes that "[d]ue respect must be accorded to the policies of each member country in regard to the recognition of states and governments."[145]

The Santiago documents were followed by further pro-democratic OAS proclamations, including a 1995 (Protocol of Washington) Charter amendment allowing recourse to suspension, by two-thirds vote of the General Assembly, of a member state "whose democratically constituted government has been overthrown

[141] "Santiago Commitment to Democracy and the Renewal of the Inter-American System," (adopted at the third plenary session held on June 4, 1991), 4th preambular paragraph.

[142] Santiago Commitment, ¶ 3b.

[143] AG/RES. 1080 (XXI-0/91) (5th plen. sess., June 5, 1991).

[144] *Id.*, 2d preambular paragraph.

[145] *Id.*, 3d preambular paragraph. In December 1992, the OAS General Assembly proposed a Charter amendment (the "Protocol of Washington"), which entered into force in 1997, providing that a member state whose "democratically elected government has been overthrown by force may be suspended from the exercise of its right to participate in the meetings of the General Assembly" and of other OAS bodies. OEA/Ser.P/AG/doc.11 (XVI-E/92) (Dec. 14, 1992). Importantly, however, the amendment does not provide for continued recognition of the ousted "democratically elected government," or cast any other aspersions on the *de facto* government's standing as the state's diplomatic and legal representative.

by force."[146] Most dramatically, in a 2001 General Assembly resolution styled as the "Inter-American Democratic Charter,"[147] the Organization proclaimed that "an unconstitutional interruption of the democratic order or ***an unconstitutional alteration of the constitutional regime that seriously impairs the democratic order*** in a member state, constitutes, while it persists, an insurmountable obstacle to its government's participation in sessions of" OAS organs.[148] Beyond suspension of the state—a measure which, by its nature, seems to presuppose that the offending regime has the status of the state's government—the IADC calls, rather vaguely (having twice referenced the OAS commitment to "due respect for the principle of nonintervention"), for such decisions as the Permanent Council and the General Assembly deem "appropriate, including the undertaking of diplomatic initiatives, in accordance with the Charter of the Organization, international law, and the provisions of this Democratic Charter."[149]

Apart from its strong stance in the exceptional 1991–94 Haitian crisis, the Organization's overall record of responses to interruptions of constitutional governance—such as have occurred in Peru, Guatemala, Paraguay, Ecuador, and Venezuela—has been less than dramatic.[150] The OAS pronouncements nonetheless potentially portend a significant departure from past positions on the attribution of international legal standing to governments, a departure emphasizing both electoral outcomes and adherence to established constitutional process over effective control through internal processes. The 2009 Honduran crisis, discussed below, provides an indication of how substantial a shift might be in the offing.

Similarly, the 2000 Constitutive Act of the African Union, best known for asserting "the right of the Union to intervene in a Member State pursuant to a decision of the Assembly in respect of grave circumstances, namely: war crimes, genocide and crimes against humanity," also espouses the principle of "condemnation and rejection of unconstitutional changes of governments."[151] In 2007, the AU adopted the African Charter on Democracy, Elections, and Governance, though very few of its

[146] OAS Charter, art. 9.

[147] Although not a "charter" in the sense of a binding treaty, the IADC can be regarded under Article 31(3)(a) of the Vienna Convention on the Law of Treaties as an authoritative interpretation of the OAS Charter. *See* Doug Cassel, "Honduras: *Coup d'Etat* in Constitutional Clothing?" 13:9 *ASIL Insight* (July 29, 2009), *available at* <http://www.asil.org/files/insight090729pdf.pdf>.

[148] OAS General Assembly, Declaration of Lima (Sept. 11, 2001), art. 19, *available at* <http://www.oas.org/juridico/english/decl_lima.htm> (emphasis added).

[149] *Id.*, arts. 19, 20.

[150] *See, e.g.*, Barry S. Levitt, "A Desultory Defense of Democracy: OAS Resolution 1080 and the Inter-American Democratic Charter," 48:3 *L. Amer. Pol. & Soc'y* 93 (2006); Dexter S. Boniface, "Is There a Democratic Norm in the Americas? An Analysis of the Organization of American States," 8 *Global Governance* 365 (2002).

[151] Constitutive Act of the African Union (July 11, 2000), art. 4(p), *available at* <http://www.africa-union.org/root/au/aboutau/constitutive_act_en.htm#top>.

members have thus far ratified the document (which requires 15 ratifications to take effect).[152] Article 25 of the ACDEG starts with a familiar call for suspension upon a finding of "an unconstitutional change of government,"[153] but unlike the OAS documents, goes on to specify a menu of responses that altogether leaves behind the principle of non-intervention:

> . . .
>
> 4. The perpetrators of unconstitutional change of government shall not be allowed to participate in elections held to restore the democratic order or hold any position of responsibility in political institutions of their State.
> 5. Perpetrators of unconstitutional change of government may also be tried before the competent court of the Union.
> 6. The Assembly shall impose sanctions on any Member State that is proved to have instigated or supported unconstitutional change of government in another state in conformity with Article 23 of the Constitutive Act.
> 7. The Assembly may decide to apply other forms of sanctions on perpetrators of unconstitutional change of government including punitive economic measures.
> 8. State Parties shall not harbour or give sanctuary to perpetrators of unconstitutional changes of government.
> 9. State Parties shall bring to justice the perpetrators of unconstitutional changes of government or take necessary steps to effect their extradition.
> 10. State Parties shall encourage conclusion of bilateral extradition agreements as well as the adoption of legal instruments on extradition and mutual legal assistance.

The very boldness of these remedies, contrasted with the realities of undemocratic and unconstitutional governance in so many of the states that voted to approve it, calls into question how seriously this instrument can be taken. At worst, the document might serve as a compact among a clique of unaccountable leaders to

[152] African Charter on Democracy, Elections, and Governance (Jan. 30, 2007), *available at* <http://www.africa-union.org/root/au/Documents/Treaties/text/Charter%20on%20Democracy.pdf>; *see* Tajudeen Abdul-Raheem, "Why No-One Will Ratify the AU Charter on Democracy," *Africa Files* (9 May 2009), *available at* <http://www.africafiles.org/article.asp?id=20794>.

[153] Article 23 defines of "an unconstitutional change of government" as:

> 1. Any putsch or coup d'Etat against a democratically elected government.
> 2. Any intervention by mercenaries to replace a democratically elected government.
> 3. Any replacement of a democratically elected government by armed dissidents or rebels.
> 4. Any refusal by an incumbent government to relinquish power to the winning party or candidate after free, fair and regular elections; or
> 5. Any amendment or revision of the constitution or legal instruments, which is an infringement on the principles of democratic change of government.

suppress challenges to one another's control. Still, the ACDEG represents an unprecedented withholding of respect for the outcome of internal processes judged to transgress international standards.

## D. THE NEW WAVE OF REJECTION OF COUP REGIMES: HONDURAS AND MADAGASCAR

Where blatantly thuggish forces impose themselves on a manifestly unwilling political community, deference to the outcomes of "internal processes" cannot be rationalized as respect for the self-determination of independent political communities. Ideological pluralism, however foundational to the international legal order, ultimately finds its limiting cases, where no internationally respected principles of public order support the governmental pretensions of narrowly self-interested cliques and glorified street gangs. The exceptional cases of Haiti and Sierra Leone might thus be seen as helping to stabilize, rather than to undermine, the general presumption in favor of the effective control criterion. Coup regimes might be subjected to diplomatic disapproval, and sanctioned for breaches of human rights obligations, including a more robustly read right to political participation, yet might still be accepted as embodying valid domestic authority for purposes of analyzing the state's rights and obligations under international law.

But new cases may point in a different direction. Most dramatic has been the international reaction to the June 28, 2009, ouster of Honduran President Manuel Zelaya. When the Honduran military, with the overwhelming support of the legislature and the unanimous support of the Supreme Court, summarily removed and exiled Zelaya in apparent defiance of the constitutional text, the international reaction to the equivocal circumstances was remarkably unequivocal: the United Nations General Assembly unanimously demanded Zelaya's immediate restoration and called "firmly and unequivocally upon States to recognize no Government other than that of the Constitutional President."[154] Accordingly, United Nations bodies refused to accept the credentials of the coup regime's representatives.[155]

The Honduran case is difficult to contain within a traditional framework. Far from holding an overwhelming popular mandate, Zelaya was a narrowly elected president nearing the end of his term, disowned by his own political party, and increasingly given to polarizing and apparently unconstitutional measures (whether for worse or, just as plausibly, for better); Honduras was a divided society.[156]

[154] G.A. Res. 63/301 (2009).

[155] Gustavo Capdevila, "Tripped Up by Honduras, UN Council Turns to Middle East," *IPS News* (Sept. 15, 2009), *available at* <http://ipsnews.net/news.asp?idnews=48452>.

[156] A CID-Gallup poll showed 46 percent opposed to the coup versus 41 percent in favor. CID-Gallup, "Honduras: 'A Divided Nation'" Public Opinion Poll, July 2009, *available at* <http://www.cid-gallup.com/Documentos/Boletin_OP_HONDURAS_71%20Englishv2.pdf>

The case for the continued recognition of Zelaya rested exclusively on an interpretation of the Honduran Constitution that, however well grounded in the text, was overwhelmingly rejected by established Honduran judicial and legislative institutions. While it is not implausible to regard the Honduran Supreme Court as both a partisan political player and a malefactor,[157] it seems incongruous for outsiders to second-guess even a highly counterintuitive constitutional interpretation issued by a foreign high court—a unanimous one, no less. As Doug Cassel notes, "Ordinarily international law imposes its own, autonomous norms for the permissible conduct of a government. Questions of domestic law—including constitutionality—are left to domestic authorities, both as a matter of their sovereign entitlements, and because they are presumed better able to interpret their own constitution."[158]

The two reasons that Cassel cites are distinct. The latter is a matter of respect for a foreign *pouvoir constitué*, on the ground that standards of legal interpretation are themselves a matter of local law. The former is a matter of respect for a foreign *pouvoir constituant*, on the ground that where permanently effective, breaches of constitutional order (whether by insurrection or by an existing regime's pattern of practice) beget their own legality.[159] For foreign courts, both of these are ordinarily rationales, not for a mere "margin of appreciation," but for judicial abstention.

However, it is not unknown for international legal questions to turn on a finding about compliance with domestic law, such as where treaty provisions provide that exceptions to specified human rights must be, *inter alia*, "non-arbitrary" and delineated in domestic law. In such circumstances, assessing a claim of violation requires an independent basis for ascertaining the requirements of domestic law. The criteria for establishing a violation might be relatively deferential, yielding to plausible claims of local expertise in interpreting local norms; interpretation of legal (including especially constitutional) norms depends on all manner of historical, ideological, political, linguistic, and jurisprudential idiosyncracies, and a high court's authority to say what is lawful counts for much, even in the face of text apparently to the contrary. Still, one cannot exclude a second-guessing of local judicial authorities on the merits, especially in cases where courts are suspected of participating in a sham.

[157] Larry Birns, director of the Washington-based Council on Hemispheric Affairs, has characterized the Honduran Supreme Court as "one of the most corrupt institutions in Latin America." CNN.com, "Police Clash with Demonstrators in Honduran Capital," June 29, 2009, *available at* <http://www.cnn.com/2009/WORLD/americas/06/29/honduras.president.arrested/index.html?iref=werecommend>.

[158] Cassel, *supra*, at 3.

[159] "Successful revolution sooner or later begets its own legality." Stanley A. de Smith, *Constitutional and Administrative Law* (London: Penguin Books, 3rd ed. 1977), at 66–67.

As Cassel points out, "In order to create a collective regional safeguard for democracy in each country, [the Inter-American Democratic Charter] sets international standards which demand (among other things) that each nation comply with its own constitution."[160] This much is established: a state's compliance with the IADC, and thus, at minimum, with OAS terms for participation, turns on a determination about compliance with domestic law. Compliance with the IADC and domestic law may also bear on the state's fulfillment of the requirements of the right to political participation under Article 23 of the American Convention on Human Rights.[161]

But here, at issue is which of two putative presidencies validly represents Honduras in the international order. From the standpoint of international law, such a controversy would ordinarily be thought to represent quintessentially a "matter essentially within the domestic jurisdiction" under Article 2(7) of the United Nations Charter and related norms of non-intervention in internal affairs. Indeed, it is hardly an exaggeration to say that if internal actors do not retain the last word on such a matter, the whole idea of a "matter essentially within the domestic jurisdiction" is now a nullity (and, some would say, a good riddance).

Herein lies a subtle but crucial distinction: States may undertake international legal obligations in respect of any subject matter whatever, but doing so does not, in itself, render breaching acts legally null and void. To be sure, contrary domestic law is not a defense to a breach of international legal obligation, but it does not automatically follow that the international order can ignore all legal facts that the breaching act purports to establish, especially as they pertain to public order within the state's territory. (For example, foreign states generally lack jurisdiction to enforce even a binding and applicable international legal norm within the territory of a fellow sovereign state, even where the latter's cooperation is unlawfully withheld, and state officials acting within national territory are ordinarily immune *ratione materiae* for their participation in acts of state that breach international obligations.) International law contains no analogue to the U.S. Constitution's Supremacy Clause; the relationship of Honduras to the international or the regional order cannot be analogized to that of Michigan to the U.S. federal government.

It is unclear how far the international system's reaction to the Honduran case entailed a literal assertion that the Zelaya Government, and not the congressionally installed Micheletti Government, represented the Honduran state for purposes of international law. For example, it is one thing for the OAS to suspend "Honduras"; it is quite another thing for states and international organizations to acknowledge a government-in-exile as exercising the authentic executive aspect of Honduran sovereignty. Interestingly, when the *de facto* regime sought to preempt suspension by

[160] Cassel, *supra*, at 3.

[161] 1144 U.N.T.S. 123, *entered into force* July 18, 1978.

withdrawing Honduras from the Organization, OAS Assistant Secretary General Albert R. Ramdin responded that "The current regime is not recognized as the legitimate government of Honduras. And so only a legitimate government can withdraw from the organization."[162] How seriously this statement was intended, and how far its implications were deliberated, remain open questions. The OAS Charter, even read in light of the IADC and related declarations, contains no language that would seem to authorize the coercive consequences that might follow from a finding that the government-in-exile bears the Honduran state's power of sovereign consent.

Two factors may render this case somewhat less profound than it initially appears. First, support for the Zelaya Government reflected an unusual alignment of interests. Governments that typically oppose intervention on principle, and have reason to fear it in practice (such as the governments of Cuba, Venezuela, and Nicaragua), happened also to be governments politically aligned with Zelaya, whereas many governments unfavorably disposed toward Zelaya (such as that of the United States) had committed themselves to a vision of the international rule of law that obliged them at least to pay lip service to demands for Zelaya's restoration. The latter group could be assured that the rhetorical posturing in this case would be unable to achieve Zelaya's restoration, while it is hardly clear that former group would be willing to live with the implications of its legal position as applied to other political circumstances.[163] Moreover, sitting governments, regardless of their constitutional or ideological basis, tend to be easily recruited to join in a political condemnation of a fellow government's irregular ouster. It is hard to know what the unanimous assent to United Nations General Assembly Resolution 63/301 says about the *opinio juris* of Cuba, one of the resolution's sponsors, let alone of Russia, China, Saudi Arabia, Myanmar, Sudan, and so on.

Second, the Honduras crisis had a near-term expiration date. Zelaya's term was coming to an end in January 2010, at which point all constitutionally grounded claims on his behalf would dissipate. The new government of President Porfirio Lobo, deriving from October 2009 elections that were not seriously marred by irregularities and boycotts, faced problems in its diplomatic reincorporation into the international system, but it did not face an internationally recognized government-in-exile that could call into question its legal capacities.

[162] Ginger Thompson & Marc Lacey, "O.A.S. Votes to Suspend Honduras Over Coup," *N.Y. Times* (July 4, 2009), *available at* <http://www.nytimes.com/2009/07/05/world/americas/05honduras.html>.

[163] Zelaya's strongest international backers—Presidents Hugo Chavez of Venezuela and Daniel Ortega of Nicaragua—have repeatedly faced objections to the constitutional propriety of their modes of governance. For example, Venezuela's 1999 constitutional revision, though accomplished with strong popular support, was accompanied by significant breaches of the then-existing constitutional order. *See* Larry Rohter, "Venezuelan Congress Fights Loss of Power," *N.Y. Times* (Aug. 27, 1999), *available at* <http://www.nytimes.com/1999/08/27/world/venezuelan-congress-fights-loss-of-power.html>.

It is instructive that while the Honduran coup regime's leader was barred from addressing the opening of the United Nations General Assembly's 2009 session, top officials of no less than 12 coup-installed governments did address that body—presided over, ironically, by the representative of Libya's 40-year coup-installed regime.[164] Apart from Micheletti, the only *de facto* leader denied permission to address the General Assembly was Malagasy President Andry Rajoelina, whom the military had installed after ousting elected President Marc Ravalomanana in March 2009. Both the AU and the Southern African Development Community (SADC) had suspended Madagascar as a result of the interruption in constitutional rule. Although Rajoelina was not permitted to address the United Nations General Assembly, the Credentials Committee neither accepted nor rejected the credentials of his government's representatives to the General Assembly, thereby provisionally permitting those representatives to participate in the work of United Nations bodies (the same solution as applied to representatives of Guinea's coup regime).[165] After a year of fruitless efforts to negotiate the Rajoelina government's relinquishment of power, the AU in March 2010 imposed extensive sanctions on Madagascar's *de facto* leaders (including travel bans and asset freezes), and urged other intergovernmental organizations to impose further diplomatic isolation.[166] Thus far, however, there has been no assertion of the existence of an alternative government with the authority to represent Madagascar.

The international reactions to the Honduran and Malagasy coups, against the backdrop of respective regional instruments hostile to unconstitutional changes of government, demonstrate the growing discomfort with a blanket conferral of international standing on whatever regime establishes effective control through internal processes. Yet these reactions remain equivocal. The international system's continuing diversity of interests and values, let alone regime types, significantly impedes so fundamental a change in international legal relations as the systematic denial to coup regimes of the legal capacity to assert rights, incur obligations, exercise powers, and confer immunities on behalf of their states in the international order.[167]

[164] Patrick Goodenough, "Regimes Arising From Coups Should Be Barred From UN Institutions, African Official Says," CNSNews.com (Sept. 29, 2009), *available at* <http://www.cnsnews.com/news/print/54694> (listing Burkina Faso, Burma, Central African Republic, Equatorial Guinea, Fiji, The Gambia, Guinea, Libya, Oman, Qatar, Sudan, and Tunisia as coup regimes represented among the speakers).

[165] UN General Assembly Credentials Committee Report, "Credentials of Representatives to the Sixty-Fourth Session of the General Assembly," U.N. Doc. 64/571 (Dec. 17, 2009), ¶ 11.

[166] UN Integrated Regional Information Networks, "Madagascar: Will AU Sanctions Be a Wake-Up Call"? (Mar. 18, 2010), *available at* <http://www.irinnews.org/report.aspx?ReportID=88477>.

[167] It is too soon, at this writing, to know the outcome of events in Côte d'Ivoire in the wake of the November 28, 2010 election, after which the Southern-based government of Laurent Gbagbo refused to yield power to the evident winner, the Northern-based opposition presidential candidate Alassane Ouattara. This case has been exceptional in that the internationally monitored election was

# Conclusion

## THE DECLINE OF THE EFFECTIVE CONTROL DOCTRINE AND THE ABSENCE OF A COHERENT SUBSTITUTE

The effective control doctrine that, in different forms, has governed the recognition of states and governments is unappealing at its core. Based on the principle of non-interference in civil strife within established international borders, the doctrine's essential logic is that in regard to internal efforts to create new states by secession or to overthrow existing constitutional orders, the international rule of law reduces to respect for the outcomes of trials by ordeal. Traditionally, international law has not established any pathway by which secession can be peacefully achieved without the consent of the original state, nor has it systematically predicated a governmental apparatus's standing to exercise the state's legal prerogatives on anything other than victory in an internal power struggle. In these fundamental ways, international law has seemed to lack a "rule of law" character.

Nonetheless, alternatives are elusive, and not merely because of *realpolitik* considerations. Appeals to the idea of "popular" rather than "state" sovereignty miss the point that opposing sides in internal conflict typically claim this mantle. The right of peoples to self-determination is associated with non-fragmentation as much as with independence; respect for majority rule presupposes an answer to the very question being contested—the "majority of whom?" problem—and respect for minority rights presupposes straightforward resolutions to clashes, not only between legitimate majority and minority interests, but also between minorities and minorities-within-minorities, between territorially concentrated and dispersed minorities, and between "national" and "non-autochthonous" minorities. Substantial sectors of the international community have an interest in avoiding the establishment of general principles that, while aiding in the solution of one crisis, will tend to destabilize local arrangements elsewhere.

Demands that local conflicts be resolved in accordance with existing domestic constitutional norms may seem to befit an international rule of law, but these demands misleadingly portray international and domestic legality as a seamless web. The international legal order as we have known it—as reflected in the language

part of an internationally brokered agreement to end an internal armed conflict that had drawn a Chapter VII intervention. *See* S.C. Res. 1880, 1893 (2009), 1911 (2010). Although the election winner's legitimacy to govern appears to be genuinely contested within the political community (along sectional lines)—the apparent run-off margin was 54 percent to 46 percent, BBC News, "Ivory Coast election: Alassane Ouattara 'beats Gbagbo,'"Dec. 2, 2010 <http://www.bbc.co.uk/news/world-africa-11903470>—the Gbagbo government is in a poor position to argue that the matter is "essentially within the domestic jurisdiction," having previously agreed, in an already internationalized context, to accept whatever electoral outcome would be certified by external monitors.

of such documents as the OAS Charter, the Friendly Relations Declaration, and the ICJ *Nicaragua* decision—is properly understood, not as a legal order of legal orders, but as a legal order of sovereign political communities that each bear an "inalienable" *pouvoir constituant*. That *pouvoir constituant* logically includes an authority (insofar as its exercise is deemed authentically attributable to its bearer) to overthrow any existing domestic order by any means.

While constitutionalism—a commitment to establish, maintain, and respect a broadly acknowledged framework for the legitimate exercise of power—is undoubtedly a crucial political virtue, the same cannot automatically be said for adherence to any particular constitutional norm or even whole constitution. Existing constitutions are artifacts of past power struggles and negotiated settlements and may preclude outcomes that are more consistent with popular will or with the protection of vital interests and rights of particular sectors.[168] It is hard to see why a particular constitutional formula to which a substantial constituency militantly objects should, purely by virtue of its having been established, have a claim to international reinforcement.

Moreover, while democratic practice cannot be sustained for any length of time without a constitutionalist ethos, it does not follow that all departures from that ethos are inimical to democracy. What counts as a democratic outcome in any given instance is highly dependent on contested normative conceptions. From one perspective, in conditions of extreme economic disparity and social stratification, liberal-democratic constitutional forms are consistent with a substantive political inequality that belies the "democratic" imprimatur; in the face of concentrations of economic and social power, a concentration of political power may be necessary to change the game. From another perspective, adherence to a particular constitutional formula may allow for demagoguery or deadlock to win the day at a critical historical moment, with potentially severe and lasting social costs. Where such assertions are facially plausible and are embraced by substantial constituencies, the words "essentially within the domestic jurisdiction," expressing the principle of sovereign equality so central to the international legal order that we have lately known, seem apt.

That said, the existence of twilight does not refute the distinction between day and night. There remains an underlying moral logic to the international legal order, and the plurality of interpretations, while substantial, is not unlimited. A cross-cutting consensus in the international community is frequently achievable, if not about what popular sovereignty is, then about what it is not. Where the outcome of

[168] As Jean d'Aspremont notes, "a coup d'etat can prove to be a *positive break from the existing order* and can bring about a desirable change in regime," especially where an elected regime's mode of exercising power vitiates its initial legitimacy. D'Aspremont, "Responsibility for Coups d'Etat," *supra*, at 473–74.

a local trial by ordeal is widely perceived to be in blatant contradiction to the notion of the state as embodying the self-determination of the entirety of the territorial population, or to the notion of the government as an authentic representative (for the time being) of the political community that the state encompasses, international institutions may repudiate that outcome and champion an alternative solution. That alternative solution, however, tends ineluctably to have an ad hoc character.

# 7

# Coming to Terms with Ruthlessness

## *State Sovereignty and International Criminal Law in Domestic Courts*

## Introduction

Among human rights-oriented scholars, arguments against unilateral exertions of power across territorial boundaries have considerable (though by no means universal) appeal as applied to unilateral threats and uses of force,[1] and perhaps even to unilateral coercive economic measures such as secondary boycotts.[2] Yet some of the same scholars who embrace restraints on those categories of exertions by individual states or "coalitions of the willing" appear to see national courts' exercises of extraordinary extraterritorial jurisdiction, nullifications of the immunity of foreign officials, and creative circumventions of *nullum crimen sine lege* as not only exempt from the pitfalls of such unilateral executive measures, but actually as a peace-building and law-developing alternative to such executive measures.

This is a fundamental mistake. Extraterritorial prosecution of foreign-state actors and forcible impositions upon foreign political communities are both conceptually and practically intertwined. Because the legal limitations on the two derive from the same jurisprudential concept, the likely consequence of the loosening of constraints in the former realm will be the erosion of constraints in the latter.

[1] *See, e.g.,* Mary Ellen O'Connell, "Opposing the New Militarism," 2008:1 *Foreign Voices* 5 (2008), <www.responsibilitytoprotect.org/index.php?module=uploads&func=download&fileId=495>; Jose Alvarez, "Notes from the President: The Schizophrenias of R2P," 23:3 *ASIL Newsletter* (Summer 2007), <http://www.asil.org/newsletter/president/pres070927.html>.

[2] *See* Andreas F. Lowenfeld, "Agora: The Cuban Liberty and Democratic Solidarity (LIBERTAD) Act," 90 *Am. J. Int'l L.* 419, 430 (1996) (asserting "that (in time of peace) the exercise of jurisdiction . . . to impose a secondary boycott . . . is contrary to international law, because it seeks unreasonably to coerce conduct that takes place wholly outside of the state purporting to exercise its jurisdiction to prescribe").

International legal constraints on the use of force are predicated not on a principle of non-violence, but on a principle of respect for a foreign state's authority within its boundaries.[3] To put the point colorfully, but without substantive exaggeration, the right against coercive intervention is the right of territorial political communities to be ruled by their own thugs and to fight their civil wars in peace. It reflects a pluralism that self-consciously sacrifices one set of genuine moral imperatives to another. It favors the creation and maintenance of a stable platform for peaceful and respectful accommodation among territorial political communities—which may be ruled, for the time being, by governments bearing incompatible conceptions of political morality—over licensing unilateral projections of power across borders in service of what might objectively be a just cause.[4] Although considerations of human rights may ground episodic exceptions to the non-intervention norm, human rights do not constitute a general qualification of the norm; rather, a state's right against dictatorial interferences in its internal affairs presumptively withstands the state's own violations of international legal norms, including human rights norms.[5]

To the extent that extraterritorial jurisdiction licenses the vilification of foreign state officials, it has the potential to undermine the platform that undergirds peaceful and respectful international relations. International efforts to secure the bases of human well-being routinely require the cooperation of political leaders to whom significant human rights violations can be attributed. Even recourse to force, both international and internal, must often be directed toward creating the conditions for a compromise that will respect the honor of the opposing party, notwithstanding the opponent's ruthless acts. Moreover, where ruthless acts have been committed with substantial popular support, particular leaders cannot be singled out for vilification without impugning underlying constituencies, thereby further complicating efforts to establish cooperation going forward. These are morally important reasons to forbear from the pursuit of retributive justice across borders, even though countervailing considerations may outweigh them in a limited set of circumstances.

Beyond being a general irritant to international relations, assertions of prosecutorial authority over the acts of foreign states within their territory, if routinized, can

[3] *See* Robert Jackson, *The Global Covenant: Human Conduct in a World of States* (Oxford: Oxford Univ. Press, 2000), at 368 ("perhaps the most fundamental [concern of modern international society] has been . . . to confine religious and ideological *weltanschauungen* within the territorial cages of national borders").

[4] "[W]hen contemplating military intervention, the United Nations (U.N.) usually has preferred not to differentiate between just and unjust reasons to intervene. Instead, the nations have favored treating all states as autonomous entities entitled to be left alone, and doing so on grounds of maintaining international peace and order, rather than advancing justice." Thomas M. Franck, "Is Justice Relevant to the International Legal System?" 64 *Notre Dame L.J.* 645, 655 (1989).

[5] See Chapter 3.

easily become an available tool for proponents of an antagonistic foreign policy.[6] Indictments could be used as a rationale for hardening the government's position against a foreign state,[7] akin to the insistence that one never negotiate with terrorists.[8] More broadly, extraterritorial prosecutions might serve as a device to discredit advocates of a peaceful settlement, purporting to reveal the fecklessness of those who counsel—or who have in earlier instances counseled—restraint and compromise in the face of a certified evil. Instead of serving as a rationale for discouraging aggressive responses, respect for international legality may be invoked as a reason to take aggressive action.[9]

Worst of all, a legal attribution of criminality to adverse regimes may tend to present international institutions with enforcement demands that such institutions, dependent on consensus among non-like-minded states, characteristically cannot fulfill. At this fork in the road, where the international legal order's procedural strictures are perceived to frustrate that same order's imperative substantive ends, violations of use-of-force norms can be rationalized as implementing the true spirit of international law.[10] Instead of furthering accountability in the exercise of power, international criminal law may furnish a rationale to disparage and to flout those international institutions and processes that are designed to hold powerful states accountable.

International criminal justice must thus respect the inherent pluralism of the international legal order or else play a part in that order's erosion. Respect for

[6] No assurance should be drawn from the fact that such proponents have, up to now, opposed international criminal justice. Should the new normative tendencies achieve dominance, those favoring projections of power by strong states in the affairs of weak states will likely adapt their rhetorical approach to exploit its possibilities. An historical precedent is the Reagan administration's remarkable shift from rejection to acceptance of human rights rhetoric in the early 1980s, and its subsequent invocation of human rights rationales in support of aggressive policies that had long preceded the rhetorical shift. See Cynthia Brown ed., *With Friends Like These: The Americas Watch Report on Human Rights and U.S. Policy in Latin America* (New York: Pantheon, 1985), 3–23.

[7] The U.S. indictment of Panamanian strongman Manuel Antonio Noriega, albeit for drug trafficking rather than human rights-related offenses, illustrates this point. *See, e.g.*, Jeff Cohen & Mark Cook, "How Television Sold the Panama Invasion"(Fairness & Accuracy in Reporting, Jan./Feb. 1990), *available at* <http://www.fair.org/index.php?page=1546>.

[8] For an exemplar of such reasoning, *see* Louis Rene Beres, "International Law Requires Prosecution, Not Celebration, of Arafat," 71 *U. Det. Mercy L. Rev.* 569 (1994).

[9] *See generally* Gerry Simpson, *Great Powers and Outlaw States: Unequal Sovereigns in the International Order* (Cambridge: Cambridge Univ. Press, 2004) (elaborating the historical tendency of the international system to cast particular states as non-right-bearing outlaws).

[10] Such invocation of universal principles in the face of institutional deadlock is brilliantly exemplified in W. Michael Reisman, "Unilateral Actions and the Transformations of the World Constitutive Process: The Special Problem of Humanitarian Intervention," 11 *Euro. J. Int'l L.* 3 (2000). That model of argumentation was arguably decisive in winning over important liberal constituencies to the Bush administration's decision to invade Iraq in 2003.

strictures associated with the international rule of law, even at the expense of substantive justice, safeguards that pluralistic order's foundations. [11]

The critique expressed herein is not directed against the International Criminal Court or (for the most part) other international criminal tribunals, nor is it directed against domestic-court exercises of extraterritorial jurisdiction over genuinely manifest atrocities. These categories all but exhaust the existing record of extraterritorial prosecution of human rights violators (though there have been exceptional cases, as discussed below). The critique is directed, rather, against the associated rhetoric of both jurists and scholars that encourages exorbitant extrapolations from actual practice. It is not an attack on how far international law has developed, but rather a call to respect how much restraint has (so far, at least) marked its actual development.

The first section below will reflect on the stigmatization of legal doctrines that tend to work in favor of "impunity." The second section will summarize the challenge that the prevalence of ruthless responses to political crisis poses to a legal order that demands both human rights compliance and forbearance from unilateral impositions. The third section will elaborate rule-of-law considerations that constrain the retrospective application of one regime's criminal law to conduct that took place under a different regime. The fourth section will speak to the special problem of observing the rule of law in accounting for enactments of past regimes that systematized extreme injustice. The fifth section will contend that the distinction between international human rights violations and international crimes needs to be rigorously observed rather than elided.

## I. Impunity as a Dirty Word

In recent years, scholars and advocates committed to the cause of international legality have almost uniformly expressed passionate enthusiasm for the burgeoning project of international criminal justice. In the international law literature, the word "impunity" appears exclusively as a pejorative, if not an epithet. Illustrative is the response of six human rights organizations to Belgium's 2003 curtailment of the reach of its penal laws: "With its universal jurisdiction law, Belgium helped destroy

[11] The reasons given above may be taken as arguments against state consent to further expansion of universal jurisdiction, or as arguments for forbearance from prosecutions that have a valid basis in existing international criminal law. Both of those questions are beyond the scope of this discussion. For present purposes, the point is that gaps in the positive criminalization of human rights violations result, not from some technical failure to have accomplished an unquestioned goal, but from countervailing considerations that ground continued resistance within the international community to an expansive license for extraterritorial prosecution. Consequently, courts have a responsibility to respect existing limitations, rather than to seek a work-around.

the wall of impunity behind which the world's tyrants had always hidden to shield themselves from justice. . . . It is regrettable that Belgium has now forgotten the victims to whom it gave a hope of justice."[12] So strong is the perceived repugnance of the term that the International Court of Justice felt the need to give rhetorical assurance that immunity does not equate to impunity, even in dicta that seemingly bolstered impunity by negative implication.[13]

Scholarship frequently suggests creative circumventions of those constraints on penal accountability that arise from a range of doctrines rooted in deference to state authority. State sovereignty is routinely cast as a realm of lawlessness that recedes insofar as international law advances, and nothing is seen to augur the advent of the international rule of law quite as much as extraterritorial prosecution of state agents for human rights and humanitarian law violations. Although the prevalent mind-set allows for controversies internal to criminal law doctrine, such as about expansive theories of what counts as personal participation in established international crimes,[14] an insistence on discerning, let alone advocating, public international law-based limitations to the reach of substantive penal norms encounters profound disfavor.[15]

[12] Human Rights Watch, "Belgium: Universal Jurisdiction Law Repealed" (Aug. 1, 2003), <http://www.hrw.org/en/news/2003/08/01/belgium-universal-jurisdiction-law-repealed>.

[13] *Case Concerning the Arrest Warrant of April 11, 2000, Democratic Republic of the Congo v. Belgium (Yerodia)*, 2002 ICJ Rep. 3, ¶ 60. This curious passage spoke of Foreign Ministers remaining subject to prosecution in foreign-state courts, after leaving office, for crimes that they committed "in a private capacity," *id.*, ¶ 61, even though private crimes in this context are obviously not of central concern, and continued immunity for crimes committed in a public capacity would amount to impunity. *See id.*, diss. op. of Judge ad hoc Van den Wyngaert, ¶.36; William A. Schabas, *The UN International Criminal Tribunals: The former Yugoslavia, Rwanda and Sierra Leone* (Cambridge: Cambridge Univ. Press, 2006), 159 & n. 31 (concluding that this language "largely overturned a somewhat more liberal ruling by the United Kingdom House of Lords in the celebrated *Pinochet* case"); David S. Koller, "Immunities of Foreign Ministers: Paragraph 61 of the Yerodia Judgment as it Pertains to the Security Council and the International Criminal Court," 20 *Am. U. Int'l L. Rev.* 7, 29 (2004) ("The Court's judgment effectively creates a substantive defense, according absolute impunity in violation of . . . the Court's own stated goal of not equating immunity with impunity."). The passage's substantive significance is doubtful (the "private capacity" language may have been intended to leave other immunity questions open), but the rhetorical incongruity is remarkable.

[14] Perhaps the most sweeping critique along these lines is Darryl Robinson, "The Identity Crisis of International Criminal Law," 21 *Leiden J. Int'l L.* 925 (2008); *see also* Alison Marston Danner & Jenny S. Martinez, "Guilty Associations: Joint Criminal Enterprise, Command Responsibility, and the Development of International Criminal Law," 93 *Cal. L. Rev.* 75 (2005); Mark J. Osiel, 'Modes of Participation in Mass Atrocity,' 38 *Cornell Int'l L. J.* 793 (2005).

[15] Some noteworthy exceptions include Henry J. Steiner, "Three Cheers for Universal Jurisdiction—Or Is It Only Two?" 5 *Theoretical Inquiries in Law* 199 (2004) (giving a mixed account of the doctrine's prospects); Madeline Morris, "Universal Jurisdiction in a Divided World," 35 *New England L. Rev.* 337 (2001) (raising concerns); *see also* Anthony Colangelo, "The Limits of Universal Jurisdiction," 47 *Va. J. Int'l L.* 1 (2005) (specifying the scope of the license that universal jurisdiction establishes). The most

Emblematic are the unidirectional "Princeton Principles," which issued from a conclave of leading figures in the field of international criminal justice. In setting forth prescriptions to expand national courts' exercise of universal criminal jurisdiction, the proclamation of Principles pointedly cautions that these prescriptions "shall not be construed as limiting the continued development of universal jurisdiction in international law."[16] The official Commentary attributes to the authors an intention "to invite rather than hinder the continued development of universal jurisdiction."[17] Thus, "[a]ll of the participants felt that the Principles not be construed... to constrain the evolution of accountability for crimes under international law."[18] The Commentary goes so far as to call for universal jurisdiction to be invoked in cases of "cruel, inhuman, and degrading treatment or punishment,"[19] even though the universal jurisdiction provisions of the Convention Against Torture expressly pertain only to the carefully circumscribed category of "torture."[20] Only one of the conclave's participants dissented from the promulgated Principles, complaining that they (1) affected states not parties to the Torture Convention or to other instruments manifesting consent to the exercise of universal jurisdiction, and (2) would remove all immunities, in respect of both personal statuses (i.e., head of state, head of government, foreign minister, and diplomat) and subject matter (acts committed within the scope of official capacity), that ordinarily apply in domestic courts.[21]

cited contrarian literature about international criminal justice comes from outside of the international law field, whether from the "New Sovereigntist" school within U.S. foreign relations law, *see* Peter J. Spiro, "The New Sovereigntists: American Exceptionalism and Its False Prophets," 79 *Foreign Aff.* 9 (2000), or from political scientists of the "realist" school, *see, e.g.,* Jack Snyder & Leslie Vinjamuri, "Trials and Errors: Principle and Pragmatism in Strategies of International Justice," 28:3 *Int'l Security* 5 (2003–04); Henry A. Kissinger, "The Pitfalls of Universal Jurisdiction," 80 *Foreign Aff.* 86 (2001).

[16] *The Princeton Principles on Universal Jurisdiction* (Princeton University Program in Law and Public Affairs, 2001), Principle 13(3), at 35.

[17] *Id.* at 41.

[18] *Id.* at 55.

[19] *Id.* at 48–49.

[20] *See* Convention Against Torture and Other Cruel, Inhuman, and Degrading Treatment or Punishment ("Torture Convention"),December 10, 1984, 1465 UNTS 85, 23 ILM 1027 (1984), arts. 5, 6 (conferring extraterritorial penal jurisdiction over acts of "torture" as defined in Article 1, but not over "cruel, inhuman, and degrading treatment" as defined in Article 16).

[21] Lord Browne-Wilkinson (best known for having issued the lead opinion in the House of Lords' final *Pinochet* judgment) elaborated on his dissenting position as follows:

> [T]he Princeton Principles propose that individual national courts should exercise such jurisdiction against nationals of a state which has not agreed to such jurisdiction. Moreover the Principles do not recognize any form of sovereign immunity: Principle 5(1). If the law were to be so established, states antipathetic to Western powers would be likely to seize both active and retired officials and military personnel of such Western powers and stage a show trial for alleged international crimes. Conversely, zealots in Western States might launch prosecutions against, for example, Islamic extremists for their terrorist activities. It is naive to think that, in

By far the preponderant view in the international criminal justice literature can be summarized as, "More is better."[22] Such a view is not entirely without merit. As to its particulars, the leading literature in the field is generally accurate and well-considered. But paradoxically, a distortion arises from the literature's predominant, and quite appropriate, focus on relatively uncontroversial cases of mass atrocities. Such contexts inspire fully justifiable efforts to overcome doctrinal obstacles to the assertion of prosecutorial authority over sovereign acts. However, those efforts tend not only to narrow the interpretation of legal limitations on the redress of injustice, but also to disparage those limitations.[23]

In particular, the anti-impunity rhetoric tends to imply sweepingly that state officials who authorize or participate in their states' violation of international legal obligations—especially human rights obligations—can be held personally accountable in foreign courts. As will be discussed below, this is the exception, not the rule, and remains so for sound reasons of principle and policy.

What, besides the purest misanthropy, could account for an approach to international law that not only acknowledges, but seeks to solidify, restraints on the pursuit of individual accountability for states' unjust and unlawful acts? The approach might appear even more curious where the author affirms that law is not reducible to a set of social facts, as some versions of legal positivism would have it, but is rather a purposive process in which moral considerations play a legitimate role.[24] It may be more

> such cases, the national state of the accused would stand by and watch the trial proceed: resort to force would be more probable. In any event the fear of such legal actions would inhibit the use of peacekeeping forces when it is otherwise desirable and also the free interchange of diplomatic personnel.
>
> I believe that the adoption of such universal jurisdiction without preserving the existing concepts of immunity would be more likely to damage than to advance chances of international peace.

*Princeton Principles*, *supra*, at 49 n.20.

[22] The prevalent attitude is expressed in such articles as Mark A. Summers, "Immunity or Impunity? The Potential Effect of Prosecutions of State Officials for Core International Crimes in States Like the United States that are Not Parties to the Statute of the International Criminal Court," 31 *Brooklyn J. Int'l L.* 463 (2006); Ellen Lutz & Kathryn Sikkink, "The Justice Cascade: The Evolution and Impact of Foreign Human Rights Trials in Latin America," 2 *Chi. J. Int'l L.* 1 (2001) M. Cherif Bassiouni, "Combating Impunity for International Crimes," 71 *U. Colo. L. Rev.* 409 (2000); Jordan J. Paust, "It's No Defense: *Nullum Crimen*, International Crime and the Gingerbread Man," 60 *Albany L. Rev.* 657 (1997).

[23] *See, e.g.*, Bassiouni, *supra*, at 421 ("The ICC reminds governments that realpolitik, which sacrifices justice at the altar of political settlements, is no longer accepted.")

[24] The methodological approach taken here, inspired significantly by the work of Lon Fuller and Ronald Dworkin, is less akin to positivism, *see* Bruno Simma & Andreas L. Paulus, "The Responsibility of Individuals for Human Rights Abuses in Internal Conflicts: A Positivist View," 93 *Am. J. Int'l L.* 302 (1999), than to the "new international legal process" theory, inasmuch as the latter considers "legal doctrine in light of the law's purposes and the polity's underlying principles," *see* Mary Ellen O'Connell, "New International Legal Process," 93 *Am. J. Int'l. L.* 334, 336 (1999) (citing the canonical work of

curious still, when the author further admits that accountability in the exercise of state power counts among legality's foremost inherent purposes, and that unlawful state acts are "committed by men, not by abstract entities."[25]

The explanation for the contrarian approach lies in the grounding purposes reflected in the United Nations Charter: the establishment of a platform for peaceful accommodation among states representing a diversity of interests and values, and the protection of weak political communities from overbearing projections of power by strong foreign states.[26] The sovereign equality of states itself represents moral purposes that, rather than being simply trumped by the project of penal accountability, persist in dynamic tension with that project.[27]

To champion the purposes associated with sovereign equality is by no means to deny that international criminal justice can serve a useful—indeed, often complementary—function. Nor can there be any doubt that, as a result of the international community's practical and rhetorical affirmations of this function, penal norms have in recent decades developed substantially within the corpus of positive international law.[28] Not only has the international system produced institutional apparatuses of its own to implement these norms, but it has increasingly "deputized" individual states to establish extraterritorial prescriptive and adjudicative jurisdiction over the most serious violations of human rights and humanitarian law.[29]

The real issues lie at the margins. Where existing positive norms of the international legal order that emphasize state authority—in particular, jurisdictional limitations, immunities, and *nullum crimen sine lege*—threaten to frustrate prosecutions of human rights violators, to what extent should interpretive creativity be brought

Henry M. Hart, Jr. and Albert Sacks). Yet in O'Connell's reading, the latter theory "not only supports the fullest accountability, but also would give international institutions the authority to decide for full accountability, despite contrary indications in positive international law." *Id.* at 351. I find this statement unexceptionable as applied to the uncontroversially atrocious cases on which she focuses, but troubling in its neglect of the countervailing purposes and principles that would properly preclude extraterritorial penal accountability in other cases.

[25] International Military Tribunal (Nuremberg), Judgment and Sentence (Oct. 1, 1946), 41 *Am. J. Int'l L.* 172, 221 (1947).

[26] "If modern international society was instituted for anything, it was to prevent unnecessary confrontations and collisions between different states that are inspired and driven by the assertion of their own preferred values." Robert Jackson, *The Global Covenant, supra,* at 368

[27] As noted in the *Yerodia* separate opinion of Judges Higgins, Kooijmans and Buergenthal—the judges most sympathetic to exterritorial prosecution—"the frequently expressed conviction of the international community that perpetrators of grave and inhuman international crimes should not go unpunished does not *ipso facto* mean that immunities are unavailable whenever impunity would be the outcome." *Yerodia, supra,* sep. op. of Judges Higgins, Kooijmans and Buergenthal, at ¶79.

[28] *See generally* Antonio Cassese, *International Criminal Law* 3–199 (Oxford Univ. Press, 2003).

[29] *See id.* at 284–98; Stephen Macedo ed., *Universal Jurisdiction: National Courts and the Prosecution of Serious Crimes under International Law* (Philadelphia: Univ. of Pa. Press, 2004).

to bear to fill gaps and to overcome barriers in the name of moral purposes? This chapter will argue that, especially where domestic courts exercise extraterritorial jurisdiction over foreign state agents, such interpretive creativity should ordinarily be resisted. Such resistance reflects, not a sterile formalism, but an affirmation that the doctrinal constraints at issue are central to the international legal order's moral project.

## II. Championing Legality in a Ruthless World

Substantive justice and the rule of law represent distinct moral projects that, while often in harmony, are sometimes in tension.[30] The rule of law, presupposing human societies beset by both conflict of interest and moral disagreement, establishes rigidities designed to promote predictability and accountability in the exercise of power. Where legal constraint lacks sufficient rigidity to withstand the pressing demands of substantive justice, especially in a "horizontal" system that relies on the more powerful states for coercive norm implementation, the strong are unleashed to pursue substantive justice as they understand it.

Working relationships in the international arena largely depend on maintaining an "agreement to disagree," not only about conflicts of interest but also about matters of fundamental justice. The international legal order thus needs to maintain a balance between ideological pluralism—accommodating inconsistent and sometimes mutually antagonistic political moralities—and an insistence on the inadmissibility of practices reprehended by an overlapping consensus of disparate conceptions of justice.

Moreover, international law's constraints on cross-border exercises of coercion and force are founded on respect for the sovereign authority of individual states. Where international law is seen to impugn that sovereign authority, and yet recourse to the trumping authority of the United Nations Security Council is unavailing (as is usual, given that body's prevalent disunity), the commitment to forbearance from self-help is inevitably strained. It is unrealistic to expect international law's insistence on the inviolability of a state's territorial integrity and political independence to be heeded where international law itself is enlisted in the project of branding that state's government as criminal.[31]

[30] *See, e.g.,* Ronald A. Dworkin, "'Natural' Law Revisited," 34 *U. Fla. L. Rev.* 165, 186 (1982) (noting the conflict between one party's "right to a better public order" and another's "right to a consistent application of the public order").

[31] *See, e.g.,* W. Michael Reisman, "Sovereignty and Human Rights in Contemporary International Law," 84 *Am. J. Int'l L.* 866, 875 (1990) (justifying "unilateral vindication of clear violations of rights when multilateral possibilities do not obtain" on the ground that "rights without remedies are not rights at all"); Reisman, "Unilateral Actions," *supra,* at 15 (2000) (contending that "as the norms in

In international criminal law, the consideration of ideological pluralism weighs most heavily in domestic court cases proceeding under the doctrine of universal jurisdiction. Unilateral assertions of extraterritorial penal jurisdiction over acts of foreign state agents are the most likely to pose a danger to the balance that international law represents,[32] thereby undermining the international legal order's indispensable functions of facilitating accommodation and precluding the strong from imposing what they unilaterally perceive as justice.

The most serious problem promises to arise in the application of putative international penal norms to cases of what I will call "ruthlessness": measures incompatible with "universal" principles of deontological morality,[33] and condemned widely in the abstract, but evaluated differentially in practice within the empirical international community, on the basis of differential regard for the ends to which these measures serve as a means. These ruthless measures constitute serious human rights violations, and some of them have been unambiguously criminalized. Many of them, however, are either (a) outside the scope of established international crimes,[34] (b) on the margins of established international crimes,[35] or (c) nominally within the

question—international human rights norms—derive from a broader decision process than the body assigned to enforce those norms, the broader decision process sustains the norms and seeks alternative modes of enforcement").

[32] "Unfortunately, considering the enormous effort and potential expense in collecting evidence, gathering witnesses, and trying accused perpetrators of horrific crimes committed extraterritorially, the motivation for almost every such national proceeding likely would have some foundation in politics or arise from a sense of judicial, and most likely Western, superiority." Anthony Sammons, "The 'Under-Theorization' of Universal Jurisdiction: Implications for Legitimacy on Trials of War Criminals by National Courts," 21 *Berkeley J. Int'l L.* 111, 137–38 (2003).

[33] For an introduction to the distinction between deontological and consequentialist approaches to morality, *see, e.g.*, J.L. Mackie, *Ethics: Inventing Right and Wrong* (New York: Penguin Books Ltd., 1977), 149–68.

[34] As noted above and discussed more fully below, the Convention Against Torture confers extraterritorial penal jurisdiction over acts of "torture" as defined in Article 1, but not over "cruel, inhuman, and degrading treatment" as defined in Article 16. *See* Torture Convention, *supra*, arts. 1, 5, 6, and 16.

[35] For example, Article 8(2)(b)(iv) of the Rome Statute of the International Criminal Court codifies the customary war crime of "Intentionally launching an attack in the knowledge that such attack will cause incidental loss of life or injury to civilians or damage to civilian objects or widespread, long-term and severe damage to the natural environment which would be clearly excessive in relation to the concrete and direct overall military advantage anticipated." The uncertainty of this norm's application to frequent occurrences in the course of armed conflicts is manifest. *See* Randall Peerenboom, "Human Rights and Rule of Law: What's the Relationship?" 36 *Georgetown J. Int'l L.* 809, 883 (2005) (expressing concern that "these exceedingly vague concepts are likely to result in outcomes determined more by power politics and contested normative views than legal considerations in many cases").

scope of existing international crimes, but not really treated as international crimes when the "good guys" are the ones committing them.[36]

Whereas the elements of the most uncontroversial international crimes themselves entail or suggest inadmissible ends,[37] ruthless measures, as herein defined, are *substantially related to cognizable governmental (or insurgent) objectives.*[38] Although presumptively wrongful in both moral and legal terms, they can be differentiated from three other categories of acts: (i) acts that represent essentially private indulgences of sadism or venality under color of governmental authority; (ii) acts explicitly or implicitly in furtherance of a governmental purpose that is ruled out by the fundamental principles of the international legal order (e.g., genocide, crimes against humanity, ethnic cleansing); and (iii) acts in furtherance of a governmental purpose less extreme, but so manifestly illegitimate that the authorities do not even assert it to justify themselves (instead relying, for example, on factual denials).[39]

As distinguished from the genuine consensus that can be found to condemn wanton cruelty, genocidal policy, and manifest cynicism, the seeming universal reprehension of ruthless measures frequently turns out, on close examination,

[36] The much-maligned *tu quoque* defense has considerable force where a standard's legal validity ultimately rests on its manifestation in patterns of actual practice. Even at Nuremberg, German Admiral Karl Doenitz was successfully defended on the count of engaging in unrestricted submarine warfare on the basis of an affidavit from U.S. Admiral Chester Nimitz, who averred that he had done the same against the Japanese. *See* Gerry J. Simpson, "Didactic and Dissident Histories in War Crimes Trials," 60 *Albany L. Rev.* 801, 806 n. 26 (1997). For an allegation of double standards in the operation of the International Criminal Tribunal for the former Yugoslavia, *see* Paulo Benvenuti, "The ICTY Prosecutor and the Review of the NATO Bombing Campaign against the Federal Republic of Yugoslavia," 12 *Euro. J. Int'l L.* 503 (2001).

[37] These include genocide (an effort "to destroy, in whole or in part, a national, ethnical, racial or religious group"), crimes against humanity (a "widespread or systematic attack . . . against [a] civilian population"), and "a plan or policy or . . . a large-scale commission" of grave breaches or other serious violations of the laws of war. Rome Statute of the International Criminal Court, Arts. 6, 7, and 8.

[38] I have elaborated on this distinction elsewhere. Brad R. Roth, "Just Short of Torture: Abusive Treatment and the Limits of International Criminal Justice," 6 *J. Int'l Crim. Justice* 215, 227–30 (2008).

[39] As Philip Soper points out, what distinguishes the objectively unjust state from "the gunman writ large" is the former's claim to be acting justly. Philip Soper, "In Defense of Classical Natural Law Theory: Why Unjust Law is No Law at All," 20 *Canadian J. L. & Jurisp.* 201, 212 (2007). Where state agents manifestly lack a good faith belief that they are acting in the public interest, the international system's respect for state authority properly offers them little shelter. Similarly, little shelter can be found where the motivating conception of the public interest, even if *bona fide,* contradicts the principle of "equal rights and self-determination of peoples" upon which the international system's respect for state authority is predicated. *See* U.N. Charter, preamble and arts. 1(2), 2(1); *see also* Djura Ninčić, *The Problem of Sovereignty in the Charter and in the Practice of the United Nations* (The Hague: Martinus Hijhoff, 1970), at 256–58 (presenting the Charter's sovereignty and self-determination norms as intertwined).

to be illusory. Affirmations of the acts' "inherent" wrongfulness often obscure deep disagreement about whether such measures could be justified in the service of what might appear—from some political or ideological standpoints, but not others—to be compelling societal needs.[40]

Ruthless measures are not the exception in violent political conflict; in the best of circumstances, they are the rule, whereas in the worst, they give way to unrestrained brutality.[41] The morally better sides in such conflicts appear to have abstained from ruthlessness only to the extent that their histories have been successfully whitewashed.[42] Complicity in ruthlessness has been endemic in liberal as well as non-liberal societies[43]; supporters of forcible measures have either known, or

[40] Opinion polls consistently demonstrate this phenomenon in regard to coercive interrogation tactics, even when they may constitute torture. *See*, e.g., Associated Press, "Poll Finds Broad Approval of Terrorist Torture: Most in U.S., Britain, France, S. Korea Say Torture Justified in Rare Instances" (Dec. 9, 2005), <http://www.msnbc.msn.com/id/10345320/> ("In America, 61 percent of those surveyed agreed torture is justified at least on rare occasions. Almost nine in ten in South Korea and just over half in France and Britain felt that way."). For a deeply reasoned, if problematic, defense of the use of torture in the interrogation of a subclass of terrorism suspects, *see* Eric Posner & Adrian Vermeule, "Should Coercive Interrogation be Legal?" 104 *Mich. L. Rev.* 671 (2006); *but see* Christopher Kutz, "Torture, Necessity, and Existential Politics," 95 *Calif. L. Rev.* 235, 263 (2007) (arguing that "the defense of necessity runs out when it confronts pre-institutional rights, whose value is not a product of an instrumental calculus").

[41] Robert S. McNamara's recent introspections have drawn attention to grisly Allied measures in World War II that decent liberal-democratic states (and the bulk of their populations) have never repudiated:

> We burned to death 100,000 Japanese civilians in Tokyo—men, women, and children. . . . Lemay said, "If we'd lost the war, we'd all have been prosecuted as war criminals." And I think he's right. He—and I'd say I—were behaving as war criminals. . . . What makes it immoral if you lose, and not immoral if you win?

Quoted in Samantha Power, "War and Never Having to Say You're Sorry," *N.Y. Times*, Dec. 14, 2003, Sec. 2, 1 at 33.

[42] As John T. Parry points out, although torture is frequently said to be at odds with U.S. historical practice, the opposite is true. *See* Parry, "Torture Nation, Torture Law," 97 *Georgetown. L.J.* 1001,1003, 1011–16 (2009) (noting systematic U.S. involvement, direct and indirect, in torture during counterinsurgent campaigns in Vietnam and Latin America) .

[43] The mainstream discourse remains far from coming to grips with the record of gross and systematic abuses that the U.S. committed directly in Korea and Vietnam, *see* Bruce Cumings, *The Origins of the Korean War, Vol. II* (Princeton Univ. Press, 1990), 753 (attributing hundreds of thousands of North Korean civilian deaths to U.S. strategic bombing); Michael Bilton & Kevin Sim, *Four Hours in My Lai: A War Crime and its Aftermath* (New York: Viking, 1992) (detailing the systematic nature of the violence that U.S. forces perpetrated against civilians in Vietnam), and by proxy in other Cold War-era conflicts, *see, e.g.*, Christopher Hitchens, *The Trial of Henry Kissinger* (New York: Verso Books, 2001); Raymond Bonner, *Weakness and Deceit: U.S. Policy and El Salvador* (New York: Times Books, 1984). But a sweeping characterization of U.S. Cold War policymakers as international criminals would miss

known that they did not want to know,[44] that those measures were inflicting and would inflict egregious suffering on the innocent. Supporters have persisted in giving aid and comfort to the perpetrators of such measures in the belief—right or wrong, reasonable or unreasonable—that the end justified the means.

It is in such cases that the international order's pluralism is most consequential. Unilateral invocations of universal justice, absent adequate positivistic substantiation, ring hollow where assessments of guilt depend on the political sympathies prevalent in the venue.[45] Such invocations pose a threat both to the integrity of international criminal justice and to the broader project of international legal order.

Accordingly, this chapter will make the case that international criminal law should eschew appeals to supra-positive moral considerations that would, without benefit of a demonstrable consensus, extend the penal law's reach in derogation of existing legal limitations. Where the purported norms providing for the exercise of extraterritorial jurisdiction, for the invalidation of immunity, or for the criminality of a government-authorized act at the time and place in question cannot by credible methods be attributed (directly or indirectly) to the affirmations of the relevant sovereign states, and where the effort to fill the gap relies on a "universal" abstract principle that enjoys no actual consensus in application—however lamentably, from a moral standpoint—the prosecutorial interest must give way.

Whatever merit there may be in deriving non-penal norms from considerations of natural justice, the legal validity of norms that identify not mere wrongfulness, but criminality—let alone the extraordinary criminality associated with "enemies of humanity"[46]—must depend on acknowledged sources of social authority. Sweeping appeals to human dignity, however properly invoked in law as a shield,[47] are

the point: hardly anyone who had a role (or, for that matter, a rooting interest) on any side of any of these conflicts is entitled to engage in flights of deontological self-righteousness.

[44] *See, e.g.,* Jack Goldsmith, "The Detainee Shell Game," *Wash. Post* (May 31, 2009) <http://www.washingtonpost.com/wp-dyn/content/article/2009/05/29/AR2009052902989.html?hpid=opinionsbox1> (arguing that seemingly more scrupulous detention policies merely end up restoring traditional U.S. reliance on "intelligence services from countries that have poor human rights records," so that "in many respects all we are really doing is driving the terrorist incapacitation problem out of sight, to a place where terrorist suspects are treated worse," while allowing us to "feel better about ourselves").

[45] See Steiner, *supra*, at 229 ("A political leader or military figure could be understood or imagined within one state or group as hero, in another as villain, within one state or group as freedom fighter, in another as terrorist").

[46] Universal jurisdiction is predicated on the idea that certain crimes establish their perpetrators as "*hostis humani generis*, an enemy of mankind." Filártiga v. Peña-Irala, 630 F.2d 876, 890 (2d Cir. 1980).

[47] In this context, I use the term "shield" to characterize the assertion of a norm to block the exercise of state power against individuals. Essentially the same assertion, of course, may afterward operate to extract reparation from the state for a violation, and would thus serve as a "sword" in the procedural

inadmissible as a sword.[48] Even the most egregious moral wrongs are crimes, in the legal sense, only when there is a requisite social, not just a moral, basis for characterizing them as such. That social basis must be established through conventionally accepted methods for attributing norms to the will of a political community that, at the time and place of the conduct, duly exerted authority. Moreover, where penal norms are applied extraterritorially, especially against persons operating under the putative authority of their own states, questions of adjudicative jurisdiction and functional *(ratione materiae)* immunity pose similar stakes—the determination on the merits being so heavily dependent on who gets to say—and must therefore be determined by similarly rigorous standards.

These proposed strictures on international criminal justice are important, not because any great number of actual prosecutions that have occurred so far have contravened them, but because they are so sharply at odds with the rhetoric that has often surrounded those actual prosecutions. The problem here is not so much that "hard cases make bad law," but rather that extreme cases generate bad dicta.[49] Both judges and commentators, in their exuberance to herald a new day of individual accountability for human rights abuse, have invoked broad propositions that, removed from their particular contexts, open the door to exercises of power incompatible with the international rule of law.[50] The goal of a more restrictive approach is not to stymie international criminal justice, but to render it safe for international legal order, thereby potentially emboldening otherwise-reluctant actors to implement it where genuinely appropriate.

sense, but the latter use can be seen as ancillary to the former. However, where the norm is invoked to hold individuals personally accountable, criminally or civilly, for acts that they committed as state agents, it is being used to authorize an imposition of state power upon them, and thus as a "sword."

[48] Beth Van Schaack, though arguing generally to the contrary, concedes that "Referring to extratextual principles is more palatable with respect to holding states responsible for breaches than it is for criminally prosecuting individuals where penal sanctions are at issue." Beth Van Schaack, "Crimen Sine Lege: Judicial Lawmaking at the Intersection of Law & Morals,"97 *Georgetown. L. J.* 119, 149 (2008).

[49] A prime example of that maxim can be found in the *Eichmann* decision, which boldly and quite unnecessarily repudiated *nullum crimen sine lege. See* Attorney General of the Government of Israel v. Eichmann, 36 *Int'l L. Rep.* 277, 282 (Sup. Ct. of Israel, May 29, 1962) ("if it is the contention of counsel for the appellant that we must apply international law as it is, and not as it ought to be from a moral point of view, then we must reply precisely from a *legal* point of view, no such rule of international law is to be found").

[50] *See, e.g.,* Prosecutor v. Furundžija, Trial Chamber, Judgment of December 10, 1998, <http://www.un.org/icty/furundzija/trialc2/judgement/index.htm>, paras. 155–56 (asserting in dicta that a prohibition's *jus cogens* character alone implies universal jurisdiction over individual violators and nullification of a state's authority to immunize or amnesty the conduct); Van Schaack, *supra,* at 192 ("International judges, it turns out, are better able to represent the moral condemnation of the international community than are states engaged in multilateral negotiations with their own interests—including ensuring impunity—at heart. And so, where the law was silent, it was made to speak.").

# III. Law and Morality in Retrospective and Extraterritorial Prosecution

## A. POSITIVISM, NATURALISM, AND THE RULE OF LAW

A pedestrian account of restrictive approaches to extraterritorial and retrospective penal accountability associates such approaches with legal positivism, and casts them in opposition to natural-law conceptions of legality. In the most sweeping and unnuanced formulation, naturalism identifies legality with immutable and rather wide-ranging principles of substantive justice, the moral truth of which suffices to establish legal validity, irrespective of any grounding in effective political authority.[51] Legal positivism, in its most straightforward formulation, asserts to the contrary that legality derives from social facts, not moral truths, so that an unjust law is law nonetheless.[52]

Thus, where violations of human dignity have reflected, rather than contradicted, the scheme of political authority in effect at the time and place of their occurrence, the archetypical naturalist would seem more disposed not only to find criminality inherent in the acts themselves,[53] but also to find the victims' humanity as sufficient justification for attributing jurisdiction to prosecutorial apparatuses lacking otherwise-established authority over the territory or the perpetrators,[54] and to nullify immunities from jurisdiction that stem from the brute fact of the perpetrators having committed the acts in service of a foreign state's sovereign authority over its national territory. The archetypical positivist, to the contrary, would insist that the immorality of the conduct does not itself provide any legal basis for imposing penal accountability, and would set exacting empirical criteria for establishing the substantive and procedural requisites to prosecution.[55]

[51] Martin Luther King, Jr.'s often-repeated quotation from St. Augustine that "an unjust law is no law at all," Martin Luther King, Jr., "Letter from a Birmingham Jail" (1963), from St. Augustine, *De Libero Arbitrio*, I, v. 11, appears to say just this, but to invoke it for that proposition is doubly misleading. First, King was concerned, not with questions of analytical or normative jurisprudence, but exclusively with those of political obligation; King was denying only that unjust laws were morally binding on the citizen. *Cf.* Soper, *supra*, at 202 (acknowledging that most theorists now interpret the maxim "as a claim in political or moral theory, not legal theory"). Second, King was not really calling for individuals to second-guess the justice of every enactment; he sought disobedience only to a specific subset of unjust laws, and then only in circumscribed ways. John Finnis has characterized the maxim as an overdramatization and distortion even of Augustine's actual meaning. John Finnis, *Natural Law and Natural Rights* (Oxford: Clarendon Press, 1980), at 363–66.

[52] *See generally* John Gardner, "Legal Positivism: 5½ Myths," 46 *Amer. J. Jurisp.* 199 (2001).

[53] *See* M. Cherif Bassiouni, "Universal Jurisdiction for International Crimes: Historical Perspectives and Contemporary Practice," 42 *Va. J. Int'l L.* 81, 99 (2001).

[54] *Id.* at 101.

[55] *Id.* at 99.

There is some rudimentary truth in these generalizations, but they obscure, if not distort, the essence of the matter. For a start, the current state of the field of analytical jurisprudence does not admit of such tidy definitions of "natural law" and "legal positivism." Each camp is itself divided on the essential meanings of these terms, and if one goes by some current accounts of the opposing positions, not only are the differences "normatively inert,"[56] but functionally, they have narrowed to near the vanishing point. The most widely held natural-law theories acknowledge that social facts very substantially constrain the project of legal interpretation,[57] and a school of "inclusive legal positivism" allows that a norm's legal validity may derive from its moral content rather than from its social source, provided that the given system's established source doctrines authorize juridical recourse to moral principles.[58] The two sides differ as to little more than their formal way of accounting for exercises of moral and political judgment that both sides accept, not only as facts of judicial behavior but as legitimate judicial practice.[59]

More importantly, the real controversies over retrospective (i.e., post-regime-change) and extraterritorial penal accountability of state agents turn not on answers to the formal question of "what is law?" but on answers to questions of political morality that are begged by terms such as "the rule of law" and "*nullum crimen sine lege*." Whether a practice is consistent with either of these principles depends on the animating purposes that one attributes to legal order.

According to Lon Fuller, law's "internal morality" requires that enactments be general, well-publicized, prospective, clear, not contradictory of other laws, susceptible of compliance, stable, and enforced in a manner congruent with

[56] Gardner, *supra*, at 202; *see also* Brian Leiter, "Beyond the Hart/Dworkin Debate: The Methodology Problem in Jurisprudence," U. of Texas Law, Public Law Research Paper No. 34 (April 2005), *available at* <http://papers.ssrn.com/sol3/papers.cfm?abstract_id=312781>, at 18.

[57] *See* Soper, *supra*, at 205; Ronald A. Dworkin, "'Natural' Law Revisited," 34 *U. Fla. L. Rev.* 165, 169 (1982); *see generally* Dworkin, *Law's Empire* (Cambridge, Mass.: Harvard Univ. Press, 1986). Dworkin's view has been aptly described as a third theory of law, intermediate between naturalism and positivism. John Mackie, "The Third Theory of Law," 7:1 *Phil. & Pub. Aff.* 4 (1977); *see also* Soper, *supra*, at 206. The same can be said of Lon Fuller's approach, which identifies law with a set of procedural requisites (law's "internal morality") rather than with conformity to a substantive conception of justice. *See* Lon L. Fuller, *The Morality of Law* (New Haven: Yale University Press, rev'd ed. 1969).

[58] *See* Gardner, *supra*, at 201; Mackie, *supra*, at 5–6; Scott J. Shapiro, "The 'Hart-Dworkin' Debate: A Short Guide for the Perplexed," U. of Michigan Public Law Working Paper No. 77 (March 2007), *available at* <http://papers.ssrn.com/sol3/papers.cfm?abstract_id=968657>, at 22–26.

[59] *See* Soper, *supra*, at 202. This is not to deny that the different approaches affect, in a more subtle way, whether and how judges confront substantive injustice. *See* Mark J. Osiel, "Dialogue with Dictators: Judicial Resistance in Argentina and Brazil," 20 *Law & Soc. Inq.* 481 (1995).

their declaration.[60] But Fuller did not regard compliance with each of these criteria of legality as a necessary condition for calling an enactment a "law." Indeed,

> in England and America, it would never occur to anyone to say that "it is in the nature of law that it cannot be retroactive," although, of course, constitutional inhibitions may prohibit certain kinds of retroactivity.... [T]here would be a certain occult unpersuasiveness in any assertion that retroactivity violates the very nature of law itself. Yet we have only to imagine a country in which all laws are retroactive in order to see that retroactivity presents a real problem for the internal morality of law.... A general increase in the resort to statutes curative of past legal irregularities represents a deterioration in that form of legal morality without which law itself cannot exist.[61]

The real question, then, is not whether a given enactment counts as "law," but whether, on the basis of a broader normative assessment, "the rule of law" is prevalent in the society in question or whether a particular measure, in its overall context, enhances or diminishes that prevalence.[62]

Fuller identified "the basic difference between law and managerial direction" as follows:

> law is not, like management, a matter of directing other persons how to accomplish tasks set by a superior, but is basically a matter of providing the citizenry with a sound and stable framework for their interactions with one another, the role of government being that of standing as its guardian of the integrity of this system.[63]

To paraphrase, what essentially distinguishes legality from its opposite—from what Locke referred to as "rule by extemporary arbitrary decree"[64]—is an overall orientation toward predictability and accountability in the exercise of power.

[60] Lon L. Fuller, *The Morality of Law, supra,* at 46–91.

[61] Fuller, "Positivism and Fidelity to Law: A Reply to Professor Hart," 71 *Harv. L. Rev.* 630, 650–51 (1958). The article was Fuller's famous response to H.L.A. Hart, "Positivism and the Separation of Law and Morals," 71 *Harv. L. Rev.* 593 (1958).

[62] Although his chief antagonist, the legal positivist H.L.A. Hart, insisted that the principles of "legality" and "the rule of law" were distinct from "law" as such, Hart's understanding of the former was essentially identical to Fuller's. *See* Jeremy Waldron, "Hart's Equivocal Response to Fuller" (unpublished paper, 2008), *available at* <www.law.nyu.edu/idcplg?IdcService=GET_FILE&dDocName=ECM_DLV_016303&RevisionSelectionMethod=LatestReleased>, citing H.L.A. Hart, "Problems of the Philosophy of Law," reprinted in H.L.A. Hart, *Essays in Jurisprudence and Philosophy* (1983), at 114.

[63] Fuller, *The Morality of Law,* at 210.

[64] John Locke, *Second Treatise of Government* (1690), ch. 11, sec. 136 ("The legislative, or supreme authority, cannot assume to its self a power to rule by extemporary arbitrary decrees, but is bound to

Predictability and accountability in the exercise of power are inherent in the project of legality for at least two reasons. First, virtually all invocations of the word "law" implicitly trade on this orientation. To use the word to describe an ordering process with the opposite orientation would violate conventional understandings of the language and thereby confuse one's audience.[65]

Second, predictability and accountability in the exercise of power are necessary, though not sufficient, conditions for the achievement of the most foundational ends associated with liberal-democratic political traditions. Predictability and accountability are, analogous to Rawls's notion of a primary good,[66] what everyone wants, regardless of what else anyone wants—insofar as "everyone," even if not a liberal or a democrat, shares those traditions' most rudimentary concerns. The first of these is that individuals have the basic capacity to organize their lives,[67] with the security that everything that is not knowably prohibited is permitted, so that they need

dispense justice, and decide the rights of the subject by promulgated standing laws, and known authorized judges; for the law of nature being unwritten, and so no where to be found but in the minds of men, they who through passion or interest shall miscite, or misapply it, cannot so easily be convinced of their mistake where there is no established judge; and so it serves not, as it ought, to determine the rights, and fence the properties of those that live under it, especially where every one is judge, interpreter, and executioner of it too, and that in his own case . . .")

[65] Jeremy Waldron reveals the point vividly as follows:

> A word like "hospital" provides a good analogy. One of the meanings given for hospital in the *Oxford English Dictionary* is "[a]ny institution or establishment for the care of the sick or wounded, or of those who require medical treatment." No one understands the term "hospital" unless he understands what hospitals are *for*. To describe one's establishment as a hospital is to hold out the promise of healing and care—even though it might turn out that the procedures actually used in a given institution making this promise are in fact harmful or hurtful to the patients. Now, if their harmfulness or hurtfulness is known and intended, that belies the sincerity of the description; we assume that Dr. Mengele is being ironic when he talks about his clinic at Auschwitz as a "hospital." But we do not withdraw the term the instant harmfulness is discovered if we are sure that the institution in question has the treatment of the sick and the wounded as its aim. So this is a case in which the analytic separability of "hospital" and "actual non-harmfulness" conceals a deeper aspirational connection between the two.

Jeremy Waldron, "Does Law Promise Justice?" 17 *Georgia State U. L. Rev.* 759, 760–61 (2001) (citation omitted). Waldron goes on to concede that "the promise of justice is not conveyed semantically by the word 'law,'" *id.* at 766, but that concession seems undue in regard to the more modest promise of an orientation toward predictability and accountability in the exercise of power.

[66] John Rawls, *A Theory of Justice* (Cambridge, Mass.: Harvard Univ. Press, 1971), at 62.

[67] As Isaiah Berlin put it, "a frontier must be drawn between the area of private life and that of public authority." Reasonable persons may well differ over the placement of the demarcation line, but liberty can be understood only as "the absence of interference beyond the shifting, but always recognizable, frontier." Isaiah Berlin, "Two Concepts of Liberty," in Berlin, *Four Essays on Liberty* (New York: Oxford University Press 1969), at 124–27. However small the space is behind that boundary, it is in that space that the individual can pursue interests and ends without regard to the preferences of state officials or others in society. *Nullum crimen* gives individuals the confidence to act freely right up to the boundary,

neither to live in terror of sudden impositions and unexpected punishments, nor to secure protection by "getting in good" with dominant officials, subordinating themselves to the latters' will.[68] The second concern is that regardless of what counts as legitimate authority in a society, the implementers of that authority—who may be untrusted, untrustworthy, or both—effectively be subjected in their purported implementation to fixed and knowable standards.

To be sure, some political orders, supported by *bona fide* (though typically hideous) political moralities, reject these concerns on principle.[69] Totalitarian orders (in the true sense associated with Hitler, Stalin, and Pol Pot) seek to mold, not to accommodate, individual will, and while they may use legal forms to hold lower officials accountable to higher ones, they have often, in practice, been satisfied if lower officials, irrespective of abuses in their exercise of delegated authority, demonstrate personal loyalty to the upper leadership. It thus would be a mistake to characterize predictability and accountability in the exercise of power as empirically universal concerns. Still, it may be fair to say that the exceptions are normatively uninteresting.

A more significant proviso is that even where predictability and accountability are core concerns of political morality, they do not have the field to themselves. There are other concerns that may, in particular circumstances, be found legitimately to be in tension with those values. One could not justifiably say that legality is absent wherever those latter concerns, such as the need for flexible response to emergency, prevail.

"The rule of law" might best be summarized as the principle that "There shall be no exercise of power, except according to law." But even were there an uncontroverted and unambiguous understanding of what counts as "law" in this context, consensus on the principle would scarcely be any the nearer.

First, one would need to specify what counts as an exercise of power. Although the present topic, prosecution, raises no problems in this area, it is worth noting that a formal devolution of authority to private actors to take decisions affecting the conditions of social life cannot properly withdraw such decisions from the subject matter, since the scope of the latter is defined not by formal categories but by underlying substantive concerns.

Second, and most daunting, one would need to determine the meaning of "according to." At one (impossible) extreme, this might mean "as dictated by": the

including to "hide behind technicalities" that permit behavior that some might find contrary to "the spirit" of the law.

[68] *See* Martin Krygier, "Marxism and the Rule of Law: Reflections After the Collapse of Communism," 15 *Law & Social Inquiry* 633, 642–43 (1990).

[69] *See generally* Ingo Müller, *Hitler's Justice* (Cambridge, Mass: Harvard Univ. Press, 1991); Harold J. Berman, *Justice in the U.S.S.R.: An Interpretation of Soviet Law*, rev'd ed. (Cambridge, Mass.: Harvard Univ. Press, 1963).

complete abolition of executive discretion. At the other (all too possible) extreme, it might mean "as authorized by," so as to be satisfied merely by an all-encompassing legislative delegation of authority to the executive organ (as in a Reichstag conferral of "all power to the Führer").[70] Law always and necessarily licenses discretionary authority[71]; "the rule of law" is achieved when law sets boundaries to such discretion that are meaningful and reasonable, given the proper ends of governance.[72] But this is quintessentially a normative question, and minds will differ widely on the requisite nature and extent of those boundaries; there is no formal standard that could conceivably resolve the controversy.

Third, one would need to determine whether any society is serious—or can afford to be serious—about the "No," the absolute claim for the illegitimacy of extralegal authority. A rule-of-law-oriented domestic political order tends to characterize the political entity's sovereignty as *constituted* by the order's legal norms, but as Carl Schmitt notoriously suggested (and as even such founders of the liberal ethos as Locke understood),[73] this is a troubled claim. An existential threat to the political order itself tends to reveal a residual constituent authority that withstands constituted order and (arguably) licenses extra-constitutional discretion.[74] The foundational Schmittian insight is that whereas norms govern in normal times, they give way in exceptional times; "sovereign is he who decides on the exception," and

[70] *See* H.W. Koch, *In the Name of the Volk: Political Justice in Hitler's Germany* (London: I.B. Tauris & Co. Ltd, 1989), 113–14 (detailing the Reichstag session of April 26, 1942).

[71] *See* William H. Simon, "Legality, Bureaucracy, and Class in the Welfare System," 92 *Yale L.J.* 1198, 1224 (1983) ("There is a law of conservation of discretion: one limits the discretion of one set of actors only by increasing that of others.").

[72] Martin Krygier refers to "a society where law *counts* in public life." Krygier, *supra*, at 644.

[73] *See* John Locke, *Second Treatise of Government* (1690), ch. 14, para. 160, on prerogative power:

> This power to act according to discretion, for the public good, without the prescription of the law, ***and sometimes even against it***, is that which is called prerogative: for since in some governments the lawmaking power is not always in being, and is usually too numerous, and so too slow, for the dispatch requisite to execution; and because also it is impossible to foresee, and so by laws to provide for, all accidents and necessities that may concern the public, or to make such laws as will do no harm, if they are executed with an inflexible rigour, on all occasions, and upon all persons that may come in their way; therefore there is a latitude left to the executive power, to do many things of choice which the laws do not prescribe. [Emphasis added.]

*See also* Clement Fatovic, "Emergency Action as Jurisprudential Miracle: Liberalism's Political Theology of Prerogative," 6 *Perspectives on Politics* 487, 491–94 (Sept. 2008) (comparing and contrasting Locke and Schmitt on this point).

[74] *See* Niccolo Machiavelli, *Discourses on Livy* [1517], bk. I, ch. 34, favoring the institution of "dictatorship," or emergency rule, on the ground that "when a similar method is lacking in a Republic, either observing the institutions (strictly) will ruin her, or in order not to ruin her, it will be necessary to break them." <http://www.constitution.org/mac/disclivy1.htm#1:34>.

sovereignty is the power to suspend valid law.[75] (One can accept this conceptual point without in any way endorsing Schmitt's own applications of it.)[76]

Thus, invocations of the rule of law necessarily raise more questions than they answer. The concept is open-textured. Formal, analytic means cannot yield determinate judgments about whether a particular measure furthers or diminishes the phenomenon's prevalence, as such judgments necessarily reflect a weighing of the range of competing normative considerations that espousal of the principle does not preclude.

## B. NULLUM CRIMEN SINE LEGE

Still, the subprinciple of *nullum crimen sine lege* lies at the core, rather than the periphery, of the rule of law. Criminal prosecutions are exercises of power not merely tolerated by law, but undertaken in the name of law. Whereas, for example, in time of war, legality may abide preventive detention measures, to be imposed temporarily on real and suspected enemies with relatively limited procedural safeguards and relatively low substantive thresholds, legality can never abide unjust convictions.[77] Undue criminal conviction differs qualitatively from other wrongful impositions, as it heaps insult upon injury; rather than treating the person as an adversary or even as a mere object, wrongful criminal conviction, in trading on

[75] Carl Schmitt, *Political Theology: Four Chapters on the Concept of Sovereignty* [1922], George Schwab trans. (Chicago: University of Chicago Press, 2005), at 5, 9.

[76] Oren Gross and Fionnuala Ní Aoláin explain the perniciousness of Schmitt's solution to the conundrum as follows: "The dictator's unlimited powers are exercisable in the context of the extreme case—i.e., the exception. However, the only logical outcome of Schmitt's collapsing together the power to decide the existence of the exception and the breadth of counter-emergency powers to be used in order to bring the exception to a conclusion, and depositing them both in the hands of one person—the sovereign dictator—is that the dictator's unlimited powers are never turned off." Gross & Ní Aoláin, *Law in Times of Crisis: Emergency Powers in Theory and Practice* (Cambridge: Cambridge Univ. Press, 2006), at 165.

[77] Thus, the Geneva Conventions, which barely regulate long-term detention for substantial categories of persons, especially in non-international armed conflict, establish a universally applicable prohibition on "The passing of sentences and the carrying out of executions without previous judgment pronounced by a regularly constituted court, affording all the judicial guarantees which are recognized as indispensable by civilized peoples." Common Art. 3, Geneva Conventions of August 12, 1949, 75 U.N.T.S. 31, *et seq.*, entered into force Oct. 21, 1950; *see also* Protocol Additional to the Geneva Conventions of August 12, 1949, and Relating to the Protection of Victims of International Armed Conflicts, 1125 U.N.T.S. 3, entered into force Dec. 7, 1978 (Protocol I of 1977), art. 75; *cf.* Korematsu v. United States, 323 U.S. 214, 244 (1944) (Jackson, J., dissenting) ("It would be impracticable and dangerous idealism to expect or insist that each specific military command in an area of probable operations will conform to conventional tests of constitutionality.... But if we cannot confine military expedients by the Constitution, neither would I distort the Constitution to approve all that the military may deem expedient.").

legality, inflicts obloquy with the pretense of objectivity and fairness. Moreover, in appropriating the symbols of legality for that purpose, distorted penal processes degrade the legitimating value of legal forms.

Violations of *nullum crimen sine lege* are quintessential abuses of legality because they so frontally defy the concern for predictability and accountability in the exercise of power. The former concern corresponds to the familiar "notice" aspect of *nullum crimen sine lege*. Much of the debate about retrospective and extraterritorial prosecution goes to this aspect, with pro-prosecutorial arguments drawing on alternative sources of notice, such as natural justice or international treaty commitments unincorporated into domestic law, to overcome the limits of positivistic sources of law authoritative at the time and place of the act.[78] Such prosecutorial strategies are often questionable in their own terms, especially given that the existence of contradictory positive law typically reflects difference of opinion over what counts as natural justice, and that notice of an international legal obligation, without more, in no way implies notice that state authorization in contradiction to the obligation will be treated as legally null and void.[79]

It is important to add, however, that *nullum crimen sine lege* is not reducible to the problem of notice. It is equally a problem of legislative and adjudicative institutions exceeding their legal authority in establishing an act's wrongfulness. A person might know that her act is condemned as criminal by some insurgent movement or hostile foreign government. She might equally know that there is a considerable chance that she will be on the losing side of the political struggle and face prosecution for the act that she commits within the authorization of the currently recognized regime. Such facts fall far short of curing the *nullum crimen sine lege* problem.[80]

[78] *See* Van Schaack, *supra*, at 156.

[79] In the United States, for example, a "controlling executive act" is given legal effect even where it violates customary international law, *see, e.g.*, Garcia-Mir v. Meese, 788 F.2d 1446 (11th Cir. 1986); Jonathan I. Charney, "The Power of the Executive Branch of the United States Government to Violate Customary International Law," 80 *Am. J. Int'l L.* 913 (1986), and statutes prevail over prior treaty commitments, The Head Money Cases, 112 U.S. 580, 598–99 (1884). Moreover, "while treaties 'may comprise international commitments . . . they are not domestic law unless Congress has either enacted implementing statutes or the treaty itself conveys an intention that it be 'self-executing' and is ratified on these terms.'" Medellin v. Texas, 128 S. Ct. 1346, 1356 (2008) (citation omitted); *see also* Charlie Savage, "Videos Shed New Light on Sotomayor's Positions," *N.Y. Times* (June 10, 2009), *available at* <http://www.nytimes.com/2009/06/11/us/politics/11judge.html?hpw> (future Supreme Court Justice recorded as saying (rather tendentiously), "Even though Article IV of the Constitution says that treaties are the 'supreme law of the land' in most instances they're not even law").

[80] On this logic, Salman Rushdie was "on notice" that Iran regarded his allegedly blasphemous literary activities as tantamount to a universal-jurisdiction crime, and therefore assumed the risk of punishment if Iran were ever to obtain jurisdiction over his person. I have elsewhere argued that the European Court of Human Rights committed a fundamental error in crediting this kind of argument in the case of former East German leaders prosecuted in the unified Federal Republic of Germany for

No basis for a criminal conviction can be found in the articulations, however morally enlightened or predictably efficacious, of an institution that lacked authority to resolve the question of the act's criminality for the time and place that the act was committed.

Where the international legal order had recognized the government and had omitted (so far) to establish the conduct as an international crime, thereby acknowledging state authority over individuals' conduct at the time and place in question, that order is estopped to criminalize, or to abide criminalization of, reliance on such state authority. To be sure, the international legal order establishes equal respect, not for governmental apparatuses as such, but for the underlying political communities. Yet those apparatuses serve as the communities' indispensable instruments for the coordination of activities establishing the conditions of social life. Members of the communities thus have good reason to regard compliance and cooperation with their recognized governments as an appropriate (whether or not obligatory) contribution to a legitimate social project. Of course, they may be morally mistaken in this and perhaps gravely so. However, international law, having acknowledged state authority at the time, cannot furnish a license to vilify, in the name of law, those who acted in reliance on that authority.

Moreover, the terms of peaceful and respectful cooperation in an ideologically diverse international community require that a prosecuting state's institutions reliably remain within the scope of the authority that international law acknowledges or establishes. Generally speaking, such institutions are not, and should not be, trusted to improvise an expansion of that authority.

Thus, *nullum crimen sine lege* should not be seen as a formalistic obstacle to the pursuit of justice. Nor is it in any way a mere artifact of legal positivism. It is itself a natural law principle—not in any mystical sense, but in the sense that it embodies concerns at the core of what it means, everywhere and always, to speak of a criminal conviction under law.[81]

establishing the Berlin Wall enforcement mechanisms. Brad R. Roth, "Retrospective Justice or Retroactive Standards? Human Rights as a Sword in the East German Leaders Case," 50 *Wayne L. Rev.* 37 (2004). The Court there stated that "anyone could have foreseen that in the event of a change in regime in the GDR these acts might constitute criminal offenses." Streletz, Kessler, and Krenz v. Federal Republic of Germany [hereinafter, *Krenz*], 49 I.L.M. 773 (March 22, 2001), *available at* <http://www.echr.coe.it/Eng/Judgments.htm>, at para. 48. This statement would as easily have validated "victor's justice" against any number of Western officials had the Communists prevailed in the Cold War.

[81] This discussion is not intended as a contribution to contemporary analytical jurisprudence. Whereas contending schools of legal philosophy might use international criminal justice to illustrate a theoretical problem, this discussion is concerned with that topic as such, and is indifferent to whether naturalism or a positivism provides an analytically superior account of the normative dilemmas that international criminal justice poses. What is important to demonstrate, however, is that the discussion's normative claims are not incompatible with a naturalist account.

## C. JURISDICTIONAL LIMITATIONS AND IMMUNITY RATIONE MATERIAE

In international criminal law, exorbitant extraterritorial assertion of prescriptive jurisdiction implicates the *nullum crimen* principle.[82] Most violations of international law lead to liability only for states as corporative entities. In support of only a small subset of states' human rights obligations does international law establish penal responsibility for individual participants in state action, and only within that range does international law license the exercise of universal jurisdiction.[83] A prosecuting state's extraterritorial penal legislation or judge-made doctrine violates *nullum crimen* where it asserts universal jurisdiction over an individual's participation in an international law violation that has not been established as an international crime.[84]

[82] *See, e.g.,* Mark A. Summers, "The International Court of Justice's Decision in Congo v. Belgium: How Has It Affected the Development of a Principle of Universal Jurisdiction That Would Obligate All States to Prosecute War Criminals?"21 *B.U. Int'l L.J.* 63, 93 (2003) ("the post-war [Geneva] conventions clearly grant states the authority to prescribe [law-of-war] violations in absentia. Otherwise, state prosecutions of offenses based on the conventions would run afoul of the principle nullem crimen sine lege.").

[83] Some scholars and jurists continue to assert, on the basis of the so-called "*Lotus* principle," *Case of the S.S. Lotus (France v. Turkey)*, 1927 P.C.I.J. (ser. A) No. 9 (7 Sept.), that exercises of extraterritorial penal jurisdiction are presumed to be permitted except where specifically prohibited. *See Yerodia, supra,* 2002 ICJ Rep. 3, diss. op. of Judge ad hoc Van den Wyngaert, paras. 48–51. In actuality, the *Lotus* "majority" opinion (only six of twelve judges, with the President voting twice) only admitted this as a possibility, never actually asserting this position definitively. *Lotus,* at 15–17 ("whichever of the two systems described above [extraterritorial criminal jurisdiction permitted unless specifically prohibited, or prohibited unless specifically permitted] be adopted, the same result will be arrived at in this particular case"); *see Yerodia,* sep. op. of Judge Guillaume, paras. 14–15. To the extent that it was ever valid, this "doctrine has fallen into obsolescence as a consequence of the development of the doctrine of jurisdiction according to which any State activity *iure imperii* requires a reasonable link." Christian Tomuschat, "Concluding Remarks," in Christian Tomuschat & Jean-Marc Thouvenin eds., *The Fundamental Rules of the International Legal Order:* Jus Cogens *and Obligations* Erga Omnes (Leiden: lineMartinus Nijhoff, 2006), 425 at 439; *but see* Summers, *supra,* at 95 (invoking the separate opinion in *Yerodia* of Judges Higgins, Kooijmans and Buergenthal to assert the continued vitality of that doctrine).

[84] *See* Colangelo, *supra,* at 14–15. And yet, although the Torture Convention's universal jurisdiction provisions expressly pertain only to acts of "torture," *see* Torture Convention, *supra,* arts. 1, 4, and 5, as distinct from "cruel, inhuman, and degrading treatment or punishment," id., art. 16, the official commentary to "Princeton Principles" calls for universal jurisdiction to be applied to the latter as well. *The Princeton Principles on Universal Jurisdiction, supra,* at 48–49. This prescription flies boldly in the face of the traditional determination in penal jurisprudence "not to fill omissions in legislation where this can be said to have been deliberate." Prosecutor v. Delalić, Mucic, Delic & Landzo (*Čelebići*), ICTY, Trial Chamber, Judgment of 16 Nov. 1998, para. 412.

A closely related limitation is the doctrine of immunity *ratione materiae*, or functional immunity.[85] This form of immunity impedes a domestic court's exercise of jurisdiction over both current and former foreign-state agents for acts that those agents committed inside their national territory within the scope of their governmental functions, except insofar as those acts have been established as international crimes.[86] Antonio Cassese construes immunity *ratione materiae*, not as a procedural bar to jurisdiction, but as a "substantive defence," available to "any de jure or de facto State agent" performing official acts, establishing that the "violation is not legally imputable to [the agent] but to his state."[87]

Cassese may overstate the case slightly; it may be more precise to characterize the doctrine as a procedural bar with substantive implications. Immunity *ratione materiae* is tied to the logic of state immunity, as it guards against the use of prosecutions and lawsuits against current and former state officials as a device to circumvent the immunities attaching to the state itself. Inasmuch as immunity *ratione materiae* exists for the state's, rather than the agent's, benefit, it is both broader and narrower in its coverage than the *nullum crimen* defense: broader, in that it applies even to those acts, committed under color of official capacity, that are crimes under the law of the agent's state[88]; narrower, in that the state (perhaps following regime change) can decide *post hoc* to waive the defense, thereby leaving the agent "hung out to dry."[89]

However, it is possible for the *nullum crimen* defense to arise directly from immunity *ratione materiae*, just as it may arise from an exorbitant assertion of extraterritorial jurisdiction. A prosecuting state's effort to establish criminal liability for a

[85] Immunity *ratione materiae* is conceptually distinct from the immunity *ratione personae*, or personal immunity, which applies exclusively to officials who conduct a state's foreign relations (including heads of state, heads of government, foreign ministers, and diplomats). Those who hold personal immunity are shielded from foreign-state legal processes altogether, irrespective of the subject matter of the controversy, but only during those officials' terms of service. *See Yerodia, supra*, 2002 ICJ Rep. 3; Cassese, *supra*, 265–67, 271–73.

[86] *See, e.g.*, Dapo Akande, "International Law Immunities and the International Criminal Court," 98 *Am. J. Int'l Law* 407, 412–13 (2004); Michael Akehurst, "Jurisdiction in International Law," 46 *Brit. Y. B. Int'l L.* 145, 240–44 (1972–73). This immunity follows from the traditional view that "[e]very sovereign state is bound to respect the independence of every other sovereign state, and the courts of one country will not sit in judgment on the acts of the government of another done within its own territory." *Underhill v. Hernandez*, 168 US 250, 252 (1897).

[87] Cassese, *supra*, at 266; *accord* Akande, *supra*, at 412–15.

[88] *See, e.g., Regina v. Bow Street Metropolitan Stipendiary Magistrate (Pinochet III)*, 1 AC 147, 203 (Lord Browne-Wilkinson: "Actions which are criminal under the local law can still have been done officially and therefore give rise to immunity ratione materiae.").

[89] *See, e.g., Pinochet III, supra*, at 265, opinion of Lord Saville ("These immunities belong not to the individual but to the state in question. They exist in order to protect the sovereignty of that state from interference by other states. They can, of course, . . . be waived by the state in question.").

noncriminal breach of international law violates *nullum crimen* even where the state's internationally recognized jurisdiction to prescribe (on, say, a "territorial effects" or "passive personality" rationale) may reach the perpetrator's conduct, so long as immunity *ratione materiae* applies to the conduct. Where the foreign perpetrator acted inside his national territory and within the scope of his official capacity, immunity *ratione materiae* blocks the prosecuting state's jurisdiction to prescribe, leaving no penal law that condemns the agent's conduct. Even if the perpetrator's state were to waive immunity *post hoc,* it would lack authority to waive the *nullum crimen* component, which would remain in place as a personal defense.

## D. THE DOCTRINE OF STRICT INTERPRETATION (LENITY)

A corollary to *nullum crimen* is the doctrine of strict interpretation: "where there is a plausible difference of interpretation or application, the position which most favors the accused should be adopted."[90] The familiar domestic law term for the doctrine is the principle of "lenity."[91]

The principle applies most straightforwardly where codification is present. As the Trial Chamber of the International Criminal Tribunal for the former Yugoslavia (ICTY) has elaborated:

> The rule of strict construction requires that the language of a particular provision shall be construed so that no cases shall be held to fall within it which do not both fall within the reasonable meaning of its terms and within the spirit and scope of the enactment. . . . The accepted view is that if the legislature has not used words sufficiently comprehensive to include within its prohibition all cases which should naturally fall within the mischief intended to be prevented, the interpreter is not competent to extend them.[92]

In international criminal law, the lack of thoroughgoing codification renders inevitable some flexibility in the application of the principle. State practice and manifestations of *opinio juris* (such as military manuals) are frequently taken to establish individual penal responsibility for "serious violations" of international

[90] Prosecutor v. Krstić, ICTY, Trial Chamber, Judgment of Aug.2, 2001, para. 502; see Cassese, *supra,* at 153–57; *see also* Rome Statute of the International Criminal Court, 2187 U.N.T.S. 90, entered into force July 1, 2002 (ICC St.), Art. 22 (2) ("The definition of a crime shall be strictly construed and shall not be extended by analogy. In case of ambiguity, the definition shall be interpreted in favour of the person being investigated, prosecuted or convicted.").

[91] Dan M. Kahan, "Lenity and Federal Common Law Crimes," 1994 *Sup. Ct. Rev.* 345 (1994).

[92] Prosecutor v. Delalić et al. (*Čelebići*), *supra,* para. 410; *see* Robinson, *supra,* at 933.

norms that, while not expressly penal in nature, have systematically admitted of penal enforcement.[93] Moreover, as Antonio Cassese points out, "gaps or lacunae" are frequently filled by resort to "*general principles* of international criminal law, or to general principles of criminal justice, or to principles common to the major legal systems of the world."[94] *Nullum crimen sine lege* does not necessarily entail *nullum crimen sine lex scripta,* even from a positivistic standpoint.

Where codification is absent, the requirement of strict interpretation needs to be applied to whatever basis the applicable legal order specifies as adequate to establish the penal standard. The substantive question remains whether there exists "a plausible difference of interpretation or application."[95] The doctrine's goal remains to provide for "fair warning" and for a barrier to "arbitrary and discriminatory enforcement."[96] Given that international criminal law has most often been addressed to egregious atrocities rather than to borderline cases, even rather woolly penal standards have frequently found relatively uncontroversial application.

Some demands for relaxation of the principle, however, derive not from the need to acknowledge informal sources of positive law, but from claims that the principle

[93] *See* Jean-Marie Henckaerts & Louise Doswald-Beck, *Customary International Humanitarian Law* (Cambridge University Press, 2005), vol. I, at 568–73, 604–05 (noting the relevance of military manuals). Most prominently, the ICTY has held "serious violations" of Common Article 3 of the Geneva Conventions to fall within its mandate; in order to qualify, the violation 'must constitute a breach of a rule protecting important values,' 'must involve grave consequences for the victim,' and 'must entail, under customary or conventional law, the individual criminal responsibility of the person breaching the rule.' *Prosecutor v. Tadić,* Appeals Chamber Decision, October 2, 1995, para. 94. The *Tadić* court's criteria, drawn from Nuremberg, emphasized 'State practice indicating an intention to criminalize the prohibition, including statements by government officials and international organizations, as well as punishment of violations by national courts and military tribunals.' *Id.* at para. 128.

[94] Cassese, *supra,* at 155. Cassese further points out that many international rules have open-ended provisions–such as "other inhumane acts of a similar character," ICC St., art. 7(1)(k)–that expressly or impliedly call for analogical reasoning to fill inevitable gaps. *Id.* at 155–56.

[95] Krstić, *supra,* para. 502.

[96] As the U.S. Supreme Court has declared:

> Vague laws offend several important values. First, because we assume that man is free to steer between lawful and unlawful conduct, we insist that laws give the person of ordinary intelligence a reasonable opportunity to know what is prohibited, so that he may act accordingly. Vague laws may trap the innocent by not providing fair warning. Second, if arbitrary and discriminatory enforcement is to be prevented, laws must provide explicit standards for those who apply them. A vague law impermissibly delegates basic policy matters to policemen, judges, and juries for resolution on an *ad hoc* and subjective basis, with the attendant dangers of arbitrary and discriminatory application.

Grayned v. City of Rockford, 408 U.S. 104, 108–09 (1972) (footnotes omitted); *see* Parry, *supra,* at 1041.

itself is flawed in failing to allow consideration of the moral context of its application. Dan M. Kahan observes that the "notice" argument for lenity

> *works well when a court is applying a statute that sits on the boundary line between socially desirable and socially undesirable conduct. . . .* Because these laws are understood to invite individuals to come right up to the line between what is a crime and what is not, obscurity as to where that line is drawn is indeed grossly unfair. *But the situation is quite different when the underlying conduct is located not on the border, but deep within the interior of what is socially undesirable. . . .* The purpose of these "interior" offenses is not so much to inform citizens of what conduct is prohibited as it is to create or increase criminal penalties for conduct that is *already understood to be absolutely forbidden by independent laws or social mores. . . .* In this context, a person who consciously seeks to come up to the statutory "line" without crossing it is not attempted to conform her behavior to the law, but rather to evade punishment for admittedly wrongful or illegal acts.[97]

The latter behavior that Kahan describes is sometimes said to be *malum in se*, as opposed to *malum prohibitum*, and therefore not entitled to the benefit of the lenity principle.[98] And indeed, where a genuine consensus of the relevant community is well known to regard the conduct as heinous, the absence of moral disagreement weighs strongly (though maybe not decisively) in favor of improvising penal standards. This solution quite plausibly applies in the international criminal justice context where, for example, state agents have inflicted cruelties, of a type unspecified in existing instruments or in expressions of *opinio juris*, that are either gratuitous or manifestly directed toward an illegitimate objective (e.g., terrorizing a local population so as to drive it from a territory)—that is, not substantially related to a cognizable governmental purpose.

This, however, is precisely where extreme cases are prone to generate bad *dicta*. Consensus on the wrongfulness of conduct viewed in isolation does not imply consensus on the wrongfulness of conduct viewed in context. Where state officials authorize acts, the authorization likely reflects some *bona fide*—even if objectively misguided or reprehensible—conception of the public interest. Except where that conception itself represents mass persecution or some similarly inadmissible goal, such acts are not *malum in se* in the relevant sense, notwithstanding that their

[97] Dan M. Kahan, "Lenity and Federal Common Law Crimes," 1994 *Sup. Ct. Rev.* 345, 400–01 (1994) (emphasis added).

[98] Jeremy Waldron, "Torture and Positive Law: Jurisprudence for the White House," 105 *Colum. L. Rev.* 1681, 1692 (2005).

*presumptive* immorality is universally acknowledged and that they trigger state responsibility for breach of an international legal obligation.[99] Even with respect to acknowledged serious human rights violations, states only exceptionally consent to subject their agents to international penal norms; absent such consent, express or tacit, states cannot be said to have authorized such external exercises of power over their agents.[100] The authority for prosecution, which needs to be specifically conferred, is to that extent withheld. As the ICTY has recognized in elaborating the principle of strict interpretation, "It has always been the practice of courts not to fill omissions in legislation where this can be said to have been deliberate."[101]

The recent U.S. controversy over penal liability for torture provides an illustration. The Torture Convention establishes international penal responsibility for individual state agents for "torture" (Article 1) but only state responsibility for "cruel, inhuman, and degrading treatment" (Article 16).[102] A U.S. penal statute implements the Convention's torture provisions (including conferral of universal jurisdiction).[103] A notorious 2002 memorandum of the Justice Department's Office of Legal Counsel purported to ascertain the statute's threshold of "severe pain or suffering."[104] It is now widely agreed that the memorandum badly mis-specified this threshold,[105] but

[99] This is true even where the international obligations in question are "non-derogable." Non-derogable means that there is no defense on the international plane to breach of the international legal obligation. It does not mean that a breaching act is *ultra vires* of state authority. *See* the discussion of *jus cogens, infra.*

[100] Beyond the general principle of strict interpretation of penal norms, there is a further rule of treaty interpretation that militates against an expansive reading of international penal standards. Treaties must be read in light of "any relevant rules of international law applicable in the relations between the parties." Vienna Convention on the Law of Treaties, 1155 U.N.T.S. 331 (1969), art. 31(3)(c). Immunity *ratione materiae* is such a relevant rule.

[101] Prosecutor v. Delalić et al. (*Čelebići*), *supra*, para. 412.

[102] *See* Roth, "Just Short of Torture," *supra*; Yuval Shany, "The Prohibition Against Torture and Cruel, Inhuman and Degrading Treatment and Punishment: Can the Absolute be Relativized under Existing International Law?" 56 *Cath. U.L. Rev.* 837, 862 (2007).

[103] 18 U.S.C. §§ 2340–2340A.

[104] Jay S. Bybee, Assistant Attorney General, "Memorandum for Alberto R. Gonzales, Counsel to the President, Re: Standards of Conduct for Interrogation under 18 U.S.C. §§ 2340–2340A," 1 August 2002, *reprinted in* Karen J. Greenberg & Joshua L. Dratel eds., *The Torture Papers: The Road to Abu Ghraib* (New York: Cambridge Univ. Press, 2005), 172. The memorandum's most notorious claim was that "Physical pain amounting to torture must be equivalent in intensity to the pain accompanying serious physical injury, such as organ failure, impairment of bodily function, or even death." *Id.* at 172. Unconvincing as this claim is, it should be noted that 18 U.S.C. §§ 2340–2340A is a universal jurisdiction statute addressed exclusively to acts occurring abroad, and thus primarily envisioned to apply to foreign state agents. Its threshold was therefore designed to identify "enemies of humanity," rather than ordinary lawbreakers.

[105] *See, e.g.*, Jose Alvarez, "Torturing the Law," 37 *Case W. Res. J. Int'l L.* 175, 197 (2006); Jordan Paust, "Executive Plans and Authorizations to Violate International Law Concerning Treatment and

there remains a question of whether the very effort to identify the threshold with precision was, in Jeremy Waldron's words, a "legally reputable enterprise."[106]

Waldron suggests that the *malum in se* nature of both torture and cruel, inhuman, and degrading treatment renders the effort to ascertain the boundary line between them both superfluous and mischievous.[107] The memorandum "failed to mention that both categories of conduct were and are absolutely prohibited" in international law.[108] It thus wrongly presupposed that interrogators "are permitted to work somewhere along the continuum of the deliberate infliction of pain, and the question is: Where is the bright line along that continuum where the specific prohibition on torture kicks in?"[109] For Waldron, then, notice of the precise location of "severity" boundary line is not only unnecessary, but a pernicious invitation to the gaming of the system:

> [W]e need to remember that the charge of torture is unlikely to be surprising or unanticipated by someone already engaged in the deliberate infliction of pain on prisoners: "I am shocked – shocked! – to find that 'waterboarding' or squeezing prisoners' genitals or setting dogs on them is regarded as torture." Remember, we are talking about precision or imprecision in regard to a particular element in the definition of torture – the severity element. The potential defendant is one who already knows that he is inflicting considerable pain; that is his intention. The question he faces is whether the pain is severe enough to constitute torture. It seems to me that the working definition in the anti-torture statute already gives him all the warning he needs that he is taking a huge risk in relying upon casuistry about "severity" as a defense against allegations of torture.[110]

Waldron's point, though persuasive in regard to the question of legal ethics with which he is primarily concerned,[111] is misleading insofar as it suggests that international criminal justice can proceed without close regard to the "severity" threshold.

Interrogation of Detainees," 43 *Colum. J. Transnat'l L.* 811, 834–35 (2005); David Luban, "Liberalism, Torture, and the Ticking Bomb," 91 Virginia L. Rev. 1425, 1454–56 (2005).

[106] Waldron, "Torture and Positive Law," *supra*, at 1705.

[107] *Id.* at 1700–09.

[108] *Id.* at 1706.

[109] *Id.* at 1705.

[110] *Id.* at 1700.

[111] Given the specific context, Waldron is correct to question the ethics of the legal project that the memorandum represented (let alone the manner in which the project was carried out). In providing perpetrators with advance notice of which wrongs do not entail criminal liability, the project constituted deliberate complicity in human rights violations. There is good reason to believe that lawyers have a professional responsibility to avoid partaking in such a project. *See* David Luban, "Torture and the Professions," *Crim. Just. Ethics* (Summer/Fall 2007), 2.

States, in distinguishing torture from cruel, inhuman, and degrading treatment, deliberately established a basis for international penal liability up to that point but no farther.[112] Short of international penal thresholds, states have maintained a monopoly of domestic authority over their agents' conduct within national territory, in full contemplation that states from time to time exercise that authority in breach of their international legal obligations. Those agents cannot properly be held responsible to a supra-positive standard of "socially desirable conduct," because states have reserved the last word on what counts as "socially desirable" for purposes of evaluating their own agents' conduct.[113]

Thus, in the zone of conduct to which states have refused to extend a positive penal norm, a locally authoritative decision to breach international obligations for the sake of a cognizable governmental purpose, such as extraction of information from alleged terrorists, vitiates the moral consensus needed to justify relaxation of the norm of strict interpretation. Lenity can arguably yield to a genuine moral consensus, but not to an illusory one.

*Nullum crimen sine lege* and the conjoined doctrines of jurisdictional limitation, immunity *ratione materiae*, and strict interpretation reflect morally significant purposes of the international legal order. This is not to deny that these principles are subject to countervailing considerations. Legality is always a matter of judgment and can never avoid the balancing of conflicting considerations of political morality. But respect for the *nullum crimen* principle creates a presumption that only an

[112] Note, however, that cruel and inhuman treatment committed against captured enemy soldiers and enemy civilians in international armed conflicts does give rise to universal jurisdiction under the terms of the Third and Fourth Geneva Conventions (Articles 130 and 147, respectively). Shany, *supra*, at 862. Moreover, while the more sweeping prohibition of cruel, humiliating and degrading treatment in Common Article 3–pertaining to all categories of persons, even in non-international armed conflicts–does not specify penal enforcement, the ICC Statute provides for penal sanctions, at least when the violations are "committed as part of a plan or policy or as part of a large-scale commission of such crimes." ICC St., arts. 8(1), 8(2)(c). In addition, "serious violations" of that Geneva standard now plausibly give rise to universal jurisdiction as a matter of customary international law. *See* Henckaerts & Doswald-Beck, *supra*, vol. I, at 568–607; Roth, "Just Short of Torture," *supra*, at 236.

There thus has arisen an apparent incongruity between the legal regimes governing cruel, inhuman, and degrading treatment in peacetime and in non-international armed conflict. A possible rationale for the distinction is that a state's invocation of armed conflict's permissive rules of engagement and detention properly imposes special liabilities for failure to observe armed conflict's strictures. I thank Norman Farrell for this insight.

[113] As John Parry's study discloses, the United States negotiated actively to limit the definition of torture, and reinforced that definition's narrowness by attaching interpretive understandings to its instrument of ratification. Parry, *supra*, at 1036–43. The purpose, Parry contends, was precisely "to preserve space for coercive interrogation." *Id.* at 1046.

extraordinary justification can overcome. *Nullum crimen* is, after all, frequently known simply as "the principle of legality."[114]

## IV. Extraordinary Circumstances: Rule-of-Law Standards in Judging the *Unrechtsstaat*

The legal philosopher Ronald Dworkin contends (quite controversially) that interpretive judgment must include, *inter alia*, an assessment of "which interpretation, all things considered, makes the community's legal record the best it can be from the point of view of political morality."[115] While there is some reason to be concerned about Dworkin's tendency, in his own normative jurisprudence, to take this abstract proposition as license to disregard inconvenient aspects of the "legal record,"[116] doubts about the probity of particular applications do not refute the proposition.[117]

Even a determination of the law of a foreign jurisdiction must be sensitive to the reason why one wants to know what that law is. Certainly a judge does not properly seek to make the legal doctrine of foreign political community the best that it can be,[118] but nor is the judge, in making a finding of foreign law, acting as a social scientist or an historian. Rather, she is implementing some norm of her own system that requires due respect for the foreign entity, and the precise respect that is due depends on the nature of the decision that confronts the court. How ambiguities should be

[114] *See* Cassese, *supra*, at 149 ("the principle of non-retroactivity of criminal rules is now solidly embodied in international law. It follows that courts may only apply substantive criminal rules that existed at the time of commission of the alleged crime.").

[115] Ronald Dworkin, *Law's Empire* (Cambridge, Mass.: Harvard Univ. Press, 1986), at 411.

[116] *See* Michael W. McConnell, "The Importance of Humility in Judicial Review: A Comment on Ronald Dworkin's 'Moral Reading' of the Constitution," 65 *Fordham L. Rev.* 1259, 1270 (1997) ("The division of labor is as follows: The Dworkin of Right Answers decides all important contested cases, while the Dworkin of Fit defends against charges of judicial imperialism.").

[117] Legal positivists, of course, reject the proposition. *See, e.g.*, Joseph Raz, *Ethics in the Public Domain: Essays in the Morality of Law and Politics* 194, 209 (New York: Oxford Univ. Press, 1994). But their fidelity *to nullum crimen sine lege*, albeit merely as "a very precious principle of morality endorsed by most legal systems," Hart, *supra*, 71 *Harv. L. Rev.* at 619, is seldom questioned. For positivists, there can be no other source of "*lege*" than the political order recognized as authoritative at the time and place of the act. Their critique of Dworkin's brand of naturalism will thus be passed over here, as will this author's reasons for rejecting that critique.

[118] *See* Jacob Dolinger, "Application, Proof, and Interpretation of Foreign Law: A Comparative Study in Private International Law," 12 *Ariz. J. Int'l & Comp. L.* 225, 240 (1995).

resolved may depend, for example, on whether a litigant is invoking foreign law as sword or as a shield.[119]

The problem takes on a special dimension when a judge in a rule-of-law-oriented system undertakes to determine the effects of law from a non-rule-of-law-oriented system.[120] This topic has engendered considerable confusion, some of it introduced by none other than Lon Fuller. In his landmark debate with H.L.A. Hart in the pages of the *Harvard Law Review* in 1958, Fuller applied his critique of legal positivism to the question of retrospective justice in post-Hitler Germany. Unfortunately, in doing so, he conflated two questions: (i) whether Nazi Germany's state security enactments and the mode of their enforcement could properly be characterized as a form, however unjust, of "law"; and (ii) whether egregious acts (other than international crimes, such as prosecuted at Nuremberg), consistent with the dictates of established political authority during the Nazi period, could justifiably be construed retrospectively as crimes.

The first question is the one that analytical jurisprudence poses. It is, for present purposes, uninteresting. Nazi Germany did not observe the rule of law, and indeed, espoused a contrary doctrine of "legality," eschewing predictability and accountability in the exercise of power, as a matter of principle.[121] The political order did, as Fuller acknowledged, engage in standard legal regulation of many fields of activity, such as inheritance and contracts (even though no legal decision was immune from political interference if state or party officials took an interest in it). In areas related to Nazism's distinctive agenda, social regulation was decidedly non-standard. Enactments provided subjects with information about what was expected of them,

[119] Additionally, a court can simply refuse to sustain a foreign law-based cause of action that contradicts a strong public policy of the forum jurisdiction, Restatement (Second) of Conflict of Laws § 90 (1969), but that rule is supposed to have "a very narrow scope of application," *id.*, § 90 cmt. a .

[120] In his concurrence in the European Court's *Krenz* judgment (upholding the Berlin Wall prosecutions), Judge Levits contended that "there is no room for other solutions" than "to apply the 'old' law, set by the previous non-democratic regime, according to the approach to interpretation and application of the law which is inherent in the new democratic political order." In his view, "Using any other method of applying the law . . . would damage the very core of the ordre public of a democratic state." *Krenz, supra*, Levits, J., concurring, paras. 7–8.

But it is hard to see why this is so in cases where nullification of unjust law operates as a sword rather than as a shield. To be sure, a liberal-democratic system must refuse applications of illiberal legal standards that would deny individuals the benefits of liberal justice. Here, however, what works the denial of liberal justice (at least *prima facie*) is the refusal to afford the defendants the protection of the standards, however illiberal, that were valid at the time and place of the conduct. *Nullum crimen* is itself a principle at "the very core of the ordre public of a democratic state." If there is a danger of eroding that core, it far more plausibly emanates from indulging the retroactive expansion of criminal liability in pursuit of material justice, a quintessential practice of illiberal regimes.

[121] *See* Müller, *supra*, at 68–81.

but entailed no promise that acts not specifically prohibited were permitted.[122] Enactments operated to hold lower-level officials accountable to higher-level ones, but they were an instrument of, not a constraint upon, the policies of the highest organs of the state and the party.[123] Legalistic mechanisms were one means of implementing the leadership's will, but extralegal means were tolerated and given retroactive "legal" imprimatur. The idea is summarized in the German term *Unrechtsstaat.*[124]

It is not clear what, precisely, is to be accomplished by asking whether this mode of order counts as "law."[125] The regime's enactments are usefully understood to have been law for some purposes, but not for others, and any sweeping answer is likely to obfuscate rather than to clarify the realities.

The second question is whether *nullum crimen sine lege* precludes prosecution of persons whose egregious conduct comported with the norms of the established order. Fuller's answer to this question plays out in the course of a famous, if not precisely factual, account of a 1949 West German prosecution of the wife of a World War II German soldier.[126] The wife had, in the wake of the failed 1944 assassination attempt against Hitler, truthfully informed the Nazi authorities of her husband's private anti-Führer grumblings, knowing—and indeed, intending, apparently for

[122] *See* Müller, *supra,* at 75.

[123] As Hans Frank, Reich Commissioner for Justice, put it in 1936: "The National Socialist ideology, especially as expressed in the Party programme and in the speeches of our leader, is the basis for interpreting legal sources." Richard J. Evans, *The Third Reich in Power* (New York: Penguin Books, 2005), at 73.

[124] For a discussion of uses and abuses of this term, *see* Jan-Werner Muller, "East Germany: Incorporation, Tainted Truth, and the Double Division," in Alexandra Barahona de Brito, Carmen Gonzalez-Enriquez & Paloma Aguilar eds., *The Politics of Memory: Transitional Justice in Democratizing Societies* (Oxford Univ. Press, 2001), 248 at 249 n.2. *Unrechtsstaat* "refers to a state that not only perpetrates systematic injustice through its laws, but also breaks its own laws. What makes the notion so charged is that all too often the concept of *Unrechtsstaat* has served to lump together the Third Reich and the DDR." *Id.* at 261. Post-reunification German courts convicted GDR officials by interpreting GDR law "in the way it might have been interpreted in a *Rechtsstaat,* in the way most favorable to human rights, when in fact the law was regularly instrumentalized for political purposes in East Germany." *Id.; see also* Howard J. De Nike, "Judges on Trial: A Cultural View of the Prosecution of East German Jurists," 18 *PoLAR (Political and Legal Anthropology Review)* 83 (1995).

[125] "[E]ither . . . Nazi Germany had law though it was very bad law or because its law was so bad it was not really law at all. Nothing turns on which way we speak so long as we make plain what further point we wish to make in speaking that way." Ronald Dworkin, "Hart and the Concepts of Law," 119 *Harv. L. Rev.* 95, 98–99 (2006).

[126] Hart invoked the case in "Positivism and the Separation of Law and Morals," *supra,* 71 *Harv. L. Rev.* at 615–21, and then Fuller commented on it at greater length in his response, "Positivism and Fidelity to Law—A Reply to Professor Hart," *supra,* 71 *Harv. L. Rev.* at 648–61. For details of the disparities between the actual case and the account of it that Hart and Fuller rendered, *see* H.O. Pappe, "On the Validity of Judicial Decisions in the Nazi Era," 23 *Modern L. Rev.* 260 (1960).

ulterior and utterly nonideological reasons—the consequence: the Nazi justice system arrested her husband, convicted him of what was then purported to be a crime, and sentenced him to death (though the death sentence was never carried out). Postwar prosecutors charged the wife under an 1871 statute, continuously in effect throughout the period, that had criminalized the illegal deprivation of a person's freedom.[127] The wife's defense, in Hart's and Fuller's telling of the story, was that the deprivation of the husband's freedom had not been illegal, as it had occurred pursuant to a pair of repressive Nazi-era statutes, from 1934 and 1938, implemented in accordance with Nazi-era standards of interpretation.[128]

Fuller's response to this case is distinctive. A classical naturalist might simply have argued that the wife's act was so substantively unjust, and her defense so dependent for shelter on a legal order that notoriously regularized egregious substantive injustice, that legality, properly so called, demanded her punishment.[129] But Fuller seems to have understood that such an approach would invite precisely the kind of subjective judgment, pertaining to the exercise of power over the most fundamental

[127] Hart, *supra*, 71 *Harv. L. Rev.* at 619.

[128] The 1934 Nazi statute criminalized, *inter alia*, "spiteful and provocative statements directed against, or statements which disclose a base disposition toward, the leading personalities of the nation," even where these statements were made in private "when the person making them realized or should have realized that they would reach the public"; the 1938 statute established the death penalty for publicly seeking "to injure or destroy the will of the German people . . . to assert themselves stalwartly against their enemies." Fuller, *supra*, 71 *Harv. L. Rev.* at 653–54. Nazi courts "quite generally disregarded" the publicity element of the latter crime. *Id.* at 654.

[129] The German legal scholar Gustav Radbruch, to whom both Hart and Fuller refer, adopted this approach. Radbruch articulated what has come to be known as his "formula" as follows:

> The conflict between justice and legal certainty may be resolved in that positive law, secured by command and force, takes precedence even when its content is unjust and unreasonable, assuming however that the positive law does not depart from justice to such an unbearable extent, that it has to give way to justice as "incorrect law." It is impossible to draw a sharper line between cases of statutory non-law and law that is still valid in spite of an inappropriate content, but a different boundary line can be drawn with greater clarity: where no attempt is even made to achieve justice, where equality, which is the heart of justice, is consciously denied in the creation of positive law, then the law is not merely to be called "incorrect," it entirely loses its character as law.

Julian Rivers, "The Interpretation and Invalidity of Unjust Laws," in *Recrafting the Rule of Law: The Limits of Legal Order*, David Dyzenhaus ed. (Oxford: Hart Publishing, 1999) 40, 42, quoting Radbruch, "Gesetzliches Unrecht.und Übergesetzliches Recht," *Süddeutsche Juristenzeitung* 105–08 (1946). The formula is alluring in the realm of thought experiments, where the mind that judges the propriety of licensing such decisions is the same one that would be entrusted with the license to decide the extent of objective immorality. Real-life conferrals of discretionary authority are less reassuring. As Radbruch himself affirmed, *id.*, the sensibility underlying the rule of law is at least distrustful of, even if it does not absolutely exclude, such empowered moralism.

human interests, that the rule of law distrustfully precludes.[130] Therefore, Fuller set out to establish that the Nazi statutes and juridical practice at issue, through their violation of law's "internal morality," lacked the formal qualities of law and so could simply be removed from the analysis, leaving only the 1871 statute condemning the wife's conduct. The 1934 and 1938 statutes were, after all, designedly vague in their proscriptions, and where even this was insufficient to serve the regime's purpose of criminalizing a "base disposition" toward the leadership, terms were routinely interpreted beyond their ordinary meaning: statements made in private were assimilated to those made in public, and the death penalty for one category of crime was transposed to a different category.[131] The statutes served as open-ended licenses to inflict severe repression on anyone manifesting opposition to the regime (all the more so, one imagines, in the wake of the 1944 assassination attempt against Hitler, which had been the subject matter of the husband's untoward comments).

Fuller's strategy for vindicating the wife's conviction, however expedient, was misconceived, for it confused the question of how the rule of law treats acts performed under a previously authoritative system with the question of whether that previous system conformed to the criteria of the rule of law. What matters for the former purposes—at least, to the extent that one does not wish to make the classical naturalist move—is the positive authoritativeness of the norms that the defendant followed, not the formal character of those norms. *Nullum crimen sine lege* places the burden on the prosecution to establish the criminality of the wife's conduct on the basis of legal norms authoritative when and where the conduct occurred. This burden derives, not from formal considerations, but from the substantive concerns about notice and authority discussed above. The pertinence of those concerns turns on whether, at the time and place of the conduct, exculpatory norms were authoritative and applicable, not on whether those norms possessed or lacked a rule-of-law character.

The proper question was whether the 1871 act rendered the wife's conduct a crime at the time of its commission, given its place alongside the enactments and officially espoused interpretive methods characteristic of the German legal order of 1944. To be sure, concealed judicial manipulations, manifesting a conscious corruption, would not affect the determination of the legal order's standards; these would have been exercises of power, but not of authority, and would have created an expectation that one could get away with an act but not an expectation that one was acting within the law. In contrast, however, idiosyncratic interpretive methods, if openly

[130] "Professor Hart and others have been understandably distressed by references to a 'higher law' in some of the decisions concerning informers and in Radbruch's postwar writings." Fuller, *supra*, 71 *Harv. L. Rev.* at 659.

[131] Fuller, *supra*, 71 *Harv. L. Rev.* at 653–55.

adopted, are undeniably part of a positive legal order.[132] The wife's conduct could be prosecuted in full compliance with *nullum crimen sine lege* if, but only if, the Nazi regime, in seeking its own legitimation, traded on the existence of a legal order within which the wife's conduct would have counted as a crime.

Subsequent commentary has revealed a plausible (though far from incontestable) account of the legal facts and the wife's conduct on which a case within such specifications could have been (and in the actual event, was) made in the postwar West German court.[133] But Fuller had no interest in making that claim, which would have fallen short of the point he was trying to establish.

Furthermore, in emphasizing the flawed character of the exculpatory norms, Fuller's theory of the case neglects the fact that the wife did no more than to report facts truthfully (so far as is reported) to officials who were, beyond cavil, duly authorized to receive such testimony. Fuller's analysis would more plausibly have had bearing on the criminal liabilities of the prosecutors and judges who applied the open-ended license,[134] deriving from the Nazi legal order's distinctive

[132] A substitution of interpretive method—attributing to words an "objective" meaning at variance with the meaning that they had in the legal culture in which they were embedded—is incompatible with the *nullum crimen* principle. No country's legal enactments can be said to have meanings so objective that their terms can be applied without regard to their context and to the overall framework within which they are routinely interpreted. Persons operating within such a framework cannot properly be left at the mercy of a hostile outsider's decontextualized semantic analysis. This author has harshly criticized the European Court of Human Rights for holding to the contrary in *Streletz, Kessler, and Krenz v. Germany, supra,* at para. 81. *See* Roth, "Retrospective Justice or Retroactive Standards?" *supra,* 50 *Wayne L. Rev. at* 50–56. For other critical accounts of the decision, see W. N. Ferdinandusse, *Direct Application of International Criminal Law in National Courts* (The Hague: T.M.C. Asser Press, 2006), at 244–48; Kenneth S. Gallant, *The Principle of Legality in International and Comparative Criminal Law* (Cambridge: Cambridge University Press, 2009), at 220–22, 375–76 (noting disapprovingly the retroactive nullification of a justificatory defense).

[133] *See* Pappe, *supra,* 23 *Modern L. Rev.* at 267–68, 271. According to Pappe, the judiciary maintained a clear understanding that convictions of this type represented a subversion of their legal duties. "To regard intimidation in the interest of the ruling party as the declared purpose of the German criminal law at the time of the death sentence, as Hart suggests, is . . . an arbitrary assumption." *Id.* at 271. Moreover, Pappe contends, the political subversion of judicial duty was notorious. "A mistaken belief in the legality of the court-martial procedure would be a defence only for a person who could not be expected to share the insights of ordinary members of the public." *Id.* at 268. In the actual case, the wife was found to have been fully conscious of the judiciary's departure from established legal standards, and in testifying in court in full knowledge of the consequences for her husband, willfully exploited that departure to her own selfish, apolitical ends. *Id.* at 268. For a contrary understanding of the openly espoused ethos of the German court system during this period, which might call into question both Pappe's analysis and the actual West German court holding, see Ingo Müller, *Hitler's Justice: The Courts of the Third Reich,* trans. D. Schneider (Cambridge, Mass., Harvard Univ. Press, 1991) 68–81.

[134] The Third Reich judges who sentenced the husband to death for maligning the Führer were not prosecuted. The reason, Pappe reports, "was not that they had been acting lawfully in the execution of public justice, but that they had the defence of intimidation, and that, therefore, no court would

"jurisprudence," to disguise an extreme act of mere political repression as the execution of a lawful sentence.[135]

The wife, however, was not responsible for implementing the German criminal code. Testifying truthfully in one's country's court system is nowhere a crime, however wicked the motivation. Morally speaking, of course, the wife's conduct can be assimilated to snitching to the neighborhood mob boss about her husband's hostility, in the hope and expectation of getting her husband "rubbed out." But unless the German government in 1944 was too evil to count as a government, or the court too manifestly corrupt to have appeared, even by standards of the prevailing ideology, as a real court,[136] the wife's *nullum crimen* defense is sound.

This is why Hart understood the Soldier's Wife Case to pose a dilemma. As he memorably put it:

> in punishing the woman a choice had to be made between two evils, that of leaving her unpunished and that of sacrificing a very precious principle of morality endorsed by most legal systems. Surely if we have learned

sentence them." Pappe regards the claim of danger to the judges as exaggerated, and the invocation of this excuse to reveal "an extremely weak point in post-Nazi judicature." Pappe, *supra*, 23 *Modern L. Rev.* at 268.

[135] *Nullum crimen sine lege* is justifiably interpreted to allow prosecution of conduct that, "at the time when it was committed, was criminal according to the general principles of law recognized by the community of nations." International Covenant on Civil and Political Rights (1966), 999 U.N.T.S. 171, entered into force Mar. 23, 1976 (ICCPR), art. 15(2). This maxim cannot properly be used to circumvent empirical dissensus about the elements of a crime or, more relevantly, about justificatory defenses; legal systems in good standing within the empirical community of nations have been known to authorize state-security-inspired extemporary measures, and it is an abuse of "general principles" to nullify the exculpatory effects of such authorization. Even so, such principles might conceivably be invoked to condemn the use of unorthodox penal jurisprudence to disguise those measures' inherent extemporary character. To portray the husband's sentence as a judicial application of law, rather than as an essentially extemporary act, seems perverse, even though the soldier could hardly have lacked notice that his grumblings about the Führer, if disclosed, would have these penal consequences.

[136] This latter was Pappe's position. Pappe, *supra*, 23 *Modern L. Rev.* at 267–68. To be sure, some Third Reich judicial processes were open to such characterization, especially those directed against foreign nationals in violation of the international law of war. One set of Nuremberg prosecutions addressed such judicial proceedings. United States v. Altstoetter, III *Trials of War Criminals Before the Nuernberg Military Tribunals under Control Council Law No. 10* (William S. Hein & Co. ed., 1997), *available at* <http//www.loc.gov/rr/frd/Military_Law/pdf/NT_war-criminals_Vol-III.pdf>. For example, defendant Guenther Joel "was convicted for using his [judicial] 'authority and duty to review penal cases from the Incorporated Eastern Territories after the occupation of Poland' . . . to give 'final authorization' to nearly 100 illegal death sentences imposed by German courts between September 10, 1942 to March 1943," sentences that the Nuremberg Tribunal found to have had "'no legal basis either under the international law of warfare or under the international common law as recognized by all civilized nations.'" Kevin John Heller, "John Yoo and the *Justice* Case," May 1, 2008 post at <http://balkin.blogspot.com/2008/05/john-yoo-and-justice-case.html>, citing *Altstoetter, supra*, at 1131, 1140–42.

> anything from the history of morals it is that the thing to do with a moral quandary is not to hide it. Like nettles, the occasions when life forces us to choose between the lesser of two evils must be grasped with the consciousness that they are what they are. The vice of this use of the principle that, at certain limiting points, what is utterly immoral cannot be law or lawful is that it will serve to cloak the true nature of the problems with which we are faced and will encourage the romantic optimism that all the values we cherish ultimately will fit into a single system, that no one of them has to be sacrificed or compromised to accommodate another.[137]

Fuller's response to this passage reveals the depth of his misunderstanding:

> I hope I am not being unjust to Professor Hart when I say that I can find no way of describing the dilemma as he sees it but to use some such words as the following: On the one hand, we have an amoral datum called law, which has the peculiar quality of creating a moral duty to obey it. On the other hand, we have a moral duty to do what we think is right and decent. When we are confronted by a statute we believe to be thoroughly evil, we have to choose between two duties.
>
> If this is the positivist position, then I have no hesitancy in rejecting it. The "dilemma" it states has the verbal formulation of a problem, but the problem it states makes no sense. It is like saying that I have to choose between giving food to a starving man and being mimsy with the borogoves. I do not think it is unfair to the positivistic philosophy to say that it never gives any coherent meaning to the moral obligation of fidelity to law. . . .[138]

But Fuller was indeed "being unjust to Professor Hart," because Hart's position was in no way predicated on the proposition that "we have an amoral datum called law, which has the peculiar quality of creating a moral duty to obey it." The relevant moral duty is not the duty of the regime's subjects to obey the enactment, but the duty of the rule-of-law-oriented court, in its retrospective analysis, to take account of the considerations of notice and authority, as discussed above. Whether or not the facts of this case justify overriding them, these are weighty considerations, rooted in the imperatives of predictability and accountability in the exercise of power. Whatever else may be said of the comparative merits of positivist and naturalist accounts of such situations, it is to the credit of Hart's positivism that it worked in this case to reveal, rather than to obfuscate, the moral dilemma.

[137] Hart, *supra*, 71 *Harv. L. Rev.* at 619–20.
[138] Fuller, *supra*, 71 *Harv. L. Rev.* at 656.

In the end, Hart allowed that leaving such egregious wrongdoing unpunished might be more intolerable than using law to punish acts that were lawful when and where committed. He was willing to entertain punishing "grudge informers" such as the soldier's wife, though he believed that the harm to legality would be better contained if the ex post facto criminalization were accomplished by overtly retroactive legislation, rather than left to a court's untethered discretionary authority.[139] That proposal, which Fuller refused to characterize as "the most nearly lawful way of making unlawful what was once law,"[140] at least addresses the accountability concern underlying the *nullum crimen* principle, ruling out the licensing of subjective reactions to the perceived moral qualities of a particular defendant.[141] Far from being obtuse about law's relationship to morality, as Fuller implies, Hart's approach provides a superior basis for identifying the moral stakes of the legal question.

Even Hart's suggestion, of course, confers on a post-regime-change legal order a doubtful authority to disrespect a defendant's adherence to a legal order internationally recognized as authoritative at the time and place of the conduct. However, it is important to note the nearly unique factors that mitigate the significance of this consideration in the case of Nazi Germany. Though Germany's government was internationally recognized, its commitment to "total war"—which entailed pan-continental aggression and multiple genocide—belies any sense of reliance, by the government or its subjects, on an international legal order according the Third Reich equal juridical respect among sovereign regimes. The Third Reich set out to destroy, and did effectively destroy, the existing international legal order; thus, those committing violence on its behalf—perhaps even those not directly involved in aggression or crimes against humanity—were arguably estopped from asserting any defense peculiarly predicated on the prosecution's obligation to recognize that regime's authority at the time and place of its effectivity within Germany, or to dignify as "lawful" the decision of the regime's subjects to abet that regime's distinctive political project.

Although the Allies rejected, prior to Nuremberg, a proposal to deny combatant privilege to *Wehrmacht* soldiers participating in their state's unlawful offensive uses of force,[142] a narrower theory of estoppel, nullifying authorizations for especially

[139] Hart, *supra*, 71 *Harv. L. Rev.* at 619.

[140] Fuller, *supra*, 71 *Harv. L. Rev.* at 661.

[141] Given the wife's plainly corrupt motive—in no way connected to a prevailing ideological view about the moral justification of draconian punishments for those privately manifesting disloyalty to the Führer—it is difficult to fault the intuition that her case should be singled out for harsh treatment. As an institutional matter, however, such assessments represent precisely the kind of subjective judgment, pertaining to the exercise of power over the most fundamental human interests, against which the rule of law distrustfully guards.

[142] *See* Telford Taylor, *The Anatomy of the Nuremberg Trials* (New York: Little Brown & Co., 1992), at 37 (on the theory proposed by Col. William C. Chanler).

ruthless means undertaken in service of a set of ends thoroughly inimical to international legal order, might be more compelling. Agents of the Third Reich were on notice that their acts were part and parcel of the "total war" that they might lose, and so, arguably, on notice that they might be judged on the basis of externally prevalent minimum standards.[143]

As Hart's ambivalence makes clear, the assertion of *nullum crimen* is the start, not the end, of the conversation about what ought to be done. But whether seen in positivist terms as a moral principle external to "law" as such, or in naturalist terms as a juridical consideration within an inherently purposive process of law determination, *nullum crimen* is a compelling principle. Whatever conclusion one might draw about disregard for *nullum crimen* in post-Third Reich prosecutions, that disregard should not be taken as a model for disanalogous cases. In particular, it should not carry over to acts undertaken under the authority of more ordinary regimes, tyrannical though they may have been, that maintained standing within an operational international legal and political order.[144]

## V. INTERNATIONAL LEGALITY AND THE CRIMINALIZATION OF ORDINARY HUMAN RIGHTS VIOLATIONS

The international rule of law is predicated on respect for states' presumptive monopoly of the last word on public order inside their respective territories. Although that monopoly no longer applies in respect to established international crimes, it continues to withstand violations of international obligations in general—including human rights obligations.[145]

[143] This estoppel might apply, in particular, to officials exercising direction under legal licenses–even ones grounded in an overt and elaborated jurisprudence—that sweepingly authorized the elimination of suspected threats to national security. Those officials could scarcely claim that the international community was bound to respect the source of this discretionary authority on the basis of the Third Reich's standing in the then-prevailing international order. One might analogize such limited respect to the legal prerogatives of Third Reich officials to the limited respect accorded to agents of an unrecognized government under the doctrine of "implied mandate." *See* Madzimbamuto v. Lardner-Burke, 1 A.C. 645, 728–29 (U.K. Privy Council, 1969) ("acts of sovereignty exercised by . . . a usurper may have an obligatory force" where exercised to avoid disorder rather than to further the usurpation).

[144] In the respect, the subsequent demise of the German Democratic Republic—generally speaking, a member in good standing of a pluralistic international order in which Marxist-Leninist and other "garden-variety" dictatorships were major participants in norm formation—posed juridical questions properly understood as very different from those posed by the demise of the Third Reich. *See* Roth, "Retrospective Justice or Retroactive Standards?" *supra*, at 41–44.

[145] "He who violates the laws of war cannot obtain immunity while acting in pursuance of the authority of the state if the state in authorizing action moves outside its competence under international law." *Judicial Decisions: International Military Tribunal (Nuremberg), Judgment and Sentences, supra*, at 221. However, these attributions of individual liability for participation in state acts typically

The establishment of an international crime requires a separate step, over and above the establishment of an international human rights norm.[146] Justice Geoffrey Robertson of the Special Court for Sierra Leone has articulated the crucial requisite for this second step as follows:

> There must be evidence (or at least inference) of general agreement by the international community that breach of the customary law rule would or would now, entail international criminal liability for individual perpetrators, in addition to the normative obligation on States to prohibit the conduct in question under their domestic law. . . . [I]t must be clear that the overwhelming preponderance of states, courts, conventions, jurists and so forth relied upon to crystallize the international law "norm" intended – or now intend – this rule to have penal consequences for individuals brought before international courts, whether or not such a court presently exists with jurisdiction over them.[147]

In the illustrative case of *Sam Hinga Norman*, Robertson's dissent asserted an insufficiency of evidence, regarding the international norm prohibiting enlistment of children in armed forces, that "by 1996 it was intended by the international community to be a criminal law prohibition for the breach of which individuals should be arrested and punished."[148] Whether or not his assessment of the evidence was

occur where "the acts were *crimes* against international law, so it is doubtful whether they apply to breaches of international law which are not crimes against international law." Akehurst, *supra*, at 243.

[146] As the ICTY has noted, "For criminal liability to attach, it is not sufficient . . . merely to establish that the act in question was illegal under international law, in the sense of being liable to engage the responsibility of a state which breaches that prohibition, nor is it enough to establish that the act in question was a crime under the domestic law of the person who committed the act." *Prosecutor v. Vasiljević*, Case No. IT-98–32-T, Judgment, paras. 196, 199 (Nov. 29, 2002), cited in Van Schaack, *supra*, at 150 n. 139. For example, the ICTY has held that for a violation of Common Article 3 of the Geneva Conventions of 1949 to qualify, the violation "must constitute a breach of a rule protecting important values," "must involve grave consequences for the victim," and "must entail, under customary or conventional law, the individual criminal responsibility of the person breaching the rule." *Prosecutor v. Tadić*, Appeals Chamber Decision, October 2, 1995, para. 94. However, as Van Schaack has pointed out, the ICTY's practice on this point has been more equivocal than this rhetoric suggests. Van Schaack, *supra*, at 154–57.

[147] *Prosecutor v. Sam Hinga Norman*, Case No.SCSL-04–14-AR72(E), Judgment of May 31, 2004, Robertson, J., dissenting (hereafter "Robertson dissent"), ¶¶ 17, 21 (*available at* <http://www.sc-sl.org/CASES/CivilDefenceForcesCDFCompleted/AppealsChamberDecisions/tabid/193/Default.aspx>). The majority opinion did not overtly depart from Robertson's criteria. See *Norman*, Majority Opinion, at ¶ 37 (citing *Tadić* on "State practice indicating an intention to criminalize the prohibition").

[148] *Norman*, *supra*, Robertson dissent, ¶ 21.

correct in that case,[149] his criterion expresses the essence of *nullum crimen sine lege* as applied to international criminal law.

In the absence of an established international crime, state sovereignty, rather than being straightforwardly displaced by international legal obligation, retains a residual presence alongside international legal obligation. Paradoxical though it may seem, renunciation of a practice does not in itself entail renunciation of the legal capacity to authorize that practice. Schmitt's notorious maxim, "Sovereign is he who decides on the exception,"[150] while debatable in application to domestic legal orders, captures the essence of the relationship between domestic and international authority wherever an international crime has not been authoritatively established: states, as represented by their recognized governments, retain the legal capacity (even though not the right) to authorize measures in violation of the state's ordinary international legal obligations.[151] In so acting, states incur responsibility for breach and render themselves susceptible to adverse legal consequences, including the (appropriately limited) countermeasures of specially affected states or of the community of states.[152] However, the cluster of constraining norms discussed above—limits to extraterritorial jurisdiction, immunity *ratione materiae,* and *nullum crimen sine lege*—shields from personal liability officials and cooperating citizens operating inside their own national territory within domestic legal mandates. Internationally-acknowledged sovereign prerogative thus operates to protect individuals who act—albeit in an internationally wrongful manner—in the state's service.

This rule applies even to norms that might plausibly be categorized as *jus cogens.*[153] Notwithstanding the indications of much scholarly commentary[154] and some

[149] For the contrary assessment, *see Norman, supra,* Majority Opinion, ¶¶ 44–51.

[150] Schmitt, *supra,* at 5.

[151] "International law . . . recognizes the power–though not the right–to break a treaty and abide the international consequences." Louis Henkin, *Foreign Affairs and the Constitution* (Mineola, NY: Foundation Press, 1972), 168.

[152] International Law Commission, Articles on State Responsibility (2001), arts. 48–54.

[153] *Jus cogens* refers to a "peremptory" norm, "accepted and recognized by the international community of States as a whole as a norm from which no derogation is permitted." Vienna Convention on the Law of Treaties, *supra,* art. 53.

[154] One source of confusion in this area is that some important scholars have popularized the term "*jus cogens* crimes." *See, e.g.,* M. Cherif Bassiouni, "International Crimes: *Jus Cogens* and *Obligatio Erga Omnes,*" 59 *Law & Contemporary Probs.* 63 (1996); Leila Nadya Sadat, "Exile, Amnesty, and International Law," 81 *Notre Dame L. Rev.* 955, 966 & n.31 (2006). These scholars use that term to highlight claims about additional legal consequences (such as the purported inadmissibility of amnesty) of certain acts that have been established to incur international criminal liability. Whatever the merit of those claims, the rhetoric has had the effect of leading less careful scholars to conflate *jus cogens* and international crimes—phenomena that do, of course, frequently coincide. *See* Bartram S. Brown,

judicial dicta,[155] a norm's *jus cogens* status does not alone establish universal penal jurisdiction or the voiding of immunities.[156] *Jus cogens* norms do have important special characteristics that imply an element of "normative hierarchy"[157]: these norms, unlike ordinary customary ones, are obligatory notwithstanding the "persistent objection" of any individual state to their formation[158]; they admit of no "circumstances precluding wrongfulness" of their violation[159]; and they limit the permissible content of treaties.[160] However, while the international system will not recognize any ill-gotten gains from a *jus cogens* violation,[161] it has not (at least, so far)

"The Evolving Concept of Universal Jurisdiction," 35 *New Eng. L. Rev.* 383, 392–93 (2001) (cautioning against the overidentification of *jus cogens* with universal jurisdiction).

Moreover, the rhetoric of *jus cogens* crimes tends to present as settled what is, in actuality, a highly contentious assertion: that the duty of states to prosecute foreign-state officials for crimes of this nature is itself a *jus cogens* obligation that overrides constraining international legal norms of a "lower" status. A prohibition's *jus cogens* status does not, in itself, imply the same status for the obligation to prosecute the offense. *See* Ferdinandusse, *supra*, at 182; Shany, *supra*, at 867. Indeed, the International Criminal Court Statute seems to counterindicate *jus cogens* status for such prosecutorial obligations, since its call for surrender of suspects expressly yields to states parties' contrary treaty obligations to non-parties. ICC Statute, Art. 98.

[155] *See, e.g., Prosecutor v. Furundžija,* Trial Chamber, Judgment of December 10, 1998, <http://www.un.org/icty/furundzija/trialc2/judgement/index.htm>, paras. 147, 155–56.

[156] *See, e.g.,* Ferdinandusse, *supra*, at 182; Shany, *supra*, at 867; Andrea Bianchi, "Human Rights and the Magic of *Jus Cogens*," 19 *Euro. J. Int'l L.* 491, 500 (2008) Several important recent decisions have, in the face of alleged *jus cogens* violations, upheld state immunity, the immunity *ratione personae* of sitting state officials responsible for diplomacy, and the immunity *ratione materiae* of state officials in civil cases. *See Case Concerning the Arrest Warrant of 11 April 2000, Democratic Republic of the Congo v. Belgium (Yerodia)*, 2002 ICJ Rep. 3 (upholding the immunity *ratione personae* of a currently serving Foreign Minister from prosecution in a foreign-state court for crimes against humanity); *Al-Adsani v. Government of Kuwait (No. 2)*, 1996 ILR 536 (House of Lords holding that state immunity precludes civil suits against foreign states for torture); *Jones v. Ministry of the Interior of the Kingdom of Saudi Arabia*, 2006 UKHL 26 (House of Lords holding that state immunity precludes civil suits against foreign officials for torture, even though those officials are subject to criminal liability); *Al-Adsani v. United Kingdom*, 34 EHRR 273 (2001) (a closely divided decision of the Grand Chamber of the European Court of Human Rights, holding that human rights law does not require a state court to void foreign state immunity in civil suits for torture). As Hazel Fox has put it, state immunity "does not contradict a prohibition contained in a *jus cogens* norm but merely diverts any breach of it to a different method of settlement. Arguably, then, there is no substantive content in the procedural plea of State immunity upon which a *jus cogens* mandate can bite." H. Fox, *The Law of State Immunity* (Oxford University Press, 2002), 525.

[157] *See* Dinah Shelton, "Normative Hierarchy in International Law," 100 *Am. J. Int'l L.* 291(2006).

[158] *See* Michael Byers, *Custom, Power, and the Power of Rules* (Cambridge University Press, 1999), at 186.

[159] ILC Articles on State Responsibility, *supra*, arts. 20–26, 50(1)(d) (peremptory norms preclude invocations of consent, self-defense, countermeasures, *force majeure*, distress, and necessity).

[160] Vienna Convention on the Law of Treaties, *supra*, art. 53.

[161] It is true that "No State shall recognize as lawful a situation created by" a "gross or systematic failure by the responsible State to fulfil" a peremptory obligation, nor may it "render aid or assistance

established that a governmental act, simply by virtue of being taken in breach of a *jus cogens* obligation, is *ultra vires* of state authority.[162]

As noted in Chapter 3, nothing logically compels the step from a norm's supremacy within the international system to the international system's denial of legal recognition to all domestic authority shielding state agents from personal liability for breach.[163] As the International Law Commission has noted, "the category of international obligations admitting of no derogation is much broader than the category of obligations whose breach is necessarily an international crime. Too close an

in maintaining that situation." ILC Articles on State Responsibility, *supra*, arts. 40–41. However, these unlawful situations "virtually without exception" involve "legal claims to territory." *Legal Consequences of the Construction of a Wall in the Occupied Palestinian Territory, Advisory Opinion*, 2004 ICJ Rep. 36 (July 9), Kooijmans sep. op., paras. 43–44; *see generally*, Stefan Talmon, "The Duty Not to 'Recognize as Lawful' a Situation Created by the Illegal Use of Force or Other Serious Breaches of a Jus Cogens Norm," in Christian Tomuschat & Jean-Marc Thouvenin, eds., *The Fundamental Rules of the International Legal Order:* Jus Cogens *and Obligations* Erga Omnes (Leiden: Martinus Nijhoff, 2006), at 99–125. The provision thus appears to be little more than a restatement of the "Stimson Doctrine," adopted in the 1930s in response to the Japanese use of force to create the satellite state of Manchukuo. *See, e.g.*, Howard Jones, *Crucible of Power: A History of U.S. Foreign Relations Since 1897* (Wilmington, Del.: SR Books, 2001), at 129. Such non-recognition follows directly from the U.N. Charter scheme, and entails no innovations.

[162] W. Michael Reisman reports (with no indication of either endorsement or disavowal):

> In human rights discourse, *jus cogens* has acquired a much more radical meaning [than that contained in the Vienna Convention on the Law of Treaties], evolving into a type of super-custom, based on transempirical sources and hence not requiring demonstration of practice as proof of its validity. This new understanding of *jus cogens* renders national law that is inconsistent with it devoid of international and national legal effect, such that national officials who purport to act on the putative authority of that national law may now incur direct international responsibility.

Reisman, "Unilateral Actions and the Transformations of the World Constitutive Process: The Special Problem of Humanitarian Intervention," 11 *Euro. J. Int'l L.* 3, 15 n. 29 (2000). In reality, "in most . . . cases where peremptory norms have been recognized, the legal consequences of this classification were essentially imperceptible." Shelton, *supra*, at 306.

[163] This proposition would entail, among other things, the "Chanler thesis," which asserted that *Wehrmacht* soldiers participating in their state's unlawful offensive uses of force lacked combatant privilege and could thus be susceptible to prosecution for their combat violence as domestic crime. *See* Taylor, *supra*, at 37. A similar idea was conveyed in the first (3 votes to 2) House of Lords decision on the immunities of former Chilean Head of State Augusto Pinochet; according to Lord Nicholls (joined by Lords Steyn and Hoffman), "it hardly needs saying that torture of his own subjects, or of aliens, would not be regarded by international law as a function of a head of state. . . . This was made clear long before 1973 and the events which took place in Chile then and thereafter." *Regina v. Bow Street Metropolitan Stipendiary Magistrate (Pinochet I)*, 1 AC 61, 109 (2000); *cf. id.* at 115 (Lord Steyn); *id.* at 118 (Lord Hoffman). In the ultimate judgment, however, at most two of seven Law Lords (Lord Millett and apparently Lord Phillips) embraced this view. *Regina v. Bow Street Metropolitan Stipendiary Magistrate (Pinochet III)*, 1 AC 147 (2000).

assimilation of the two notions may be an attractive simplification, but it does not appear to be conceptually acceptable."[164]

This is the essential reason why, in the case of Chilean ex-dictator Augusto Pinochet, the ultimate decision of the British House of Lords found susceptibility to prosecution abroad only for those acts of torture committed after the Torture Convention came into force for Chile.[165] Even though the decision acknowledged torture to have been a violation of customary international law, and indeed a violation of *jus cogens*, long before the treaty's effective date, an exemption from immunity was effected only upon the positive establishment of universal jurisdiction over foreign-state officials operating inside their national territory and within official capacity.[166] In the wake of the Torture Convention and state practices pursuant and parallel to it, official torture by now likely constitutes a universal-jurisdiction crime under customary international law as well, but this was not clearly so with respect to earlier periods (including, regrettably, the mid-1970s, when the bulk of the Chilean atrocities took place).

Beth Van Schaack has nonetheless discerned a tendency in international tribunals to elide the distinction between international obligations and international crimes, and thus between state responsibility and individual culpability. She observes that, for example, the ICTY has imputed individual criminal responsibility even with respect to Geneva norms that fall outside of the Conventions' "grave breaches" regime.[167] Yet it is important to note that even Justice Robertson's positivistic approach to *nullum crimen sine lege* does not exclude subsequent attributions of

[164] International Law Commission, Commentary to the Draft Articles on State Responsibility (Art. 19) (1996) (*available at* <http://www.lcil.cam.ac.uk/Media/ILCSR/rft/Sr19.rtf>), para. 62; *see also* Michael Byers, *Custom, Power, and the Power of Rules, supra,* at 184–185 n. 95.

[165] An additional reason concerned the principle of "double-criminality" in British extradition law—i.e., the need for British law, as well as Spanish law, to have established torture as a universal jurisdiction crime—but that aspect of the holding was not predicated on an interpretation of international law. *See Pinochet III, supra,* at 189 (opinion of Lord Browne-Wilkinson).

[166] The lead opinion made the point as follows:

> I have doubts whether, before the coming into force of the Torture Convention, the existence of the international crime of torture as jus cogens was enough to justify the conclusion that the organisation of state torture could not rank for immunity purposes as an official function. At that stage there was no international tribunal to punish torture and no general jurisdiction to permit or require its punishment in domestic courts. Not until there was some form of universal jurisdiction for the punishment of the crime of torture could it really be talked about as a fully constituted international crime. But in my judgment the Torture Convention did provide what was missing: a worldwide universal jurisdiction.

*Pinochet III, supra,* at 204–05 (opinion of Lord Browne-Wilkinson).

[167] Van Schaack, *supra,* at 154 & n. 162, citing Prosecutor v. Delalić et al. (*Čelebići*), *supra,* para. 176 ("While 'grave breaches' must be prosecuted and punished by all States, 'other' breaches of the Geneva Conventions may be so.").

penal responsibility to initially non-penal norms, so long as patterns of state practice and manifestations of *opinio juris* properly evidence an authoritative decision of the international community to this effect. Positivism insists that a norm's legal validity derives from its social source rather than its moral content[168]; it does not limit cognizable sources to treaties and legislation.

More troubling is Van Schaack's observation that "Tribunals have reasoned that, when conduct shocks the conscience of the international community, no formal notice of its penal consequences is necessary to prosecute offenders."[169] Insofar as "no formal notice" here means dispensing with the need, not merely for official promulgation, but for the positive establishment of crimes, on grounds of the acts being *mala in se*,[170] this directly contradicts Robertson's orthodox position, which he articulates with eloquence as follows:

> Here, the Prosecution asserts with some insouciance that "the principle of *nullem crimen sine lege* is not in any case applied rigidly, particularly where the acts in question are universally regarded as abhorrent and deeply shock the conscience of humanity." On the contrary, it is precisely when the acts are abhorrent and deeply shocking that the principle of legality must be most stringently applied, to ensure that a defendant is not convicted out of disgust rather than evidence, or of a non-existent crime. *Nullem crimen* may not be a household phrase, but it serves as some protection against the lynch mob.[171]

Although Robertson's endorsement of the moral significance of positive law is stirring, it needs some qualification. Rigidity in this field is a virtue, not for its own sake, but because it responds to a vital moral interest. The problem is not that it is wrong to prosecute "conduct that shocks the conscience of the international community"; the problem is that it is too easy so to characterize the conduct of disfavored actors.[172]

[168] Gardner, *supra*, at 199.

[169] Van Schaack, *supra*, at 156.

[170] Van Schaack cites, for example, this characteristically equivocal language from the ICTY Appeals Chamber: "Although the immorality or appalling character of an act is not a sufficient factor to warrant its criminalization under customary international law, it may in fact play a role in that respect, insofar as it may refute any claim by the Defence that it did not know of the criminal nature of the acts." *Milutinovic*, Case No. IT-99–37-AR72, Decision on Dragoljub Ojdanic's Motion Challenging Jurisdiction: Joint Criminal Enterprise, para. 42, quoted in Van Schaack, *supra*, at 156.

[171] Robertson dissent, *supra*, at para. 12 (footnote omitted).

[172] The *Norman* case itself was by no means as morally clear-cut as Justice Robertson's formalistic argument suggests. The defendant led the Sierra Leone Civil Defense Force against a rebel group, the Revolutionary United Front (RUF), notorious for the grotesquerie of its mass atrocities. *See* Michael Nesbitt, "Lessons from the Sam Hinga Norman Decision of the Special Court for Sierra

Where individuals commit ruthless acts on behalf of political causes to which one is unsympathetic or indifferent, the acts "shock the conscience." Where the acts are thought to be necessary expedients in the service of a compelling societal end, they turn out not to be so shocking, after all.[173] The hypothesized conscience of the international community is deontological; the empirical conscience of the international community, I submit,[174] is consequentialist. The ends of the "good guys" are widely perceived to justify their means; acts undertaken to further the cause of the "bad guys" are inevitably viewed less charitably.[175] In an international system that reconciles a wide-ranging (though not unlimited) plurality of political moralities, it is dangerous to make generalizations about specific measures that "shock the conscience" irrespective of their political justifications. Universal-jurisdiction-based prosecutions that could proceed by appeals to conscience would inevitably generate widely varying results, depending on the political sympathies prevalent in the venue.

The global system's pluralism is, above all, a pluralism of conflicting consequentialist moralities. There is typically no dispute about the *presumptive* wrongfulness of the acts in question. Indeed, inasmuch as these are acknowledged as human rights violations, there is no legally cognizable dispute that the wrong suffered by the

Leone: How Trials and Truth Commissions Can Co-exist—Part 1/2," 8:10 *German L.J.* (Oct. 1, 2007), *available at* <http://www.germanlawjournal.com/article.php?id=866>. Not only was Norman widely regarded as a hero in Sierra Leone, but given the dire moral consequences of defeat in that conflict, it is hardly clear that enlisting child soldiers to maximize his force's fighting capacity was truly, in its context, shocking to the conscience. One might imagine that a village in danger of being overrun by the RUF would sooner muster its children to the collective defense than leave its children at the mercy of the marauders. This consequentialist argument is inadmissible in the presence of a firmly established and strict penal norm, but to the extent that the penal standard is being improvised by appeal to moral consensus, the point can hardly be considered immaterial.

[173] Some supporters of the Bush administration have contended that U.S. constitutional jurisprudence governing cruel, inhuman, and degrading treatment or punishment prohibits—as "conscience-shocking"—only "conduct intended to injure in some way unjustifiable by any government interest." *Chavez v. Martinez*, 538 US 760, 775 (2003). Although this is probably a somewhat misleading account of the constitutional doctrine, the doctrine plausibly establishes a sliding scale, evaluating harsh measures differentially in light of varying governmental needs.

[174] *See* Chapter 4.

[175] As the conflicted responses to the excesses of the 1999 NATO bombing of Serbia bear out, successful campaigns in the service of well-regarded causes will seldom draw determined outrage, let alone criminal proceedings. See Benvenuti, *supra*; *see also* Human Rights Watch, *Civilian Deaths in the NATO Air Campaign* (Feb. 2000), *available at* <http://www.hrw.org/reports/2000/nato/Natbm200.htm#P39_994>, #P88_14845> ("In its investigation Human Rights Watch has found no evidence of war crimes" despite finding that the purpose of "the bombing of state Serb Radio and Television headquarters in Belgrade on April 23 . . . seems to have been more psychological harassment of the civilian population than to obtain direct military effect").

victims cannot simply be cancelled out by a countervailing social benefit.[176] There is nonetheless frequent dispute as to whether, in particular cases, exceptional circumstances justify inflicting the wrong upon that set of victims, dispute that typically reflects differential regard for the conceptions of legitimate and just public order that underlie the claims of justification.[177]

The system's default position is that a state retains the sovereign capacity to authorize the act, thereby taking collective responsibility for the violation and shielding state agents from personal liability. Only where the international community of states comes to acknowledge the violation as an international crime is the state deemed to have renounced this sovereign capacity.

This step occurs most often with respect to those measures—for example, genocide, crimes against humanity, and gross or systematic violations of the laws and customs of war—that, far from being substantially related to cognizable governmental ends, entail or suggest, by their very nature, either rogue activity or ends that the international community has authoritatively repudiated (such as "ethnic cleansing"). The phenomenon has extended, typically by express consent, to other specific measures as well (including, for example, torture and the use of chemical weapons), but the international community, as it stands currently, is very far from having sweepingly criminalized state recourse to ruthless means.[178]

Whereas human rights norms should be read expansively to realize their object and purpose, international penal norms need to be read narrowly as derogations of affirmative legal limitations.[179] It would be highly distortive to transplant the expansive logic of human rights protection—appropriate to the use of law as a shield—to the very different task of identifying candidates for international vilification.[180] The problem is all the worse where state agents' status as "enemies of humanity" will be left open, through the removal of immunity *ratione materiae*, to determinations

[176] On "uncancelled wrongs" from the standpoint of moral philosophy, see Steven Lukes, *Moral Conflict and Politics* (Oxford Univ. Press, 1991), at 192–93.

[177] The philosophical aspects of these disputes are too complex to cover in this space. For present purposes, it is enough to notice the sociological aspects. A ready illustration can be found in the vituperative disputes that rage among liberal intellectuals who sympathize, respectively, with the Israeli and Palestinian causes. *See, e.g.*, Malvina Halberstam, "Belgium's Universal Jurisdiction Law: Vindication of International Justice or Pursuit of Politics?" 25 *Cardozo L. Rev.* 247 (2003).

[178] For greater elaboration of the point, see Roth, "Just Short of Torture," *supra*, at 232–34.

[179] *See* Vienna Convention on the Law of Treaties, *supra*, art. 31(3)(c) (treaty interpretation must take into account "any relevant rules of international law applicable in the relations between the parties").

[180] And indeed, the need for the distinction cuts both ways. Were all breaches of human rights obligations to be regarded *ipso facto* as international crimes, it would follow logically, but perversely, that any practice that is a not an international crime is not a breach of state obligation. To interpret the standard restrictively, as appropriate where the focus is on the wrongdoing of the perpetrator, would then have the effect of diluting the standard of state obligation toward the victim.

by those adverse to the governmental ends for which the ruthless means were invoked.

Yet, as Darryl Robinson, has noted,

> a technique commonly used in ICL is (i) to adopt a purposive interpretive approach; (ii) to assume that the exclusive object and purpose of an ICL enactment is to maximize victim protection; and (iii) to allow this presumed object and purpose to dominate over other considerations, including if necessary the text itself.[181]

Such an approach might be tolerable in the service of giving full effect to an international consensus that was real and manifest to the perpetrator at the time of the conduct, even if the requisite articulations of *opinio juris* lagged somewhat behind. But insofar as it would give effect to illusory consensus, and license partisan judgments in the name of universality, it would offend considerations fundamental to the international rule of law.

International penal norms represent the limits of a qualified pluralism. They place certain acts and actors beyond the pale, while otherwise leaving in place an agreement to disagree, not merely about peripheral matters, but about matters of freedom and tyranny, life and death. By observing positivistic standards in discerning the reach of international penal norms, jurists implement whatever overlapping consensus and compromise have been established among bearers of differing moral sensibilities. In this way, they avoid exaggerations of the scope of accord, exaggerations well suited to the pursuit of a partisan agenda.

## Conclusion

The foregoing chapter intends a radical statement, albeit in service of a set of moderate prescriptions. The target of that statement is not international criminal law as it has generally operated in practice, but the exuberant rhetoric that has frequently accompanied that practice. The sweeping promise to "end impunity" for human rights violations should be a source of anxiety rather than enthusiasm, for it may well portend, not predictability and accountability in the exercise of power, but rather quite the opposite. To romanticize penal processes as holding perpetrators accountable to victims obscures their more typical tendency to hold the losers of political conflicts accountable to the winners. Human rights advocates, of all people, should think twice before identifying with winners as against losers, and before

[181] Robinson, *supra*, at 934.

engaging in advocacy that may conveniently aid in legitimating the impositions of the powerful.[182]

*Nullum crimen sine lege* and related doctrines that limit extraterritorial jurisdiction and confer immunity *ratione materiae* are not inconvenient obstacles to be circumvented but crucial safeguards to be respected. These doctrines respond to the reality that the international community remains beset by serious moral disagreement, both about what count as just ends and about which harsh measures those ends might justify in circumstances of high-stakes political conflict. In such a world, in which very few hands are truly clean, unilateral invocations of universal principles must be viewed skeptically, and associated exercises of power treated guardedly. Prosecutions undertaken in the name of the international community must establish a requisite social, and not merely a moral, basis for condemning acts—including acknowledged human rights violations—as crimes, and for holding their state-authorized perpetrators as subject to individual penal responsibility.

An over-assertive approach to international criminal justice, to be pursued unilaterally in domestic justice systems, is troubling because it risks undermining what is arguably most valuable about international law. International law provides a framework for accommodation among the non-like-minded and a normative basis for mobilizing broad opposition to the self-righteous violence of the powerful (even as it licenses uses of force where there is genuinely no reasonable alternative). Penal processes aim to identify villains, consequently to exclude them as bearers of recognized authority, and thus as partners in negotiation and accommodation. Appropriate though such outcomes are in an important subset of circumstances, it is dangerous to distract from the deeper truth that peace means peace with others as they are, not as we might like for them to be. One must seek peace, not always with the gentle, but often with the ruthless. A repudiation of that truth risks setting in motion, willy-nilly, a new ruthlessness to end all ruthlessness.

[182] Darryl Robinson astutely points out the potential misfit between a "human rights liberalism" that views such international criminal cases from the standpoint of the prosecution and a "criminal law liberalism" that views them from the standpoint of the defense. Robinson, *supra,* at 931. But it remains disconcerting that human rights advocates should identify with prosecutorial authority, or for that matter, with the winning side of political conflicts. This may be attributable to a peculiar historical moment, with views having been forged by the experience of an extraordinary series of relatively peaceful transitions from authoritarian to liberal regimes. This author's more pessimistic frame of mind reflects the influence of a different set of historical episodes, and a self-conscious identification with losers, rather than winners, of political conflict.

# 8

# Concluding Observations

## *The Enduring Need for a Pluralist Global Legal Order*

## Introduction

The earlier chapters articulate and defend a particular conception of international legal order. This conception emphasizes the foundational principle of the United Nations Charter-based order, the sovereign equality of states, as an institutional response to persistent disagreement about what constitutes a legitimate and just territorial public order. While by no means excluding international legal norms that bind states in the conduct of their internal affairs, this principle nonetheless poses substantial barriers both to the recognition and to the implementation of such norms. Above all, in a horizontal legal system where enforcement capacities are decentralized, the principle militates against powerful states' penchant for invoking universal principles to rationalize unilateral (and typically self-serving) impositions upon weak states.

On the above account, respectful accommodation among territorial political communities is predicated on a "bounded pluralism" in regard to clashing political moralities. It is morally irresponsible to eschew respectful accommodation, not because the truth of political morality is culturally relative or because moral truth is unachievable on ontological or epistemological grounds, but because pluralism is needed to satisfy an objective moral interest in coexistence and cooperation. The fact that human beings systematically and profoundly disagree about justice has morally significant consequences, irrespective of the truth of the matter.

If the operative theme of international legality is understood to be bounded pluralism rather than "transcendent justice," sovereignty-oriented constraints on the establishment and implementation of international norms appear as a fundamental premise of, rather than a mere impediment to, the project of international legality. These constraints reflect morally significant considerations that must be given due regard in assessing the appropriateness of international action, whatever the moral appeal of the proposed action. Due respect for these constraints is a moral obligation that must, at the very least, be balanced against any obligation to pursue justice in territorial political communities other than one's own.

Yet, as the earlier chapters on humanitarian intervention, on international responses to secessions and coups, and on international criminal justice indicate, the ground beneath this pluralist approach to global order has undoubtedly shifted, if to an uncertain extent. In the formative period of the United Nations Charter-based order, a balance of First, Second, and Third Worlds undergirded pluralistic doctrines. Geostrategic and ideological struggle between the liberal-democratic and the revolutionary-socialist states, combined with the rival blocs' need to woo the uncommitted, created the conditions for acknowledgment of the legal inviolability of weak states and for a qualified neutrality of international institutions on the legitimacy of particular systems of internal public order.

By contrast, the period from the end of the Cold War to the beginning of the Global War on Terrorism—the period from 11/9 (the November 9, 1989, fall of the Berlin Wall) to 9/11 (the September 11, 2001, World Trade Center and Pentagon attacks)—was a period in which international order could be, and was, radically reimagined. Western initiatives faced far less resistance in international fora, and many post-colonial state apparatuses, no longer able to exploit superpower competition to their advantage, became exposed as catastrophically ineffective and worse. Meanwhile, exuberance about the possibilities of a New World Order, whether or not extending to claims about "the end of history,"[1] suggested the irrelevance of many earlier policy concerns that had recommended a greater modesty of mission.

The period after September 11, 2001, has seen a restoration of some of the pluralism-relevant characteristics of the Cold War period, both for reasons related to the ensuing Global War on Terrorism—above all, the Iraq War, the attendant rise in global distrust of the United States, and the decidedly mixed results of external impositions in the targeted states—and for a host of coincidental reasons, including, *inter alia*, China's ever-increasing influence, Russia's renewed geopolitical assertiveness, Islamist political movements' enhanced profile (and, in some countries, electoral performance), and a socialist-populist resurgence in several Latin American countries (led by Venezuela). Yet while variants of Islamic political theology have led the way in reintroducing the question of pluralism in the international order, the greatest global ideological clash of the current period is not a clash among blocs within the international order, but a confrontation between leading elements of that order and extreme Islamist non-state actors totally alienated from the international community of states. International law has renewed significance as a

[1] Francis Fukuyama notoriously argued at the end of the Cold War that we had arrived at "the end of history as such; that is, the end point of mankind's ideological evolution and the universalization of Western liberal democracy as the final form of human government." Fukuyama, "The End of History?" *The National Interest* (Summer 1989), pp. 3–4.

framework of accommodation among non-like-minded states, but also renewed significance as a "fighting faith," as against forces widely viewed as both practically unappeasable and morally unacceptable.[2]

This chapter will attempt no sweeping prediction about future events. It will, however, argue that as against practicable alternatives, sovereign equality, however seemingly outmoded, still has much to recommend it as a foundational principle of international public order. In particular, the chapter will answer moral objections associated with efforts (1) to substitute a liberal-democratic for a pluralist international approach to internal public order, and (2) to substitute "an end to impunity" and "no safe havens" for interstate peace and respectful accommodation as public international law's preeminent theme.[3] It will contend that insofar as human rights advocates reject the global pluralism with which this book is concerned, they figure to empower what they themselves should identify as the wrong interests and values. It will remind those advocates of insights from the not-so-distant past that have tended to be neglected or forgotten, as international moralism's reach has come to exceed its grasp.

## I. Eschewing Liberal-Democratic Norms as the Basis for Acknowledging State Authority

As has been noted in a vast literature, democracy has increasingly come to be regarded as a human right and as a legal norm of the international order.[4] The right to political participation, once virtually nullified by a failure of the international community to reach accord on any of the details—including on whether a one-party state that tolerated no organized opposition could nonetheless be held to have

[2] *Compare* S.C. Res. 1373 (2001), requiring that states "[p]revent and suppress the financing of terrorist acts;" *with* G.A. Res. 42/159 (1987), bearing the tellingly cumbersome title, "Measures to prevent international terrorism which endangers or takes innocent human lives or jeopardizes fundamental freedoms and study of the underlying causes of those forms of terrorism and acts of violence which lie in misery, frustration, grievance and despair and which cause people to sacrifice human lives, including their own, in an attempt to effect radical changes." Although the definition of terrorism remains fudged, *see, e.g.*, Alex Schmid, "Terrorism—The Definitional Problem," 37 *Case W. Res. J. Int'l L.* 375, 388 (2005); Jarna Petman, "The Problem of Evil and International Law," in Jarna Petman & Jan Klabbers eds., *Nordic Cosmopolitanism: Essays in International Law for Martti Koskenniemi* (Martinus Nijhoff Publishers/Brill Academic Publishers: Leiden, 2003), 111, there is no question that a particular brand of terrorism, at least, has been identified as an enemy to the international order.

[3] *See, e.g.*, Jamie Mayerfeld, "Ruthlessness, Impunity, and the Effacement of International Human Rights Law," 8 *Santa Clara J. Int'l L.* 289 (2010) (criticizing the article from which Chapter 7 is adapted).

[4] *See generally* Gregory H. Fox & Brad R. Roth eds., *Democratic Governance and International Law* (Cambridge University Press, 2000) (collection presenting a range of views on related questions).

satisfied the norm—has achieved far greater determinacy in international pronouncements. That determinacy is further reflected in the practices of international agencies that have monitored and, in some cases, organized electoral processes in those states that have either invited external monitoring or have been subject to binding Security Council mandates.[5]

What matters most from the standpoint of sovereignty, however, is not the existence of a presumptively authoritative norm, but the persistence of a government's residual authority, as promulgator of the last word on public order in the territory, to suspend the local operation of a valid international norm. The crucial issues arise in dynamic rather than static contexts, in crisis rather than in normalcy. Even where a norm achieves universal and binding status, sovereign remains "he who decides on the exception"—not in the sense of establishing a valid international legal defense to breach, but in the sense of creating legal facts that, notwithstanding the breach, are not subject to nullification or coercive recourse by any external authority.

As discussed in Chapter 6, articulations of a new democratic norm coexist uneasily with intergovernmental bodies' statements and practices reaffirming the long-standing norm against foreign intervention in the internal affairs of states. To alter the essential logic of the pluralist global order, a democratic entitlement would need three components: (1) a determinate standard for what counts as a genuinely participatory process; (2) a determinate standard governing the relationship between the mandated participatory mechanisms and the actual exercise of political power; and (3) an affirmation that the sovereign rights of the territorial political community—above all, against foreign intervention—can cognizably be asserted (in the name of popular will) only by a government formed in compliance with these determinate standards.[6] Yet this third step—the disapplication of the effective control doctrine—has been taken only in the rarest of circumstances, where (as in Haiti in 1991–94 and Sierra Leone in 1997–98) a governmental apparatus has done far worse than to violate a formal standard of free and fair elections.[7]

[5] *See* Gregory H. Fox & Brad R. Roth, "Democracy and International Law," 27 *Rev. Int'l Studies* 327 (2001).

[6] *Id.* at 336.

[7] At this writing, a new test case looms in the aftermath of the November 28, 2010, Côte d'Ivoire election. The Southern-based government of Laurent Gbagbo, defeated at the polls by 54 percent to 46 percent according to a count affirmed by international monitors, BBC News, "Ivory Coast election: Alassane Ouattara 'beats Gbagbo,'" Dec. 2, 2010 <http://www.bbc.co.uk/news/world-africa-11903470>, has refused to yield power to the Northern-based opposition movement led by Presidential candidate Alassane Ouattara. This case, too, would be exceptional in that while the election winner's legitimacy to govern appears to be genuinely contested within the political community (along sectional and other lines), the election was part of an internationally-brokered agreement to end an internal armed conflict that had drawn a Chapter VII intervention. *See* S.C. Res. 1880, 1893 (2009), 1911 (2010).

Indeed, while multiparty elections have proliferated, reflecting a widening expectation of a democratic basis for governmental legitimacy, so too have blatant electoral cheating and circumventions of electoral mandates proliferated; these latter have frequently drawn international condemnation but rarely a denial of a government's ultimate authority. A one-sided interpretation of international law in this area—presenting still-open questions about legal norms of democracy and popular sovereignty as though they have been definitively resolved—may lend a false imprimatur to a coercive interventionism that contradicts important elements of the international legal order.

Moreover, proposals for a fundamental reform of the international legal order to accommodate such an interventionism—a reform that would delegitimate and cast into international outlawry political projects inconsistent with a hegemonic conception of democratic values—should be viewed warily. Though superficially attractive, assertions of a new, "democratic" criterion for the international legal standing of governments—and, consequently, armed oppositional movements[8]—pose dangers, not only to international peace and security, but also to popular self-determination within weak states. Outside observers tend to equate democracy with freedom and power for those members of foreign societies with whom they personally identify, and outside assessments of internal political conflicts are highly susceptible to the partisan manipulations of both local elites and their foreign patrons.[9] Efforts to transcend partisanship through the establishment of politically and ideologically neutral "democratic" specifications turn out to be unavailing.[10]

Democratic entitlement advocates are faced with two options in asserting democracy as a determinate norm of international law. The first is to deem "free and fair elections" (defined as including not merely a fair vote count, but also effective protections against infringements of civil and political liberty in the preelectoral period) the necessary and sufficient condition of democratic legitimacy, to the

[8] The democratic entitlement's pioneer, Thomas M. Franck, while explicitly opposing unilateral forcible measures against noncomplying governments, did propose "that legitimate governments should be assured of protection from overthrow by totalitarian forces through concerted systemic action after—and only after—the community has recognized that such an exigency has arisen." Thomas M. Franck, "The Emerging Right to Democratic Governance," 86 *Am. J. Int'l L.* 46, 91 (1992).

[9] Anyone who believes that this potential is purely hypothetical should examine the work of the Human Rights Bureau of the United States State Department with respect to the Central American crises of the 1980s. The literature on this episode is vast, but one concise critique of the political manipulation of human rights compliance assessments can be found in Americas Watch, *Human Rights in Nicaragua: Reagan, Rhetoric and Reality* (New York: Americas Watch, 1985).

[10] Instructively, the U.S. Supreme Court characterizes a "political question" as one from which courts should abstain on account of, *inter alia*, "a lack of judicially discoverable and manageable standards for resolving it . . . or the impossibility of deciding without an initial policy determination of a kind clearly for nonjudicial discretion." Baker v. Carr, 369 U.S. 186, 217 (1962).

exclusion of any consideration of the broader social context.[11] The second is to identify "democratic" governance with some substantive conception of "good" governance, with "free and fair elections" serving in a generally supportive, but not primary, role.

The first approach fails to acknowledge that "free and fair elections" achieve general acceptance as the arbiter of political conflict only where antecedent questions have been resolved. Where there is no agreement in the society about what fates electoral outcomes should be permitted to determine—whether that agreement be embodied in a written constitution subject to authoritative interpretation by a constitutional court, or in time-honored constitutional custom reflecting a perceived covenant of the living, the dead, and the yet to be born, or in the manifest legacy of "the revolution"—the stakes of electoral competition can be intolerably high, with the vital interests or even the very survival of significant sectors of the society on the line.[12] Where the losers militantly oppose the outcome, electoral numbers alone provide little basis for condemning their opposition.

Although "one person, one vote" may appear to have moral standing as an egalitarian rule of decision, this is so only where the rule translates in practice to influence over collective decisions on the part of each in proportion to how those decisions affect his or her life. Where, for example, a predatory majority can skew the burdens and benefits of public decisions against a minority, there is no moral reason why the minority is bound to accept the outcome. Agreement is frequently elusive on such matters as the degree of influence to which each is entitled regarding which decisions, as well as what nondecisions count as collective decisions. Procedure alone thus supplies no reason to regard free and fair electoral outcomes as inherently democratic.[13]

Indeed, democracy, while often imagined as reducible to decision procedures, is inherently a teleological concept. Supposedly-democratic procedures are

[11] For a critique of the prevailing vision as identifying the democratic norm with a "low-intensity democracy" that emphasizes electoral competition among elites at the expense of mass participation and empowerment, see Susan Marks, *The Riddle of All Constitutions: International Law, Democracy, and the Critique of Ideology* (Oxford Univ. Press, 2000), at 50–75.

[12] For a classic examination of such problems, see Arend Lijphart, "Consociational Democracy," 21 *World Pol.* 207 (1969).

[13] In defining democracy in essentially procedural terms, the democratic entitlement school follows the contemporary comparative politics literature in rejecting teleological definitions—ideas about popular will and the common good—that render democratic performance inherently unmeasurable by social science techniques. *See* Samuel Huntington, *The Third Wave: Democratization in the Late Twentieth Century* (Norman, Okla.: Univ. of Oklahoma Press, 1991), at 5–13. Yet political scientists justify this sterile definition, so much at odds with the term's role in both classical theory and popular morality, by purporting to lighten the term's normative baggage–that is, by identifying democracy as, at most, one of many political virtues. *Id.* at 10. The democratic entitlement school restores the normative baggage, but without the necessary teleological counterpart.

themselves derived from expectations about those procedures' capacity to effectuate a set of social goals associated with the democratic ideal. However enamored one may be of a certain set of procedures, one cannot sensibly insist upon those procedures while simultaneously conceding that adherence to them will doom the very goals for which they were established. Yet disagreement remains endemic as to the precise nature of the democratic goals and as to the order of priority of goals that, in any particular context, may conflict.

Put simply, we do not know what democracy ***is*** unless we know what it is ***for***, and we do not genuinely agree on what it is for.[14] One's assessment of the democratic quality of a political act—e.g., the Algerian coup to preempt the electoral victory of illiberal Islamists in 1992, Boris Yeltsin's unconstitutional dispersal of the Russian legislature in 1993, the Dayton High Commissioner's removal of Republika Srpska's elected ethno-nationalist president in 1999, the multifarious actions on both sides of the Venezuelan crisis of 2002, the Hamas electoral victory in the Occupied Palestinian Territories in 2006, the legislatively and judicially backed Honduran coup d'etat in 2009—turns ultimately on whether one sees it as serving (long-term) democratic ends.[15]

Thus, democratic entitlement advocates find themselves driven to the second approach, wherein the entitlement is a right, not to governance conducted according to a given set of procedures, but to such governance as is calculated in any given instance to further the establishment of a "truly" democratic society.[16] But to the extent that democratic entitlement advocacy reflects a particular substantive political vision, it departs from any claim to grounding in the international system's

[14] Although functioning constitutional democracies are marked by some combination of overlapping consensus and compromise among ideological tendencies, the democratic idea itself cannot actually transcend ideological difference. The libertarian and the socialist, the multiculturalist and the ethno-nationalist, the secularist and the religious conservative do not hold common understandings of democracy, although they may hold common understandings of a constitutional compact that is binding by virtue of the express, tacit, or imputed consent of the existing political factions.

[15] In societies that are sufficiently polarized (especially on a socioeconomic or ethno-national basis), defeat for one's own substantive conception has morally and practically unacceptable consequences, and thus civil wars can occur in which either side can plausibly be identified with democracy. Or, the tendency to civil war can be suppressed by the imposition of a dictatorship (which literally denotes emergency rule, except that the emergency tends to become purportedly perpetual) that will be supported (provisionally) by some democrats and militantly opposed by others.

That is not to say that neither side is wrong, nor that neither side should lose. It is to say that in the assessment, appeals to "democracy" beg the question. Thus, if interpretations of democracy were to be the basis for determining external behavior toward internal conflicts, the result would be the very free-for-all that international law has endeavored to forestall.

[16] Franck's later work on the democratic entitlement indicated a move in this direction. See Thomas M. Franck, "Democracy, Legitimacy, and the Rule of Law: Linkages," New York University School of Law, Public Law and Legal Theory Working Paper Series, Working Paper 2 (1999), *available at* <http://papers.ssrn.com/paper.taf?abstract_id=201054>

underlying social facts. Assertion of that vision as a compulsory international norm would amount to a call for a liberal-democratic crusade, a drive to impose a specific worldview that has yet to find general acceptance.

Moreover, the particular vision of the democratic entitlement advocates tends to reflect the social position of those with whom they identify. One finds in the democratic entitlement literature a strong emphasis on protection of individual liberty from governmental encroachments,[17] yet remarkably little emphasis on socioeconomic conditions. Obscured are the vast inequalities of power that mark the reality of liberal-democratic practice—even in the most developed nations, let alone in less developed countries where economic disparity and social stratification tend to empty formal political equality of much of its real-world significance.[18]

By contrast, one might reasonably posit as the essence of democracy the effective equality of power in social decision-making.[19] The decisions that are made in political processes both reflect and affect distributions of economic, social, and cultural power—the ability of individuals and groups to control the conditions of their own lives and to impose conditions on the lives of others. One might say, therefore, that a country is truly democratic only where the interests and/or opinions of the lower half of the socioeconomic ladder have commensurate weight in shaping the conditions of social life. On this view, fidelity to familiar electoral procedures should be subject to the overarching purpose of substantive social empowerment of the less well-off. It therefore follows that authoritarian and coercive devices calculated to break the effective hold of socioeconomic elites may, under certain conditions, be more democratic than "free and fair elections"—which, for structural reasons, would inevitably ratify the status quo.

Given the failure to emphasize equality of power as the democratic criterion, the familiar claims for the benefits of liberal-democratic institutions to individual freedom (typically the *summum bonum* of the democratic entitlement advocates)

[17] *See, e.g.*, Thomas M. Franck, *The Empowered Self: Law and Society in the Age of Individualism* (New York: Oxford Univ. Press, 2000).

[18] Today, purported democratization often goes hand in hand with the upward redistribution of income and the downward redistribution of risk, with the reduction of public goods so as to make the quality of life more dependent on market success, with creating opportunities for the strong to opt out of relationships that contribute to the well-being of the weak, and with undermining the stability and self-government of workplaces and local communities. More and more decisions are being excluded from the realm of even nominal accountability to those affected by them. Meanwhile, more and more people vote in more and more elections that decide less and less.

[19] Literal political equality—in the sense that the decisions affecting social life (assuming we could say what those are, distinguishing properly public from inherently private or intra-associational decisions) are a product of the equal input of all those affected by them (or perhaps, in proportion to how much their lives are affected, assuming that we could determine objectively what counts as what quantum of affectedness)—is not even conceivable, let alone practicable or desirable. Democracy is a metaphor. The question is whether the metaphor is an apt one in any given instance.

are ideologically skewed. Those sectors of society that have weight in political decision-making—whether through direct participation or not, whether through pluralistic processes or not—tend to win the conditions of freedom relevant to those sectors. Barriers to state encroachment on the individual are the primary conditions of freedom for those with command over resources, whereas the primary condition of freedom for the have-nots is an end to economic deprivation and insecurity and to social disempowerment and exclusion. The success of liberal-democratic institutional forms in securing the former has not been matched by success in securing the latter. (Concededly, the alternatives tried so far have been disappointing in the latter regard while being disastrous in the former.)

In short, democracy presents still-open questions at its very core. When one affirms that the term "democracy" demarcates the moral high ground in political struggle, one must also acknowledge that the word encompasses a wide range of political virtues as variously perceived, at which point democracy's presence or absence largely ceases to be an empirical question.

To be sure, some clarity is achievable, at least, as to what democracy is not. One need only to invoke "Democratic Kampuchea" to point out that unambiguous cases of undemocratic practice exist and are readily discernible. But the "democratic" merits of real-life political struggles in diverse lands are seldom so reliably judged from abroad. That the most blatantly tyrannical systems of government should be excluded from international legal protections does not imply that international legal protections should be reserved for one particular governmental model.

An international legal norm of "democratic governance," even if developed and applied ingenuously, portends external impositions at odds with plausibly democratic interests. The still greater danger is that an illusory consensus on the meaning of democracy will lend itself to partisan manipulation, with universal values invoked on behalf of particular interests and, ultimately, unilateral action. "Democratization" is all too frequently a rationalization for measures aimed at the destabilization of geostrategically adverse regimes, which may be no more undemocratic than friendly regimes exempted from such measures.

Democratic entitlement advocates frequently respond by touting democratization's potential contribution to the conditions of global peace. They cite (by no means uncontroverted) studies purporting to establish that democracies virtually never go to war with one another.[20] But whatever its empirical merits, the "democratic peace" thesis transitions poorly from empirical finding to normative prescription.[21] The empirical evidence is a long way from establishing that the

[20] *See generally* Michael E. Brown, Sean M. Lynn-Jones & Steven E. Miller eds., *Debating the Democratic Peace* (Cambridge, Mass.: MIT Press, 1996).

[21] For some complicating factors, see, .e.g., Edward D. Mansfield & Jack L. Snyder, *Electing to Fight: Why Emerging Democracies Go to War* (Cambridge, Mass.: The MIT Press, 2005); Errol A. Henderson,

adoption of anti-pluralist and interventionist policies by intergovernmental organizations and powerful states will make peace more prevalent. Arguably, the conditions that underlie stable liberal democracy are more likely to explain the peace finding than is democratization as such. If some discrete set of internal factors separately produces both democratic institutions and peaceful conduct toward other democracies, external imposition of democratic institutions alone would not necessarily produce a peaceful disposition. Moreover, proponents of the "democratic peace" thesis concede that democracies do commit aggression—an unsurprising fact, given that war-related policymaking in liberal democracies frequently circumvents or violates liberal-democratic norms. It would be a great step backward if international law could be invoked as a justification for imposing homogeneity, by economic coercion or force, in the name of some grander vision of global harmony.

If such a democratic norm as has achieved international standing furnishes no workable standard for gauging the legitimacy of authority within sovereign states, still less does it provide criteria for recognizing seceding entities or establishing the nonconsensual dissolution of federal states. Democracy presupposes rather than establishes the boundaries of political community. To give effect to the voice of the people requires an antecedent decision about which populations have a right to be heard on the question—the very matter being contested.[22]

Unquestionably, democratic principles are relevant to any gauge of whether the interests and values of a particular region's inhabitants (or a majority thereof) have been systematically deprived of their appropriate weight in the decisions conditioning the territory's social life. But again, except in the rare case, the question of appropriate weight is likely to give rise to conflicting "democratic" assessments among even the most sophisticated and scrupulous external observers, let alone those who may be influenced by self-interest, cultural affinity, manipulative media accounts, or other distortive factors.

None of this is to deny that a further proliferation of liberal-democratic institutions and processes would, other things being equal, be a benefit to popular empowerment, to global peace and security, and to the reconciliation of internal factions. The problem is that strategies to advance such a proliferation in violation of the

"Disturbing the Peace: African Warfare, Political Inversion and the Universality of the Democratic Peace Thesis," 39 Brit. J. Pol. Sci. 25 (2008).

[22] Should the fate of Northern Ireland be decided by a vote of (a) the population of the Six Counties, (b) the population of the island of Ireland, (c) the population of the United Kingdom of Great Britain and Northern Ireland, or (d) the population of the British Isles? In early 1992, should some majority-Serb portion of Bosnia and Herzegovina have been carved out—based on pre-dislocation demographic concentrations—for the purpose of soliciting a decision on that portion's fate, or should its fate have been controlled by the will of the entire Bosnian population, or by the will of the entire population of what by then remained of the larger Yugoslav entity?

sovereign equality principle can well be anticipated, all things considered, to produce overall costs to those aims that exceed the benefits. Consistent application of such strategies across the universe of cases, in the face of morally and practically significant variables, would produce detriments of one kind; leaving these strategies on the shelf, available to be implemented at the discretion of great powers where they see fit, would produce detriments of another kind.

As elaborated in Chapter 6, the sovereign equality regime establishes baselines for international practice in taking cognizance of the last word on public order in a given territory. Although extraordinary conditions, perceived in common from a wide range of ideological standpoints, can justify divergence from those baselines, there is little reason to believe that the substitution of liberal-democratic for pluralist criteria would prove salutary.

## II. Locating Anti-Impunity at the Periphery, Not the Core, of the International Legal Order

International criminal law is widely seen as, in Kenneth Anderson's words, "perhaps the signal achievement in public international law since 1990 and the end of the Cold War."[23] This characterization is owing, not to any noteworthy power of criminal justice institutions nor to any conspicuous political impact of specific prosecutions, but to that project's potential "'structural' implications . . . for international law, politics, and institutions more generally."[24]

Yet, as Anderson's critique indicates, the project's potential implications for international law have not thus far been fully realized. Indeed, for Anderson, the institutions of international criminal justice have an uncertain practical—and moral—significance in the absence of an international community that is ready, willing, and able to respond forcibly to ongoing atrocities.[25] In confronting crises in the former Yugoslavia and Rwanda in the early 1990s and in Darfur more recently, international actors established mechanisms for prosecuting crimes *post hoc* while declining to undertake a war to stop the perpetrators in real time. The international peace and security order's failure to accomplish what international criminal law establishes to be imperative constitutes, for Anderson, both a moral failure and an

[23] Kenneth Anderson, "The Rise of International Criminal Law: Intended and Unintended Consequences," 20 *Euro. J. Int'l L.* 331, 331 (2009).

[24] *Id.* at 332.

[25] Nuremberg, he reminds us, "was a lovely hood ornament on the ungainly vehicle that liberated Western Europe, but it was not a substitute for D-day." *Id.* at 335 (quoting an unnamed senior British military lawyer).

unbearable jurisprudential tension. Ultimately, he seems to imply, that tension will be resolved by reform to the peace and security order.

Anderson's point is trenchant. There is an inherent tension between the spirit of international criminal justice, which cannot abide impunity, and the present international law of peace and security, which effectively demands that impunity be abided in the absence of an extraordinary political consensus. A natural resolution of this tension would be found in *de jure* or *de facto* reforms to the peace and security order that would allow the international community's avenging angels to circumvent Security Council obstructionists. That logic is foreshadowed in W. Michael Reisman's affirmation of the legitimacy of the 1999 Kosovo campaign: "as the norms in question—international human rights norms—derive from a broader decision process than the body assigned to enforce those norms, the broader decision process sustains the norms and seeks alternative modes of enforcement."[26]

This natural resolution of the tension, however, is cause for trepidation. The danger is not that humanitarian interventions lacking a Security Council mandate will find validation in an emergent legal doctrine; indeed, as suggested in Chapter 5, some such development may be needed precisely to avoid a broader delegitimation of strictures against intervention. The danger is that the international criminal justice project's spirit portends a justification of the exception that will fatally undermine the rule.[27]

The post-World War II order, as constructively amended in the era of decolonization, established the priority of peace and respectful cooperation among juridically equal states; the ethos was one of ideological pluralism and forbearance, qualified only by a Security Council mechanism requiring an extraordinary cross-cutting consensus. That the system leaves unredressed all but the most extraordinary injustices occurring within state boundaries is not an aberrant consequence; the system, mindful that great-power predation has typically flown the flag of righteousness, prioritizes the impeding of impositions.

Proposed doctrines of humanitarian intervention ordinarily seek to cover the extreme case while leaving the basic premise of non-intervention intact. They seek to avert impending humanitarian catastrophe (which often can be perceived in common from a broad range of ideological and cultural perspectives), not to authorize forcible recourse against wrongdoing as such.

[26] W. Michael Reisman, "Unilateral Actions and the Transformations of the World Constitutive Process: The Special Problem of Humanitarian Intervention," 11 *Euro. J. Intl L.* 3, 15 (2000).

[27] As suggested in Chapter 5, support for the unauthorized Kosovo campaign ended up undermining opposition to the subsequent Iraq campaign because the take-away message was not that a narrow exception must be designed to avert widely anticipated and imminent humanitarian catastrophe, but that "the law is an ass," and should not be allowed to get in the way of doing the right thing (as perceived by the strong).

If international criminal justice comes to be perceived as displacing the United Nations. Charter's peace and security scheme as the centerpiece of international order, the genie of empowered moralism will be let out of the bottle of legal constraint. The danger arises less from developments of actual legal doctrine—and all the less still from the actual, quite modest exertions of international tribunals—than from what Anderson appropriately calls international criminal law "as social practice,"[28] including the ever more conspicuous advocacy for domestic-court exercises of universal jurisdiction. As slogans such as "an end to impunity" and "no safe havens" become prevalent in the rhetoric of international law advocates, accommodation and restraint inevitably become cast as vices rather than virtues, to the detriment of the international legal order's most practicable mission.

As argued in Chapter 7, a legal attribution of criminality to adverse regimes will tend to present international institutions with enforcement demands that such institutions, dependent on consensus among non-like-minded states, characteristically cannot fulfill. At this fork in the road, where the international legal order's procedural strictures are perceived to frustrate that same order's imperative substantive ends, violations of use-of-force norms can be rationalized as implementing the true spirit of international law. Paradoxically, instead of furthering its presumed mission of furthering accountability in the exercise of power, international criminal law may end up furnishing a rationale to disparage and to flout those international institutions and processes that are designed to hold powerful states accountable.

Whether or not they risk degenerating into show trials, international criminal prosecutions are, by their very nature, morality plays. Where the moral lesson involved represents a genuine consensus—or more to the point, an insistent near-consensus—of the international community as a whole, such trials may be salutary (as they have been in, for example, making "ethnic cleansing" a globally recognizable term of opprobrium). However, where extraterritorial jurisdiction is vested in the national courts of 190-odd states, international criminal law has all too great a potential to lend itself to partisan festivals of self-righteousness.

As Amrita Kapur has eloquently put it, a "'seal of justice' that merely vindicates victors' actions through a wholesale condemnation of the vanquished party's wrongs, does not provide meaningful truth or justice."[29] What Kapur did not note, but might have, is that recent developments in international criminal law have dispersed to national courts the resources for just such a wholesale condemnation, which may be used retrospectively to discredit those who had previously advocated peace or restraint, and which may be used prospectively to place a not-yet-vanquished state in the cross-hairs.

[28] 28 Anderson, *supra*, at 331.

[29] Amrita Kapur, "The Rise of International Criminal Law: Intended and Unintended Consequences: A Reply to Ken Anderson," 20 *Euro. J. Int'l L.* 1031, 1040 (2009).

International criminal law "as social practice" is associated with two problematic assertions about the role of penal processes in post-conflict transitions. The first is that an authoritative condemnation of perpetrators is an essential element of post-conflict efforts to reaffirm the dignity of victims. The second is that peace and reconciliation are necessarily predicated on—and therefore, perhaps, should be held hostage to—the authoritative triumph of a particular moral judgment about the acts of conflict participants.[30]

If one has in one's mind's eye morally unambiguous conflicts, where one side used atrocious means in the service of a manifestly evil end, both of these assertions seem plausible. Insofar as the project of international criminal justice limits its ambitions to such circumstances—and there are enough of these to sustain a full docket—it poses no threat to other values associated with the international rule of law.

But as discussed in Chapter 7, many armed conflicts involve, on one or both sides, informed persons of good faith and sound reason who endorse the use of ruthless methods for what they regard as an indispensable greater good. Ruthless acts have often been committed, not because of a "culture of impunity," but because actors (and their constituencies) believed, non-pathologically, that presumptively wrongful acts were justified in the effort to avert what they regarded as a morally worse overall outcome.[31] (The Israeli-Palestinian conflict might be seen as

[30] For a clash of views on these topics, see Juan E. Mendez, "National Reconciliation, Transnational Justice, and the International Criminal Court," 15 *Ethics & International Affairs* 25 (2001); Brad R. Roth, "Peaceful Transition and Retrospective Justice: Some Reservations. A Response to Juan E. Mendez," 15 *Ethics & Int'l Aff.*45 (2001).

[31] In a recent online debate, Kapur criticizes my stance as follows:

> Roth makes a bold distinction between "atrocious means in the service of a manifestly evil end" and the non-pathological use of ruthless methods. I contest the relevance and usefulness of such a distinction on the basis of a multi-disciplinary analysis . . . . Further, I characterize ICL as the preferred tool . . . for minimizing the commission of ruthless acts, whether on pathological or non-pathological grounds specifically because "ordinary people.without any particular hostility can become agents in a terrible destructive process". . . .

Amrita Kapur, "The Rise of International Criminal Law: A Further Rejoinder to Roth and Anderson," EJIL:Talk! (Jul 8, 2010), available at <http://www.ejiltalk.org/the-rise-of-international-criminal-law-a-further-rejoinder-to-roth-and-anderson/>, quoting Kapur, *supra*, at 1036 n.29.

The very fact that the distinction at issue could be characterized as "bold" indicates the extent of the clash of intuitions. On my reading of events, ruthlessness is here to stay, and not merely at the margins of international life; it is an attribute, not solely of those who are and will be remembered as criminals, but also of those who are and will be remembered as fighters in a noble cause. "Destructive processes," on this reading, are not distinctively products of criminality but part of the landscape of violent political contestation (though patent criminality often compounds the destructiveness of these processes). My formulation is not an effort to excuse ordinary people who committed patently egregious acts "without any particular hostility"; it is an effort to avoid vilifying those whose involvement in ruthlessness was indistinguishable from that of those who are exempted from such vilification because they happened to have been on the currently favored side.

quintessential in this regard, but even the question of which conflicts fall into this category turns on one's political attitudes.)

Among the conclusions that follow from this observation is that the potential target list for the project of international criminal justice is too rich. The problem is not simply the danger that the typically hoped-for expansion of domestic-court invocation of universal jurisdiction will produce frivolous prosecutions or legally unjustified convictions. Rather, the problem is precisely that fully sound cases could, in principle, be brought against a very wide range of actors, including those widely identified (both rightly and wrongly, perhaps) as the "good guys." And yet in practice, prosecutions will almost always be reserved for the politically unpopular and strategically uninfluential.

International criminal justice enthusiasts are not, of course, heedless of the prospect for the partisan abuse of penal processes. Their answer to this danger is to insist narrowly on procedural fairness.[32] A commitment to procedural fairness, however, implies nothing at all about political neutrality in the exercise of prosecutorial discretion nor anything about neutrality in application of law to fact as between cases involving favored and disfavored political causes. Worse, procedural fairness sometimes appears to be defined narrowly enough to allow its coexistence with dubious substantive doctrinal innovations, such as "*in dubio pro humanitate*"[33] and extended conceptions of complicity and "joint criminal enterprise."[34] Where the institutional focus is on individual acts—and even more narrowly, on the injustices suffered by individual victims[35]—rather than on broader historical contexts and global systems, and where

[32] According to Kapur, "the likelihood of 'partisan festivals' is lowered by a greater commitment to neutrality, as expressed through procedural fairness." Kapur, "Conceptual Distinctions between the ICJ Project and Its Constituent Processes: A Reply to Brad Roth and Ken Anderson," EJIL:Talk! (May 11, 2010), *available* at <http://www.ejiltalk.org/conceptual-distinctions-between-the-icj-project-and-its-constituent-processes-a-reply-to-brad-roth-and-ken-anderson/>. I am not sure to whose "commitment to neutrality" Kapur is referring (apart from the ICC, where the cautious institutional design appears likely to preclude all but the most unambiguous cases).

[33] For critiques of such an approach to penal liability, *see, e.g.*, Tamás Hoffmann, "The Gentle Humanizer of Humanitarian Law: Antonio Cassese and the Creation of the Customary Law of Non-International Armed Conflicts," in Carsten Stahn & Larissa van den Herik eds., *Future Perspectives on International Criminal Justice* (The Hague: TMC Asser/Cambridge University Press, 2010), 58, *available at* <http://papers.ssrn.com/sol3/papers.cfm?abstract_id=1531703>; Darryl Robinson, "The Identity Crisis of International Criminal Law," 21 *Leiden J. Int'l L.* 925 (2008).

[34] *See* Alison Marston Danner & Jenny S. Martinez, "Guilty Associations: Joint Criminal Enterprise, Command Responsibility, and the Development of International Criminal Law," 93 *Cal. L. Rev.* 75 (2005); Mark J. Osiel, 'Modes of Participation in Mass Atrocity,' 38 *Cornell Int'l L. J.* 793 (2005).

[35] It may seem intuitive that a wrong suffered is the flip side of a wrong committed; "injury," after all, entails the combination of harm and injustice. It may also seem an advance for human rights if injustices suffered are attributed to individual wrongdoing rather than to impersonal and complex social systems.

Both of these intuitions are, in my view, fundamentally problematic. They are undoubtedly appropriate where the baseline is harmony—the basic conditions of a dignified human existence being

*tu quoque* objections are ruled out of order, there are endless opportunities to affix black hats to disfavored political actors, with windfalls to partisan political agendas.

As noted in Chapter 7, these dangers do not weigh heavily in respect of the limited range of uncontroversially atrocious cases to which extraterritorial prosecutions have up to now, for the most part, been limited. But extreme cases, from Nuremberg and Eichmann onward, have tended to generate extravagant dicta that will be turn out to be regrettable if applied unilaterally in contexts that are sites of serious moral and political contestation.

Over time, the international legal system has made substantial progress in setting boundaries to the state-authorized conduct that it will abide, and in establishing mechanisms of retributive justice to reinforce those boundaries. These mechanisms, judiciously managed, may make a significant contribution in strengthening the global commitment to combat genocide, crimes against humanity, and gross and systematic violations of the laws and customs of war.

Nonetheless, continued broadening of the scope of the effort is less likely to further than to undermine accountability in the exercise of power.[36] In a decentralized legal and political order, where transnational implementation depends primarily on

initially present for all, but then disturbed by discrete, direct, and deliberate acts, which can clearly be seen to breach uncontradicted or categorically prevailing duties. But if the baseline is turbulence, with those basic conditions largely absent or threatened, as a result of both discrete incursions and systemic deprivations, the nature and balance of the duties confronting those responding to that turbulence becomes controvertible among informed persons of good faith and sound reason. Ruthless acts are undertaken in a name of the creating, securing, or restoring conditions of a dignified human existence, especially for those to whom one (as a leader or servant of a discrete political community) owes special duties.

Human rights advocates understandably recoil from this latter way of understanding the world, since it is associated with bloodletting in the name of aims that so often turn out to be empty abstractions. As the saying goes, you can break many eggs without ever making an omelette. It may or may not be salutary to respond by asserting the categorical priority of negative duties ("first, do no harm"). But given the real-world prevalence of support for ruthlessness in crisis conditions, the sweeping identification of serious human rights violations with crimes—judgmentalism fashioned into a sword rather than a shield—seems less than salutary, especially where sustaining it requires hypocrisy about the actions of one's own heroes.

[36] Moreover, maintaining the distinctness of the categories of human rights violations and international crimes serves an important human rights purpose. If all breaches of human rights obligations were ipso facto international crimes, it would follow logically, but perversely, that any harsh practice that is not an international crime is not a breach of state obligation. Even in a purely domestic context, such a conflation of standards is problematic, as courts in a criminal proceeding would undoubtedly interpret the standard restrictively, as appropriate where the focus is on the wrongdoing of the perpetrator; that restrictive interpretive approach would then have the effect of diluting the standard for human rights compliance, which is more properly governed by considerations of the harm and indignity to be avoided, rather than the wrong to be punished. Courts addressing rights violation might be unduly reluctant to find a violation were penal consequences necessarily to follow. There are a great many cases where rights violations should be recognized, even though the perpetrators should not be held guilty of criminal wrongdoing. For more on this theme, see Brad R. Roth, "Just Short of Torture: Abusive Treatment and the Limits of International Criminal Justice," 6 *J. Int'l Crim. Justice* 215 (2008).

voluntaristic exertions, conferrals of universal jurisdiction are akin to hunting licenses. These may, at their present early stage of operation, appear to provide weapons to the weak against the strong, but in the longer run, the strong are better positioned to exploit these weapons. Universal jurisdiction encourages fantasies about holding to account officials of strong and influential states, but in reality, such states have the political clout to shield those officials, as well as the capacity to employ judicial processes to focus one-sided attention on foreign crises in which they have a stake and to vilify foreign leaders whom they wish to depose. Perhaps just as importantly, rhetoric that associates international legality primarily with bringing wrongdoers to justice, rather than primarily with maintaining peaceful and respectful relations among bearers of conflicting political moralities—with the cross-border exercise of power rather than with restraint on power—furnishes legitimation to agendas that are, on the whole, unlikely to serve humanitarian aims.

The point here is not to predict an impending free-for-all of domestic-court exercises of extraterritorial jurisdiction against foreign-state officials. Even if the scholarship of enthusiasts has laid a groundwork for such an eventuality, positive international law, faithfully construed, remains quite constraining. Moreover, expansive theoretical designs face formidable obstacles in practice. It may be that predictably ill-fated initial moves against officials of influential states will prompt more and more states to limit their courts' capacity to exercise extraterritorial penal jurisdiction altogether. It may even be that in filling a manifest gap in the global legal order, the International Criminal Court will serve, contrary to the hopes of many of the Court's strongest supporters, to suppress rather than to stimulate appetites for domestic-court prosecutions of foreign-state officials.

The point, rather, is that it should not be lamented if international criminal justice, notwithstanding all of the exuberant rhetoric, remains peripheral to the operation of the international legal order. Prosecutions should not be used to win a live political argument; they should be used where a genuine (and not an illusory or hypocritical) consensus of a diverse international community identifies conduct as beyond the pale. The piercing of the veil of sovereignty by courts of a coequal state is an extraordinary recourse; it should be reserved for extraordinary circumstances.

## A Final Word

Global pluralism is a moral, not merely a practical, imperative. Would-be reformers of international order must accept that internal struggles over competing conceptions of legitimate and just public order cannot always be contained by liberal constitutional solutions and that recourse to ruthless means, while often objectively unjust, is a fact of political life that unbridled interventionism cannot eradicate—and may well exacerbate. Such reformers must acknowledge the unique stake of a territorial political community's members in the collective decisions that condition life in their society, and the inherent untrustworthiness of even well-intentioned and thoughtful (let alone self-interested, arrogant, or sophomoric) outsiders poised to impose unilateral implementations of supposed universal standards. Moreover, such reformers must serve the moral interest in international coexistence and cooperation by strengthening, not weakening, the institutional basis for good-faith accommodation among the non-like-minded.

All of this can occur without any abandonment of moral judgment. Pluralism is not skepticism or relativism. To uphold limitations on transnational prosecution or forcible intervention is not to refrain from condemning or sanctioning breaches of legal obligations, just as to insist on consent-based methods for ascertaining states' legal obligations is not to abjure more wide-ranging standards for evaluating states' performance of their moral duties. A moral approach to international relations does not require—and properly conceived, does not permit—unleashing the strong to impose justice as they understand it.

# Table of Cases

# Index